SCOTTISH SOCIETY IN THE SECOND WORLD WAR

SCOTTISH SOCIETY IN THE SECOND WORLD WAR

Tradition, Tension, Transformation

MICHELLE MOFFAT

EDINBURGH
University Press

Edinburgh University Press is one of the leading university presses in the UK. We publish academic books and journals in our selected subject areas across the humanities and social sciences, combining cutting-edge scholarship with high editorial and production values to produce academic works of lasting importance. For more information visit our website: edinburghuniversitypress.com

© Michelle Moffat, 2023, 2025

Edinburgh University Press Ltd
13 Infirmary Street,
Edinburgh, EH1 1LT

First published in hardback by Edinburgh University Press 2023

Typeset in 10/12 ITC New Baskerville by
Cheshire Typesetting Ltd, Cuddington, Cheshire

A CIP record for this book is available from the British Library

ISBN 978 1 3995 2253 3 (hardback)
ISBN 978 1 3995 2254 0 (paperback)
ISBN 978 1 3995 2255 7 (webready PDF)
ISBN 978 1 3995 2251 9 (epub)

The right of Michelle Moffat to be identified as author of this work has been asserted in accordance with the Copyright, Designs and Patents Act 1988 and the Copyright and Related Rights Regulations 2003 (SI No. 2498).

Contents

List of Figures	vi
List of Abbreviations	vii
Glossary	ix
Acknowledgements	x

	Introduction: A 'Grand, Unified Collective'?	1
	Prologue: Scotland on the Eve of War	17
1	'Here Come the Keelies': The Government Evacuation Scheme in Scotland	28
2	'What That Boy Needed Was a Real Good Thrashing': Scotland's Moral Crisis, 1940–5	63
3	'A War of Their Own': Discontent and Subversion on the Scottish Home Front	93
4	'We Here in Scotland Can Also Take It': Morale in Scotland, 1939–45	125
5	The Great Escape: Scottish Wartime Holidays	160
6	Leisure and Pleasure: Scottish Responses to War's Disruption of Everyday Life	186
7	'Scotland's Fighting Fields': The Transformation of Rural Scotland	225
	Epilogue: A Story Worth Telling?	256

Bibliography	259
Index	271

Figures

1.1	Map of Scotland's evacuation zones	33
1.2	Two evacuees from Glasgow	36
1.3	Edinburgh schoolchildren prepare for evacuation	37
2.1	'Weeding and watering': boys' and girls' garden in a city graveyard	85
2.2	'Making a wheelbarrow': boys' and girls' garden in a city graveyard	86
2.3	'At work': a model housing scheme	90
3.1	Group photograph of workers at Imperial Chemical Industries factory	98
3.2	Thomas Johnston, Secretary of State for Scotland, with female industrial trainees	99
3.3	D. McLintoch and four other Bevin Boys just after training	122
4.1	'Clydeside carries on': the March 1941 Blitz	137
5.1	Open-air dancing at the Ross Bandstand, Edinburgh	164
5.2	Members of the Cowgate Boys' Club go camping	169
5.3	'Where shall we go this summer?'	170
6.1	'Music for the Fleet'	200
6.2	Tanks at Edinburgh Castle for War Savings week, 1941	205
6.3	Wings for Victory plane, Glasgow, 1943	206
6.4	Lord Alness sticking a savings stamp on a bomb, 1943	210
7.1	'A picturesque scene from last month's great freeze-up'	233
7.2	Personnel of the Canadian Forestry Corps moving a log, 1943	243
7.3	A band from the Honduran Timber Corps playing in Tranent	247

Abbreviations

AEC	Agricultural Executive Committee
ARP	air raid precautions
AWM	Australian War Memorial
BHFU	British Honduran Forestry Unit
BUF	British Union of Fascists
CEMA	Council for the Encouragement of Music and the Arts
CO	Conscientious Objector
CP[GB]	Communist Party [of Great Britain]
ENSA	Entertainments National Service Association
FR	M-O File Report
GCA	Glasgow City Archives
GES	Government Evacuation Scheme
GJRC	Glasgow Jewish Representative Council
HC Deb	Hansard, House of Commons Debate
HI	MoI's Home Intelligence Division
HL Deb	Hansard, House of Lords Debate
IAC	Industrial Campaign to Counter Communism in Scotland (also known as Industrial Areas Campaign)
IRA	Irish Republican Army
IWM	Imperial War Museum
JD Stats	NRS, HH60/427, Juvenile delinquency, statistics
M-O	Mass-Observation
MoI	Ministry of Information
NFU	National Farmers' Union
NOFU	Newfoundland Overseas Forestry Unit
NRS	National Records Scotland
POW	prisoner of war
PWD – IR	Police War Duties – Intelligence Report
R	M-O respondent
RIO	MoI Regional Information Officer
RSSPCC	Royal Scottish Society for the Prevention of Cruelty to Children
SED	Scottish Education Department
SHD	Scottish Home Department
SIR: JD	NRS, HH60/422, 'Ministry of Information, Special Intelligence Report: Juvenile Delinquency (Scotland)'
SJAC	Scottish Jewish Archives Centre

SMT Magazine	*SMT Magazine and Scottish Country Life*
SNO	Scottish nationalist organisations
SNP	Scottish National Party
SWG	Scottish Women's Group on Public Welfare
TC	M-O Topic Collection
TNA	The National Archives
WDIC	Western District Information Committee
(S)WLA	(Scottish) Women's Land Army
WTC	Women's Timber Corps

Glossary

Bailie   civic officer in local government, similar to post of magistrate or alderman. At the time of print, Glasgow had seventeen bailies.
Close   a private alleyway or thoroughfare.
Kirk   chiefly 'church', used in reference to the Church of Scotland.
Provost   civic head of regional Scottish councils, analogous to mayor or magistrate.

Please note, I have used contemporary terms and place names in keeping with primary sources. For example, when referring to lumberjacks from what was then British Honduras (now Belize) I have used the term 'British Hondurasians'. This is now an archaic term, but was suitable in the Second World War. In addition, I have used contemporary regional place names when referring to Scottish constabulary reports (where appropriate), such as 'Zetland' for what is now known as Shetland.

Acknowledgements

It brings me great pleasure to see this project to completion, and I am grateful to all those who have supported me along the way. This book began as a doctoral thesis at the University of Otago (New Zealand), and I am grateful to the History Programme, Humanities Division and Bamforth estate for generously providing funding for aspects of this research. Many thanks are due to my doctoral supervisors, Angela McCarthy and Mark Seymour, for their wisdom, guidance and attention to detail, and for assisting me in forging a new path that has brought much fulfilment.

I would also like to thank my editorial team at Edinburgh University Press, and the anonymous reviewers whose comments have strengthened this work. In addition, thanks to Juliette Pattinson, Tom Brooking, Glyn Harper, Catriona Macdonald, Jeremy Crang, Alan Malpass and Sir Tom Devine for their invaluable advice at various stages in the preparation of this manuscript. I must also acknowledge the assistance of archival and library staff in Scotland, especially at National Records Scotland where particular thanks are due to Liz and the retrievals staff.

Sections of this manuscript have appeared in print in my article '"Scotland's fighting fields": the mobilisation of workers in rural Scotland during the Second World War', *Rural History* 33, no. 2 (2022): 231–249, doi:10.1017/S0956793322000024 © The Author(s), 2022. Published by Cambridge University Press. Reprinted with permission.

For the use of archival and photographic material, I thank the Imperial War Museum, the National Library Scotland, Library and Archives Canada, the Church of Scotland and Historic Environment Scotland. I am also grateful to East Lothian at War, the National Mining Museum Scotland and the Devil's Porridge Museum, who have kindly donated material. Further information about any of the images in this work is welcome.

I warmly acknowledge the support of friends, family and colleagues, especially Julia Mallett, Christina Evans and the crew at the History Programme. Thanks also to W. D. and Diane Fitzharding-Jones, whose dear and generous support has helped this publication across the line. Finally, a heartfelt thank you to Adam, who has been a steadfast champion and enabler of dreams. To all, the completion of this project by no means indicates you will stop hearing about wartime Scotland!

I dedicate this book to the people of Second World War Scotland, in whose shoes I have walked for the past five years, and in remembrance of the victims of the 1941 Glasgow and Clydeside Blitz.

INTRODUCTION

A 'Grand, Unified Collective'?

In early 1940, Scottish author Ian Macpherson mulled over the sacrifices made during times of war by his small Highland village, Dalwhinnie. Looking at the village's Memorial to the Great War, Macpherson stated '[t]he immense sacrifice of men that Dalwhinnie made in the last war, and the offering of men it has already made in this, do in my view epitomise Scottish country experience'. Macpherson also noted that the names of half of the adult male population of the village were inscribed on the memorial stone, conveying a sense of the degree to which the previous war had impacted Scotland, its pall still hanging over parts of the country. 'Would not Britain as a whole count war terrible if every town and city and every quiet village had lost half its men in the last year, or any war?' Macpherson mused. He added '[h]ow strangely, how impossibly indeed, the Highlands have contributed to the growth of our Empire and the preservation of our liberties. How little they have gained themselves, excepting glory.'[1]

Despite these heavy sacrifices, upon the outbreak of the Second World War the village offered its remaining men in service. In Macpherson's words, a 'disproportionate share of its children' were sent to fight in the new conflict, leaving behind only women, children and the elderly. He was quick to emphasise that the war was

> taken quietly, as a thing for granted, because people are not only passionately convinced of its justice, but also of its necessity. They feel that our world suffers from a cancer which, unremoved, will rot us and at last destroy all. There is no flag-waving . . . But the passion is there; the spirit is as wild, proud, and eager as ever.

Macpherson concluded, however, 'the lesson of the last war is so recent, so vivid still, a great many of us find it difficult really to feel we are at war again, as if the past had never been.'[2]

The musings of this Scottish novelist illustrate several themes central to this book. Firstly, the themes of legacy and identity are reflected in Macpherson's lamentations of the sacrifices Scotland made in the Great War, and the willingness of Scots to support the Second World War. Additionally, undercurrents of tension and discontent are exposed

---

[1] Ian Macpherson, 'A Scottish village in war-time', *SMT Magazine and Scottish Country Life* (hereafter *SMT Magazine*), April 1940, 26.
[2] Ibid., 27–9.

by his suggestion that if Scotland's losses had similarly affected other British villages they would be more prominently remembered. Finally, Macpherson alluded to transformation: to Scotland's previously important role in the British Empire, and to the ways the Great War reshaped Scotland's people and communities. These themes infused Scottish experiences of war, and they form the backbone of *Scottish Society in the Second World War*.

Until now, though, details of Scotland's experience of the Second World War have remained largely hidden. Previous academic literature on the British home front has been relatively London-centric, with little consideration of Britain's constituent nations.[3] Works by Wendy Ugolini, Martin Johnes and Russell Davies have advanced the conversation about Welsh wartime identities, and Guy Woodward has written about wartime culture in Northern Ireland but, beyond these, there remains much ground to be covered.[4] This is a significant oversight as Britain comprises four diverse nations and is essentially 'a cultural, if not political, "multi-nation"'.[5] Here, I argue that a multi-national state needs multi-national histories if it is to truly understand its people and their lived experiences. This is particularly important in the case of Scotland, where there is a significant dearth of research on home front life during the Second World War. Notable exceptions include Jeremy Crang's work on home defence and military preparations, Alison Chand's study of reserved workers in Clydeside and T. M. Devine's broad overview in *The Scottish Nation*.[6] Geoffrey Field's *Blood, Sweat and Toil* also touches upon a range of relevant themes, including evacuation, trade unionism and female workers.[7] Further to these works, a number of texts consider aspects of Scotland at war, though broader

---

[3] Important exceptions include Angus Calder, *The People's War: Britain 1939–45* (London: Jonathan Cape, 1969); Sonya O. Rose, *Which People's War? National Identity and Citizenship in Wartime Britain 1939–1945* (Oxford: Oxford University Press, 2003); Geoffrey G. Field, *Blood, Sweat and Toil: Remaking the British Working Class, 1939–1945* (Oxford: Oxford University Press, 2011); Wendy Ugolini and Juliette Pattinson (eds), *Fighting for Britain? Negotiating Identities in Britain During the Second World War* (Bern: Peter Lang, 2015).

[4] Wendy Ugolini, *Wales in England 1914–1945. A Social, Cultural, and Military History of the Two World Wars* (Oxford: Oxford University Press, forthcoming); Martin Johnes, *Wales Since 1939* (Manchester: Manchester University Press, 2012); Russell Davies, *People, Places and Passions – Pain and Pleasure: A Social History of Wales and the Welsh, 1870–1945* (Cardiff: University of Wales Press, 2015); Guy Woodward, *Culture, Northern Ireland, and the Second World War* (Oxford: Oxford University Press, 2015); see also Ch. 6 in Rose, *Which People's War?*

[5] Rose, *Which People's War?*, 197.

[6] See Jeremy A. Crang, 'The Second World War' in Edward M. Spiers, Jeremy A. Crang and Matthew J. Strickland (eds), *A Military History of Scotland* (Edinburgh: Edinburgh University Press, 2012): 559–99; Alison Chand, *Masculinities on Clydeside: Men in Reserved Occupations, 1939–1945* (Edinburgh: Edinburgh University Press, 2016); T. M. Devine, *The Scottish Nation: 1700–2000* [1999] (London: Penguin, 2006).

[7] Field, *Blood, Sweat and Toil*.

Introduction 3

studies of society and culture on the home front are sparse.[8] Beyond these contributions, there exists a budding body of non-scholarly work and local histories.[9]

While there is coverage of the war years in some general texts on twentieth-century Scotland, these have been criticised for failing to address the 'contradictions and complexities' of the war years.[10] Catriona Macdonald claimed that this oversight arose as the Second World War 'disrupts the comfortable grand narratives on which many of these texts are built'.[11] With regards to lived experiences, as Lynn Abrams and Callum G. Brown argued, much of modern Scottish history is driven by 'the political or national(ist) narrative', while the history of the Scottish everyday remains relatively untapped.[12] Besides T. C. Smout and Sydney Wood's 'real history of ordinary people doing everyday things', few studies have focused on the banality of 'normal' life.[13] There is a clear need for academic texts considering both Scottish everyday life and the lived experience of war.

This book addresses these oversights with a study of Scottish society during the Second World War. Drawing on a rich selection of fresh archival material, it explores the lived experiences of those in Scotland, shedding light on everyday life and work in a time of war. It poses the questions: how

---

[8] Juliette Pattinson, Arthur McIvor and Linsey Robb, *Men in Reserve: British Civilian Masculinities in the Second World War* (Manchester: Manchester University Press, 2017); Linsey Robb, *Men at Work: The Working Man in British Culture, 1939–1945* (Cham: Palgrave Macmillan, 2015); Wendy Ugolini, *Experiencing War as the "Enemy Other": Italian Scottish Experience in World War II* (Manchester: Manchester University Press, 2011); David Smith, 'Official responses to juvenile delinquency in Scotland during the Second World War', *Twentieth Century British History* 18, no. 1 (2007): 78–105; John Stewart and John Welshman, 'The evacuation of children in wartime Scotland: culture, behaviour and poverty', *Journal of Scottish Historical Studies* 26, no. 1–2 (2006): 100–120.

[9] Trevor Royle, *A Time of Tyrants: Scotland and the Second World War* [2011] (Edinburgh: Birlinn, 2019); Seona Robertson and Les Wilson, *Scotland's War* (Edinburgh: Mainstream Publishing, 1995); Ian Nimmo, *Scotland at War* (Edinburgh: Archive Publications/The Scotsman, 1989); Les Taylor, *Luftwaffe Over Scotland: A History of German Air Attacks over Scotland, 1939–45* (Dunbeath: Whittles Publishing, 2010); John MacLeod, *River of Fire: The Clydebank Blitz* (Edinburgh: Birlinn, 2011); I. M. M. MacPhail, *The Clydebank Blitz* (Dumbarton: West Dunbartonshire Libraries, 1974); Elaine M. Edwards (ed.), *Scotland's Land Girls: Breeches, Bombers and Backaches* (Edinburgh: NMS, 2010); Lorne A. Wallace (ed.), *Here Come the Glasgow Keelies* (Dunning: Dunning Parish Historical Society, 1999).

[10] Catriona M. M. Macdonald, '"Wersh the wine o'victorie": writing Scotland's Second World War', *Journal of Scottish Historical Studies* 24, no. 2 (2004): 105; Christopher Harvie, *No Gods and Precious Few Heroes: Twentieth-Century Scotland* (Edinburgh: Edinburgh University Press, 1998); Ewen A. Cameron, *Impaled Upon a Thistle: Scotland Since 1880* (Edinburgh: Edinburgh University Press, 2010); Catriona M. M. Macdonald, *Whaur Extremes Meet: Scotland's Twentieth Century* (Edinburgh: John Donald, 2009).

[11] Macdonald, 'Wersh the wine', 105.

[12] Lynn Abrams and Callum G. Brown, 'Introduction: conceiving the everyday in the twentieth century', in Lynn Abrams and Callum G. Brown (eds), *A History of Everyday Life in Twentieth-Century Scotland* (Edinburgh: Edinburgh University Press), 10–11.

[13] T. C. Smout and S. Wood, *Scottish Voices 1745–1960* (London: Collins 1990), 1.

did everyday life and work look like in wartime Scotland? How did Scots respond to war's influence on their lives? Did pre-war tensions and divisions shape wartime experiences? How was national identity conceptualised at a time when messages of British unity were promoted? This study makes an important contribution to our understanding of Scotland's war years, and to scholarship on Scottish everyday life. It also reinserts the voices of Scots and those living in Scotland into the narrative of Britain's Second World War years.

Community

Two concepts are particularly pertinent to this book: community and identity. Both held a central place in wartime discourse, and have generated much historiographical discussion in the years since. The Second World War 'heightened national consciousness' and promoted discussion on the composition of national character.[14] This also included a focus on citizenship and the ideal behaviours of those in the British national community. In August 1940, as the Battle of Britain raged, Prime Minister Winston Churchill addressed the British public:

> The whole of the warring nations are engaged, not only soldiers, but the entire population, men, women and children. The fronts are everywhere. The trenches are dug in the towns and streets. Every village is fortified. Every road is barred. The front line runs through the factories. The workmen are soldiers with different weapons but the same courage . . . If it is a case of the whole nation fighting and suffering together, that ought to suit us, because we are the most united of all the nations.[15]

These themes of unity, suffering and courage permeated the British home front. Authorities regularly promoted the vision of Britain as 'a unified community of ordinary people', doing their bit, suffering and sacrificing for the greater good of the war effort.[16] The emphases on the collective and on the notion of equality of sacrifice were also viewed as a way to foster social cohesion, raise public morale and, ultimately, stimulate commitment to that effort.[17] This picture of a unified British nation, bound by collective

---

[14] Richard Weight and Abigail Beach, 'Introduction' in Richard Weight and Abigail Beach (eds), *The Right to Belong: Citizenship and National Identity in Britain, 1930–1960* (London: I. B. Tauris, 1998), 8.

[15] Hansard, House of Commons Debate (hereafter HC Deb), 20 August 1940, vol. 364, cols 1160–1.

[16] Rose, *Which People's War?*, 6; Corinna M. Peniston-Bird, '"All in it together" and "backs to the wall": relating patriotism and the people's war in the 21st century', *Oral History* 40, no. 2 (2012): 72.

[17] Tom Harrisson, *Living Through the Blitz* (London: Collins, 1976), 324; Robert Mackay, *Half the Battle: Civilian Morale in Britain During the Second World War* (Manchester: Manchester University Press, 2002), 141, 226, 248–50.

Introduction

identity and notions of sacrifice, is interrogated throughout *Scottish Society in the Second World War*.

Historians have reminded us that wartime rhetoric is an artificial construct, useful for nation-building in a time of conflict. Lucy Noakes observed that in British popular conceptions of the wartime nation 'all internal divisions disappear. Conflicting interests of class, race, politics and gender are collapsed together to create a picture of a unified nation.'[18] This picture, of course, does not reflect reality and, as Angus Calder stated, the idealised vision of wartime Britain was 'sentimentalised and sanitised', and papered over the more divisive aspects of the home front.[19] These stark realities included anti-social behaviour and delinquency, gender conflict, industrial unrest and class divide.[20] Similar signs of discord were present on the Scottish home front, and will be examined in many of the chapters of this work.

The wartime focus on internal cohesion and a 'national' community is part of nation-building. Nations are, in effect, imagined political communities, psychological constructs and 'fantasy structures' useful for creating feelings of solidarity among members of society.[21] In her influential text *Which People's War?* Sonya Rose pointed out that the idea of the nation as a unitary 'we' was a 'politically and emotionally powerful vision', fostering the urge to be part of 'a grand, unified collective', and bringing an imagined sense of communal identity.[22] She pointed us in the direction of two key aspects of wartime rhetoric: not only was the promotion of community an important political tool, but individual notions of the collective were malleable, easily shaped around desired attributes.[23] British wartime collective identity included the assumption of internal homogeneity. At times, this idealised picture of social and ethnic sameness led to hostility towards those perceived as different, or as community outsiders.[24]

---

[18] Lucy Noakes, *War and the British: Gender and National Identity, 1939–91* (London: I. B. Tauris, 1998), 6.
[19] Peniston-Bird, 'All in it together', 69–70; Angus Calder, *The Myth of the Blitz* [1991] (London: Pimlico, 2008), xiv, 2, 43.
[20] Calder, *People's War*; Calder, *Myth of the Blitz*; Harold L. Smith, *Britain in the Second World War: A Social History* (Manchester: Manchester University Press, 1996); Stuart Hylton, *Their Darkest Hour: The Hidden History of the Home Front 1939–1945* (Stroud: Sutton, 2003); Field, *Blood, Sweat and Toil*.
[21] Benedict Anderson, *Imagined Communities: Reflections on the Origin and Spread of Nationalism*, rev. edn (London: Verso, 1991), 6–7; Renata Salecl, 'The fantasy structure of nationalist discourse', *Praxis International* 13, no. 3 (1993): 213–23, here 217; Katherine Verdery, 'Whither "nation" and "nationalism"?', *Daedalus* 122, no. 3 (1993): 37–46.
[22] Rose, *Which People's War?*, 9–11.
[23] Ibid.; Anderson, *Imagined Communities*; Craig Calhoun (ed.), *Social Theory and the Politics of Identity* (Oxford: Basil Blackwell, 1994).
[24] Paul Ward, *Britishness Since 1870* (London: Routledge, 2004), 124.

Historians have suggested the very process of building the national community requires the suppression of other groupings that also provide a sense of identity, such as gender, race or ethnicity.[25] While war is a time for unity, it may also be a time for excluding those who are not seen to display particular characteristics. To this end, research on the British home front has uncovered evidence of anti-Semitism, racial prejudice towards Black American GIs and poor treatment of aliens such as Italians and Germans.[26] Moreover, insightful contributions on this topic have been made by Wendy Ugolini and Wendy Webster, who sought to reinsert migrant experiences into narratives of war, and Gail Braybon and Penny Summerfield, who explored the challenges faced by female workers in traditionally masculine industries.[27] Similarly, the difficulties experienced by 'outsiders' are further explored here in Chapters 1 and 7, in which I argue Scottish responses to evacuees and migrant workers exposed community tensions and social divisions, actively challenging wartime motifs of unity and community.

On the British home front, these powerful notions of community were also accompanied by ideas about 'correct' behavioural norms.[28] The focus on moral virtue, 'decency' and character was a resurgence of ideas that had proliferated during the Great War.[29] These concerns were tied to underlying notions of civic virtue and rational self-control, in which the community-minded individual was expected to exert restraint for the greater good of the collective.[30] As Churchill suggested in his speech

---

[25] Mary Poovey, 'Curing the "social body" in 1832: James Phillips Kay and the Irish in Manchester', *Gender and History* 5, no. 2 (1993), 196–211; Rose, *Which People's War?*, 72.

[26] Tony Kushner, *The Persistence of Prejudice, Antisemitism in British Society during the Second World War* (Manchester: Manchester University Press, 1989); Graham Smith, *When Jim Crow met John Bull: Black American Soldiers in World War II Britain* (New York: St Martin's Press, 1988); Sonya O. Rose, 'Girls and GIs: race, sex, and diplomacy in Second World War Britain', *International History Review* 19, no. 1 (1997): 146–60; Ugolini, *'Enemy Other'*; Lucio Sponza, *Divided Loyalties: Italians in Britain during the Second World War* (Bern: Peter Lang, 2000).

[27] Wendy Ugolini, '"When are you going back?": Memory, ethnicity and the British home front', in Lucy Noakes and Juliette Pattinson (eds), *British Cultural Memory and the Second World War* (London: Bloomsbury, 2014): 89–110; Wendy Webster, *Mixing It: Diversity in World War II Britain* (Oxford: Oxford University Press, 2018); G. Braybon and P. Summerfield, *Out of the Cage: Women's Experiences in Two World Wars* (London: Routledge, 2012); Penny Summerfield, *Reconstructing Women's Wartime Lives: Discourse and Subjectivity in Oral Histories of the Second World War* (Manchester: Manchester University Press, 1998).

[28] On the First World War see Angela Woollacott, '"Khaki fever" and its control: gender, class, age and sexual morality on the British homefront in World War I', *Journal of Contemporary History* 29, no. 2 (1994): 325–47; Susan R. Grayzel, *Women and the First World War* (London: Taylor & Francis, 2002).

[29] J. M. Winter, 'British national identity and the First World War', in S. J. D. Green and R. C. Whiting (eds), *Boundaries of the State in Modern Britain* (Cambridge: Cambridge University Press, 1996): 261–77, here 262, 268.

[30] Rose, *Which People's War?*, 85–91; 'Family in trouble' in Field, *Blood, Sweat and Toil*; David Morgan and Mary Evans, *The Battle for Britain: Citizenship and Ideology in the Second World War* (London: Routledge, 1993); George L. Mosse, *Nationalism and Sexuality: Middle-Class Morality and Sexual Norms in Modern Europe* (Madison: University of Wisconsin Press, 1985).

during August 1940, citizens were expected to sacrifice and to 'do their bit'. Within the portrayal of the good citizen, the pursuit of pleasure was frowned upon and self-interest was viewed as 'antithetical to the wartime spirit'.[31] Rose suggested a focus on internal enemies is a natural response to a perceived threat to internal unity, especially at times when national solidarity is 'highly charged'.[32] Across wartime Britain, notions about active or 'correct' citizenship resulted in a wave of panic about juvenile delinquency, alcohol consumption – particularly by women – and perceived sexual immorality.[33] Discussions about self-control and virtue also proliferated in wartime Scotland. These ideas are further explored in Chapter 2, which interrogates moral panics, conceptions of 'bad' citizens and underlying concerns about communal and national identity.

The wartime focus on sacrifice and forgoing pleasure has proven particularly pervasive, infusing cultural memory of the Second World War. The power of this message of sacrifice was made evident in a 2017 study by Juliette Pattinson, Arthur McIvor and Linsey Robb, who discovered many former war workers still foreground themes of sacrifice and graft, and insist they had no time during the war for leisure and pleasure. The historians concluded that the absence of leisure in wartime memories is attributable to the centrality of work life, and that discussion of pleasure conflicted with powerful narratives of 'graft and sacrifice'.[34] In this work, I argue that leisure and pleasure were a valuable – and central – part of wartime life. This is the focus of Chapters 5 and 6, where I have sought to reinsert daily pleasures into the narrative of life on the home front.

To conclude, motifs of unity, community and good character were an intrinsic part of the British home front. As Sonya Rose summarised, popular representations of wartime unity serve a particular purpose – they foster an urge to be part of 'a grand, unified collective'.[35] In other words, these images have power as they allow individuals to feel part of something bigger. They also create a sense of belonging and security, which is particularly important in times of turbulence. *Scottish Society in the Second World War* interrogates these wartime conceptions of community, seeking to understand how an emphasis on unity played out in a fragmented Scottish nation.

Identity

Character and virtue have long been linked to conceptions of national identity. Richard Weight and Abigail Beach explained that from the

---

[31] Rose, *Which People's War?*, 71.
[32] Ibid., 72–3.
[33] See Chs 3–4 of Rose, *Which People's War?*; Sonya O. Rose, 'Sex, citizenship, and the nation in World War II Britain', *The American Historical Review* 103, no. 4 (1998): 1147–76; Summerfield, *Women's Wartime Lives*.
[34] Pattinson, McIvor and Robb, *Men in Reserve*, 243–5.
[35] Rose, *Which People's War?*, 7.

eighteenth century, ideas of 'an immutable national character' brought 'a reassuring sense of what it meant to be British'.[36] During the uncertain times of the Great War these introspective visions of Britishness gained particular importance, satisfying 'a deep yearning for national self-understanding and reassurance'.[37] As explained above, these conceptions of national character, and how the ideal British community should look, were also a crucial part of official rhetoric during the Second World War. Identity-formation in the war years centred around events such as the evacuation from Dunkirk of the fighting forces, and the Blitz. Dunkirk, and its associations with plucky courage and success in the face of impossible odds, quickly became 'entrenched in the national psyche', 'crucial' to conceptions of Britishness.[38] Similarly, perceptions of stoicism, good humour and a 'we can take it' mentality in the face of Nazi air raids became part of this lauded national character. A wide range of scholarship has examined perceptions of Britishness in wartime, and interrogated the durability of these motifs in cultural memory of the Second World War.[39]

While some scholars grapple over questions of British identity, others note there has been 'remarkably little' attention paid to wartime conceptions of identity within Britain's constituent nations.[40] Rose argued that, despite the official emphasis on unity and Britishness, war, in fact, activated 'expressions of cultural distinctiveness' in Scotland and Wales.[41] In contrast, Paul Addison brushed aside such claims of difference, stating the Second World War was 'the culminating moment' in the history of multi-national Britain and there was 'little friction between the Scots and the Welsh on the one hand and Whitehall and Westminster on the other'.[42] He also claimed many anti-war nationalists were viewed as 'crackpots'.[43] Likewise, journalist Trevor Royle in *A Time of Tyrants* claimed the war years were 'the high point

---

[36] Weight and Beach, 'Introduction', 2.

[37] Julia Stapleton, *Englishness and the Study of Politics: The Social and Political Thought of Ernest Barker* (Cambridge: Cambridge University Press, 1994), 4.

[38] Mark Connelly, *We Can Take It! Britain and the Memory of the Second World War* (Harlow: Pearson Longman, 2004), 90; Peniston-Bird, 'All in it together', 69.

[39] See Rose, *Which People's War*; Noakes and Pattinson, *British Cultural Memory*; Noakes, *War and the British*; Penny Summerfield, 'Dunkirk and the popular memory of Britain at war, 1940–58', *Journal of Contemporary History* 45, no. 4 (2010): 788–811; Peniston-Bird, 'All in it together'; David Edgerton, 'The nationalisation of British history: historians, nationalism and the myths of 1940', *The English Historical Review* 136, no. 581 (2021): 950–85.

[40] Wendy Ugolini and Juliette Pattinson, 'Negotiating identities in multinational Britain during the Second World War', in Ugolini and Pattinson, *Fighting for Britain?*, 3; Martin Johnes, 'Wales, history and Britishness', *Welsh History Review* 25, no. 4 (2011): 596–619.

[41] Rose, *Which People's War?*, 231.

[42] Paul Addison, 'The impact of the Second World War' in Paul Addison and Harriet Jones (eds), *A Companion to Contemporary Britain 1939–2000* (Oxford: Blackwell Publishing, 2005): 3–22, here 12.

[43] Ibid.

of modern British unionism', a time when Scots 'embraced a sense of British nationhood as at no other period in the country's history'.[44]

The novel archival evidence contained within *Scottish Society in the Second World War* challenges these conclusions, and supports Rose's interpretation that war unleashed aspects of cultural difference. This is particularly evident in Chapters 3 and 4, which examine unrest, anti-government sentiment and morale. These chapters explore conceptions of national identity, and find that friction within the Union and frustration with Whitehall were expressed in a range of ways. While the war years could, perhaps, be considered 'the high-water mark of Britishness', in Scotland there existed significant undercurrents of discontent and strong connexion with Scottish identity.[45]

But what exactly did it mean to be Scottish during the Second World War? After all, the nation was geographically vast and internally diverse. Archival research deployed throughout this book reveals that popular wartime conceptions of nationhood tended towards cliché, including martial attributes, tartanry, Highlandism and stereotypes of the stoic Scot and braw lad. The legacy of union with England in 1707 also fed into wartime conceptions of Scottishness. Marinell Ash claimed that, in the act of union, Scottish history was subsumed by Britain and, as a result, there was 'an increasing emphasis on the emotional trappings of the past', arguably 'compensation for the loss of a distinctive Scottish identity'.[46] Similarly, novelist William McIlvanney suggested that 'when a country loses the dynamic of its own history, the ability to develop on its own terms, its sense of its past can fragment and freeze into caricature'.[47] Certainly, the extent of wartime tropes of imagined Scottishness at times appeared close to exaggerated parody.

Furthermore, wartime concepts of nationhood had little consideration for diversity. In times of war, claimed Sonya Rose, 'representations of national identity . . . subsume or deny the significance of other identities'.[48] This was certainly the case for members of the Italian diaspora in Scotland, 'traumatically constructed as the "enemy within"'.[49] Alongside ethnicity, wartime identity could also be constructed along lines of gender or class, among other factors. In his examination of the home front, Geoffrey Field proposed that feelings of fraternity and identity transcended national

---

[44] Royle, *A Time of Tyrants*, 338.
[45] Paul Addison, 'National identity and the Battle of Britain', in Barbara Korte and Ralf Schneider (eds), *War and the Cultural Construction of Identities in Britain* (Amsterdam: Rodopi BV, 2002): 225–40, here 235.
[46] Marinell Ash, *The Strange Death of Scottish History* (Edinburgh: Ramsey Head Press, 1980), 10.
[47] Quoted in David McCrone, 'Tomorrow's ancestors: nationalism, identity and history', in Edward J. Cowan and Richard J. Finlay (eds), *Scottish History: The Power of the Past* (Edinburgh: Edinburgh University Press, 2002): 253–71, here 256.
[48] Rose, *Which People's War?*, 9.
[49] Wendy Ugolini, '"Spaghetti lengths in a bowl?" Recovering narratives of not "belonging" amongst the Italian Scots', *Immigrants & Minorities* 31, no. 2 (2013): 214–34, here 215.

boundaries, running along lines of occupation and giving workers across Britain a sense of belonging to a national working class.[50] In contrast, Alison Chand's study of reserved workers in wider Glasgow concluded that local, shared history was a more powerful identity marker than that of class more broadly. She stated that while 'collective subjectivities' were shared by men in similar industrial occupations across Britain, the 'bedrock of identity' for Clydeside workers came from 'the "reservoir of human life" surrounding them on an everyday basis'.[51] These differing conclusions illustrate the complexity of identity, not only in Scotland but also across the multi-national state of Britain.

Historians have warned we should not assume national identity is fixed and singular, and they suggest dual or hybrid identities should be given greater consideration.[52] Likewise, sociologist David McCrone asserted it is possible to be both Scottish and British, and for identity to be construed as dual and complementary.[53] Nonetheless, as this monograph demonstrates, expressions of Britishness or discussions of what it meant to be British were not a strong part of the lived experience of war in Scotland. As the following chapters discuss, while a sense of belonging to a shared British community may have been an unspoken part of Scottish experiences of war, wartime conversations about nationhood predominantly revolved around conceptions of Scottishness. In exploring these experiences and constructs of identity, this study offers new insights into Scottish society during the Second World War.

Sources

A significant amount of original archival work has been undertaken in the preparation of this monograph. These archival sources can be broadly categorised into four groups: published material, official documents, life writing and the records of special interest groups. Lucy Noakes and Juliette Pattinson have noted that memory of the Second World War has become 'increasingly visible, and contested', and Geoff Eley has astutely pointed out that remembrance of the war 'requires no immediate experience of those years'.[54] To account for these difficulties I have focused almost exclusively on records created during the war years, in an attempt to understand how contemporaries perceived their

---

[50] Field, *Blood, Sweat and Toil*, 80.
[51] Chand, *Masculinities on Clydeside*, 131.
[52] Wendy Ugolini, '"The band of brothers": the mobilisation of English Welsh dual identities in Second World War Britain', *Journal of British Studies* 60, no. 4 (2021): 822–47.
[53] McCrone, 'Tomorrow's ancestors', 260.
[54] Lucy Noakes and Juliette Pattinson, 'Introduction: "Keep calm and carry on": the cultural memory of the Second World War in Britain', in Noakes and Pattinson, *British Cultural Memory*, 2; Geoff Eley, 'Finding the people's war: film, British collective memories and World War II', *The American Historical Review* 106, no. 3 (2001): 818–38, here 818.

experiences, devoid of the influences of time, 'popular memory' and selective amnesia.[55]

Newspaper articles are the main type of published source used throughout this work, though magazines and publications by special interest groups are also utilised. Publications provide details of events, outline official information, regulations and responses, and also illuminate mass culture, through such features as advertisements, government propaganda, editorials and letters. A valuable source of newspaper articles was discovered in Scottish Home Department files, wherein civil servants curated scrapbooks on selected topics, clipping newspaper reports from publications across Scotland. While this source may be subject to the beliefs or biases of the persons who gathered these articles, nonetheless they have provided access to a wide range of additional publications that were not otherwise accessible to the author. Aside from this source, I searched online newspaper databases, using keywords such as 'Clydeside', 'bombing' or 'blitz', and newspapers were browsed on and around important dates, such as 13 March 1941.

Privately produced publications, such as the magazine of Edinburgh's Scottish Motor Traction group (SMT), were another important source of information on wartime experiences. *SMT Magazine and Scottish Country Life* (hereafter *SMT Magazine*) was a monthly publication established by SMT in the 1920s, featuring articles on Scottish history and culture, natural features and, during the war years, articles and photographs of home front life and events. The magazine provides a rich glimpse into Scottish culture and conceptions of national identity, and also gives important insights into lived experiences, such as through feature stories on evacuees or 'Land Girls'. This source has some limitations though, particularly as many of its home front features and photographs appear to have originated from the Ministry of Information (MoI). More generally, privately produced publications should also be used with a view to their intended readership and distribution figures. I was unable to establish distribution figures for *SMT Magazine*, though letters to the editor came from across Britain, the frontline fighting forces and diaspora networks in Canada, South Africa, Australia and New Zealand. This demonstrates the reach of this publication, though further production details would give a better-rounded picture of its scope of influence.

Official sources

The second main category of sources utilised within this book is those produced by official bodies. This includes files from Scottish government departments such as the Scottish Home Department (SHD) or Department of Health for Scotland, as well as Whitehall-located bodies

---

[55] Noakes and Pattinson, 'Keep calm', 5–7, 15.

such as the Ministry of Home Security, or transcripts of Parliamentary debates at Westminster. I also utilised intelligence documents originating from authorities in both Whitehall and Scotland. These sources are useful in giving background information about schemes or campaigns, as well as restrictions and regulations. Most importantly, these sources provide inside access to secret propaganda campaigns and programmes to influence public morale, and they reveal official responses to public actions.

The MoI and MoI's Home Intelligence (HI) Division compiled their reports from a wide range of individuals and bodies, providing insight into a broad section of British society. As a result, these documents are an excellent source of information on public mood and behaviour. They also demonstrate the ways officials responded to Scottish actions and show the manoeuvrings that took place behind the scenes to influence the public. Reports on public opinion and morale, such as HI reports, have some shortcomings. They can be impressionistic and may have been shaped by those who ordered or gathered the intelligence. Nonetheless, they provide a unique glimpse into public attitudes and behaviour.[56] Historians Paul Addison and Jeremy A. Crang wrote that while a single morale report offers only 'a glimpse' of life, the cumulative effect over time provides 'a continuously evolving narrative and a coherent version of events'.[57] These intelligence summaries also convey regional diversity across Scotland and the existence of localised dissent, themes that will be further explored in Chapters 3 and 4.

In addition to these official sources, this research also relies on the previously untapped source of Scottish constabulary reports, held at National Records Scotland. This archive is a significant discovery and provides unparalleled information on Scottish wartime experiences. Regular reports by regional chief constables assess home front conditions, subversive behaviour, industrial discontent, air raid action and morale. As such, these documents are a valuable foil to HI reports, which have been extensively mined in research on the London home front. Additionally, these records provide concrete data on attendances at subversive meetings, and public reaction to anti-government or anti-war sentiment. Moreover, the reports, authored by chief constables from all regions of Scotland, provide insight into local experiences and perceptions of war, and were written by authorities with an understanding of local background and circumstances.

As with any source, these reports may be subject to the bias of their authors, and certain chief constables seemed to value the process more than others, affecting the length and detail of reports. Ultimately, though, this is a valuable discovery, and the contents of these records provide the best insight currently available into the Scottish home front in the Second

---

[56] Paul Addison and Jeremy A. Crang, *Listening to Britain: Home Intelligence Reports on Britain's Finest Hour — May to September 1940* (London: Vintage Books, 2011), xi.

[57] Ibid., xvi–ii.

World War. These documents were searched by topic, such as 'Reactions to war conditions', keywords and on dates relating to important events, such as the Clydeside apprentices' strike in early 1941. Many are also arranged by location, so this allowed for comparisons between regions and across time.

Life writing

In addition to official and published sources, this book draws upon a range of life writings to examine wartime society in Scotland. These include diaries, letters, private papers and responses to questionnaires. Life writings offer illuminating insights into everyday life during a time of global crisis. They also reveal private thoughts and feelings about the war and its disruption of everyday life. In addition, they provide details of personal opinions, friction and overt hostilities, which writers may not have been comfortable publicly expressing.

Life writings are, at times, problematic. Many of the diaries examined for this research were written for Mass-Observation (M-O) and, while the social history organisation published selected findings, writers were guaranteed anonymity. However, James Hinton has pointed out that while M-O diaries may have been composed privately, their authors often had 'a sense of audience', and may have curated their entries with this in mind.[58] This does not necessarily make these diaries any less reliable as a source, reminded Summerfield in *Histories of the Self*. She further noted that life writing reveals the agency of the author and reflects contemporary social conventions and attitudes.[59] Hinton also claimed diaries allow authors to experiment with notions of self, including the rational and emotional or public and private, and through this raw introspection the historian can observe 'selfhood under construction'.[60] In this sense, using personal writing helps to uncover not only details of the Scottish home front but the nature of the individuals that made up Scottish wartime society. As Abrams and Brown have pointed out, testimonies add richness, complexity and the personal to our knowledge of the everyday.[61] These sources also corroborate or act as a foil for other sources.

This research utilises twenty-three diaries written by Scots or diarists residing in Scotland during the war, ten collections of letters, and four collections of private papers. In addition, it uses a pool of seventy-eight respondents to M-O questionnaires, residing in Scotland when their replies were composed. M-O searches included all respondents residing in Scotland in any year between 1939 and 1945 (inclusive). Additional diaries

---

[58] James Hinton, *Nine Wartime Lives: Mass-Observation and the Making of the Modern Self* (Oxford: Oxford University Press, 2010), 6.
[59] Penny Summerfield, *Histories of the Self: Personal Narratives and Historical Practice* (Abingdon: Routledge, 2019), 64–5.
[60] Hinton, *Nine Wartime Lives*, 7.
[61] Abrams and Brown, 'Conceiving the everyday', 11.

and letters were gathered from the BBC 'WW2 People's War' website using the same criterion, and in response to advertisements I placed with newspapers and magazines. These provided a small but relatively representative sample of the Scottish population, including roughly even numbers of male and female, urban and rural, employed and unemployed authors. Based on the authors' occupations, educational qualifications and self-identification of class, there were higher numbers of educated and middle-class respondents, and few non-educated and working-class Scots. There were also few 'others' such as Catholic or Irish Scots. While insight into these members of society was gathered through other sources, it is hoped that future studies will encompass a broader range of lived experiences.

It is important to note this is a small sample group and findings may be limited. I have taken a *bricolage* approach, though, believing that when layered with other primary sources the value of a small sample group is not lost.[62] By employing a range of sources, I have been able to make comparisons between official and private interpretations of events or morale status, uncover regional variation within Scotland, and contrast with scholarship about war experiences elsewhere in Britain.

Interest groups

Finally, this monograph also draws upon documents, records and publications of special interest groups. These include political or cultural organisations, such as the Scottish National Party; religious groups, particularly the Church of Scotland; and advocacy groups, including the Scottish Temperance Alliance. Documents, annual reports, correspondence and meeting minutes have further illuminated home front activities in Scotland during the Second World War. Such records also expose the complex factors at play in Scottish society, revealing hidden motivations and concerns exposed or exacerbated by war. For example, records of the Synod of the Church of Scotland reveal concerns about secularisation, and divulge the multi-faceted tactics used to win hearts and minds during the war years.

In addition to these types of document, an important source of information was reports produced by M-O. These included special reports authored by investigators on topics such as drinking, morale in Glasgow and 'the Clyde situation'.[63] In contrast to directives and diaries, which were composed entirely by public volunteers, these studies were produced by combining reports authored by trained investigators with

---

[62] Ibid., 1, 12.
[63] M-O, Topic Collection (TC) 85: Scottish drinking, 11 October 1940; TC600: Morale in Glasgow and apprentice strikes, 7 March 1941; File Report (FR) 932: The Clyde situation, October 1941.

those by amateur social commentators.⁶⁴ Critics have asserted that M-O's wartime reports are infused with the pre-conceived notions of their authors, particularly regarding class, and that topical reports produced for Whitehall's MoI may reflect the agendas of that organisation.⁶⁵ In contrast, others state that one of M-O's great strengths was its independence, and its trained observers reported on seen behaviour and overheard conversations 'regardless of any official accounts, departmental feelings or published glosses', even to the extent of inspiring 'strong hostility' at Cabinet level.⁶⁶ Potential limitations notwithstanding, M-O files are 'a rich vein of raw material',⁶⁷ and a resource 'for which there is no parallel or substitute'.⁶⁸

However, records created by special interest groups should be viewed with extra caution. Not only are they subject to the biases of their authors, but they are created with a view to influencing policy, shaping public behaviour and, as we shall see in Chapter 2, persuading authorities such as the police to act on issues of concern. We must also recognise these groups are not necessarily representative of wider society. This is especially the case with groups such as the Scottish National Party, which had a membership of 10,000 in 1934 and had declined to 2,000 in 1939.⁶⁹ These sources, however, enrich our understanding of Scottish life and society, and detail the causes, values and issues with which citizens were concerned. They also expose undercurrents, and reveal the pressures such groups placed on authorities and lawmakers.

In summary, the difficulty of examining lived experiences and individual subjectivities is that, as M-O founder Tom Harrisson pointed out, 'no one is privately typical of anyone else'.⁷⁰ Individual sources, while not representative at the base level, nonetheless provide access to a broader cultural world and allow historians to 'teas[e] from unique stories insights into more general historical processes'.⁷¹ It is my hope that future studies of the lived experiences of war will be able to address any shortcomings.

---

[64] Dorothy Sheridan, 'Researching ourselves? The Mass-Observation project', in Ruth Finnegan (ed.), *Participating in the Knowledge Society* (London: Palgrave Macmillan, 2005): 138–51, here 138.
[65] Brad Bevan and John Griffiths, 'Mass-Observation and civilian morale: working-class communities during the Blitz 1940–41', *Mass Observation: Observational Papers* 8 (1998), 2, 4–5.
[66] Bevan and Griffiths, 'Mass-Observation', 2; Harrisson, *Living through the Blitz*, 15.
[67] Mackay, *Half the Battle*, 11.
[68] Paul Addison, 'Introduction', *The British People and World War II: Home Intelligence Reports on Opinion and Morale, 1940–1944*, Reel 1 (University of Sussex, 1983), 8.
[69] Christopher Harvie, *Scotland and Nationalism: Scottish Society and Politics 1701 to the Present*, 4th edn (Abingdon: Routledge, 2004), 31.
[70] Harrisson, *Living through the Blitz*, 254.
[71] Hinton, *Nine Wartime Lives*, 17.

Chapter outline

Following a prologue which examines Scotland's economy, politics, society and culture on the eve of war, the subsequent chapters are organised thematically. These themes have been chosen as they represent common aspects of home front life, and therefore provide a comprehensive look at Scottish wartime society. Scotland is a country of extremes with wide variations between regions, and, of course, not all wartime experiences are homogenous. Nonetheless, this research draws out and explores the commonalities of wartime life as well as sketching a picture of Scottish culture in the mid-twentieth century.

Chapters 1 and 7 explore wartime measures and their effects on local communities, through studies of the official evacuation scheme, and the rural sector's response to ambitious targets for food and forestry production. These chapters both utilise diaries to assess people's more personal understandings of their new roles, as well as newspaper and official reports to chart discontent and friction related to these new measures. This theme of community friction is further interrogated in Chapter 2, which investigates the moral panic over juvenile delinquency. This chapter also delves into underlying anxieties about changing social and gender norms, secularisation and questions of identity.

As this introduction has established, values of civic virtue, sacrifice, support for the war effort and British 'national' identity were considered important aspects of home front life and community participation. Chapters 3 and 4 use life writings, questionnaire responses and intelligence reports to examine the place of these attributes on the Scottish home front. These chapters chart strike action, unrest and anti-government activity, and examine the factors that influenced morale in Scotland. Likewise, Chapters 5 and 6 interrogate notions of graft and sacrifice. Archival sources including letters, diaries, questionnaire responses, government reports, newspapers and magazines are used to explore both everyday life and leisure, and holidays. These chapters conclude Scots had ample time for leisure and pleasure, and displayed a particular determination to holiday during a time of national and global crisis.

This book examines Scottish society and culture during the Second World War. It also explores interactions between history, internal divisions, and national identity, and interrogates the ways these factors influenced Scottish responses to war. Moreover, this book charts the ways war changed Scotland and, in doing so, it also uncovers the uncertainties that permeated Scottish society at this time: relating to nationhood, to cultural identity, to Scotland's place within the Union and towards the country's future.

PROLOGUE

Scotland on the Eve of War

To assess the ways in which the Second World War shaped Scotland, we must first explore Scottish life and society on the eve of war. By gaining an appreciation of pre-war Scotland, we are better able to understand the responses Scots made to war, and the underlying tensions, traditions and priorities that underpinned Scottish life at this time. Moreover, as explained in the Introduction, most previous research on the British home front has concentrated on life and culture in England, and more specifically on London. There is an extensive historiography on England's economy, politics, society and culture in the interwar period, and this existing research has enabled historians to make judgements about the changes war brought to Britain.[1] Consequently, an understanding of pre-war Scotland will bring greater comprehension of the ways war impacted everyday life, as well as illuminating differences in wartime experience between Scotland and Britain.

Scotland in the interwar period was a nation wrought with what sociologists Catherine Bromley and David McCrone have called 'fissiparous

---

[1] See for example, on the economy, Roderick Floud and Paul Johnson (eds), *The Cambridge Economic History of Modern Britain*, Vol. 2: *Economic Maturity, 1860–1939* (Cambridge: Cambridge University Press, 2008); S. N. Broadberry, *The British Economy between the Wars, A Macroeconomic Survey* (Oxford: Blackwell, 1986); Neil K. Buxton and Derek H. Aldcroft (eds), *British Industry between the Wars: Instability and Industrial Development, 1919–1939* (London: Scolar Press, 1979). On politics: Chris Wrigley (ed.), *A Companion to Early Twentieth-Century Britain* (Oxford: Blackwell, 2003); Paul Addison, *The Road to 1945: British Politics and the Second World War* (London: Jonathan Cape, 1975); Richard Thurlow, *Fascism in Britain: From Oswald Mosley's Blackshirts to the National Front* (London: I. B. Tauris, 1998); A. J. P. Taylor, *English History, 1914–1945* (Oxford: Oxford University Press, 1965). On society: Martin Daunton (ed.), *The Cambridge Urban History of Britain*, Vol. 3: *1840–1950* (Cambridge: Cambridge University Press, 2001); John Benson, *The Working Class in Britain, 1850–1939* (London: Longman, 1989); Selina Todd, 'Young women, work, and leisure in interwar England', *The History Journal* 48, no. 3 (2005): 789–809; Richard Overy, *The Twilight Years: The Paradox of Britain Between the Wars* (London: Penguin, 2010); Daniel Todman, *The Great War: Myth and Memory* (London: Hambledon, 2005); Jay Winter, *The Great War and the British People* (London: Macmillan, 1985). On culture: Martin Pugh, *'We Danced All Night': A Social History of Britain Between the Wars* (London: The Bodley Head, 2008); Peter Borsay, *A History of Leisure: The British Experience since 1500* (Basingstoke: Palgrave Macmillan, 2006); Stephen Humphries, *Hooligans or Rebels? An Oral History of Working-Class Childhood and Youth, 1889–1939* (Oxford: Blackwell, 1981).

tendencies'.² Virtually every sector of society was divided and existing schisms widened along economic, political, social and cultural lines. These divisions were complex and often overlapped, reflecting historical tensions and underlying uncertainty about Scotland's identity and place in a changing world. This prologue explores these themes of economy, politics, society and culture to establish a picture of Scottish life and society on the eve of war.

Economy

At the beginning of the twentieth century, the Scottish economy flourished. A global industrial powerhouse, Scotland was a world leader in the production of textiles, ships, locomotives and steel.³ Scottish goods were traded across the world, and Glasgow stood as the second city of the British Empire, after London.⁴ The Scottish economy was reliant on manual labour, in which over 70 per cent of the workforce were employed at the turn of the century.⁵ In the Glasgow region, textiles and clothing were major employers and, in 1911, 17 per cent of Glasgow's industrial employment was in these two industries.⁶ Scotland's dependence on heavy industry led to increased levels of urbanisation, and the vast numbers of Scots and Irish immigrants seeking work swelled the population of the western counties to 44 per cent of the national population.⁷ The city of Glasgow was particularly popular, mostly as a result of greater employment opportunities, and on the eve of the Great War it contained 1 million of Scotland's nearly 5 million inhabitants.⁸ In 1911, nearly one in two employed male workers in Scotland found work in the wider Glasgow and western region now known as Strathclyde.⁹ For many of these inhabitants, wages were low and life depended on seasonal employment that could be erratic, for example as a result of fluctuations in shipping demand.¹⁰

Scotland's economy, though, was overly reliant on these heavy industries, and depended on overseas markets for the coal, jute, locomotives

---

² Catherine Bromley and David McCrone, 'A nation of regions?', in John Curtice, David McCrone, Alison Park and Lindsay Paterson (eds), *New Scotland, New Society? Are Social and Political Ties Fragmenting?* (Edinburgh: Polygon, 2002), 167.
³ Clive H. Lee, 'Scotland, 1860–1939: growth and poverty', in Floud and Johnson, *Economic History of Modern Britain*, 428.
⁴ Lee, 'Scotland, 1860–1939', 428; W. Hamish Fraser, 'Introduction', in W. Hamish Fraser and Irene Maver (eds), *Glasgow*, Vol. II: *1830 to 1912* (Manchester: Manchester University Press, 1996), 3.
⁵ Arthur McIvor, 'The realities and narratives of paid work: the Scottish workplace', in Abrams and Brown, *History of Everyday Life*, 105.
⁶ John Butt, 'The industries of Glasgow', in Fraser and Maver, *Glasgow*, Vol. II, 98–9.
⁷ Devine, *Scottish Nation*, 252.
⁸ Ibid., 253, 259.
⁹ Richard Rodger, 'The labour force', in Fraser and Maver, *Glasgow*, Vol. II, 166.
¹⁰ Fraser, 'Introduction', 4.

and ships produced in its factories and yards.[11] In the first decade of the twentieth century this would come to present a problem, as increased international competition and mechanisation threatened these industries and Scotland's reliance on them. This decline was halted, though, with the arrival of the Great War. On the eve of war the shipyards of Glasgow's River Clyde produced almost one-fifth of the world output of shipping tonnage, including battleships and cruisers for the Admiralty.[12] Jute and linen factories once again prospered as canvas for tenting and sandbags for frontline trenches were in demand. Other war supplies such as ships and iron for railways and munitions brought a surge in demand for Scotland's commodities.[13]

In the words of Richard J. Finlay, 'if the Scottish economy had been unbalanced before 1914, the wartime boom pushed it into an unsustainable trajectory'.[14] In the years following the Great War, Scotland was unable to sustain this prosperity and its main industries resumed their decline. Inflation ran rampant and as a result the cost of living almost doubled between 1914 and 1920.[15] In response to the collapse in key industries, high unemployment plagued sectors such as mining and manufacturing. Between 1923 and 1930, Scottish unemployment averaged 14 per cent, compared to a UK average of 11.4 per cent.[16] By 1931, male unemployment in Scotland had risen sharply to 39 per cent, well above the UK average of 22 per cent.[17] Further, nearly 28 per cent of Scotland's unemployed had been out of work for over twelve months. This figure was the highest in the UK.[18] The resulting poverty was severe and between 1929 and 1936 numbers on poor relief rose by 76 per cent. In contrast, UK figures showed only a 13 per cent increase over the same period.[19] Moreover, Scottish real earnings were lower than the British average, with one estimate placing the Scottish per capita income in 1938 at 89 per cent of the British average.[20] In response, many Scots sought better opportunities in other lands and

---

[11] Devine, *Scottish Nation*, 254.

[12] Ibid., 250, 265.

[13] Clive H. Lee, 'The Scottish economy and the First World War', in Catriona M. M. Macdonald and E. W. McFarland (eds), *Scotland and the Great War* (East Linton: Tuckwell Press, 1999), 12–14.

[14] Richard J. Finlay, 'The interwar crisis: the failure of extremism', in T. M. Devine and Jenny Wormald (eds), *The Oxford Handbook of Modern Scottish History* (Oxford: Oxford University Press, 2012), 573.

[15] Angela Turner and Arthur McIvor, '"Bottom dog men": disability, social welfare and advocacy in the Scottish coalfields in the interwar years, 1918–1939', *The Scottish Historical Review* XCVI, 2, no. 243 (2017), 187–213, here 192.

[16] Harvie, *No Gods*, 47.

[17] Scotland's Census, '1931', https://www.scotlandscensus.gov.uk/1931 (accessed 6 March 2019). (In contrast, Devine gives a figure of 29% in *Scottish Nation*, 268.)

[18] Cameron, *Impaled Upon a Thistle*, 52.

[19] Harvie, *No Gods*, 47.

[20] Devine, *Scottish Nation*, 271.

emigration soared to unprecedented levels, as will soon be discussed in greater detail.

During the years of depression, workplace discontent raged. Many workers were on a piece-rate payment system in which wages were linked to production output, and this was viewed by some workers as a way for employers to consolidate their power over employees. In the coal mining industry more than half of employees were on a piece-rate system, and in engineering this was almost universal.[21] In addition, workers expressed both fear and antagonism towards foremen, who had the power to make decisions over hiring and firing and production processes, and managed the day-to-day activity within a workplace.[22] Again, this was evidence of the power imbalances present in many of the heavy industries that dominated Scotland's economy. When the Second World War upended this system, as Chapter Six will investigate, this would radically alter workplace relations in Scotland.

In the later 1930s as preparations for the future conflict were put into place, Scotland's heavy industries were thrown a lifeline. In the surge for rearmament, the British government invested heavily in industries such as coal, iron, steel and shipping. Scotland would play a key part in Britain's war effort, with one-quarter of wartime shipbuilding taking place on the River Clyde.[23] In addition, the revival of Scotland's industries led unemployment to fall to 1.6 per cent by the outbreak of war.[24]

Politics

The political situation in interwar Scotland was closely linked to the country's economic fortunes. The unstable interwar period saw the end of Scotland's Liberal tradition and signalled a period of great turbulence across the political spectrum. Before the Great War, the Scottish Liberal Party had enjoyed a long hegemony, promoting the values of respectability, sobriety, self-improvement and education. In short, liberalism represented 'Scottish values'.[25] The challenges of war and the subsequent economic downturn brought the end of this Scottish political tradition and the rise of new elements such as socialism, conservatism, fascism and nationalism.

In the industrial Clydeside, working-class stress and frustration with the government proved fertile ground for socialist ideas. From 1914 to 1920, the Liberal government appeared indifferent to working-class frustrations, which spilled over into a series of strikes over dilution (the reliance on

---

[21] W. Knox, 'Class, work and trade unionism in Scotland', in A. Dickson and J. H. Treble (eds), *People and Society in Scotland*, Vol. III: *1914–1990* (Edinburgh: John Donald, 1992), 115.
[22] Ibid., 114. See also A. Moffat, *My Life with the Miners* (London: Lawrence & Wishart, 1965).
[23] Crang, 'The Second World War', 559.
[24] Harvie, *No Gods*, 52.
[25] Devine, *Scottish Nation*, 285.

semi- or unskilled labour for mass production), overcrowding, rent hikes and poor work conditions.[26] In the 1920s, the Communist Party of Great Britain (CPGB) gained support, having a solid member base in Glasgow and mining areas such as Fife. There was also a move by communists to infiltrate the Labour Party during the 1920s, which proved 'a serious headache' for Labour officials.[27] Thus, communist influence was not limited to those who supported the CPGB. After a change in policy in the 1930s, Scottish support for communism waned, though the Party retained its hold in traditional heartlands such as Fife and Clydebank.[28]

In addition to communism, the interwar period saw the rise of socialist agitators such as the Clyde Workers' Committee, the Independent Labour Party, suffragettes and the Glasgow Trades Council.[29] These groups appeared sympathetic to workers' causes, and in response the socialist ideals of the Labour Party grew in appeal. Clydeside workers felt the Liberal Party no longer represented their interests, while Labour seduced with its promotion of working-class causes such as better housing and working conditions, and ideas that workers should receive a greater share of national wealth.[30] In the 1918 elections, Labour gained one-third of Scottish votes, ten times more than any previous result, and by 1922 was the largest party in Scotland.[31] Socialism provided a voice for the Scottish working class when traditional liberalism seemed to have failed it.

The success of the Labour Party was also driven by two other factors. Firstly, the 1918 Franchise Act redistributed Scottish electoral boundaries, intending to create constituencies of equal population size. As a result, the urban industrial areas of Glasgow and the central belt gained seats. Because these areas contained large populations of working-class voters who felt socialism represented their interests, the Labour Party was 'much assisted' by this process.[32] Adding to this was the issue of Irish Home Rule. Previously, Irish Catholic immigrants had shown strong support for the Liberal Party who supported Home Rule, but when the Liberals failed to stop the partitioning of Ireland in 1920, Irish Catholic support for the Party dropped. The key beneficiary was the Labour Party. At this time, Catholic voters made up around 20 per cent of the electorate, a significant new support base for the Labour Party.[33]

[26] The three biggest disputes were the 1915–16 strikes over dilution; the 1915 strikes in protest at rising house rents; and a 1919 strike calling for a forty-hour working week. After each, the government cracked down on socialist publications and key figures of the movement.
[27] I. G. C. Hutchison, *Scottish Politics in the Twentieth Century* (Basingstoke: Palgrave, 2001), 60–62.
[28] Ibid., 97–8.
[29] Devine, *Scottish Nation*, 311.
[30] Finlay, 'Interwar crisis', 572.
[31] Devine, *Scottish Nation*, 311–12.
[32] Hutchison, *Scottish Politics*, 30.
[33] Michael Fry, *Patronage and Principle: A Political History of Modern Scotland* (Aberdeen: Aberdeen University Press, 1987), 148; Devine, *Scottish Nation*, 312.

The turbulent days of the interwar period also saw the rise of middle-class radicalism. During the Great War inflation had devalued savings and salaries, and post-war government regulation was seen as a threat to small business-owners. The middle class was also concerned that unemployment relief was draining government resources, while those who owned property were affected by wartime rent freezes.[34] With the rise of Labour in the central belt, and the spectre of Red Clydeside still looming, some middle-class voters found security in nationalist and fascist politics.

The main organisation dedicated to fascism in Scotland was the British Union of Fascists (BUF). Run by Oswald Mosley and his Blackshirts, the party had a small amount of success in Scotland, mainly in pockets such as Dumfriesshire, Aberdeen, Edinburgh and Glasgow.[35] In Leith and Edinburgh party meetings and rallies came under attack from the radical group Protestant Action, who were famous for violent attacks on Catholics, and who sought to stamp out extremism.[36] Ultimately, the BUF was run from London and failed to capitalise on Scottish interests. At its peak in 1934, there were around 1,000 Scottish members, though the Union soon declined in popularity.[37] While this party might not have amounted to much in Scotland, its brief popularity showed that radical groups were able to gain a foothold in a country divided by issues of class, race and religion.

As we shall read shortly, during the interwar period Scotland struggled with identity and questions of nationhood. For some Scots, there were concerns that 'the best of the nation' had emigrated and, when combined with heavy Great War casualties and strong Irish immigration, there arose a feeling the Scots as a race were dying out.[38] This unease over the state of the Scottish nation led to the creation of the National Party of Scotland and the Scottish Party, who aligned to form the Scottish National Party (SNP) in 1934. These parties shared a desire for some form of Scottish Home Rule, though this was somewhat appeased when the government instituted administrative devolution in 1937.[39] Richard Finlay stated the Nationalists did not achieve greater success as all were 'dogged by inability to form a consensus'.[40] Adding to this, the SNP was concerned at the risk of fascist nationalism and issued a public statement condemning fascism, which upset its more right-wing followers, thus alienating part of its support base.[41]

---

[34] Finlay, 'Interwar crisis', 576.
[35] Stephen M. Cullen, 'The fasces and the saltire: the failure of the British Union of Fascists in Scotland, 1932–1940', *The Scottish Historical Review* 87, no. 2 (2008), 309–10.
[36] Ibid., 325.
[37] Ibid., 315.
[38] Finlay, 'Interwar crisis', 578.
[39] Ibid., 579.
[40] Ibid., 578.
[41] Cullen, 'The fasces', 320.

With the fragmentation of many political opponents, the Unionists were in an enviable position. The party enjoyed success as a result of its superior organisation skills, operating with 'vitality and élan', and making strong appeals to women and youth.[42] It also benefited from healthy party membership and, consequently, financial contributions were high.[43] In addition, support came from the Church of Scotland, the legal system and the press. The Unionist Party worked hard to consolidate their power and, as a result, were 'remarkably successful' and enjoyed 'undisputed supremacy' in the interwar period.[44]

The stand-out features of Scottish politics in the interwar period are the end of the Liberal tradition, the rise and fall of Labour and the fractious nature of political parties at this time. It is clear that economic crisis undermined political certainty, maintaining a turbulence that would carry through to the late 1930s. In addition, fringe and radical elements were able to gain a foothold, exploiting existing social grievances.

Society

While Scots were grappling with the changing economic and political situation, the face of society was changing and divisions further widening. One of the key social changes in the early twentieth century came as a result of mass emigration. Between 1850 and 1930 approximately 2 million Scots emigrated and, as a result, the country regularly ranked in the top four European countries exporting migrants.[45] Furthermore, in the years between 1904 and 1913 Scotland had the highest emigration rates per capita of any European country.[46] This trend did not subside after the Great War, and numbers of Scots seeking opportunities elsewhere continued to increase. Between 1921 and 1931 emigration figures were double what they had been in each decade to 1911.[47]

While many of these Scots left for foreign lands, others migrated internally. During the nineteenth century, many rural Scots had moved to cities for better employment opportunities. T. M. Devine estimated that, at that time, up to one-third of the entire population of the Hebrides and western Highland mainland permanently migrated.[48] This was devastating for rural communities, which lost not only heads of population, but rural traditions and culture.[49]

---

[42] Hutchison, *Scottish Politics*, 42.
[43] Ibid., 42.
[44] Devine, *Scottish Nation*, 316, 326.
[45] Angela McCarthy, *Personal Narratives of Irish and Scottish Migration, 1921–65: 'For Spirit and Adventure'* (Manchester: Manchester University Press, 2007), 15.
[46] Devine, *Scottish Nation*, 263.
[47] Ibid., 269.
[48] Ibid., 418–19.
[49] T. M. Devine, *The Scottish Clearances: A History of the Dispossessed* (Milton Keynes: Penguin, 2019), 3, 11–13.

This internal migration, combined with arrivals from countries such as Ireland, resulted in growing levels of urbanisation. By the early 1900s, more than one in three Scots lived in the 'big four' cities of Glasgow, Edinburgh, Dundee and Aberdeen.[50] For those in the working class, life was characterised by overcrowding, poor nutrition and high rates of disease. Overcrowding was particularly common amongst those who lived in inner-city tenements. In 1911, 8.6 per cent of Scotland's population lived four to a room and, by 1931, over 35 per cent of Scots lived with more than two persons per room. In England and Wales at this time, the comparable figure was only 6.9 per cent.[51] Overcrowding was acute in poor districts, especially in Glasgow, where the density of persons per acre was twice that in Edinburgh and Dundee.[52] Conditions in the 'grossly overcrowded' Scottish tenements were said to be responsible for lice and high rates of typhus, cholera and lung disease.[53] This was partly a result of poor sanitation and inferior housing. These slum tenements saw multiple families sharing one toilet or a single water tap, densely packed together in housing that had inadequate ventilation and drainage.[54] As a result, tenants frequently used closes and stairs for toileting, which became 'filthy and evil smelling'.[55] Living with such inadequate levels of sanitation, it is hardly surprising disease spread quickly and cleanliness was difficult to achieve.

Not only were many urban Scots living in overcrowded conditions or inadequate housing, but their nutrition was also suffering. In the early years of the twentieth century, working-class diets began to move away from traditional oats, milk and fish, to meals high in sugar and low in fresh vegetables, fat or protein.[56] Studies in Glasgow revealed porridge, broth and potatoes were disappearing from the city diet. As a result, rates of juvenile undernourishment were high, tooth decay was on the increase and city children showed lower height and weight than their peers in the country.[57] In addition, in the mid-1930s infant mortality in Scotland was higher than in all other western European countries, except Spain and Portugal.[58] This was mostly attributed to poor nutrition, overcrowding and disease.[59] A study by famous Scottish scientist John Boyd Orr found that 20 per cent of Scottish families had a diet that was deficient in all areas (protein, fat,

---

[50] Devine, *Scottish Nation*, 253.
[51] James G. Kellas, *Modern Scotland* (London: George Allen & Unwin, 1980), 26.
[52] Devine, *Scottish Nation*, 341.
[53] W. Hamish Fraser and Irene Maver, 'The social problems of the city' in Fraser and Maver, *Glasgow*, Vol. II, 353; Devine, *Scottish Nation*, 337.
[54] Fraser and Maver, 'Social problems', 376–7.
[55] Ibid., 376–7.
[56] Ibid., 361.
[57] Harvie, *No Gods*, 73; Fraser and Maver, 'Social problems', 361.
[58] Cameron, *Impaled Upon a Thistle*, 127.
[59] Ibid.

calories, vitamins and minerals). Across wider Britain, in contrast, only 10 per cent of families fell into this group.[60]

Not all Scots were impoverished, of course and, for those in the middle classes, the interwar period was a time of some security and upward mobility. During these years, middle-class unemployment was at a low 5 per cent and income rose around 15 per cent for those in steady employment.[61] Moreover, there was a boom in suburban bungalow-building, which meant the middle classes could live further away from their place of employment.[62] In contrast to working-class 'rough culture' of drink, gambling and football, middle-class Scots were more likely to subscribe to the Kirk's idea of 'rational recreation'.[63] Many became involved in church and voluntary groups, and the temperance movement. As a result of these differences in experience, the class gap again began to widen in Scotland, as it had in earlier times.[64] Historian Christopher Harvie has defined this period as having a class-consciousness to an 'almost pathological degree'.[65]

Alongside the growing chasm between the classes, religious and ethnic tension was also rife. Much of this tension was directed at Catholics, of whom there was a significant population in the west of Scotland. Large numbers of Irish had immigrated in the mid-nineteenth century in response to the Great Famine, and many of these were Catholic.[66] Further, Catholics were inclined to have larger families, so overall population was, naturally, greater.[67] The Irish Catholic population tended to concentrate in particular districts or towns where there were jobs in heavy industry, such as in the east end of Glasgow, Airdrie and Coatbridge.[68] In 1930, while 26.2 per cent of the Scottish population identified as Church of Scotland, 11.2 per cent were Catholic.[69]

During the interwar period, sectarianism increased in intensity. Roman Catholics came under greater criticism from the Kirk, which had historically been hostile towards Catholicism, and Protestant Action groups.[70] Irish Catholics were the subject of special attention, and were targeted not only for their religion, but for their alleged intemperance, squalor and

---

[60] John Foster, 'A proletarian nation? Occupation and class since 1914', in Dickson and Treble, *People and Society*, 223.
[61] Devine, *Scottish Nation*, 268.
[62] Ibid., 348–9.
[63] Callum G. Brown, 'Popular culture and the continuing struggle for rational recreation', in T. M. Devine and R. J. Finlay (eds), *Scotland in the Twentieth Century* (Edinburgh: Edinburgh University Press, 1996), 215–16.
[64] Ibid., 210, 216–17.
[65] Harvie, *No Gods*, 85.
[66] Devine, *Scottish Nation*, 252.
[67] Harvie, *No Gods*, 68.
[68] Devine, *Scottish Nation*, 487.
[69] Harvie, *No Gods*, 85.
[70] Devine, *Scottish Nation*, 491.

supposed deviance.[71] At the forefront of this criticism was the Church of Scotland, which waged a persistent campaign against the 'menace' of Irish Catholic immigrants.[72] In 1923, the Church published a pamphlet entitled 'The menace of the Irish race to our Scottish nationality', outlining the ways in which Irish Catholics were taking 'Scottish' jobs, subverting Presbyterian values and bringing criminality and intemperance to the country.[73] Grassroots anti-Catholic leagues also sprang up, sometimes resorting to violence to get their message across. This religious strife continued into the 1930s, though it had lessened by the time war broke out in 1939.[74]

Culture

Alongside the turbulence, uncertainty and division experienced at political, economic and social levels, interwar Scotland was marked by cultural crisis. Prior to the Great War, Scotland's identity had been closely tied to its place in the British Empire. In its heyday Scotland was one of the world's leading industrial nations, Glasgow was second city of the Empire and its explorers, missionaries and colonialists were proudly sent to far-away locations.[75] This global prominence was a source of national pride.

Further aspects of Scotland's pre-war identity were based on Highlandism and the military tradition. In the late eighteenth century, tartanry and imagined Highland traditions had become popular with Lowland elite and London society.[76] Adding to this legend was the heroic reputation of Highland regiments during conflicts such as the Napoleonic Wars. Scotsmen in these regiments became known for loyalty, courage, daring and virility.[77] Highlanders, wrote Tom Devine, were no longer barbaric or inferior, but a 'standard-bearer for long-held beliefs about the martial virtues of the Scottish nation'.[78] In addition, tartanry was 'an alluring myth for a society searching for an identity amid unprecedented economic and social change'.[79]

During the Great War, these themes of Highlands, tartanry and warriors of old were again drawn upon. Military recruiting campaigns relied heavily on such imagery. Most featured kilted soldiers and drew upon ideas

---

[71] Finlay, 'Interwar crisis', 583.
[72] T. M. Devine, 'Introduction', in T. M. Devine (ed.), *Scotland's Shame? Bigotry and Sectarianism in Modern Scotland* (Edinburgh: Mainstream, 2000), 7.
[73] Devine, *Scottish Nation*, 499.
[74] Tom Gallagher, *Glasgow: The Uneasy Peace: Religious Tension in Modern Scotland* (Manchester: Manchester University Press, 1987), 5.
[75] Richard J. Finlay, 'National identity in crisis: politicians, intellectuals and the "end of Scotland", 1920–1939', *History*, 79, no. 256 (1994), 242.
[76] Devine, *Scottish Nation*, 223–4.
[77] Ibid., 234, 238–40; Finlay, 'National identity', 242.
[78] Devine, *Scottish Nation*, 240.
[79] Ibid., 245.

of loyalty and ancestry.[80] Similarly, home front campaigns used themes of military and Highland identity. One campaign by the Scottish War Savings Committee featured William Wallace and a message that by buying national war bonds the public could 'help to defend [their] life and liberty'.[81] By the end of 1915, 2.4 million British men had volunteered for the armed forces and, of this total, 13 per cent were Scottish.[82] More than 100,000 Scots perished in the conflict, and this took a sharp toll on Scottish communities.[83] In addition, many men returned disabled or incapacitated, others suffered as a result of unemployment and homelessness, and some Highland veterans felt cheated out of traditional land rewards.[84]

Factors such as these augmented the identity question, and Scotland as a country seemed to have lost its self-confidence.[85] With the decline of both the British Empire and Scotland's role as industrial world leader, the country seemed cast adrift, its identity in tatters. In addition, after the heavy sacrifices made during the Great War, military attributes were no longer held in such high esteem.[86] With the 1920s and 1930s bringing a range of changes to Scottish politics, economy and society, for many there was a reassessment of Scottish identity. Within a narrow section of society, there was a push for cultural reawakening and a revival of the Scots language, but for others it was a time of uncertainty and of wondering if Scottish culture might just be a 'hollow tartan sham'.[87]

In summary, the interwar period brought widespread change to Scotland. The economy was devastated by the decline of industry, unemployment raged and there was a haemorrhage of population. In addition, these years were characterised by sectarianism, poverty, political turbulence and questions of identity. This period of unrest and uncertainty revealed a 'crisis of national insecurity', exposing the underlying concern that the Scottish identity and culture was slipping away.[88] For some, Scotland's strength would be found in her place within Britain; for others, the Union reduced Scotland to a 'subordinate province' and the solution lay in devolution and the nationalist movement.[89] Thus, Scotland stood on the edge of the Second World War riven by internal division and grappling with insecurity. As the following chapters will explore, these legacies carried into the war years, shaping Scottish responses and experiences.

[80] Imperial War Museum (IWM), PST 12148, 'Argyll and Sutherland Highlanders', 1914.
[81] IWM, PST 10079, 'Help to defend your life and liberty', 1918.
[82] Trevor Royle, 'The First World War', in Spiers et al., *Military History of Scotland*, 512–13.
[83] Royle, 'First World War', 529–30.
[84] Ibid., 530; Ewen A. Cameron and Iain J. M. Robertson, 'Fighting and bleeding for the land: the Scottish Highlands and the Great War', in Macdonald and McFarland, *Scotland and the Great War*, 90, 97.
[85] Finlay, 'National identity', 242, 244.
[86] Ibid., 255.
[87] Ibid., 244.
[88] Devine, *Scottish Nation*, 498.
[89] Finlay, 'National identity', 255; Fry, *Patronage and Principle*, 148.

CHAPTER ONE

'Here Come the Keelies': The Government Evacuation Scheme in Scotland

With the outbreak of the Second World War in September 1939,[1] plans were enacted across Britain that saw over one-and-a-half million people evacuated from densely populated areas to safer rural areas. These evacuees were billeted with local families, but in the days and weeks afterward, hosts and evacuees struggled to integrate, and gossip about the new arrivals proliferated. The following story was spread through one rural village in Scotland:

> A small boy from a Glasgow dock-tenement . . . refused to eat certain kinds of food because he was not in the habit of eating them. His foster-mother tried every means of persuasion and coaxing, at last in her desperation declaring that God would be very angry if he did not take his food. The boy still refused. That night a storm of thunder and lightning broke over the district, and during it the woman felt impelled to go upstairs to see how the boy was getting on. To her horror the small bedroom was empty. Hurrying downstairs to the other rooms she discovered him in the kitchen, gloomily eating. Before she could speak he remarked with a sulky frown, 'It's an awfu' fuss He's makin' ower three prunes, eh?'[2]

Such stories were commonplace, as rural hosts tried to make sense of the alien arrivals. This chapter explores these receptions and perceptions, examining the responses of Scottish hosts and communities to the evacuation. It focuses exclusively on those evacuated via the official Government Evacuation Scheme (GES), though a significant portion of evacuation took place outside that framework.[3]

Operation Pied Piper, Whitehall's plan to relocate vulnerable persons from cities to 'safer' areas during the Second World War, was marred by

---

[1] 'Keelie': Scots slang: an urban ruffian; lower-class town or city dweller, esp. Glaswegian. *Collins English Dictionary* (Glasgow: HarperCollins, 2019).
[2] John Clark, 'Notes on a village at war', *SMT Magazine*, February 1941, 20.
[3] This included school parties evacuated to homesteads and residential schools, or overseas to the Dominions via the Children's Overseas Reception Board. The Scottish Education Department (SED) estimated up to 7,000 children were privately evacuated during the first year of the war: see SED Report, 1939–1940, quoted in Scottish Women's Group on Public Welfare (SWG), and Minna Galbraith Cowan, *Our Scottish Towns: Evacuation and the Social Future* (Edinburgh: W. Hodge & Co., 1944), 5.

weak planning, poorly delivered and plagued by interpersonal conflict. Histories of evacuation in Britain have highlighted the official scheme's logistical glitches and the negative public reactions to verminous and ill-equipped evacuees, though many of these scholarly works concentrate on the evacuation of Londoners or those in other regions of England.[4] There are also important contributions on other types of wartime evacuation, such as the June 1940 civilian evacuation of the Channel Islands and child evacuations via the Children's Overseas Reception Board.[5] Further, this rich historiography benefits from research into the psychological and physical health impacts of child evacuation, while studies of evacuation through the lenses of class and motherhood, by Geoffrey Field and Maggie Andrews, are similarly insightful.[6] Moreover, a large body of popular history explores experiences and memories of former evacuees, those both on the official scheme and evacuated by private arrangement.[7]

In the immediate post-war years academic literature was dominated by assertions that the GES's exposure of working-class poverty, including poor health and housing, had prompted drastic social change and resulted in the creation of Britain's Welfare State.[8] This idea was popularised by social

---

[4] See Richard Titmuss, *Problems of Social Policy* (London: HMSO, 1950); Calder, *People's War*; Royle, *Time of Tyrants*, 202–3; A. M. Preston, 'The evacuation of schoolchildren from Newcastle upon Tyne, 1939–1942: an assessment of the factors which influenced the nature of educational provision in Newcastle and its reception areas', *History of Education* 18, no. 3 (1989): 231–41; S. J. Hess, 'Civilian evacuation to Devon in the Second World War', PhD diss., University of Exeter, 2006.

[5] On the Channel Islands see Gillian Mawson, *Guernsey Evacuees: The Forgotten Evacuees of the Second World War* (Stroud: History Press, 2012); on CORB see Michael Fethney, *The Absurd and the Brave* (Lewes: Book Guild, 1990); Claire L. Halstead, 'From lion to leaf: the evacuation of British children to Canada during the Second World War', PhD diss., University of Western Ontario, 2016; Edward Stokes, *Innocents Abroad* (St Leonards: Allen & Unwin, 1994).

[6] Catherine Calvin, Jeremy Crang, Lindsay Paterson and Ian Deary, 'Childhood evacuation during World War II and subsequent cognitive ability: the Scottish Mental Survey 1947', *Longitudinal and Life Course Studies* 5, no. 2 (2014): 227–44; D. Foster, S. Davies and H. Steele, 'The evacuation of British children during World War II: a preliminary investigation into the long-term psychological effects', *Aging & Mental Health* 7, no. 5 (2003): 398–408; James Rusby and Fiona Tasker, 'Long-term effects of the British evacuation of children during World War 2 on their adult mental health', *Aging & Mental Health* 13, no. 3 (2009): 391–404; Field, *Blood, Sweat, and Toil*; Maggie Andrews, *Women and Evacuation in the Second World War: Femininity, Domesticity and Motherhood* (London: Bloomsbury, 2019).

[7] See Martin L. Parsons, *'I'll Take That One': Dispelling the Myths of Civilian Evacuation 1939–45* (Peterborough: Beckett Karlson, 1998); Mike Brown, *Evacuees: Evacuation in Wartime Britain 1939–1945* (Stroud: Sutton, 2005); John Welshman, *Churchill's Children: The Evacuee Experience in Wartime Britain* (Oxford: Oxford University Press, 2010); Julie Summers, *When the Children Came Home: Stories of Wartime Evacuees* (London: Simon and Schuster, 2012); Gillian Mawson, *Evacuees: Children's Lives on the WW2 Home Front* (Barnsley: Pen and Sword, 2014).

[8] Arthur Marwick and Harold Chapman, *The Home Front: The British and the Second World War* (London: Thames and Hudson, 1976); W. J. Mommsen (ed.), *The Emergence of the Welfare State in Britain and Germany, 1850–1950* (London: Croom Helm and German Historical

policy analyst Richard Titmuss, in his volume of the official history of the Second World War, which included figures from the GES in Scotland. He believed the extreme poverty exposed by evacuation had outraged the public, leading to the beliefs that public resources should be shared more equitably and the state should take greater responsibility for the health and housing of those in need. Titmuss claimed this fuelled inquiry and proposals for reform 'long before victory was even thought possible'.[9] Such ideas were promoted by other historians including Arthur Marwick, who stated that evacuation brought home 'the terrible inadequacies of existing social institutions' and war 'tipped the balance of circumstances' in favour of social change.[10]

The view of evacuation as catalyst for social change dominated analyses of the social history of the Second World War until revisionists began to re-examine wartime society and claims about its metamorphosis. In 1986, influential social historians John Macnicol and José Harris questioned the belief that evacuation directly brought about progressive change in British society. Both argued that while the GES exposed politicians to symptoms of inner-city poverty, this did not result in a swing in attitudes nor a lobby for increased state intervention.[11] Rather, Macnicol argued, it was incorrect to say a fundamental ideological shift had occurred when the evidence more strongly suggested that evacuation reinforced existing social divides, including the middle-class belief that nothing could change the working class, an 'incorrigible underclass of [the] personally inadequate'.[12]

In recent times, historians have given a more balanced interpretation of the evacuation's impact on British society. American historian Sonya Rose noted the post-war emergence of a new 'structure of feeling' concerned with addressing problems of social and economic inequality made 'painfully clear' by the evacuation.[13] Similarly, John Welshman, an expert in social policy and public health, argued there was powerful evidence for 'profoundly altered attitudes to state welfare', driven by evacuation's exposure of social problems.[14] As regards Scotland, Welshman and his colleague

Institute, 1981); Arthur Marwick, 'People's war and top people's peace? British society and the Second World War', in A. Sked and C. Cook (eds), *Crisis and Controversy: Essays in Honour of A. J. P. Taylor* (London: Macmillan, 1976): 148–64.

[9] Titmuss, *Social Policy*, 508.

[10] Marwick, 'Top people's peace?', 155; Marwick and Chapman, *Home Front*, 181.

[11] John Macnicol, 'The effect of the evacuation of schoolchildren on official attitudes to state intervention', in Harold L. Smith (ed.), *War and Social Change: British Society in the Second World War* (Manchester: Manchester University Press, 1986), 24; José Harris, 'Political ideas and the debate on state welfare, 1940–45', in Smith, *War and Social Change*, 258.

[12] Macnicol, 'Evacuation of schoolchildren', 27. See also R. Lowe, *The Welfare State in Britain Since 1945* (London: Macmillan, 1993); José Harris, 'Some aspects of social policy in Britain during the Second World War', in Mommsen, *Welfare State*, 247–60.

[13] Rose, *Which People's War?*, 62, 70.

[14] John Welshman, 'Evacuation and social policy during the Second World War: myth and reality', *Twentieth Century British History* 9, no. 1 (1998), 53.

John Stewart, in one of the few works dedicated to the Scottish evacuation, concluded the scheme drew attention to the plight of the urban impoverished and proposed its remedy, without interpreting poverty as a result of poor parenting or social inadequacy, as it was viewed in England.[15]

This chapter considers whether it was really the case that Scots avoided attributing to parental or societal defect the poverty exposed by evacuation. It asks how did Scottish hosts receive and perceive evacuees? Which factors explain those reactions? Beginning with the broader context of the GES in Scotland, the chapter then addresses the ways Scottish hosts received and perceived evacuees. Finally, it explores the underlying factors prompting host perceptions and responses.

Aside from Stewart and Welshman's article, Scotland has received little exposure in scholarship on the wider British evacuation.[16] What is available relies heavily on the work of William Boyd, an educationalist from Glasgow University who carried out a wartime survey on evacuation, and the war history written by Titmuss.[17] Adding to this narrow picture, Titmuss relied heavily on Boyd's survey when making claims about evacuation in Scotland. While Boyd's survey is comprehensive, this over-reliance on one source has resulted in a rather one-dimensional picture of the evacuation. To add richness to our knowledge of the GES in Scotland, this chapter utilises, alongside Boyd's valuable survey, a range of fresh archival sources, including personal papers and diaries, documents from Scottish government departments and articles from Scottish newspapers and magazines. Material is also included from the relatively untapped source of intelligence reports authored by the Scottish constabulary. Although utilising memoirs of the evacuation, this chapter is predominantly grounded in contemporary sources, and foregrounds host experiences of evacuation, seeking to understand motivations and pre-existing grievances that drove – and exacerbated – responses and sites of tension.

Background to the Scottish evacuation

Originally proposed in the 1920s, the idea of a pre-emptive public evacuation was intended to avoid civilian casualties in the event of enemy

---

[15] Stewart and Welshman, 'The evacuation of children'.
[16] Exceptions include Jo Jack, 'The impact of Second World War evacuation on social welfare in Scotland', MPhil thesis, University of Stirling, 2017; and J. M. Lloyd, 'The Scottish school system and the Second World War: a study in central policy and administration', PhD diss., University of Stirling, 1979; Mattie Turnbull, *Days of Apprehension and Adventure: Experiences of Scottish Evacuees During World War Two* (Pittsburgh, PA: Dorrance, 2016). Local histories also provide valuable insight, including Wallace (ed.), *Here Come the Glasgow Keelies*.
[17] William Boyd, *Evacuation in Scotland: A Record of Events and Experiments* (Bickley: University of London Press, 1944). Boyd and Glasgow University students surveyed teachers and helpers involved with evacuation, and compiled studies of other forms of evacuation, such as to camps and hostels.

air attack. Officials also believed bombing raids would damage schools and public facilities, and there would be a large amount of 'panic flight' from cities, clogging main transport routes. Estimates were initially based on German air raids on Britain in the Great War, and later revised after joint German and Italian bombings of civilians in the Spanish Civil War.[18] In 1938 the Committee on Evacuation, a sub-committee of Whitehall's Air Raid Precautions Department, announced a plan for a large-scale civilian evacuation programme. Under this plan, those from large industrial areas in England could voluntarily evacuate to safer parts of England or Wales, and vulnerable populations from Scottish cities would be moved to the surrounding countryside. While Scotland would be part of the wider British evacuation scheme, the Scottish Education Department (SED) and the Department of Health for Scotland would take responsibility for its organisation and implementation in Scotland.[19] This reflects other aspects of wartime administration, in which some powers were devolved to Scottish institutions. In evidence of the unequal footing of Britain's constituent nations, this did not happen in Wales.[20]

Scotland was divided into 'evacuation areas', with densities of population of 14,000 per square mile or more and seen as vulnerable to enemy attack; 'neutral areas'; and 'reception areas', which were generally in the countryside, away from key cities and coastlines, and had much lower population densities (see Figure 1.1).[21] Initially, Dundee, Rosyth, Edinburgh, Glasgow and Clydebank were deemed the most vulnerable to enemy attack and so the evacuation would begin from these areas.[22] After air attacks during 1940, the Firth of Forth, Inverkeithing, North Queensferry and South Queensferry were added to the list of evacuation zones. Further, after heavy bombings around the mouth of the River Clyde, Port Glasgow, Greenock and Dumbarton in 1941, these areas joined the list.[23]

In 1939, the Department of Health for Scotland surveyed available accommodation in Scottish reception areas, and instructed householders to prepare to host evacuees. Some of the census-takers were overly enthusiastic and in Dumfriesshire one man, owner of a house with nine rooms, was informed he would have to take twenty-eight children, while the owner of a mansion in Renfrewshire was told he would be given fifty.[24]

---

[18] Macnicol, 'Evacuation of schoolchildren', 10; National Records Scotland (NRS), ED24/1, Government Evacuation Scheme, 3 August 1941. For details about air raids in Britain during the Great War see Susan R. Grayzel, *At Home and Under Fire* (Cambridge: Cambridge University Press, 2012).

[19] John Anderson, *Report of Committee on Evacuation* (London: HMSO, 1938); Alexander J. Belford, 'Evacuation in Scotland: a record' in Boyd, *Evacuation in Scotland*, 3, 4.

[20] Rose, *Which People's War?*, 197–8, 235, 238.

[21] NRS, ED24/201, Map of Scotland's Government Evacuation Scheme.

[22] Belford, 'Evacuation in Scotland', 6.

[23] Ibid., 6; NRS, ED24/1. Government Evacuation Scheme, 3 August 1941.

[24] John Third, 'The early stages of evacuation' in Boyd, *Evacuation in Scotland*, 44.

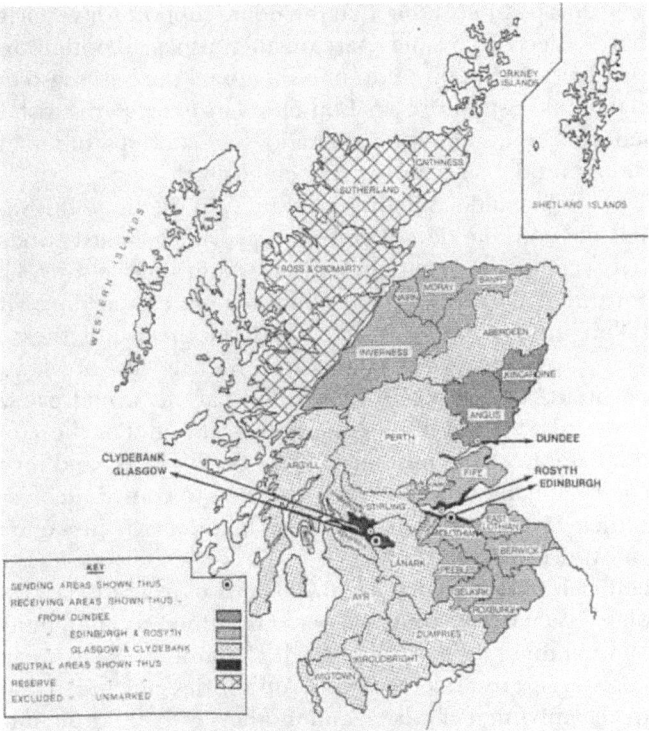

Figure 1.1 Map of Scotland's evacuation zones. (Source: National Records Scotland, ED24/201.)

In spite of such imposing estimates, Scots in reception areas appeared to receive the scheme positively. Numbers of objections to receiving evacuees were very small, and responses were recorded as 'excellent', 'most willing' and 'generous'.[25] In Renfrewshire an assistant billeting officer found only two out of eighty households unwilling to take evacuees, and in one (unnamed) large town 64 per cent of those surveyed were willing.[26] A similar survey of available accommodation was carried out by authorities in England and Wales where it was decided there was available accommodation for 4,800,000 people, though homeowners claimed up to a sixth of rooms were reserved for evacuating friends and relations.[27]

One of Dr Boyd's researchers noted concern that potential hosts were often given the impression that billeting evacuees was compulsory. This was based, Boyd's researcher suggested, on the belief evacuation 'would never

---

[25] Ibid., 45–6, 49.
[26] Ibid., 46.
[27] Titmuss, *Social Policy*, 37.

take place'.[28] It is possible, then, that the noted support for receiving evacuees may have reflected possible coercion and misplaced optimism that one might never be called upon to do one's national duty. It is also important to note that 'in almost every case' householders expressed a wish for unaccompanied children, perhaps foreshadowing later discontent at being asked to house mothers accompanying children.[29]

Hosts were to be paid a billeting allowance, in the hope this would ease the burden on householders. Hosts who provided 'board' (lodging and food) to unaccompanied school children would receive a weekly rate of 10s. 6d. for one child or 8s. 6d. per child for more than one. Those who provided 'lodging' (sleeping quarters) for mothers and their children would receive 5s. per week for each person over the age of 14, and 3s. for those aged under 14.[30] It was intended that parents would pay what they were able towards the cost of billeting their children. For those on higher incomes that amount was considered to be 6s. per week, and for those on lower incomes the amount they were expected to contribute was 'proportionate to their financial resources'.[31] This amount was the same for hosts in Scotland, Wales and England.

British officials estimated that 3,500,000 persons from England and Wales would wish to evacuate, and 500,000 persons within Scotland, though it was unclear on what these figures were based.[32] In June 1939 Glaswegians were asked to register interest in evacuation. Authorities concluded that around 165,000 unaccompanied children, and mothers with children, intended to evacuate, along with 7,500 others such as pregnant women and those with physical or mental disabilities. Parents also indicated that 20,000 children would be privately evacuated, with around 46,000 children remaining in the city.[33] In Scotland, categories of persons eligible for evacuation included school children, pre-school children and their mothers, expectant mothers, 'cripples', mentally handicapped children and the blind.[34] These groups were also evacuated in England, though not to the same extent. Based on figures in the official war history, in England mothers with children and expectant mothers made up around 33 per cent of the total evacuees in September 1939, while in Scotland the corresponding figure is

[28] Third, 'Early stages', 46.
[29] Ibid., 47.
[30] Glasgow City Archives (GCA), D-TC 8/10/61. In October 1939 householders were paid 10s. 6d for evacuees aged over 16. In May 1940, rates for older children increased, and in May 1942 rates for hosting children aged 5–10 were increased to 10s. 6d.
[31] Belford, 'Evacuation in Scotland', 5, 24–25; Titmuss, *Social Policy*, 39. This required a calculation, taking into account net income, minus rent, and costs for additional children. Half of the resulting amount would be the billeting charge.
[32] Titmuss, *Social Policy*, 33; Hansard, HC Deb, 21 November 1939, vol. 353 col. 1104. Titmuss gave a figure of 360,000 for Scotland.
[33] GCA, D-TC 8/10/61, Letter from R. Allardyce, evacuation officer (Glasgow) to parents, March 1939; GCA, D-TC 8/10/62, untitled document, 23 June 1939.
[34] Ibid.

closer to 56 per cent.[35] The much higher percentage of evacuee mothers accompanying young children is a notable difference between the GES in Scotland and that in England and Wales.

Operation Pied Piper begins

While trial runs were held in summer 1939, as late as 30 August the Prime Minister rejected calls to begin the evacuation of vulnerable persons, saying it was not 'necessary or advisable' for civilian evacuation to begin.[36] With further deterioration of the situation in Europe, public notices were hastily placed in newspapers announcing civilian evacuation would take place immediately, from 1 to 3 September. Operation Pied Piper was under way, and on 3 September Britain declared war on Germany.

During the first three days of September 1939, over 1.5 million Britons evacuated, including 175,812 Scots (see Figures 1.2 and 1.3).[37] Despite the generous predictions by Scottish authorities that 500,000 would evacuate, numbers only amounted to 49 per cent of those who had registered, with a mere 34 per cent of those in priority classes. In Glasgow, where in June over 170,000 had indicated they planned to evacuate, only 120,000 turned up. Organising authorities in Edinburgh reported 'considerable indifference' towards the scheme, as a mere 32,000 departed. This was only 28 per cent of city school children, and one-third of the expected number. In Dundee figures were slightly higher, with nearly 50 per cent of the 37,000 who had registered leaving the city. In total, around 62,000 unaccompanied children were evacuated in Scotland, and 97,500 mothers with young children.[38] These figures were lower than authorities had anticipated, leaving them wondering why so many would desire to remain in potentially dangerous cities.

As the Scottish scheme came under the auspices of the SED, children of school age were evacuated in school groups with teachers acting as helpers. Some teachers remained in reception areas to teach their classes, though responsibility for evacuees was delegated to local head teachers.[39] Evacuations of the sick and disabled took place by separate arrangement, including on 6 September when 300 blind persons were evacuated

---

[35] Belford, 'Evacuation in Scotland', 5, 31; Titmuss, *Social Policy*, 103.
[36] 'No evacuation yet', *The Scotsman*, 30 August 1939, 10; 'Evacuation of pupils: 1700 children take part in Edinburgh school test', *The Scotsman*, 5 July 1939, 12.
[37] Titmuss, *Social Policy*, 103; Hansard, HC Deb, 21 November 1939, vol. 353 col. 1104.
[38] NRS, *2011 Census: First Results on Population Estimates for Scotland – Release 1A* (December 2012); Total Population: Edinburgh City, *A Vision of Britain through Time*, accessed 12 October 2018, http://www.visionofbritain.org.uk/unit/10211104/cube/TOT_POP; Titmuss, *Social Policy*, 103; Third, 'Early stages', 53; Belford, 'Evacuation in Scotland', 31.
[39] GCA, D-TC 8/10/61, 'Government Evacuation Scheme, letter to parents in Glasgow', no date.

Figure 1.2 Two evacuees from Glasgow. (Source: *The Scotsman*, 2 September 1939. National Library Scotland.)

from Glasgow to locations in the wider west of Scotland region.[40] Mass evacuations of schools and asylums also took place, including the Thomas Burns Home for Blind Women, which evacuated all female inmates to Haddington. In addition, blind adults working at the Royal Blind Asylum and School in Edinburgh were able to evacuate alongside others in the city scheme. Evacuation was not compulsory, though, and workers were permitted to remain behind, with the public asked to give them 'kindly consideration and help' in the event of air raids.[41] Further, Scottish hospital patients were evacuated from medical facilities in case the beds would be needed to accommodate air raid victims. *The Scotsman* reported that 600 patients vacated the Royal Infirmary in September 1939, 'some of whom were on

[40] 'Blind leave for safety: success of Glasgow evacuation scheme', *The Scotsman*, 7 September 1939, 3.
[41] 'Workshops for blind remaining open in Edinburgh', *The Scotsman*, 13 September 1939, 6.

Figure 1.3 Edinburgh schoolchildren prepare for evacuation. (Source: *The Scotsman*, 2 September 1939. National Library Scotland.)

the operating table only two days ago', and the *Glasgow Herald* reported that around 200 hospitals across Scotland would follow suit.[42] In November that year, the Secretary of State for Scotland confirmed the evacuation of hospitals had continued, making available 12,000 beds.[43]

As in Scotland, numbers of evacuees in England were low, and fewer than half of those who had registered evacuated.[44] Two main factors have traditionally been considered as the cause of the low turnout across Britain. The first is that people simply did not see the need to evacuate, as the initial evacuation took place before war was declared on Germany, when there appeared to be little direct threat to Britain's shores and the government was keen to allay fears.[45] As mentioned earlier, the Prime Minister had announced on 30 August that it was not necessary to begin evacuation and so, when the announcement to evacuate followed only two days later, it would be fair to assume many did not feel there was any present danger. Secondly, the evacuation announcement came at the end of long summer holidays, leaving many families ill-prepared while others were still on vacation.[46]

These explanations do not stand up under close analysis, however, as numbers turning up for evacuation did not show a sudden surge on 3 September, the day after the government declared war on Germany, when it would surely have been clear that the threat was real. Nor was there public demand for further evacuation when all were back from summer holidays and with sufficient warning. It seems more likely turnout was low as those who had the means to do so had already arranged private evacuation, and that those who remained simply did not believe the possible danger was enough to warrant uprooting their lives. Scottish chief constables noted public sentiment that conditions would be 'no more dangerous' at home than in other areas, and felt this view of relative safety deterred people from evacuation.[47]

The main way the Scottish experience of evacuation differed from the rest of Britain is in the number and timing of wartime evacuations carried out under the official government scheme. In England, there were three main waves: the first in early September 1939; the second after the fall of France in June 1940; and the third in June 1944 after renewed air attacks

---

[42] Hansard, HC Deb, 21 November 1939, vol. 353 col. 1093; '600 patients removed: Edinburgh Royal Infirmary clearance', *The Scotsman*, 1 September 1939; 'Evacuation of hospitals: many Scots patients sent home', *The Glasgow Herald*, 1 September 1939.

[43] Hansard, HC Deb, 21 November 1939, vol. 351 col. 1110.

[44] Titmuss, *Social Policy*, 103.

[45] 'The evacuation decision', *The Scotsman*, 1 September 1939.

[46] Hansard, HC Deb, 1 November 1939, vol. 114 cols 1603, 1608; Belford, 'Evacuation in Scotland', 31.

[47] NRS, HH55/23, Police War Duties – Intelligence Report (hereafter PWD – IR), 16 August 1940: City of Glasgow; 30 August 1940: City of Edinburgh, City of Glasgow.

on London.[48] In comparison, after the initial three-day evacuation in September 1939 Scottish authorities arranged a supplementary registration from 11 to 17 September, for school children only. Few signed up, and those who did were evacuated on public transport over the following weeks.[49] In February 1940 the Scottish Department of Health announced that another period of evacuation would take place the following month. This time, no mothers or pre-school children would go, and schools would evacuate as a unit. In conjunction, billeting allowances were raised, and arrangements were made for registered children to undergo thorough medical inspections, to counter the issues experienced in early September 1939.[50] The final official evacuations in Scotland took place after heavy bombing of industrial areas around the River Clyde, in March and May 1941. This saw vulnerable populations from Port Glasgow, Dumbarton and Greenock join those from Glasgow and Clydebank in fleeing to safer areas.[51] In contrast with England and Wales, in Scotland there were no further official evacuations beyond 1941. In addition to having separate administrative bodies for the scheme, Scotland's evacuations also ran on a different timeline. This reveals the different priorities and dangers in wartime Scotland, distinct to those in England.

How did hosts receive and perceive evacuees?

Householders in reception areas had been told they must contribute to the war effort by helping vulnerable city folk escape from areas that would be targets for German bombers. In the scheme's early days most homeowners willingly volunteered rooms for accommodating evacuees, though some were coerced and told they would be fined or imprisoned if they did not agree to host.[52] Whatever the motivation for taking in evacuees, authorities, no doubt, anticipated hosts would willingly do their duty and welcome evacuees with kindness and hospitality.

There were many reports of Scottish hosts welcoming the new arrivals in just this manner. In Glasgow Eileen Offley, a secretary, noted her manager had received six child evacuees from a working-class part of the city and was 'delighted' with the additions to his family. Another colleague was 'well pleased' with his evacuees, and had given them 'a very hearty welcome'. Miss Offley also observed that 'many women in receiving areas had gone to great pains to make the little ones happy'.[53]

---

[48] Welshman, *Churchill's Children*, 151; 'Another wave of evacuations', Imperial War Museum, https://www.iwm.org.uk/history/the-evacuated-children-of-the-second-world-war (accessed 15 October 2018).
[49] Belford, 'Evacuation in Scotland', 33.
[50] Ibid.
[51] Ibid, 6.
[52] Third, 'Early stages', 46; Welshman, *Churchill's Children*, 65.
[53] Mass-Observation (M-O), Diarist 5390 (Glasgow), 1, 4, 9 September 1939.

Other examples of host kindness came from across Scotland. In Campbeltown, on the Kintyre peninsula, friendly hosts taught local evacuees to ride ponies and in Macduff, on the north-east coast, teachers formed a club for evacuees and local children to meet up for games, crafts and dancing and established a space where evacuees could complete their homework in peace.[54] The selflessness of host teachers was also applauded by Dr Boyd and his team at Glasgow University, who noted teachers had given up many hours of their time to prepare for new arrivals.[55] An article in *The Scotsman* concluded teachers in reception areas had done 'a great deal more than what is normally required', including taking lessons on communal feeding so they could provide meals for groups of evacuees.[56] Volunteers such as those from the Women's Rural Institute and Women's Voluntary Services also showed hospitality, generously providing many meals for evacuees and those accompanying them, as well as sourcing blankets and catering equipment for their comfort.[57]

Stories of host kindness were also presented in Parliament. In the House of Commons Mr Campbell Stephen, the MP for Glasgow Camlachie, shared a story of Glasgow evacuees who had been sent to Inveraray, a coastal town in the district of Argyll and Bute. There, 150 women and children evacuees had arrived, tired and hungry, to be told there had been a mix-up in arrangements and there was no available accommodation. While they spent their first night in a cold hall, locals soon rallied and arranged for some condemned properties to be opened, collecting furniture and carpets, cleaning and making the properties generally fit for habitation. In this case, locals were reportedly 'anxious to be as helpful as possible'.[58] Alongside this story of host kindness, the MP added he had heard many stories of positive receptions for evacuees arriving in new destinations. He told the House of Commons '[f]riends have told me how kindly their children have been treated and how well they are getting on. The spirit on the part of many of the people has been admirable.'[59]

For some hosts, the evacuation scheme was a success and they soon settled into a new routine with their evacuees. Positive stories came from across Scotland, including Campbeltown, where one local noted that a few women had 'become really attached to the children, especially when they have been able to help them a great deal, cleaned them and given them good food and seen the results'.[60] Another woman wrote to *The Scotsman* to report evacuees in her village were happy, showed an appreciation

---

[54] M-O, Diarist 5374 (Campbeltown), 24 April 1941; *SMT Magazine*, February 1940, 51.
[55] Third, 'Early stages', 51.
[56] 'Education to go on: plans already made in receiving areas in Scotland', *The Scotsman*, 1 September 1939.
[57] Third, 'Early stages', 51.
[58] Hansard, HC Deb, 14 September 1939, vol. 351 col. 810.
[59] Ibid.
[60] M-O, Dir.(ective for) November 1939, R(espondent) 1534 (Campbeltown).

for country life and were able to enjoy blackberrying for the first time in their lives. She also quoted one youngster who wished the war would not end quickly, as she wished to stay in her new location, and another who remarked to her hostess '[w]ell, if heaven is anything like this it'll be a lovely place'.[61] These stories of kindness and welcome, of contentment and positive influence, show the official evacuation scheme at its best. They are the embodiment of a benevolent population caring for its weaker members, perhaps the ideal vision foreseen by directors planning the evacuation. This, though, was not the full story.

'Limp', 'truculent', 'stupid': host perceptions of evacuees

'The shade has been expressed rather more than the light', complained John Colville, then Secretary of State for Scotland, as the House of Commons debated the topics of Scottish education and evacuation on 21 November 1939.[62] That day, MPs reported that across Britain gossip was flying and accusations raging as hosts expressed not kindness and welcome but great shock and disgust at unwell, lazy and feckless evacuees. There were also strong expressions of hostility in Scotland, where hosts railed against the scheme that had brought such unsavoury folk to their homes. This section explores the details of the 'shade', and the resulting host resentment.

The early signs of host unrest in Scotland came immediately as the first evacuees arrived in reception areas. Hosts were shocked to see large numbers of mothers alongside pre-school children, a fact that had not often been made clear to them beforehand. Authorities, apparently, had not considered that families might wish to reside together, and hosts were taken aback by large families who refused to be separated.[63] In Kilmarnock, for example, the 'chief trouble' was said to be in billeting mothers with children, as many with families of seven or eight children had arrived, too many to accommodate with a single host. In another case a Glaswegian mother refused all offers of accommodation, unless she and her thirteen children could be housed together.[64] 'The mothers would not separate from their children', an Ayrshire man commented, 'and one can hardly blame them.'[65] Not only were hosts expected to give up their homes and their privacy but, in many cases, Scottish hosts were expected to accommodate entire city families, minus only the father. This must have brought much unease to hosts who may have pictured receiving one or two grateful children, and instead found their houses full of visitors.

---

[61] 'Letter to the Editor from "Materfamilias"', *The Scotsman*, 14 September 1939.
[62] Hansard, HC Deb, 21 November 1939, vol. 353 col. 1107.
[63] Third, 'Early stages', 47; M-O, Dir. November 1939, R1363 (Prestwick, Ayrshire).
[64] 'Billeting difficulties: mothers with children', *The Scotsman*, 6 September 1939, 5.
[65] M-O, Dir. November 1939, R1363 (Prestwick).

Another factor prompting shock was the poorly condition of evacuees. On the face of it, this appeared to be a result of the journeys to reception areas, often long and without toilets or food, resulting in tired, bedraggled evacuees and helpers.[66] For example, one journey from Glasgow to Aberdeenshire was so plagued by delays that evacuees did not arrive at their allocated village until 12:30 a.m. One helper spoke of the twelve-and-a-half-hour journey, normally less than four hours by train, as 'the most depressing, deplorable and disgusting journey I have ever had the misfortune to make'.[67] One can only imagine the condition of a party of children, some of whom had become train-sick, after a day of travel with minimal food or rest stops.

Hosts across Britain were also shocked at the state of evacuee clothing and footwear, much of which was ragged or inadequate for country life. Problems were recorded from Liverpool to London while, in Newcastle, one in five children arrived in reception areas with inadequate clothing.[68] In contrast, the severe poverty of Scottish evacuees from Glasgow and Clydebank was revealed in Dr Boyd's surveys, which found that 39 per cent of child evacuees had clothing in a 'bad' or 'deplorable' state.[69] Some Scottish hosts were shocked that those in evacuation areas would dress their children so shabbily, while others seemed surprised that city-dwellers could live in such poverty.[70] Others viewed things more cynically, spreading rumours that city mothers had sent children in rags in the hope they would be given new clothing in receiving areas. Glaswegian Miss Offley reported hearing many such stories, including that of one family who were all sent in shoes too small in the hope of claiming new ones from billeting authorities, and the story of one mother who had apparently told her children 'see you get new clothes and shoes when you arrive'.[71] This caused much frustration among hosts, who perceived it as ingratitude and worried they might have to pay for new items out of their own purse. One host complained he could not afford new clothes for his ragged evacuees, and that their father was working double time at John Brown's shipyard in Clydebank and would be receiving far more than the host's billeting allowance.[72] The host felt resentment towards the father who, he felt, should be made to pay for his children's upkeep.

Adding to the shock over large family size and the poor appearance of evacuees, hosts were horrified to discover that many were verminous and in poor health. Some areas carried out health examinations of arriving

---

[66] Third, 'Early stages', 55.
[67] Ibid., 55.
[68] Daniel Todman, *Britain's War: Into Battle, 1937–1941* (Oxford: Oxford University Press, 2016), 252; Field, *Blood, Sweat, and Toil*, 15.
[69] Third, 'Early stages', 57.
[70] Hansard, HC Deb, 21 November 1939, vol. 353 col. 1107.
[71] M-O, Diarist 5390 (Glasgow), 9 September 1939.
[72] Ibid.

evacuees and the statistics were grim. In England, 8 to 35 per cent of London evacuees were verminous, while figures ranged from 22 to 50 per cent of Merseyside evacuees. Again, Scottish figures were more severe, with vermin found on 30 to 90 per cent of evacuees.[73] In Stirling, out of 827 children, 201 had either vermin, scabies or septic sores. Of accompanying adults, 14 per cent were infected with similar ailments.[74] Another village reported that, among its contingent from a school in the city slums, 50 per cent had 'dirty heads' (a common phrase for head lice), 30 per cent had impetigo and 20 per cent seemed to be incontinent.[75] There were even rumours of evacuated mothers bringing venereal disease to households and some were sent home because of this.[76] To deal with vermin, hosts had to burn children's clothing, cut lice-ridden hair and bathe evacuees in disinfectant. One woman commented wryly that while it was easy to treat children, it was not quite as simple to de-louse evacuee mothers.[77] The extra work of dealing with lice, and the disgust at overall rates of disease, added to host dissatisfaction and prejudice in Scotland.

As well as disease, evacuee toilet habits caused much talk among hosts. This was a particular problem for evacuees from Glasgow, where water closets were often one per tenement block in the city. It was not uncommon for slum-dwellers to use a bucket or pile of newspapers as a toilet.[78] This lack of familiarity with modern sanitation caused many hosts to view evacuees with revulsion, believing them to be coarse and uncultured. The questionable toilet habits of evacuees were best represented in one of the most famous stories of the evacuation, that of a Glasgow mother who admonished her son: 'Johnnie, don't use the lady's carpet – use the surround!'[79] Bedwetting was also common. Boyd's data from across Scotland showed this problem occurred in between 1 and 33 per cent of Scottish evacuees, with a mean occurrence of 12 per cent.[80] This brought further costs for hosts, who needed to acquire waterproof linings or replace ruined bedding. In Kincardine, a doctor wrote to his local Member of Parliament complaining about the insanitary tendencies of evacuees. He complained that their habits were 'indescribable', and said he had been notified of many cases where carpets, mattresses and bedding had been destroyed owing to 'the primitive habits of these evacuees'.[81] Certainly the generosity of hosts was stretched to its limits by the arrival of certain evacuees who were seen as ragged, verminous and insanitary.

---

[73] Field, *Blood, Sweat, and Toil*, 16–17.
[74] Third, 'Early stages', 62–3. At this time, 'vermin' often referred to lice.
[75] Aberdeen University Review, 238, quoted in SWG, *Our Scottish Towns*, 18.
[76] Hansard, HC Deb, 18 June 1940, vol. 362 col. 116.
[77] M-O, Diarist 5390 (Glasgow), 9 September 1939.
[78] Fraser and Maver, 'Social problems', 377.
[79] SWG, *Our Scottish Towns*, 2.
[80] Third, 'Early stages', 65.
[81] Hansard, HC Deb, 14 September 1939, vol. 351 col. 818.

Once the shock over evacuee condition had subsided, Scottish hosts had to deal with a growing horror at evacuee habits, misbehaviour and vices. The most common host gripes about evacuee children and mothers had to do with poor behaviour, over which complaints came thick and fast. One M-O diarist worked for the Postal Office in Aberdeen, where he was able to read the contents of letters and postcards. In September 1939, he reported reading of 'some of the tougher slum kids refusing to eat anything but fish suppers, breaking crockery, hen-houses, etc.'[82] The same diarist heard that evacuees in Kintore had 'pulled rowans off trees in garden & put them through mangle, pulled wallpaper off walls, swung on chandelier & brought it down & roof'.[83] The Scottish Women's Group on Public Welfare (SWG) also reported stories of evacuees gathering the farmer's eggs and using them as ammunition, plucking hens, decapitating turkeys and throwing stones at dogs.[84] Hosts reacted in horror to this terrible misbehaviour, devoting hours to its discussion and repeating the most sensational tales.[85]

Over time, some children settled down while others continued to cause trouble. Some hosts had difficulty dealing with misbehaving evacuees, as their removal required the permission of local head teachers, who oversaw billeting in many areas, and if the teachers were not willing to act there was no official recourse. One woman found her evacuees smoking and stealing but upon complaint she found the head teacher unsympathetic and refusing to give permission for the evacuees to be removed from the lady's household. The upset host later met with both the Provost and the Director of Education, who were unable to assist. She also provided a doctor's certificate to the head teacher, saying she was on the verge of a nervous breakdown, and her husband threatened to have the Sheriff evict the boys. No change in the situation was observed.[86] After receiving no help from numerous authorities, the host must have felt powerless to change her difficult situation.

This powerlessness was not felt by a couple whose story featured in the *Our Scottish Towns* report. A young couple tried giving every excuse to avoid taking any evacuees: the rooms of their house were too small; their mother-in-law was coming; their brother was visiting to sit exams. In the end, they were made to take two girls. Unhappy with this arrangement, the couple packed the evacuees into the family car and drove them home to their parents.[87] Such a direct approach was uncommon, though as we shall see shortly it was not uncommon for disgruntled evacuees to take themselves home.

---

[82] M-O, Diarist 5232 (Aberdeen), 5–9 September 1939.
[83] Ibid., 15 September 1939.
[84] SWG, *Our Scottish Towns*, 20.
[85] M-O, Diarist 5390 (Glasgow), 9 September 1939; Hansard, HC Deb, 21 November 1939, vol. 353 col. 1107.
[86] M-O, Diarist 5374 (Campbeltown), 15–20 May 1941.
[87] Aberdeen University Review, 241, quoted in SWG, *Our Scottish Towns*, 11.

Hosts were not only critical of evacuee misbehaviour, but also of their naïveté about country conditions and diet. In one (unnamed) village, locals sneered at the evacuees' words for coastal features: anything in the sea was called 'fish', rocks were known as 'bricks' and children were overheard calling fishermen's skiffs 'motorboats'.[88] One small boy, arriving with his mother at a village in Inverness-shire, complained of the strange smell when he got out of the train, to which another boy replied '[w]hisht, it's only the fresh air'.[89] Hosts also found it amusing that some evacuees were scared of country animals, such as sheep. 'We'd never seen trees or anything like that ... this was just nothing but green, no buildings or nothing', one former evacuee recounted. He added, '[w]hen I looked out the window all I could see was these white things and the place was full of them ... I was terrified in case these white animals should all gang up on us and eventually attack us'.[90]

Hosts were also critical of the fussiness of urban evacuees, though they were somewhat intrigued by the unusual habits. The city folk were noted for their fondness for a fish supper, jam sandwiches and refusal to eat anything they had not encountered before.[91] In Renfrewshire a woman on the Education Committee mentioned that among their local evacuees some had not previously tasted fruit, others had never used a knife or fork, and most 'have difficulty in grasping what soup is'.[92] The SWG felt that many urban housewives simply could not imagine life without the pie-shop or the 'wafer-man', and seemed to have forgotten even 'elementary knowledge' of cooking.[93] While hosts managed to find some amusement at the peculiar eating habits of evacuees, underlying it was a budding feeling of resentment towards the strange city folk. Hosts often exhibited open hostility towards the behaviour and attitudes of evacuee mothers. The MP for Kincardine, a county south of Aberdeen, reported that evacuee mothers in his area were becoming well known for their fondness for red wine, and this spending on alcohol had, in some cases, resulted in children being deprived of food.[94] In addition, the SWG claimed many of the women had come for a free holiday, as some had never had a holiday before. 'I don't want to go home, not me – the first holiday I've had for sixteen years', one evacuee reportedly said.[95]

Evacuee women were also referred to as demanding, lazy and feckless, and called 'parasitic' by the SWG for making frequent requests for free

---

[88] Clark, 'Notes on a village', 20.
[89] Hansard, HC Deb, 30 July 1941, vol. 373 col. 1431.
[90] Francis O'Hagan, 'Enquiry skills in history: the Blitz and evacuation', *Citizenship, Social and Economics Education* 9, no. 1 (2010): 69–80, here 76.
[91] Third, 'Early stages', 71; M-O, Diarist 5232 (Aberdeen), 15 September 1939.
[92] M-O, Diarist 5390 (Glasgow), 17 September 1939.
[93] SWG, *Our Scottish Towns*, 13.
[94] Hansard, HC Deb, 14 September 1939, vol. 351 col. 819.
[95] SWG, *Our Scottish Towns*, 9.

clothing or wanting to have everything done for them.⁹⁶ Mothers were criticised for always having money for 'packets of fags' or 'the pictures', as well as showing a fondness for dancing, drink and obscene language.⁹⁷ Scots surveyed by Dr Boyd also criticised evacuee mothers, labelling them 'limp', 'truculent' and 'stupid', and there were a few mentions of women who expected breakfast in bed or to be taken to the cinema by their hosts.⁹⁸ Such stories appeared regularly in primary sources examined for this chapter, and it would be fair to say this was representative of the way many city mothers conducted themselves in reception areas. Their behaviour and remarks certainly went a long way towards exacerbating the developing host hostility.

Many Scottish hosts also felt ungrateful evacuees were taking advantage of their hospitality. The Lord Provost of Perth observed that, owing to the behaviour of evacuees, the goodwill of householders had been lost.⁹⁹ Similarly, the Women's Institute believed the campaign had unfairly burdened rural women across Scotland. The group expressed anger, rather than pity, towards verminous slum mothers and their bedwetting children, believing the evacuation was little more than 'dictatorship to the Housewife'.¹⁰⁰ It seems that local Scottish women, tasked with feeding and housing indifferent or slothful women and their children, found themselves unable to show kindness and welcome, growing in ill-feeling towards the evacuees.

'No enthusiasm for future arrivals': lasting hostility

Even though many in the initial wave of maladjusted evacuees returned home, host hostility did not die down. In contrast to Boyd's findings that over time most Scottish householders were hospitable to evacuees, sources examined for this chapter revealed increasing levels of host discontent with the scheme, and an unrelenting hostility towards receiving evacuees. One example of this strong feeling came from Banff, a seaside town in the north-west of Scotland. Upon hearing that a supplementary evacuation would occur in mid-September 1939, town councillors agreed to inform the Department of Health for Scotland that the town was unanimous in its reluctance towards evacuation and did not want any further evacuees. This enmity was based on townsfolk experience with their first group of evacuees, the council noted. This experience was said to have been 'so unfortunate that practically no householder in the town will agree to take in evacuees', and as a result any more who were sent would only be

---

⁹⁶ Ibid., 9, 11, 16.
⁹⁷ Ibid., 12.
⁹⁸ Third, 'Early stages', 69.
⁹⁹ NRS, ED24/7, 8 November 1939.
¹⁰⁰ R. Minns, *Bombers and Mash: The Domestic Front 1939–1945* (London: Virago Press, 1980), 21.

accommodated in public halls.[101] Host reluctance was partly based on the 'vermin and general filth' of previous evacuees and the perception that many mothers who arrived had acted as if they were on 'a holiday at Government expense'.[102] These townsfolk were united in their resistance to further arrivals of evacuees.

Across time, host hostility moved from grumbles and gossip to outright defiance of the authorities. In February 1940, when it was advised that another official wave of evacuations might take place, the Department of Health for Scotland sent forms to receiving areas to gauge available space for new evacuees. In Fife, 22,000 forms were sent but only 300 were returned, of which 67 were refusals. In Perth, out of 18,700 requests, only 413 acceptances were received. Other areas had similar results.[103] Miss Offley in Glasgow noted that in Stirling the police had to persuade some hosts to take in evacuees, as the locals had been expecting 'innocent helpless little mites' and were unhappy with those who turned up.[104] Similar resistance was recorded in the town of Bridge of Allan, near Stirling, when *The Scotsman* reported residents had held a meeting in protest against receiving additional Glaswegian evacuees. The excuses ranged from having a population of retired folk, who should not be pressed to take lively young children, to the assertion that several householders depended on letting rooms for an income. The claim was also made that several people had become seriously ill because of the trouble of looking after evacuees, and one woman had worried herself to death. The scheme was labelled 'dictatorial', and residents urged the government not to resort to 'Draconian powers' in forcing residents to comply.[105]

Scottish resistance to the scheme did not decrease with time, even in response to adverse events in evacuation areas. In early May 1940 as Germany invaded Western Europe, Prime Minister Churchill warned the public 'we have before us an ordeal of the most grievous kind'.[106] Despite the grave situation, Scottish chief constables continued to note public hostility towards evacuees. Even when faced with the possibility that city children might suffer during air raids, those in reception areas remained resistant to the scheme. At that time, the Chief Constable for Dundee stated his belief that 'much difficulty and hostility [would] be experienced should any attempt be made to have the children in vulnerable areas evacuated to reception areas where ... practically without exception the householders are most unwilling to have this duty imposed upon them'. Similar sentiment was noted in other reception areas. In Perthshire and Kinross-shire,

---

[101] 'Evacuees in Banff: householders' refusal after "unfortunate" experience', *The Scotsman*, 14 September 1939.
[102] Ibid.
[103] Belford, 'Evacuation in Scotland', 34.
[104] M-O, Diarist 5390 (Glasgow), 9 September 1939.
[105] 'Evacuation scheme: Bridge of Allan protests', *The Scotsman*, 20 March 1940, 10.
[106] Hansard, HC Deb, 13 May 1940, vol. 360 cols 1502–3.

public notification of future evacuee arrivals caused 'expressions of bitter disappointment' and in the city of Perth both the local authority and most of the public were said to be 'strongly averse' to receiving evacuees, especially 'in view of their former experiences'. Constables in Moray and Nairn stated the evacuation was 'not looked upon with favour', in Ayr the scheme was 'not at all popular' and in Argyllshire there was 'no enthusiasm' for future arrivals. The chief constable of Inverness-shire reported that owing to previous experience the public did not want a repeat, and Dunbartonshire householders were relieved the last lot of evacuees had gone home and did not want more, 'chiefly on account of their uncleanliness and destructive habits'.[107] As these officials documented, strong host opposition to receiving evacuees was expressed from a broad section of Scottish reception areas.

Later that year, the SS *City of Benares*, a transport carrying evacuee children to Canada, was torpedoed with the loss of over 250 passengers and crew, including 77 out of 90 evacuees, several whom were Scots.[108] As a result, the Children's Overseas Reception Scheme was put on hold permanently. It seems this tragedy may have caused a temporary softening in attitudes towards evacuees in Scotland, as chief constables reported the public 'now recognise the need to evacuate', were 'generally prepared to receive' evacuees, and adverse comments were absent compared to the previous few months.[109] This change of heart did not last long. After the Blitz on Glasgow and Clydebank in March 1941, public opposition to evacuation was once again observed. These heavy air raids brought much damage to property and the loss of over 1,200 lives.[110] In response, the official evacuation scheme was reopened and there was a surge in both official and private evacuations. One might assume those in reception areas would welcome the new arrivals, fleeing from a danger that was no longer hypothetical, yet sources reveal little softening of attitudes towards evacuees. For example, after a number of child evacuees arrived in Peeblesshire, local constabulary noted that householders were 'still reluctant to accept them'. Similarly, in Berwickshire 'great difficulty' was experienced in finding hosts, mostly owing to previous experiences.[111]

Hostility was also reported from reception areas after other bombing raids. In May 1941, after the intensive bombing of Greenock and Port Glasgow in which nearly 300 people were killed and more than 10,000

---

[107] NRS, HH55/21, PWD – IR, 10 May 1940: City of Dundee, Perthshire and Kinross-shire, City of Perth, Moray and Nairn, Ayr Burgh, Argyllshire, Inverness-shire, Dunbartonshire.
[108] 'Bereaved Scottish families', *The Scotsman*, 27 September 1940.
[109] NRS, HH55/23, PWD – IR, 27 September 1940: City of Edinburgh, Berwickshire. Compared to HH55/21 and HH55/23 IR from May and August 1940.
[110] MacPhail, *The Clydebank Blitz*, 80.
[111] NRS, HH55/28, PWD – IR, 20 June 1941: Peeblesshire, Berwickshire.

injured, evacuations resumed across Scotland.[112] Public reluctance to evacuation was again observed. Despite the severity of the Luftwaffe attacks in the west, a billeting officer in Haddington struggled to find homes for evacuees from Edinburgh. The man spent a whole day knocking on doors and, in the end, resorted to compulsory measures to find accommodation for the children.[113]

Such examples give a strong impression of Scottish resistance and hostility towards the evacuation scheme. This is especially noteworthy in that opposition continued even after destructive air raids and mass casualties. This contrasts with experiences in England and Wales, where hosts were said to have softened towards evacuees who arrived in subsequent waves after air raids in England.[114] Conversely, resistance towards the Government Evacuation Scheme by those in Scottish reception areas was so strong that opposition to evacuees was expressed even when the lives of urban Scots – including vulnerable children – were directly threatened. This was a clear departure from the intended hospitality and willingness to host, a sign the official projection of the scheme did not meet with reality and had quickly gone awry. Those in rural Scotland frequently demonstrated resistance to the official evacuation scheme, and many were unwilling to accommodate their fellow countrymen in the face of danger.

Explaining host reactions

While hosts struggled with evacuees and demonstrated resistance to the scheme, evacuees also found the process difficult. On 14 September 1939 Mr Campbell Stephen, representative for Glasgow Camlachie, reported to the House of Commons that he believed up to 50 per cent of Scottish evacuees on the GES had returned from reception areas, a mere fortnight after the start of the campaign. Stephen felt there must have been profound mistakes in the implementation of the scheme to have had such a high failure rate.[115] Just one month later, the Secretary of State for Scotland confirmed that more than half of Scottish evacuees under the official scheme had returned home. By Christmas this was up to three-quarters.[116]

Out of the Scottish contingent of evacuees, unaccompanied children were more likely to stay on in receiving areas. In November 1939, an average of 60 per cent of unaccompanied children evacuated via the

---

[112] NRS, HH36/5, Raids on Clydeside, Edinburgh Civil Defence Headquarters report, 31 July 1941.
[113] NRS, HH55/28, PWD – IR, 20 June 1941: East Lothian.
[114] Field, *Blood, Sweat, and Toil*, 27; A. Marwick, *Class, Image, and Reality in Britain, France and the USA since 1930* (Oxford: Oxford University Press, 1980), 218.
[115] Hansard, HC Deb, 14 September 1939, vol. 351 col. 810.
[116] Hansard, HC Deb, 21 November 1939, vol. 353 col. 1104; Boyd, 'Parents and evacuation', in Boyd, *Evacuation in Scotland*, 96.

official scheme remained in reception areas. This varied by region, and some counties had 80 per cent of unaccompanied children stay on while others had fewer than 50 per cent remaining. Only 21 per cent of unaccompanied Edinburgh children had returned to the city by late November, while over half of Clydebank children had returned home. Of the original 1,989 Clydebank evacuees, all bar 112 had returned home by the time of the March 1941 Blitz, in which Clydebank was badly bombed.[117]

Like Clydebank evacuees, Scottish mothers who evacuated with their children were much more likely to abandon the scheme. An official return from January 1940 showed 87 per cent of women with pre-school children had returned home.[118] Comparative data from England and Wales shows most mothers with children had returned home by the end of January 1940. For child evacuees, however, rates of return in England and Wales were lower than those in Scotland and, while figures varied by region, by January 1940 generally more than half of evacuees remained in reception areas. In some locations figures were high, such as Devon where an average of 75 per cent of children on the official scheme remained with their hosts in early 1940.[119] At that time, the same percentage of Scottish evacuees had abandoned the scheme. Across Britain, Operation Pied Piper was a mixed success.

While it is clear Scottish evacuees fled reception areas in their droves, the reasons for their departure were varied. MPs and authorities debated the high return rate, and some wondered whether those closest to home returned more quickly, though there was not a clear set of data to support this interpretation.[120] Other sources revealed evacuees departed in response to the unwelcoming attitude of hosts. In Fife, local MP Mr Gallacher told Parliament the evacuation was the most farcical thing he had ever known, as city-based mothers and children now had 'a natural horror for anything which suggested evacuation', owing to their bad experiences in reception areas. Gallacher said landladies of boarding-houses who desired empty rooms for well-paying summer guests had 'made life like hell' for the September evacuees, to encourage their departure before the busy season. He claimed the boarding-house keepers turned evacuees out into the street on cold days, insulted them, and other locals would even

---

[117] Hansard, HC Deb, 21 November 1939, vol. 353 col. 1104; Belford, 'Evacuation in Scotland', 31.
[118] Belford, 'Evacuation in Scotland', 31.
[119] Field, *Blood, Sweat, and Toil*, fn. 17; Titmuss, *Social Policy*, 172; Susan Isaacs, Sibyl Clement Brown and Robert H. Thouless, *The Cambridge Evacuation Survey: A Wartime Study in Social Welfare and Education* (London: Methuen, 1941), 18; Preston, 'Evacuation of schoolchildren'; Hess, 'Civilian evacuation to Devon', 173–4.
[120] Hansard, HC Deb, 21 November 1939, vol. 353 col. 1106; HC Deb, 14 September 1939, vol. 351 col. 816.

stop to 'cock a snook at the "vacs"' when encountered in the streets, leaving them feeling most unwelcome.[121]

The evidence presented in this chapter has shown that while some Scottish hosts extended hospitality to evacuees, the wider response was one of hostility and resistance to the scheme. The following section will explore the key factors that may have prompted Scottish hosts to receive and perceive evacuees in this manner: economic and social concerns, religious tensions, country versus city and class conflict. It begins with an assessment of the influence of economic and social concerns on Scottish responses to evacuees.

'Two women cannot share a sink': economic and social concerns

At a fundamental level, host hostility arose out of the difficulty of providing hospitality to strangers for a sustained period. While potential hosts were 'practically unanimous' in their generosity and willingness to provide board for evacuees when questioned in February 1939, this goodwill began to dissipate within days of the arrival of evacuees later that year.[122] Despite hosts' good intentions, it was difficult to open one's home to strangers, especially if those strangers were poorly behaved and appeared ungrateful for the hospitality extended. Further, the arrival in reception areas of large numbers of evacuees put a strain on local resources. In many rural areas, purses were already strained after the interwar depression, and this was exacerbated by food shortages during the Second World War. One example of this came from Ross and Cromarty, a Highland region to which some evacuees had fled after the Clydebank Blitz in March 1941. The local chief constable reported there were existing shortages of common foodstuffs in Stornoway, in the Western Isles, and housewives billeting airmen from the Royal Air Force had already complained about 'meagre supplies'.[123] The arrival of a large number of evacuees further served to increase the problem of food shortage in the district, no doubt adding to tensions there. Other problems were reported in Kincardine, where weekends brought a great influx of 'motor cars bearing Dundee registration numbers, packed to overflowing with people who had come "for a hurl", . . . to see their friends in the country'. This was, reported the local MP, 'an invasion which caused a raid on the larders of a great many people'.[124] These visiting friends and family members added additional costs to the extra expense of feeding evacuees, which further strained relationships between evacuees and hosts.

Alongside these economic difficulties, women in reception areas struggled to share their home territory with evacuees. In a House of Commons

---

[121] Hansard, HC Deb, 29 May 1941, vol. 371 cols 2069–70.
[122] Third, 'Early stages', 46.
[123] NRS, HH 55/27, PWD – IR, 28 March 1941: Ross and Cromarty.
[124] Hansard, HC Deb, 14 September 1939, vol. 351 col. 816.

debate on evacuation in September 1939, two MPs agreed 'two women cannot share a sink', while another reported hearing that in Essex separate kitchens were being designed for evacuees because of the failure of host and evacuee mothers to work together.[125] In Scotland, as numbers of evacuee mothers were higher this situation was more pronounced. A diarist in Ayrshire reported that in 'many' homes evacuee mothers treated their hosts 'like landladies or servants'. He also relayed the story of a local host whose evacuee mother made comments such as 'we'll away out for the afternoon now – you can have our tea ready for 5.30'.[126] Another host in Glasgow complained that every time she went to put on dinner she could not as the evacuee mother was using all her pots.[127] Feelings of resentment grew rapidly for hosts who felt their homes and their privacy had been invaded. For some hosts, the war was not being fought overseas but within their own kitchen.

One explanation for this hostility may be found in cultures of exchange and gratitude. Throughout history, theologians and philosophers have portrayed gratitude as a 'manifestation of virtue – an excellence of character . . . essential for living life well'.[128] To some, the absence of gratitude is seen as a moral defect and, when linked to social hierarchy, ingratitude could be perceived as an offence towards one's 'social betters'.[129] In Parliament on 21 November 1939 the Secretary of State for Scotland said '[e]veryone recognises the real sacrifices that have been made by the receiving householders. No one on the home front has done more than the housewives who opened their homes to the children.'[130] It seems the only ones who did not acknowledge the sacrifices made by hosts were the evacuees themselves. The behaviours reported earlier – demanding, parasitic, a free-holiday mentality and placing unfair obligations on housewives – all came across with a distinct whiff of evacuee ingratitude.

Anthropologically, the culture of gift exchange often relies on the assumption the receiver of the gift will reciprocate in due course, creating a debt of gratitude. The problem comes when the recipient does not express thanks for the gift, essentially reneging on an unspoken social contract.[131] Behavioural scientist Aafke Komter claims that gratitude is essential to the function of society, creating cohesion and community. She wrote 'without

---

[125] Ibid., cols 830, 849.
[126] M-O, Dir. November 1939, R1363 (Prestwick).
[127] Ibid., R1574 (Glasgow).
[128] R. A. Emmons, 'The psychology of gratitude: an introduction', in R. A. Emmons and M. E. McCullough (eds), *The Psychology of Gratitude* (New York: Oxford University Press, 2004), 3.
[129] Aafke Elisabeth Komter, 'Gratitude and gift exchange' in *Psychology of Gratitude*, 196; E. J. Harpham, 'Gratitude in the history of ideas', in *Psychology of Gratitude*, 26.
[130] Hansard, HC Deb, 21 November 1939, vol. 353 col. 1108.
[131] Komter, 'Gratitude and gift exchange', 196; Harpham, 'History of ideas', 27; see also Barry Schwarz, 'The social psychology of the gift', *The American Journal of Sociology* 73, no. 1 (1967): 1–11; Marcel Mauss, *The Gift* (English translation: Cohen & West, 1954).

the ties created by gratitude, there would be no mutual trust ... and no grounds for maintaining the bonds of community.'[132] When this concept is applied to the host and evacuee relationship, it is revealing. The lack of gratitude expressed by some evacuees, and the reluctance of hosts to extend hospitality, indicates that the bond of community was not strong and is evidence of underlying societal divide.

'A golden opportunity': religious tensions

In parts of England and Wales, religious differences played a part in tensions between evacuees and host communities. These included difficulties in accommodating the religious activities of Catholic evacuees, sent from Liverpool to rural north Wales and from London to Cornwall; and providing kosher food and religious instruction for Jewish children billeted across England.[133] In Scotland, where pre-war society had shown division along sectarian lines, did religion influence host perceptions of evacuees? To this end, how did host communities respond to Irish Catholics from Glasgow and Clydebank?

Primary sources examined for this chapter reveal only traces of sectarianism in relation to the evacuation campaign. Diaries revealed little evidence of religious tension, with only three authors mentioning religion in their notes about the evacuation scheme. These include Miss Offley and Mr Foulds, who both noted Catholic evacuees had been placed in Protestant villages and some were having difficulty getting to mass. Further, Miss Mellon commented that locals in her village were all impressed by their Catholic evacuees hiring a bus to go *'en masse* to Mass'.[134] These diarists recorded no criticism of these evacuees practising their religion; rather, the villagers admired their enterprising nature or were sympathetic to their difficulties. The only negative comment was recorded by Glaswegian Miss Offley, who noted that locals who complained about dirty evacuee children blamed this on their being Irish Catholics.[135] She did not expand further on this point. Few other comments about Irish or Catholic evacuees were made by other diarists.

Other archival sources do reveal some evidence of friction. In the main, criticisms were linked to Catholic evacuees being placed in Protestant households, and the resulting clashes over worship services and dietary requirements. Dr Boyd's study of the evacuation scheme concluded that the difficulty arose from 'host tactlessness' and annoyance at having to reschedule meals, rather than overt sectarian hostility. In addition,

---

[132] Komter, 'Gratitude and gift exchange', 195, 211.
[133] Field, *Blood, Sweat, and Toil*, 20–21.
[134] M-O, Dir. November 1939, R1363 (Prestwick); Diarist 5390 (Glasgow), 5 September 1939; Diarist 5374 (Campbeltown), 21 April 1941.
[135] M-O, Diarist 5390 (Glasgow), 11 September 1939.

Boyd noted that out of 295 parental complaints about evacuation, only 5 related to hosts displaying anti-Catholic sentiment.[136] An examination of Scottish constabulary reports reveals host complaints were expressed from all reception areas in Scotland, and frustrations were not limited to areas hosting evacuees from Glasgow and the Clydebank region.[137] Resentment about hosting evacuees, therefore, was directed towards evacuees from all sending areas.

While Scotland's historic Protestant/Catholic divide might have been a factor in friction between hosts and evacuees, there is little evidence of this in primary sources studied for this chapter. Instead, sources reveal tension between Protestant hosts and non-Christian evacuees. Soon after mothers and children began their evacuation to the Scottish countryside in 1939, an article in the Church of Scotland's *Life and Work* magazine complained about the resulting 'invasion of our homes', and referred to hosts as experiencing a 'severe drain on their nervous resources'.[138] Christian hosts were aghast at the lack of religious adherence of many of their guests, and one wrote a piece in *Life and Work* describing her shock at her evacuee who, rather than saying bedtime prayers, simply turned over to sleep 'with a "Cheerio", accompanied with a wave which signified my dismissal from the bedroom'.[139] Furthermore, the president of the Kirk's Woman's Guild told of a relative who was hosting four little boys who 'simply died of laughing' when their host suggested saying prayers before bed.[140]

In response to this perceived ungodliness, Kirk leaders and members chose to use the evacuation as an opportunity for evangelism. The November 1939 edition of *Life and Work* featured numerous anecdotes of evacuees beginning to pray with their hosts and evacuation was said to be 'a golden opportunity . . . to restore the sacred rite of family prayers'.[141] Another parish chose to move its evening service to Sunday afternoons and tailor it towards children, to appeal to the high numbers of young evacuees in the village.[142] In addition, in the town of Stirling, north-west of Edinburgh, the Home Board of the Church of Scotland sent two Church Sisters to visit evacuees, and 'assure the mothers of the Church's friendship

---

[136] Third, 'Early stages', 68; Boyd, 'Parents and evacuation', 119.

[137] Host complaints came from Banff, Dundee, Fife, Stirling, Perth, Ayrshire, Glasgow, Perthshire and Kinross-shire, Moray and Nairn, Ross and Cromarty, Edinburgh, Haddington, Argyllshire, Ayr, Kincardine, Peeblesshire, Berwickshire, Dunbartonshire and East Lothian. Resentment came from all receiving areas, not just those hosting evacuees from Glasgow and Clydebank. See NRS, HH55/21–28, PWD – IR, 10 May 1940, 16 and 30 August 1940, 27 September 1940, 6 December 1940, 20 June 1941.

[138] G. J. Jeffrey, 'The renewal of family life: one result of A. R. P.', *Life and Work*, November 1939, 454.

[139] Ibid.; M. H., 'What shall we teach them?', *Life and Work*, November 1939, 461.

[140] 'The Woman's Guild: notes from the President's diary', *Life and Work*, November 1939, 476.

[141] M. H., 'What shall we teach them?', 461–2.

[142] A. R. P., 'From town to village', *Life and Work*, November 1939, 468.

and help, and to invite them into the fellowship'. Mothers were also encouraged 'whenever possible' to attend Church services.[143] It is unclear what the evacuee response to this evangelism was, though.

In comparison, the Jewish community was more vocal about its frustration with Christian evangelism towards Jewish evacuees. In September 1939 a Jewish official wrote to the Glasgow Jewish Representative Council (GJRC) to note his objections to Jewish evacuees in Perthshire being required to attend local churches on Sundays and to go to school on Jewish religious holidays.[144] The official was also upset as he had made prior arrangements with local authorities for the children to be excused from school to observe religious festivals. He arranged with the GJRC for a Jewish religious teacher to visit the district 'to safeguard the religious welfare of the children', and further investigate the issue.[145]

Lack of religious education in Christian areas was also a problem for evacuees from the Edinburgh Hebrew Congregation.[146] These concerns were quickly addressed and by November 1939 all 440 Jewish evacuees across Scotland were receiving 'some form of Hebrew education', though they remained living with their local hosts.[147] Soon afterward, leaders of the GJRC decided Jewish children should be housed in hostels that could better cater to their religious needs. The first, catering for 60 evacuees in the town of Skelmorlie, was completed in May 1940.[148]

Alongside problems with religious education, evacuation also brought complications for Jews who wanted to observe religious laws relating to food. In September 1939 an article in the *Jewish Chronicle*, a London-based Jewish newspaper, noted the concerns of Britain's Chief Rabbi over the ability of evacuees to keep kashrut.[149] He reminded parents that 'in a national emergency such as the present' all that was required was to refrain from eating forbidden meats and shellfish.[150] This was not as easy as it sounded, as the Chief Rabbi later specified that forbidden meats included 'any meats, even from a clean animal, that have not been slaughtered, prepared, or cooked according to Jewish rites'.[151] This meant any porcine products were forbidden, as well as meat that had not been killed by the

---

[143] G. A. Henderson, 'The Church and the evacuees', *Life and Work*, November 1939, 460–61.
[144] Scottish Jewish Archives Centre (SJAC), Minutes of the Glasgow Jewish Representative Council (GJRC), 20 September 1939; SJAC, 'Report on school children evacuated to Perthshire from Annette Street P. School', n.d.
[145] Ibid.
[146] SJAC, Edinburgh Hebrew Congregation, Minutes of Council, 24 October 1939.
[147] 'Glasgow news', *Jewish Chronicle*, 6 October 1939, 14 and 17 November 1939, 19–20.
[148] SJAC, Minutes of the Executive of the GJRC, 4 February 1940, 7 May 1940.
[149] Kashrut is the practice of keeping kasher/kosher, religious dietary purity laws. See Badatz Igud Rabbonim, 'What does kosher mean?', http://www.koshercertification.org.uk/whatdoe.html, accessed 19 February 2020.
[150] 'Jewish evacuees: emergency ruling on observance of food laws', *Jewish Chronicle*, 8 September 1939, 16.
[151] 'Religious observance in war-time', *Jewish Chronicle*, 15 September 1939, 12.

laws of Shechita, or any meals that combined meat and dairy, among other things.[152] These laws must have been difficult for evacuees to observe when living and eating in the homes of non-Jewish Scots. In response, the Glasgow Queen's Park Hebrew Congregation arranged to make and deliver four kasher dinners per week to evacuated children nearby, so they could observe religious customs.[153]

Additional research into archives from Scotland's Catholic and Jewish communities may further illuminate host–evacuee relationships in Scotland. At present, though, the theory that Scottish host hostility may have been prompted by religious tension is not borne out by the sources. In contrast to England, where research by Geoffrey Field and Tony Kushner revealed anti-Catholic and anti-Semitic sentiment towards evacuees, in Scotland a brief analysis of sources suggests host frustrations were not driven by religion.[154] Antagonism was not directed towards Catholic or Irish Catholic evacuees in particular, and while tensions arose between Jewish evacuees and evangelising hosts, or those who prevented observation of Jewish religious laws, this did not spill over into hostility as it had in parts of England.[155] Rather, the Jewish community's constructive response and attempts to resolve the problems may have quashed any rising discontent. Certainly, sectarian friction caused day-to-day difficulties for hosts and evacuees but, overall, there were other forces at play that had a greater role in the breakdown of these relationships.

'The quiet but deep pleasures of country life': country versus city

One of those forces was the divide between urban and rural, and the accompanying view that country was better than city. Differences between urban and rural life were a factor in host–evacuee friction across Britain, but the issue was particularly pronounced in Scotland.[156] There, the divide was long-established, with claims of the inferiority of city life arising in the nineteenth century when rates of disease, malnutrition and infant mortality were significantly higher in Scottish cities, and overcrowding and squalor were rife in impoverished urban slums.[157] Further, in overcrowded city tenements with poor sanitation, disease spread more quickly. Inner-city Glaswegian slums were among the most overcrowded and

---

[152] Shechita requires a trained *shochet* to kill the animal by making a 'rapid and expert transverse incision . . . which severs the major structures and vessels at the neck'. Exsanguination must follow. See Badatz Igud Rabbonim, 'What does kosher mean?'; Shechita UK, *A Guide to Shechita* (2009), 5.

[153] 'Glasgow news', *Jewish Chronicle*, 6 October 1939, 14.

[154] Kushner, *Persistence of Prejudice*; Field, *Blood, Sweat, and Toil*, 20–4.

[155] Field, *Blood, Sweat, and Toil*, 22–4.

[156] Ibid., 14–16; Todman, *Into Battle*, 250; Calder, *People's War*, 42; Rose, *Which People's War?*, 56–7, 198–9, 207–10.

[157] Devine, *Scottish Nation*, 341–4.

impoverished in Britain, and Scottish infant mortality rates were some of the worst in Europe. In addition, urban diets were known to be poor, and studies found that badly nourished Glaswegian juveniles were lower in weight and height than their rural peers.[158] Scottish health officials firmly believed that country air, diet and conditions were better for heath – both physical and intellectual.[159] These sentiments were echoed by other members of society.

This well-established view of rural superiority was reflected in reports by hosts and authorities in Scottish reception areas, who were quick to note the benefits of country life for evacuees. The Church of Scotland said that for those 'who applied themselves' to life in the country, there was improvement in health and physique.[160] The Scottish Women's Group was similarly positive, and reported 'abundant testimony [of] clean, lovable little visitors, who came, rejoiced in the country life, made good physically, prospered in school, and in some cases wept bitterly on the parental summons to return home'.[161] Officials also promoted the view that country life was better for evacuees. One example came from the Secretary of State for Scotland who said country-based evacuees were 'definitely gaining in health', and publicly announced that fresh air, better sleep and good food would benefit the children's health and physique.[162] Officers of the SED also felt the country had improved the health of evacuees, and a March 1940 report stated rural air had brought 'considerable benefit, moral as well as intellectual' for the evacuees who had 'tasted the quiet but deep pleasures of country life'.[163]

Hosts also seemed to take special pleasure in 'curing' evacuees of the afflictions of the city. An example of this was given to Parliament, from a letter written by a host:

> I am beginning thoroughly to enjoy reaping some reward. I know few greater satisfactions than to see these children from the slums getting some colour into their cheeks; putting on weight; growing daily less noisy and better mannered; to see their minds opening to new interests and healthy forms of fun; and to watch them discovering that life can hold lots of excitement apart from gangster fights, petty thieving and escapes from the cops.[164]

---

[158] Cameron, *Impaled Upon a Thistle*, 127; John Foster, 'A proletarian nation? Occupation and class since 1914', in *People and Society in Scotland*, Vol. III, 201–40, here 223; Fraser and Maver, 'Social problems', 353–5, 361.

[159] Irene Maver, 'Leisure time in Scotland during the nineteenth and twentieth centuries', in John Beech, Owen Hand, Mark A. Mulhern and Jeremy Weston (eds), *Scottish Life and Society: The Individual and Community Life* (Edinburgh: John Donald, 2005), 178.

[160] Church of Scotland, 'Report of the Committee on Church and Nation', May 1941.

[161] SWG, *Our Scottish Towns*, 20.

[162] Hansard, HC Deb, 21 November 1939, vol. 353 col. 1099.

[163] NRS, ED24/42, 'The educational position in Scotland – March 1940'.

[164] Hansard, HC Deb, 21 November 1939, vol. 353 col. 1107.

Perhaps evident in this was an element of a saviour complex, of hosts desiring to rescue city children from a perceived life of crime, disease and poverty.

Despite the desire of hosts to rescue evacuees from their 'inferior' city life, many evacuees seemed to care little for the benefits of the country. Overheard evacuee complaints included, 'there's too much grass about', and '[a]t nicht it wis hills, jist hills! and in the mornin' it wis hills again, hills and hills!'[165] In addition, evacuees were disappointed by the lack of ice-cream stores and unavailability of fish and chips in their new country villages, things they had enjoyed in the city.[166] Evacuees in one small west Highland village referred to their new home only as 'a place which was all hills and lacked tram-cars'.[167] This came as a surprise to one local who noted that writer Robert Lynd had described the village as 'the last sight a Christian's eyes are likely to tire of'.[168]

In addition, many evacuees missed the entertainments that accompanied city life. Eileen Offley's charwoman told her employer that many local families had given up on evacuation as 'they don't like the country'.[169] Miss Offley also heard elsewhere that evacuees had 'a dislike for country [and] they want to go to the cinema'.[170] Other stories came from Wigtown, where one group of evacuees near Stranraer said the villages they had been placed in were too small, and from Glenluce, where evacuees complained they were too far from home and there were no picture houses.[171] At that time, Glasgow had over 100 cinemas, and one study of West Lothian children found 36 per cent attended the cinema weekly, with one-quarter attending more than once per week.[172] Dancing was also a popular form of entertainment for city youngsters, and by the mid-1930s Glasgow had over 150 registered dance halls.[173] Such entertainments were mostly absent from country life, adding to the evacuee perception of boredom and dissatisfaction.

The evacuee rebuff of what hosts perceived as the unquestionable fact of country superiority, a view shared by the church, authorities and medical personnel, was not well received. Hosts felt it was a rejection of good common-sense, and the return of evacuees to their city life was, in a way, seen as a slap in the face for rural hosts, convinced they had offered evacuees the chance to escape an unhealthy, inferior life in the city. This rejection of the country lifestyle and its benefits added further weight to host resentment of evacuees.

---

[165] Third, 'Early stages', 71; SWG, *Our Scottish Towns*, 1.
[166] SWG, *Our Scottish Towns*, 13.
[167] Clark, 'Notes on a village', 20.
[168] Ibid.
[169] M-O, Diarist 5390 (Glasgow), 7 September 1939.
[170] Ibid., 9 September 1939.
[171] 'Billeting difficulties: mothers with children', *The Scotsman*, 6 September 1939.
[172] Devine, *Scottish Nation*, 360.
[173] Ibid.

'It's too posh for me': class conflict

Conflict between the social classes was a further significant factor prompting host hostility towards evacuees. Alongside religious tension, class division had flourished in Scotland during the 1920s and 1930s. As explained earlier in this work, the economic depression had brought high rates of working-class unemployment, which hit those in Scotland's industrial heartland especially hard. The middle classes did not suffer as badly, with middle-class unemployment rarely over 5 per cent.[174] After the Great War, a separate working-class culture had further developed in Scotland, with a focus on leisure pursuits such as football, and a rise in support for the Labour Party.[175] The separate cultures and the differing effects of economic depression widened the gap between working- and middle-class Scots. Further differences were borne out in religion, place of residence and family size, which were often interlinked. Both Catholic and working-class families tended to be larger, having an average of five to seven children, while middle-class families generally had fewer than five. The 1911 census found that one in five (often working-class) women aged between 22 and 26 had over ten children, which hosts in reception areas discovered with shock as some arrived in evacuation parties.[176] These differences, brought into the homes of hosts, were easy to notice and comment upon.

In Scotland, the class-divide was obvious to all, and this manifested itself in evacuees feeling uncomfortable and believing they were being judged, and middle-class hosts expressing hostility towards their social inferiors. In Edinburgh, one man reported hearing 'many grumbles about children of one class being billeted on people of a lower class'.[177] In Prestwick a student reported one of the difficulties with evacuation had to do with class: 'children coming from upper middle-class homes were put into working class homes when in the same town poor children were being put into large houses. The result was that both sets of children were uncomfortable.'[178] The student also mentioned evacuee mothers feeling unsettled in their new billets, with comments such as 'it's too posh for me', 'it's too clean' and 'you can't be yourself here'. Elsewhere, evacuees asked to take their 'pieces' outside to eat at the kerb, as it felt too strange to sit inside at the table.[179] Uncomfortable, one evacuee family went so far as to ask their host if they could sleep in her lobby, as the large furnished room they had been given was 'too grand'.[180] The differences were obviously too great for this family, unwilling to remain in accommodation in which they felt unsettled.

---

[174] Ibid., 268.
[175] W. Hamish Fraser, 'The working class', in Fraser and Maver, *Glasgow*, Vol. II, 343.
[176] Devine, *Scottish Nation*, 328–9, 334, 349, 524–5.
[177] M-O, Dir. November 1939, R1302 (Edinburgh).
[178] Ibid., R1363 (Prestwick).
[179] M-O, Diarist 5390 (Glasgow), 17 September 1939.
[180] Ibid., 9 September 1939.

Differences were also notable in how evacuees perceived sanitary facilities. As mentioned earlier, there were problems with evacuees using carpets, bedding and buckets as toilets, leading many hosts to perceive them as dirty. This is exemplified in the story of one evacuee billeted with the town provost of Aberfeldy in Perthshire. On his first night, in a panic he climbed out of a window and onto the Provost's house roof, calling out '[h]elp, help! They're trying to droon me!' It turned out the Provost had run a bath for the child, who had never had a proper bath before. At the evacuee's home in an inner-city tenement, several families shared a tin tub for bathing and he was thus unfamiliar with a fixed bath.[181] As late as 1951, only 57 per cent of Scottish households had access to a fixed bath, and one-third of households shared a W. C.[182] Standards of sanitation differed widely, especially for evacuees from inner-city slums, and the exposure of such habits was a shock to hosts.

One aspect to the derision of middle-class hosts was the belief, lingering from the Victorian period, that slum inhabitants were 'slothful, drunken and feckless', enduring squalor as a result of 'personal failure and defects of character', 'worse off than wild animals'.[183] These ideas were linked to views on superiority of the country, and surprise that many who had been given the opportunity to escape either returned to their situation or were dissatisfied with what hosts perceived as a better one. One factor that exacerbated this perception was that urban families who had the means to do so often arranged for the private evacuation of children. This meant those who were evacuated on the government scheme generally came from families who were more impoverished. When such children were sent to board with middle-class hosts, the differences in social class were more pronounced, leading hosts to feel that all city-dwellers were of a similar ilk, perhaps again playing on their belief that the city was inferior to the country. As the SWG pronounced, '[t]o the average observer of Scottish character there is . . . a broad difference between the country and the town bred person . . . the basic fact of extreme poverty normally reacts in a deleterious manner on the character and morale of those subject to it for long periods'.[184] This was a view echoed by many middle-class hosts.

When evacuees were billeted with working-class hosts, there were fewer complaints and an absence of the hostile views reported in many sources examined for this chapter. In one mining village, the hosts of already-crowded working-class homes showed a greater response to taking evacuees, and in Stirling and Kilmarnock it was said there was no trouble with evacuees when billeted in poor areas similar to their own homes. 'Here, kind

---

[181] Lesley Roberts, 'Scots evacuees remember dramatic World War II operation', *Daily Record*, 29 August 2009.
[182] Devine, *Scottish Nation*, 529–30.
[183] Ibid, 344; Fraser and Maver, 'Social problems', 353.
[184] SWG, *Our Scottish Towns*, 22, 24.

is living with kind', the observer commented.¹⁸⁵ In addition, constabulary reports from the central industrial belt of Scotland, with a much higher proportion of working-class hosts, did not report complaints about hosting evacuees. There was some comment that these homes were glad to have the extra wages from a billeting allowance, and that adding one or two mouths to an already large family did not make much difference to costs.¹⁸⁶ In contrast, middle-class hosts seemed concerned about the effect of class cross-pollination. 'What will be the outcome of this mixing of the classes?' one diarist pondered, adding '[t]here is a popular view that it will open the door to communism'.¹⁸⁷ A young diarist in Ayrshire echoed these sentiments, telling M-O the problems had greatly to do with 'marked class difference', and if similar classes had been placed together this discomfort would have been absent.¹⁸⁸ From the comments expressed by middle-class hosts, it becomes clear that much of their discomfort was based on the differing social class of their evacuees, and that when evacuees were placed with hosts of a similar social class there was an almost total absence of complaint.

Similar findings were observed in studies of evacuation in England and Wales. Field noted that evacuation was least successful when children were placed in homes of the upper middle class; Hess observed that, in Devon, 'the vast majority' of children were placed in working-class homes and, as a result, abandonment of the scheme was very low; while Titmuss concluded that socially matched evacuation had the greatest chance of success.¹⁸⁹ This 'profound clash of cultures' was the main cause of evacuee–host tension in England and Wales, and this was, likewise, the case in Scotland.¹⁹⁰

John Stewart and John Welshman concluded that the Scottish evacuation scheme exposed urban poverty and, in contrast to England, Scots blamed structural problems for this poverty, rather than attributing it to behavioural or individual factors. Stewart and Welshman stated there was 'no evidence' that, in Scotland, poor parenting and the 'problem family' were blamed for evacuee poverty.¹⁹¹ The evidence presented in this chapter categorically refutes this interpretation. Many of those in reception areas fervently blamed the health, condition and behaviour of evacuees on their social background. They also viewed evacuee manners and sanitary habits as a sign of poor parenting common to city-dwellers. Above all, in Scotland the evacuation seemed to expose existing social divisions and reinforce class divides. I have already mentioned one diarist's comment, 'there is no

---

¹⁸⁵ M-O, Dir. November 1939, R1363 (Prestwick); M-O, Diarist 5390 (Glasgow), 9 September 1939.
¹⁸⁶ Third, 'Early stages', 62.
¹⁸⁷ M-O, Diarist 5390 (Glasgow), 9 September 1939.
¹⁸⁸ M-O, Dir. December 1939, R1363 (Prestwick).
¹⁸⁹ Preston, 'Evacuation of schoolchildren', 234–5; Field, *Blood, Sweat, and Toil*, 29; Hess, 'Civilian evacuation to Devon', 184; Titmuss, *Social Policy*, 392–3.
¹⁹⁰ Todman, *Into Battle*, 250.
¹⁹¹ Stewart and Welshman, 'Evacuation of children', 100, 119.

trouble [when] kind is living with kind'.[192] This harks back to the interpretation proposed by Macnicol, that the British evacuation 'served to reinforce existing analyses of working-class poverty'.[193] The contemporary sources used in this chapter suggest this was also the case in Scotland. In particular, diaries, newspaper articles and Chief Constables' reports that discussed evacuation did not portray hosts as being so concerned about urban poverty that they called for social welfare reform. Rather, evacuation seemed to increase the ill-feeling and resentment of the middle classes towards those of the working class.

Through exploring host reactions to evacuees, this chapter has shown that divisions in Scottish society ran deep. The evacuation was intended to protect vulnerable urban Scots from harm and ease pressure on authorities in the event of air raids, which were expected to be frequent and damaging. Research contained in this chapter reveals that even in the face of these potential risks, rural Scots found the evacuation scheme to be inconvenient, and resisted having to host these evacuees – their fellow Scots. This demonstrates that social schisms were of greater impact on behaviour than fears about the war and its effect on the daily lives of other citizens. In the words of Captain McEwen, MP for Berwickshire and Haddington, the GES was an 'earthquake in the social life of Scotland', bringing great shock to hosts whose homes and communities were 'invaded' by fellow Scots who had different outlooks, backgrounds and religions.[194]

---

[192] M-O, Diarist 5390 (Glasgow), 9 September 1939.
[193] Macnicol, 'Evacuation of schoolchildren', 27.
[194] Hansard, HC Deb, 21 November 1939, vol. 353 col. 1173.

CHAPTER TWO

'What That Boy Needed Was a Real Good Thrashing': Scotland's Moral Crisis, 1940–5

Nine boys, who with 31 others ran away from an approved school, appeared at Perth Juvenile Court yesterday before Sheriff Valentine, and admitted 15 charges. All aged 16 except one of 15, the boys were stated to have committed a theft in Angus then gone to Inverness-shire and returned down the Great North Road towards Perth. At Murthly they broke into Rohallion House, occupied by Lady Helena Mariota Carnegie, and stole over 50 articles, including money. Among the 150 stolen articles in all were tinned fruit, champagne, wine, brandy, and siphons of soda water. Three motor cars, a motor van, and nine bicycles were also taken by the boys. With regard to the 31 other boys who escaped . . . some of them had returned to the school, but many were still at large. The boys took the motor vehicles and after the petrol supply ran out abandoned them.[1]

This story was one of many about delinquent juveniles that saturated the Scottish press during the Second World War.[2] What came to be known as 'the moral crisis' was sparked by an official report in 1940 that revealed alarming increases in youth crime across Britain. Those official statistics noted there had been a 41 per cent increase in the number of British children aged under 14 found guilty of indictable offences in the first year of war. Furthermore, among those aged 14 to 17, there had been a 22 per cent rise.[3] In Scotland, the situation looked even more serious as there had been a 26 per cent increase in juvenile crime over the previous

---

[1] 'Runaway boys stole cars, champagne', *Dundee Courier and Advertiser*, 13 August 1941 in NRS, HH60/421 – Juvenile delinquency 1939–42, press and Hansard cuttings. Quotation in chapter title from Hansard, HC Deb, 21 July 1943, vol. 391 col. 989, comments of a Glaswegian sheriff to Mr Francis Watt, MP for Edinburgh Central.
[2] Titles included 'Runaway boys stole cars, champagne', *Dundee Courier and Advertiser*, 13 August 1941; 'Boy offenders: Glasgow delinquency problem', *Glasgow Herald*, 20 May 1942; 'Girl gangsters robbed people in black-out', *Daily Express*, 1 April 1942; 'Church warns: war life ruining children', *Daily Express*, 9 May 1941; 'We're breeding a race of rogues', *Daily Express* 13 March 1941; 'Boy's "day out" on stolen money', *Edinburgh Evening News*, 24 June 1942; all contained within NRS, HH60/421 – Juvenile delinquency 1939–42, press and Hansard cuttings.
[3] Geoffrey Field, 'Perspectives on the working-class family in wartime Britain, 1939–1945', *International Labor and Working-Class History* 38 (1990), 12.

year.⁴ From that time onwards, the British home front was in the grip of a moral panic, with the church, local authorities, parliamentarians and law and order officials displaying an obsession with the notion Britain was descending into degeneracy, plagued by drunkenness, juvenile delinquency and sexual immorality. In Scotland, there were frequent reminders in newspapers of shocking crimes, such as the one above from August 1941. This wave of delinquency and immorality captured Scottish attention, and started a debate that would rage throughout the following years of the Second World War.

A number of historians have discussed Britain's wartime preoccupation with behaviour and morals.⁵ This includes a wealth of scholarship on sexuality, the gendering of leisure and the policing of women's behaviour, by authors such as Penny Summerfield, Gail Braybon, Nicole Crockett, Claire Langhamer and Sonya O. Rose.⁶ Geoffrey Field concluded the wartime panic about delinquency more generally was linked to social judgement of the working class and those who were seen to be part of the 'problem family' phenomenon.⁷ Along similar lines, in 2007 David Smith published a study of official responses to Scottish juvenile delinquency during the war. He found that delinquency in Scotland, while considered to be primarily a result of the social disorganisation caused by war, was also linked to the breakdown of the family.⁸ In Smith's opinion, topics such as 'the neglectful mother', 'abnormal home life' and 'bad environment' gave reformist professionals and officials an opportunity to 'publicise the inadequacies' of Scotland's cities and those who dwelled in them.⁹ Sociologist John Macnicol has agreed with these interpretations, writing that the perceived decline in wartime morality created a resurgence in ideas of biological determinism, eugenics and belief in the existence of an underclass, or '*residuum*'.¹⁰ Often impoverished and welfare-dependent, without regular employment, the underclass was seen as being ruled by pleasure, drink and

---

⁴ Smith, 'Official responses', 82.

⁵ Claire Langhamer, '"A public house is for all classes, men and women alike": women, leisure and drink in Second World War England', *Women's History Review* 12, no. 3 (2003): 423–43; Pamela Cox, *Gender, Justice and Welfare: Bad Girls in Britain, 1900–1950* (Basingstoke: Palgrave Macmillan, 2003); Christine Gledhill and Gillian Swanson (eds), *Nationalising Femininity: Culture, Sexuality and Cinema in World War Two Britain* (Manchester: Manchester University Press, 1996); John Costello, *Love, Sex, and War: Changing Values, 1939–1945* (London: Collins, 1985).

⁶ Braybon and Summerfield, *Out of the Cage*; Summerfield, *Women's Wartime Lives*; Penny Summerfield and Nicole Crockett, '"You weren't taught that with the welding": lessons in sexuality in the Second World War', *Women's History Review* 1, no. 3 (1992): 435–54; Penny Tinkler, 'Cause for concern: young women and leisure, 1930–50', *Women's History Review* 12, no. 2 (2003): 233–62; Rose, 'Girls and GIs'.

⁷ Field, 'Working-class family', 12–14.

⁸ Smith, 'Official responses', 78–9.

⁹ Ibid., 86–7, 101.

¹⁰ John Macnicol, 'Reconstructing the underclass', *Social Policy and Society* 16, no. 1 (2017), 103.

idleness, possessing poor parenting skills and ill-disciplined children: 'a menace and a disgrace to the community'.[11] For Macnicol, the moral panic served as a thinly veiled attack on the underdog: the working class.

These criticisms link back to Victorian social hygiene ideas and notions of hereditary morality. Greta Jones has argued that, even in the mid-twentieth century, much of British society remained obsessed with ideas of heredity. For those considered unable to help themselves, it was believed that cleaning up their insanitary environment, curtailing unsuitable leisure and entertainment pursuits, and the 'removal of evil influences' would assist them into an improved position in society.[12] Concerns over morality are also linked to the prominence of religion in British life, and notions of Christian respectability and behavioural norms. In Scotland, Callum Brown has written much about the chief voice of morality in Scotland – the Church of Scotland – which had long been considered the authority on 'correct' behaviour and appropriate recreational activities.[13] Sonya Rose, in her landmark study of the British home front, wrote of the wartime obsession with the romantic behaviour of women, lurid headlines on teenage girls running wild and, in general, the 'widespread perception that a wave of "moral laxity" was engulfing the country'.[14] For Rose, this puritanism was linked to the struggle over women's sexual emancipation and the outdated notion that society was the keeper of a woman's body.[15] As Brown pointed out, on the eve of war strong notions of 'correct' behaviour governed Scottish society. When the early years of the war brought a barrage of reports of delinquent and immoral behaviour, Scottish authorities, interest groups and the church began to panic. This resulted in much public discussion on what might explain these immoral tendencies.

Historians have focused on what wartime delinquency reveals about gender relations, sexual norms and welfare reform in Second World War Britain, without giving attention to the influences behind concerns over morality, or exploring differences in responses across Britain.[16] This chapter aims to redress this with a focus on Scotland, examining a range of primary sources to discover which causes and remedies were voiced by contemporaries, and what this tells us about society, religion and identity in wartime Scotland. The chapter will examine the espoused causes of degeneracy and the suggested ways to exorcise the demons from a delinquent population. Through examining the perceptions held by contemporaries,

---

[11] Ibid., 103. See also J. Welshman, *Underclass: A History of the Excluded, 1880–2000* (London: Continuum, 2006).

[12] Greta Jones, *Social Hygiene in Twentieth-Century Britain* (London: Croom Helm, 1986), 11.

[13] Callum G. Brown, *The People in the Pews: Religion and Society in Scotland since 1780* (Glasgow: Economic and Social History Society of Scotland, 1993), 32.

[14] Rose, *Which People's War?*, 74–5.

[15] Ibid., 83, 91, 287.

[16] For example, Rose, *Which People's War?*; Summerfield and Crockett, 'You weren't taught that'; Field, 'Working-class family'.

we discover a resurgence of the Victorian obsession with an uncivilised *residuum*, concerns about national unity during war and signs of the Kirk losing its grip on modern Scotland.

Its first half explores the factors proposed as responsible for wartime delinquency and immorality in Scotland, and the methods suggested to treat the supposed scourge. As R. S. Sindall has pointed out, wartime crime statistics varied widely across Scotland and are, moreover, 'a measure, not necessarily of what was happening, but what people *believed* was happening' (emphasis mine).[17] With this in mind, if the delinquency situation was not as close to crisis point as many believed, why then did Scottish officials, church leaders and interest groups allow themselves to become so affected by the issue? The second half of this chapter will further examine this question, seeking to understand the social factors underlying the moral panic, and what these influences might reveal about Second World War Scotland, as compared with the rest of Britain.

Scottish beliefs about wartime delinquency

From 1940 onwards, Scottish youth delinquency pervaded news reports. Alongside youthful crimes and misdemeanours were reports of increased rates of drinking by youths, industrial workers and those in the armed services. There were also numerous reports of young girls 'consorting' with men, and a resurgence of venereal disease among both servicemen and those who provided sexual services. By 1942, newspapers were producing a flood of articles proclaiming moral delinquency was at dangerous levels. These included such sensationalist headlines as 'Juvenile courts: extraordinary figures', 'Boy offenders: Glasgow delinquency problem', 'We're breeding a race of rogues' and 'Girl gangsters robbed people in black-out'.[18] Alongside these scandalous articles, parties such as the church, the police, probation officers and social workers held a range of conferences and meetings to consider the best methods to deal with the weighty problems of Scottish delinquency and immorality. These newspaper articles, meetings and reports culminated in a mood of panic, and public belief in a situation rapidly spiralling out of control.

In late 1941, statistics on Scottish juvenile offences were released by the authorities. During the previous year, the rates of offenders found guilty of misdemeanours had risen by 26 per cent from the 1939 figures.[19] Further, since 1939 crimes committed by Scots aged under 14 had risen by

[17] R. S. Sindall, 'Criminal statistics of nineteenth-century cities: a new approach', *Urban History Yearbook* (1968): 28–36, here 34.

[18] 'Juvenile courts: extraordinary figures', *The Scotsman*, 28 November 1942; 'Boy offenders: Glasgow delinquency problem', *Glasgow Herald*, 20 May 1942; 'We're breeding a race of rogues', *Daily Express*, 13 March 1941; 'Girl gangsters robbed people in black-out', *Daily Express*, 1 April 1942.

[19] NRS, HH60/425, memo from Anderson to Aglen, 11 December 1941.

52 per cent. This seemed an extraordinary and shocking rise. In July 1942 Thomas Johnston, the Secretary of State for Scotland, spoke to Parliament of his alarm at the increase in juvenile crime. 'There is an increase of 3,500 cases over the last pre-war year, and that is an increase of 22 per cent', Johnston revealed.[20] When combined with an official circular on juvenile offences that referred to statistics as 'striking', 'marked' and 'disquieting', this added to the general mood of alarm.[21] The circular, produced by the SED and the SHD, was distributed to education authorities, juvenile organisations, councils and representatives for the courts. According to the authors, juvenile delinquency arose out of a range of 'war conditions': shorter school hours; greater opportunity for 'misdirected activity'; less parental control owing to fathers and mothers on war work; high war wages bringing new temptations; and the black-out providing 'a cloak for delinquent action'. The reports also stated that the war had produced anxiety and excitement in the young, as well as restlessness and 'destructive instincts'.[22] The fact that these two Scottish departments released a joint official circular on juvenile delinquency reveals this was a matter the authorities took seriously.

In response to this perceived wave of delinquency, lawmakers, officials, the Kirk and the public proposed factors they believed were responsible for this deluge. These factors causing wartime delinquency can be roughly categorised as ill-discipline, lack of self-control, personal inadequacy and the defective family. While war might have opened the gates for delinquency, these other factors were said to be assisting its passage. This chapter will explore the factors said to be responsible for Scottish delinquency, beginning with ill-discipline.

'Too much slackness': ill-discipline

The new temptations and situations created by war afforded multiple opportunities for degenerate behaviour. The general feeling was that those who were lacking in self-discipline took advantage of these wartime conditions to engage in delinquent activities. This accusation, prompted by the alarming crime statistics of 1940, was largely levelled at juveniles. During the war, many youths received less supervision than in pre-war years. Rural Scottish classrooms often operated on a half-day rota to allow teaching of evacuees, while city schools were generally requisitioned for military purposes or closed temporarily in areas deemed at high risk of air raids.[23] Furthermore, working fathers were required to undertake longer hours and, as the war dragged on, mothers were called to take on employment.

---

[20] Hansard, HC Deb, 8 July 1942, vol. 381 col. 795.
[21] NRS, HH60/427, SED Circular No. 215 and SHD Circular No. 4740, *Juvenile Offences* (Edinburgh: HMSO, 1941), 1–4.
[22] Ibid.
[23] Hansard, HC Debs 21 November 1939, vol. 353 cols 1088–92; 18 June 1940, vol. 362 cols 73–7; 30 July 1941, vol. 373 col. 1459.

These changes resulted in young people spending many hours of the day and evenings without adult supervision.

During this time undisciplined youngsters seemed determined to make the most of wartime disruption in order to engage in mischief. One columnist reported that, without supervision, unsettled youths 'often find an outlet in activities which do not meet with the approval of law-abiding citizens, and unruly behaviour ... becomes characteristic'.[24] Similarly, in a report to the Edinburgh Town Council, Bailie Baird stated there was 'a lamentable lack of discipline among a certain section of young people to-day'.[25] The bailie added that 'what had made Scotland great in the past was discipline, and there was too much slackness and easygoing to-day'.[26] An MoI investigator agreed, noting there had been a 'notable relaxation in home discipline' and, in youths, 'the results have been wilfulness and wantonness'.[27]

Reports of ill-disciplined youth emerged from across Scotland, and spanned the duration of the war. In Clydebank young delinquents were said to be roving around houses left derelict by enemy bombing, 'taking full advantage of the blitzed houses for their wild adventures'.[28] In Paisley, a gang of seven girls used the darkness provided by the black-out to rob unwary pedestrians.[29] MoI also collated numerous complaints regarding youths making the most of the black-out to engage in 'insanitary behaviour in the streets'. Moreover, the youths were damaging gardens and private property, and this was viewed by MoI officials as 'a purely war-time manifestation' of delinquency.[30]

Observers felt war had encouraged youths to engage in destructive behaviour.[31] Glasgow Springburn MP Agnes Hardie claimed in 1943

> there is a war mentality. Children see the results of bombs being dropped, buildings being blown up and everything destroyed. I am told that some of the smashing of shelters – which I am not justifying – is due to the fact that those responsible are playing at commando raids.[32]

A report of this sort of destructiveness came from Dundee, where a group of juvenile offenders were charged in court with causing £50,000 worth of damage to air raid shelters.[33] In 1944 MoI cautioned '[t]he fighting spirit

---

[24] L. R. R., 'Woman's View column: youth marches on', *Edinburgh Evening Dispatch*, 21 October 1942.
[25] 'Use of birch', *The Scotsman*, 9 January 1942.
[26] Ibid.
[27] NRS, HH60/422, 'Ministry of Information, Special Intelligence Report: Juvenile Delinquency (Scotland)' (hereafter 'SIR: JD Scotland'), 25 January 1944, 5.
[28] Ibid.
[29] 'Girl gangsters robbed people in black-out', *Daily Express*, 1 April 1942.
[30] SIR: JD Scotland, 3.
[31] Ibid.
[32] Hansard, HC Deb, 21 July 1943, vol. 391 col. 964.
[33] 'Juvenile offenders', *Dundee Courier*, 9 October 1942.

is rampant . . . Almost 100 per cent of the spontaneous play of small boys is of the Commando type'.[34]

In 1943 The London Midland and Scotland Railway Company reported a wave of malicious damage to train carriages. In the Glasgow area alone, carriages had 1,200 window straps torn or cut, upholstery in over 300 compartments had been slashed and 'considerable damage' had been done to mirror glass, blinds and other fittings.[35] Major Malcolm Speir, the chief officer for the company, said society needed to appeal to youths to regain their 'spirit of "service for others" and "playing the game"'.[36] Cinema managers across Scotland complained of similar malicious damage, much committed by youths attending sessions in the afternoon or evening. One manager believed picture houses were being used as babysitters, saying '[t]he cinema has become more of a habit than a treat as parents seem to send them there to get them out of the way'.[37] The MoI reported in 1944 that cinema managers 'all over Scotland' felt similarly, having experienced an increase in damage caused by youths. This damage included reports of 'insanitary behaviour' and petty theft, and more serious 'malicious damage' such as knives being used to tear seats, and lavatory fittings being destroyed.[38] At a Glasgow cinema in the district of Govan, cinema owners reported delinquents had slashed seats with razors and knives, leaving 2,000 out of 2,500 seats destroyed.[39] War appeared to have unleashed a torrent of ill-discipline.

During the war, citizens were meant to be acting for the greater good, working together to win the war rather than wantonly engaging in crime and destruction.[40] Scottish delinquents, therefore, were showing ill-discipline at a time when restraint was most important. Many observers felt the way to deal with this crisis of ill-discipline was to punish offenders more harshly, in the hope this might deter delinquents from reoffending. One common refrain was to bring back the birch and mend young offenders with corporal punishment. As the following examples suggest, those who advocated birching believed harsher punishment was necessary to instil discipline in those who lacked it. 'A good "clouting" would do some of them no harm', stated a Mr Hardie, at a meeting of the Edinburgh Town Council in 1941.[41] The Town Council also heard that probation officers and bailies were at their wits' end over dealing with troublesome youths, and alternative

---

[34] SIR: JD Scotland.
[35] NRS, HH60/422, 'Criminal interference with the war effort: this sabotage must be stopped!', 10 January 1943.
[36] Ibid.
[37] SIR: JD Scotland, 2.
[38] Ibid.
[39] 'City ordered the birch 110 times', *Glasgow Herald*, 26 November 1943.
[40] See Rose, *Which People's War?*
[41] Comments from Mr Hardie, 'Juvenile delinquency: serious problem in Edinburgh', *The Scotsman*, 6 June 1941.

measures such as approved schools and probation had 'utterly broken down'.[42] In 1943, a sheriff in Glasgow lamented that a young delinquent was put on probation, which would leave him feeling he had got away with his crimes. The juvenile courts were a farce, the sheriff complained, and 'what that boy needed was a real good thrashing'.[43]

Some parents of delinquents even requested harsh punishment be given to their offspring. One father in Greenock asked the justices at Greenock Juvenile Court to order his son to be birched for theft.[44] The Court agreed, and it became only the second time a sentence of birching had been ordered there. A Dundee mother felt similarly about her 10-year-old, who appeared in court charged with theft in June 1942. She asked the courts to 'thrash' the boy, saying he had given her a heart attack with his 'carrying on'. She also admitted, 'I have whipped him until he has dropped. He just defies me.'[45] This leaves one wondering what she thought the courts could achieve that she had not already tried.

Many members of the public argued passionately for the use of the birch as a way of curbing the wave of wartime ill-discipline. A Mr Norman Macdonald from Auchterarder wrote to *The Scotsman* in February 1942, stating

> nobody has yet told us why corporal punishment is 'brutal', 'inhuman', 'cruel' and even 'repellent' . . . People whose hearts rule their heads are a public danger . . . Many of our people are going soft and, worse still, making the youngsters softer. [He alleged that if birching was abandoned,] Manliness will soon be replaced by effeminacy.[46]

Holding similar sentiment was well-known lawyer and judge Edward Salvesen, who wrote to the editor with his views on juvenile delinquency in 1941. Delinquency was 'a menace to the morals of the growing generation', Lord Salvesen claimed, adding that he had compared the statistics, and Scotland had eight times as many juvenile delinquents as England.[47] In his opinion, birching had 'fallen into disuse through false sentimentality, but statistics show that a continuous decrease in the number of birchings awarded has been followed by a steady increase in juvenile delinquency'.[48] It is difficult to know whether Salvesen's figures were accurate, as easily comparable statistics were not kept by the SHD.[49]

---

[42] 'Birching of boys', *Edinburgh Evening Dispatch*, 24 November 1941.
[43] Comments of a Glaswegian sheriff to Mr Francis Watt, MP for Edinburgh Central, Hansard, HC Deb, 21 July 1943, vol. 391 col. 989.
[44] 'Father's request to court', *Glasgow Herald*, 31 March 1940.
[45] 'Boy who would not go to school', *Daily Record*, 25 June 1942.
[46] 'Letter to the editor from Norman Doran Macdonald (Auchterarder)', *The Scotsman*, 5 February 1942.
[47] 'Letter to the editor by Edward Salvesen', *The Scotsman*, 7 March 1941.
[48] Ibid.
[49] The SHD kept a file of statistics on juvenile delinquency, but each measured a different topic including charges laid against juveniles, charges successfully proved, percentage increases/decreases as part of total youth population. This makes comparisons difficult,

In contrast, others fought against the claim that harsher punishments were necessary to fix Scotland's broken morals. Dr Boyd, the famous educationalist, protested against birching and said it did not have a deterrent effect on delinquents so should be abolished. He also asserted his pride in Fife County's record of not birching a single delinquent in the eleven years prior to 1940.[50] In 1942, the Edinburgh Town Council debated delinquency and corporal punishment. Speaking against birching, Councillors Munro, Trainer and Woolburn referred to the practice as 'fiendish', 'no deterrent' and said it 'savoured of the Middle Ages', while Mr Gilzean claimed Edinburgh's record on birching was 'a shame to the whole community. Not even Nazi Germany or Fascist Italy looked upon this as we looked upon it', he claimed.[51] Nonetheless, the Council voted 29 to 23 to retain the birch for punishment.

Even when physical discipline was used it was not always the deterrent some made it out to be. *The Daily Express* reported on 31 March 1941 of the court appearance of three boys charged with housebreaking. Just thirty days earlier, the boys had been birched for previous crimes but, clearly undeterred, that same day had gone on to break into another house.[52] As observers had suggested, war might provide a youngster with the opportunity to commit crime, but a lack of personal discipline provided the motive.

'Crumbling of moral fibre': self-control

While ill-discipline and corporal punishment received most attention, a lack of self-control was also touted as a cause of wartime delinquency. According to *The Times Educational Supplement*, the cause of Scotland's rising levels of youth immorality was 'an ever-increasing desire for pleasure'.[53] Whether youngsters or adults, those who overindulged in alcohol and engaged in sexual intercourse outside marriage were seen by many church leaders and parishioners as having poor morals, showing ill-discipline and being unable to control their base urges.[54] This was problematic at a time when Britons were being called upon to devote themselves wholeheartedly to the war effort. According to critics, these forms of delinquency were problems of self-control, and only complete abstinence from alcohol and sex could control such immoral tendencies. The situation was urgent, concerned groups pleaded, and war was a time for control over the self, not for indulging in the pursuit of pleasure.

and the SHD itself recommended the help of a statistician to interpret its data. See NRS, HH60/427, Juvenile delinquency, statistics (JD Stats).

[50] 'Juvenile delinquency: birching should be abolished', *The Scotsman*, 13 February 1942.
[51] 'Use of the birch', *The Scotsman*, 9 January 1942.
[52] 'Birching did not cure boys', *Daily Express*, 31 March 1941.
[53] 'Juvenile crime: increase in Scotland', *The Times Educational Supplement*, 12 April 1941.
[54] Callum G. Brown, *Religion and Society in Twentieth-Century Britain* (London: Routledge, 2014), 200–203; Summerfield and Crockett, 'You weren't taught that', 440.

The Church of Scotland, police and temperance groups were distressed at what they saw as a growing 'drink problem' fostered by war conditions. For members of the armed forces, those in the auxiliary services or labourers at aerodromes or forestry encampments, there was not always much in the way of entertainment, particularly in remote parts of Scotland. These personnel became known for indulging in alcohol in village public houses, or when in cities on leave, as Chapters Six and Seven will discuss.[55] Furthermore, the rise of the female drinker caused particular aggrievement to moralisers. This behaviour was investigated by John Mack, who undertook a study into drinking in Scotland, on behalf of MoI. Mack noted new types of female drinkers, such as office girls who would have a drink by themselves after work, groups of young women drinking in 'the more respectable or better-class bars' and the 'modern Amazon . . . who tries to emulate their male colleagues' by slapping their mates on the back and ordering 'a pint of the best'.[56] Mack felt these behaviours were only representative of a small number of women, but were a result of 'the new freedom' women had gained during war, of which 'something can be said in its favour. There is no secrecy about it, no embarrassment. It is a plain open practice of drinking as and when they please.'[57]

The Scottish Temperance Alliance railed against the increased drinking of young men and women in the armed forces, and expended much effort lobbying the government to speak out against the wartime consumption of liquor and the Sunday drinking laws. According to the group, 'there is no more disgusting feature of our public life than the irrational adulation of beer'.[58] The Church of Scotland's Women's Temperance Association fought along similar lines, showing marked vehemence towards Sunday drinking – 'a social cancer'.[59] One of the group's most vocal claims was that because alcohol retarded nerve reaction it would slow production rates for those working in essential war industries. In its annual report for 1940 the group concluded: 'in a war which demands mobility, high technical skill and sound health, as well as the highest degree of morale and efficiency, the production and consumption of alcoholic beverages should be restricted'.[60]

Over the subsequent years of the Second World War, both groups expended much energy lobbying the government to curb drinking during wartime and legislate against the sale and consumption of alcohol.[61]

[55] NRS, HH55/27, Report by Chief Constable of West Lothian, 28 March 1941; NRS, HH55/29, Report by Chief Constable of Berwickshire, 15 August 1941.
[56] M-O, TC85: 'Scottish drinking, Report by John A. Mack on public opinion and the drink question in Scotland', 25 September 1940, 4–5.
[57] Ibid., 5.
[58] Scottish Temperance Alliance, *Scottish Temperance Reformer*, 31 July 1944.
[59] NRS, CH1/17/1, Women's Temperance Association, Annual Reports 1940 and 1942.
[60] Ibid., 1940.
[61] 'Alcohol in war-time', *Life and Work*, February 1941.

There was little sympathy from the Scottish authorities, though. When temperance advocates forwarded a copy of *The Scottish Temperance Reformer* to officials at the SHD, this received little support. Mr Fairgrieve, an official at the SHD, forwarded the newspaper to Glasgow's chief constable M. McCulloch, highlighting a selected article and noting that it misrepresented the law.[62] The article put 'the worst possible construction' on police drunkenness figures and, he wrote, 'I am not disposed to attach much weight' to it.[63] The chief constable agreed, making the apt observation that the publication's editor had 'placed the best construction [on the figures] so far as affects the cause which he espouses'.[64]

Alongside drunkenness, war also brought an increase in sexual immorality. The black-out was seen to provide the ideal cover for those engaging in 'immoral acts', and the presence of British and foreign servicemen supplied many willing participants to consort with young women. 'Immorality was so rampant that even the police were appalled by its dimensions', the Glasgow Presbytery said in 1942.[65] That same year, Violet Roberton, a Glasgow bailie and chairperson of the Scottish Committee of the British Council for Social Hygiene, spoke out about the problem of teenaged girls who were 'apt to follow after [troop] movements' or loiter in locations where there were large populations of industrial workers.[66] Sub-Lieutenant Austin, speaking in the House of Commons, also railed against 'the diseased mentality of these young girls that allows them to throw themselves at the heads of the troops'.[67] Glasgow and Edinburgh both experienced problems with a significant number of teenage girls and 'dead-end girls' with no jobs or permanent housing who took up with Allied soldiers, and showed 'a general looseness in moral conduct'.[68]

Kirk leaders also frequently spoke out against wartime immorality and the lack of self-control shown by the Scottish people. In 1943 official figures stated there had been a 70 per cent rise in venereal disease across Britain.[69] In response, the Women's Temperance Association stated this was 'all too clear evidence of a serious decline in moral standards'.[70] Alongside this, Reverend A. S. Kydd of the Church of Scotland added his thoughts on rising levels of immorality: '[t]he alarming increase in the incidence of venereal disease . . . is intimately connected with the moral standards which

---

[62] NRS, HH60/485, Drunkenness, letter from Fairgrieve to McCulloch, 21 August 1944.
[63] Ibid.
[64] NRS, HH60/485, Drunkenness, letter from McCulloch to Fairgrieve, 25 August 1944.
[65] 'Nation's youth: drinking on the increase', *The Scotsman*, 4 October 1942, 3.
[66] NRS, ED 39/23, Social and community services: behaviour of girls and women in wartime, 'Welfare of girls: greater need of parental control' (newspaper name unclear), 19 November 1942.
[67] 'Juvenile crime blamed on high wages', *Glasgow Herald*, 3 November 1945.
[68] 'Dead-end girls are problem no. 1', *Daily Express*, 10 April 1945; NRS, ED39/23, 'City of Glasgow Police: memo on women police patrols', 14 October 1942.
[69] Field, *Blood, Sweat, and Toil*, 202.
[70] NRS, CH1/17/1, Women's Temperance Association, Annual Report 1943.

prevail in the community and with the tone and quality of its social life'.[71] Again, it seemed to observers that the conditions brought by war, such as the black-out, lack of parental supervision and the presence of servicemen, had encouraged some Scots to exhibit a lack of control and engage in behaviour perceived as immoral.

Some Scottish authorities introduced practical measures to protect 'such members of the community as might be enticed into moral danger'.[72] In 1942, the assistant chief constable of Glasgow wrote of his distress at reports of drinking, sex and the rise of venereal disease, acknowledging that 'the crumbling of the moral fibre of our young men and women' needed greater attention than the police could reasonably give.[73] The following year, the Glasgow constabulary appointed an 'Emergency Officer for Youth' to help deal with the problem, and a number of policewomen had some success 'helping them back on the right road again'.[74] Similarly, in Edinburgh the constabulary formed a Women's Auxiliary Police Corps, tasked with preventing teenaged girls from 'loitering in the vicinity of Service Men's Clubs, or frequenting open spaces, gardens, railway stations, etc., particularly at late hours'.[75] While these measures helped the situation, an article in the *Daily Express* in 1945 noted 'Scotland's dead-end girls are getting fewer – but there are still a sufficient number to keep the authorities worried'.[76] In response to these claims, a Glasgow police chief replied that the situation had actually improved 'considerably', and that the policewomen had 'helped to clean up what once was a big wartime problem'.[77]

The most common method advocated as a measure of curing wartime immorality was abstinence from both sex and alcohol. By practising self-control, church and temperance advocates believed the individual could control their immoral desires. The Church of Scotland advocated 'the need for clear, reverent teaching of the true function of sex in human life'.[78] Further, a Kirk associate, Robert Sutherland, MD, suggested adolescents should be taught the 'personal and social reasons for self-control and

---

[71] Church of Scotland, General Assembly 1944, Report by the Committee on Church and Nation: appendix on venereal disease.
[72] 'Dead-end girls are problem no. 1', *Daily Express*, 10 April 1945; 'Women police', *Edinburgh Evening Dispatch*, 20 October 1943.
[73] NRS, ED39/23, 'Memo on women police patrols'.
[74] NRS, ED39/23, letter from Mary Cohen to Secretary of State for Scotland, 19 October 1942.
[75] 'Women constables to protect young girls in Edinburgh streets', *Edinburgh Evening Standard*, 20 October 1943; NRS, HH60/427, *Report on the State of Crime and the Police Establishment in the County of the City and Royal Burgh of Edinburgh 1944* (Edinburgh: Mackenzie and Storrie, 1945).
[76] 'Dead-end girls are problem no. 1', *Daily Express*, 10 April 1945.
[77] Ibid.
[78] Church of Scotland, General Assembly 1944, Report by the Committee on Church and Nation: appendix on venereal disease.

chastity'.[79] Abstinence was also advocated in official advertisements, such as a public leaflet authorised by Secretary of State Johnston. The 1943 leaflet on venereal disease stated '[f]ree and easy sex behaviour must mean a risk of infection and cannot be made safe ... Clean living is the only way to avoid infection: abstinence is not harmful.'[80]

To further encourage youths to show self-control and abstain from bad influences, interest groups held rallies and gave talks in schools. In 1943 alone, the Women's Temperance Association group gave lectures at twenty-eight schools in Edinburgh, thirty-nine in Berwickshire and twelve in Wigtownshire.[81] With a similar purpose in mind, the Scottish Temperance Alliance held rallies and temperance days, such as in Kilmarnock on 15 July 1944 which featured a junior choir and pipe band, gymnastic displays by a local Boys' Brigade troupe and the crowning of a Temperance Queen, Miss Elizabeth Stevenson.[82] By the promotion of such events, temperance adherents believed that the young could learn self-control and thus avoid the opportunities war had provided for engaging in immoral or delinquent behaviour. In this matter, the war provided these interest groups with an ideal platform to spread their message and further their aims.

'A diseased mentality': personal inadequacy

While ill-discipline and poor self-control were touted as two factors in wartime delinquency, another theory was that the delinquent individual suffered from personal inadequacy. For those who felt that low intelligence or poor wellbeing resulted in delinquent tendencies, psychological examination was proposed as a first step in treatment. Proponents of the new sciences of psychiatry and behavioural psychology advocated the use of child guidance clinics, instead of alternatives such as corporal punishment or probation. Significant developments in this area had come about in the early twentieth century and were related to new ideas on the psyche and individual wellbeing.[83]

In Scotland, proponents of clinics to treat delinquents included Dr Boyd who was medical superintendent of Fife District Asylum at that time. He urged the establishment of a child guidance clinic to treat delinquents in Fife, as did the Education Committee in Ayr, which advised the SHD that it wanted similar clinics for Ayr county.[84] *The Times* also reported a councillor

---

[79] Ibid.
[80] 'Display ad: ten plain facts about venereal diseases', *The Scotsman*, 26 February 1943, 3.
[81] NRS, CH1/17/1, Women's Temperance Association: Annual Report 1943.
[82] Scottish Temperance Alliance, *Scottish Temperance Reformer*, 31 July 1944, 43.
[83] Jones, *Social Hygiene*, 7–8; Douglas A. Kramer, 'History of family psychiatry: from the social reform era to the primate social organ system', *Child and Adolescent Psychiatric Clinics in North America* 24, no. 3 (2015): 439–55.
[84] 'Delinquency problem: Fife child guidance clinic project', *The Scotsman*, 2 September 1942; NRS, HH60/428, letter from Mr Hepburn at Ayr County Council, 22 July 1942.

in Lanarkshire as having 'advocated in the strongest terms' the setting up of clinics for the psychological treatment of offenders.[85] The Notre Dame Clinic in Glasgow was one clinic putting these modern methods of psychology into practice. In the clinic, therapists 'watch the young patients carefully, and the treatment is always by the path that leads right into the child's mind. They win his friendship, discover the fear or the longing that causes delinquency and then apply the cure', reported journalist Nicol Jarvie in the *Scottish Daily Express*.[86]

Such progressive approaches were also advocated by some well-read members of the public. For example, an A. A. Wilson from Edinburgh wrote to *The Scotsman* urging greater reliance on clinics where 'the psychologist would trace the contributory causes' of delinquency, such as relevant child diseases, birth order, general intelligence, emotional conditions or level of extraversion.[87] Modern ideas and treatments such as these were seen as being able to help delinquents to understand their behaviour, and to find methods for treating the delinquent tendencies that war had released.

Some authorities warned that those who showed delinquent tendencies were not always of average ability and were often 'feeble-minded', 'socially maladjusted' and, in the case of young girls who threw themselves at servicemen, possessed a 'diseased mentality'.[88] An MoI officer also suggested the wartime closure of schools was 'a calamity [for] backward children' who would express their frustrations in 'undisciplined and anti-social behaviour'.[89] James Barrie, the Probation Officer for the county of Fife, found that in 1940 below-average intelligence was a contributing factor in over 8 per cent of all cases before Fife's juvenile court.[90] More alarming were figures provided by the president of the Edinburgh branch of the National Federation of Business and Professional Women, Elspeth Macleod. In a letter to the editor of *The Scotsman* in 1942, she pointed out that a study of 200 child delinquents found 82 per cent 'mentally backward' and a further 8 per cent 'mentally defective'.[91] The study also found mental impairment was five times more common in delinquents than in the control group of non-delinquent children.[92] Macleod concluded with a hope that 'knowledge and understanding' would result in more tolerance being shown towards 'the wrong-doer'.[93]

---

[85] 'Juvenile crime: increase in Scotland', *The Times Educational Supplement*, 12 April 1941.
[86] Nicol Jarvie, 'We're breeding a race of rogues', *Scottish Daily Express*, 13 March 1941.
[87] 'Letter to the editor from A. A. Wilson', *The Scotsman*, 28 January 1942.
[88] NRS, HH60/426, notes on SED debate on juvenile delinquency, 21 July 1943; HC Deb 02 November 1945 vol. 415 col. 809.
[89] SIR: JD Scotland, 2.
[90] NRS, HH60/425, 'Report on Delinquency on the County of Fife'.
[91] 'Letter to the editor from Elspeth Macleod', *The Scotsman*, 16 January 1942, 7.
[92] Beatrice Edyell, 'Review of *The Young Delinquent* by Cyril Burt', *International Journal of Ethics* 36, no. 4 (1926): 424–9.
[93] 'Letter to the editor from Elspeth Macleod', *The Scotsman*, 16 January 1942, 7.

In early 1942, a conference between the Board of Education, the Home Office and the Scottish Office was held to consider the topic of juvenile delinquency. The conference opened with a discussion of maladjusted youth, which 'might be defined as a child with a mental kink which was likely to yield to special treatment'.[94] Unfortunately, this special treatment was unlikely to be given as there was a severe shortage of professionals across Britain. In 1941, P. McCowan, a Dumfries psychiatrist, wrote to the Secretary of State for Scotland to offer his suggestions on approaches to Scotland's moral crisis. 'I was struck by the relative backwardness of extra-mural psychiatry in Scotland', he wrote, quoting a British Medical Association Report that noted there were only 8 psychiatric out-patient clinics in Scotland, compared to 167 in England, and 10 child-guidance clinics in Scotland, only 1 with a full-time psychiatrist.[95] McCowan maintained youth gang leaders were often mentally and morally defective, or severely psychopathic, and 'psychiatric abnormalities' were at least partly responsible for 'all forms of social degradation in adults and children'.[96] To Scots who thought similarly, defective tendencies were already present in the individual and had merely been fomented by war.

'Birch the parents': the defective family

Another factor commonly proposed as responsible for exacerbating wartime delinquency in Scotland was the defective family. Some argued wartime crime and immorality was directly related to the offender's family situation and background. Authorities often blamed rising delinquency in Scotland on parental neglect or absence. The SED and SHD agreed that with the growing need for industrial workers, 'more mothers are likely to be engaged in war work, and their absence from home will probably increase the tendency towards juvenile neglect and delinquency'.[97] Chief Constable William Whyte from Stirlingshire agreed, stating it was 'fairly obvious' that wartime family situations were responsible for immoral behaviour: fathers were away on service, mothers were working, there was a 'general all-round laxity of control' and, above all, 'war seemed to engender a relaxing of self-discipline and an indifference to social obligations'.[98] Similarly, the author of a women's column in the *Edinburgh Evening Dispatch* lamented that teenagers

> present a special problem in war-time . . . The slackening of home influence, with fathers in the Forces and mothers often engaged in

---

[94] NRS, HH60/425, conference held at Alexandra House on juvenile delinquency, 7 January 1942.
[95] NRS, HH60/426, letter from P. McCowan, 30 July 1941.
[96] Ibid.
[97] NRS, HH60/427, *Juvenile Offences*, 1–4.
[98] 'Juvenile crime: increase due to war conditions', *Edinburgh Evening Dispatch*, 21 October 1943.

some form of war work which leaves less time to be devoted to home duties, has a definite effect on young people.[99]

In addition, the Secretary of State for Scotland suggested the late-night duties of fathers and brothers engaged in air raid precautions (ARP) or fire-watching meant youths had fewer adults at home to control wayward behaviour.[100]

In 1942, the Royal Scottish Society for the Prevention of Cruelty to Children (RSSPCC) announced a study into the problem of delinquency. The society linked such behaviour to a lack of adequate parental control, and stated that misbehaviour was 'aggravated by the absence of so many fathers on war service'.[101] Other organisations, such as the Notre Dame Child Guidance Clinic, warned the absence of a father 'may disorganise the whole pattern and logical development of a child's life', and things such as sleeplessness could be traced as 'emotional and nervous reactions' to the departure of a father from a home.[102] Furthermore, the clinic's director stated that the break-up of the stability of the home was 'causing a graver threat to healthy child life than any amount of blitzing'.[103]

Some Scots argued that delinquent behaviour was fostered in the home environment and innate to the 'degenerate' working classes.[104] As discussed in the Prologue, a sense of class division was prevalent in pre-war Scottish society and this tradition contributed to views on causes of delinquency. The belief in inbuilt, heritable deficiencies among members of the working class pervaded much of the discussion on wartime degeneracy.[105] This harked back to Victorian times when there arose a belief that the lowest members of the working-class were an underclass, diseased, sinful and unintelligent, and in need of rescue from their immoral ways.[106] This *residuum* was considered 'a menace and a disgrace to the community', and especially susceptible to 'evil influences'.[107]

Scotland's wartime delinquency gave ammunition to those who believed immorality was an inbuilt weakness of the *residuum*. For example, Margaret Macpherson, a Scottish Liberal MP writing as a columnist for the *Glasgow Evening Citizen*, claimed a rise in delinquent behaviour was due not only to the war, but also a result of the 'stunted mentality and low standard of morality of the parents'.[108] Macpherson's article also quoted a representative

[99] 'Woman's View column: youth marches on', *Edinburgh Evening Dispatch*, 21 October 1942.
[100] 'Youth in wartime: problem of parental control', *The Scotsman*, 11 July 1942.
[101] 'Juvenile delinquency: lack of parental control', *Glasgow Herald*, 30 September 1942.
[102] 'Fathers on service: upsetting effect on child behaviour', *Glasgow Herald*, 19 March 1943.
[103] Ibid.
[104] Macnicol, 'Reconstructing the underclass', 103.
[105] Field, *Blood, Sweat, and Toil*, 98; Field, 'Working-class family', 10–11.
[106] Brown, 'Rational recreation', 210–11.
[107] Macnicol, 'Reconstructing the underclass', 103; Jones, *Social Hygiene*, 11.
[108] Margaret Macpherson, 'Delinquency as a matter of form', *Glasgow Evening Citizen*, 17 August 1943.

from the RSSPCC who said a high percentage of delinquent parents and children 'are of subnormal intelligence', and that one of the principal causes of delinquency was life in the slums.[109] According to some, the roots of wartime immorality were to be found in the home, with the delinquent as the product of 'an utterly useless generation of parents'.[110] The Rev. Canon William Hall of the Episcopal Church in Scotland provocatively commented in early 1942 that rather than punishing youths for their waywardness, 'would it not be better to birch the parents, the teachers, yes, and the clergy in whose care the delinquent has been?'[111] Similarly, Dr Boyd asserted, 'undoubtedly, the real cause of delinquency is to be found in the home', while the Glasgow chairman of the RSSPCC stated that child delinquents were 'nearly all the victims of parental neglect or of "dangerous" home surroundings (i.e. of low morality)'.[112]

In 1944, MoI compiled a special report on *Juvenile Delinquency in Scotland*. Its investigators championed the theory of the unsuitable home, claiming child-guidance clinics showed 'over and over again' home life was responsible for low morals, and in 75 per cent of delinquency cases offenders came from 'unsatisfactory homes'.[113] It seemed 'unsatisfactory' could mean many things: poor parental skills, disease and insanitary environments, or tolerance of crime. For example, the County Probation Officer for Fife stated that in juvenile crimes resulting in a sentence of probation, trouble 'in the home life' was a factor in 90 per cent of cases.[114] He explained that the 'broken home' meant a 'lack of parental interest, control or understanding, and various other parental defects'.[115] The Lord Provost of Edinburgh, Sir Henry Steele, also agreed the fault lay in the home. He claimed '[s]ome part of the blame must rest with the parents, who . . . did not fully appreciate their responsibilities, and failed to exercise the necessary measure of control in the training of the young'.[116] In this camp, while war provided the spark, irresponsible parents were the fuel.

The first section of this chapter has considered the explanations espoused by various Scots for wartime crime and delinquent behaviour. As demonstrated by the sheer number of conferences, meetings, newspaper columns, investigations, intelligence reports and letters to the editors of newspapers debating wartime delinquency, many sectors of society felt Scotland was a country at the point of moral crisis. As Greta Jones and Callum Brown suggested, many in pre-war Britain still held Victorian ideas

---

[109] Ibid.
[110] 'Juvenile delinquency: birching should be abolished', *The Scotsman*, 13 February 1942; 'Birch the clergy', *Edinburgh Evening Dispatch*, 11 February 1942.
[111] 'Birch the clergy', *Edinburgh Evening Dispatch*, 11 February 1942.
[112] 'Delinquency as a matter of form', *Glasgow Evening Citizen*, 17 August 1943.
[113] SIR: JD Scotland.
[114] NRS, HH60/425, 'Report on delinquency on the County of Fife'.
[115] Ibid.
[116] 'Juvenile delinquency: serious problem in Edinburgh', *The Scotsman*, 6 June 1941.

of appropriate behaviour.[117] As such, wartime immorality and delinquency presented a challenge to these ideas of morality. The next section of this chapter will further explore the underlying factors that stoked the fires of outrage over wartime degeneracy in Scotland.

Why did Scotland's wartime delinquency engender such panic?

As the first half of this chapter reveals, concerns about morality and behaviour during wartime were common among those who were preoccupied with morality and law and order. These Scots felt strongly about the factors that might have prompted these degenerate actions and what should be done to curb this behaviour. But was the situation as bad as perceived? To confuse this picture, during the timeframe of the war, statistics and investigations regarding Scottish drunkenness, immorality and juvenile crime revealed mixed results.

On one hand, very little attention was paid to the fact that offences committed by Scottish 14- to 17-year-olds were at lower rates in 1940, 1941 and 1942 than in 1938.[118] Additionally, the number of those under 14 years old found guilty of offences only rose 6.6 per cent between 1940 and 1943.[119] Further, the percentage of Scottish young people found guilty of crime was never more than 1.8 per cent of the total juvenile population between 1939 and 1946.[120] Some officers of the law felt that much of this crime should be reclassified as misconduct or naughtiness, and dealt with outside the courts.[121] To this end, figures supplied by the Edinburgh constabulary revealed that, in 1944, four-fifths of juvenile offenders found guilty had been convicted for crimes of dishonesty, including theft, housebreaking and fraud, which were at the less serious end of the scale.[122]

It is difficult to be certain whether the rise in juvenile crime was attributable to the war and the opportunities it provided, or this trend was influenced by another factor. From 1943, Scottish juvenile crime continued to abate and, by 1947, as a percentage of all crime, juvenile offences were down to pre-war levels.[123] W. F. Arbuckle of the SED wrote to Thomas Johnston in 1947, stating that the 'considerable improvement' in juvenile crime in Glasgow could be attributed to 'the return of the fathers from the Forces and the release of many of the mothers from employment'.[124] This echoed the argument that youth misbehaviour was closely related to lack of supervision.

---

[117] Jones, *Social Hygiene*, 11; Brown, *People in the Pews*, 32.
[118] JD Stats 1938–43, n. d.
[119] Ibid.
[120] Ibid., and 1944–6.
[121] Smith, 'Official responses', 82.
[122] JD Stats, SHD: Juvenile delinquency in Edinburgh, 29 March 1945.
[123] Ibid., SHD: Juvenile delinquency, 1943–7.
[124] Ibid., letter from Arbuckle to Johnston, 12 February 1947.

In regards to increased alcohol consumption, there was limited evidence to support the claims of temperance campaigners. A 1940 investigation by M-O concluded there was some legitimate public unease about alcohol consumption among young women, servicemen and industrial workers. The report concluded, though, that higher levels of drinking were often related to boredom and lack of alternative entertainments, and as long as these could be provided, the problem would abate.[125] In addition, apprehensions for drunkenness in Edinburgh, for example, were lower in all years between 1940 and 1944 than they had been in 1939.[126] In fact, wartime apprehensions in the city for drunkenness were lower than those in all years from 1919 to 1930.[127] Furthermore, chief constables' reports from 1940 to 1944 revealed that levels of drunkenness across Scotland were not generally considered by their officers to be a cause for concern.[128] The only exceptions to this came from areas with high proportions of servicemen, or labourers from Ireland and Newfoundland.[129] As Chapter Six will reveal, general public alcohol consumption was affected by shortages of supply and Sunday restrictions on travelling to obtain drink. In summary, though, there is no clear evidence that the war was causing Scots to turn to drink.

Finally, in relation to immorality, from 1942 onwards there was an increase in reports from Scottish police, youth workers and bailies about young girls who 'chase after American and other soldiers in our cities'.[130] There is no doubt this was a serious problem, particularly in areas such as Glasgow city, where reports of attempts to curb the behaviour were numerous.[131] The full story, however, was not so clear-cut. Statistics on illegitimate births in Scotland during the war are not the smoking gun we might expect them to be. Between 1940 and 1944 illegitimate births as a percentage of all live births were never higher than 7.87 per cent, and while higher than the years 1933 to 1939, are similar to those from 1927 to 1932.[132] Moreover, an article from 1944 revealed in Edinburgh arrests of 'professional prostitutes' had declined during the war, and in Inverness

---

[125] M-O, TC85: Scottish drinking, 1–6.
[126] NRS, HH60/427, *Report on Crime in Edinburgh 1944*, 21.
[127] NRS, HH60/427, 'graph showing the trend of drunkenness in Edinburgh during the last forty years', in *Report on Crime in Edinburgh 1944*.
[128] See NRS, HH55/7–42, PWD – IR, 1939–45.
[129] NRS, HH55/35, Report by Chief Constable of Moray and Nairn, 6 November 1942; NRS, HH55/37, Reports by Chief Constables of Moray and Nairn, and Inverness Burgh, 18 June 1943.
[130] The National Archives (TNA), INF 1/293, MoI Scotland, Special Intelligence Report: Juvenile delinquency, 5 January 1944, 3.
[131] See 'Juvenile crime blamed on high wages', *Glasgow Herald*, 3 November 1945; NRS, ED39/23, Social and community services: behaviour of girls and young women in wartime. This was also a problem in Wales: see Johnes, *Wales Since 1939*, 14.
[132] M-O, TC3_2860, Illegitimate births in Scotland, 25.

none had been arrested in the three years before 1944.[133] This may not mean that concerns over sexual immorality were unwarranted, though, as while prostitution arrests were lower this may have been because men were meeting their sexual needs for no cost with other young women who were chasing after them.

Prostitution and sex outside marriage certainly were happening, and the resurgence of venereal disease provided further evidence of this. It was, largely, temperance groups and the Kirk who raised the outcry to fever pitch, referring to rates of venereal disease as being 'heavily increased', 'alarming', 'very disquieting', a 'national scourge' and an 'evil'.[134] At an initial glance, the figures did, indeed, appear much increased. In 1941, syphilis cases were 50 per cent higher among the general population than in 1939, and 70 per cent higher for those in the armed services.[135] Two years later, the Ministry of Health confirmed there was a 70 per cent rise in venereal disease across Britain.[136] One historian reminds us that, while percentage increases seem high, in reality the aggregate numbers were much less alarming.[137] It is also worth remembering that moral campaigners were always concerned with rising rates of sexually transmitted diseases as these were historically linked to prostitution and sin.[138]

While there was some cause for concern in data on Scottish wartime drinking, sexual immorality and juvenile crime, the picture was not as desperate as the public panic would suggest. Some figures from the early years of the war were alarming but, as the war continued, these levels did not continue their increase. Other statistics were in line with those from the previous twenty years. As we know, statistics can be used to justify any argument and, as David Smith has stated, the data do not matter if the Scottish public *perceived* there to have been an increase in degeneracy.[139] Sensationalist newspaper headlines and vocal temperance groups helped to promote a picture of desperately spiralling rates of delinquency and immorality. While these figures may have been exaggerated, for those caught up in the storm of panic the situation appeared critical.

So why were delinquency and morality so important to Scots, and why did the furore reach such a pitch if crime and drunkenness were not as serious as first claimed? This section will consider two underlying aspects of

[133] 'You must not let them down', *Daily Record*, 28 February 1944.
[134] NRS, CH1/17/1, Women's Temperance Association, Annual Report 1943; Church of Scotland, General Assembly 1944, Committee on Church and Nation, 'Report on venereal disease', and Reverend A. S. Kydd, 'Venereal disease'; Church of Scotland, General Assembly 1943, Report of the Committee on Temperance; 'You must not let them down', *Daily Record*, 28 February 1944.
[135] Field, *Blood, Sweat, and Toil*, 202.
[136] Ibid.
[137] Ibid. Field does not give the exact numbers, and an additional search proved fruitless.
[138] Adrian Bingham, 'The British popular press and venereal disease during the Second World War', *The Historical Journal* 48, no. 4 (2005), 1059.
[139] Smith, 'Official responses', 85–6.

discussions on wartime morality that exacerbated the growing sense of crisis in Scotland. The first of these factors is the wartime rhetoric of national sacrifice and 'the greater good', in which there was no place for delinquent behaviour.[140] The second will cover the Kirk's concerns about delinquency, and how these played into fears about growing Scottish secularisation.

'An ordeal of the most grievous kind': sacrificing for the greater good

One important aspect of life on the British home front was the emphasis on solidarity and sacrifice. 'We have before us an ordeal of the most grievous kind. We have before us many, many long months of struggle and of suffering', stated Winston Churchill in May 1940. 'Come then, let us go forward together with our united strength.'[141] As the prime minister had urged, total war required total sacrifice. If the war was to be played out in the streets and in the factories, with civilians as combatants on the front line, then certain codes of behaviour would be required and public energy could not be wasted on fighting internal enemies.[142] This resulted in a rhetoric of corporeal sacrifice or, as Sonya Rose has summarised, a nation of 'reasonable citizens who willingly and with good humour sacrificed their private and personal interests and desires for the collective good'.[143] Within this rhetoric of sacrifice, the needs of the community must come before the self, and anything that was not 'for the greater good' or did not advance the war effort should be cast aside.

In this idealised picture of a united corps of people who would put aside the self for the greater good of the whole, any signs of disease in the social body had to be expunged. This idea may originate in the Bible's Book of Matthew which states '[i]f your right hand causes you to sin, cut it off and cast it from you'.[144] This imagery is particularly relevant during war which is, Rose suggests, a time 'for identifying and excluding those who do not exemplify particular national virtues'.[145] On the Scottish home front, as in England, those who committed misdemeanours, overindulged in alcohol or engaged in sexual intercourse outside marriage were seen to have their own selfish interests at heart, instead of the needs of the community.

One aspect to public concerns over delinquency was the fear that self-serving behaviour might hamper the war effort. The Kirk's Committee on Temperance argued alcoholic beverages were not essential to national morale and, in fact, their consumption 'in a time of critical warfare' was

---

[140] In wartime, Britain was often called 'a nation' and citizens throughout Britain were called upon to fight 'for the nation'.
[141] Hansard, HC Deb, 13 May 1940, vol. 360 cols 1502–3.
[142] See Mackay, *Half the Battle*, 3–4; Pattinson, McIvor and Robb, *Men in Reserve*, 262.
[143] Rose, *Which People's War?*, 79; see also Noakes, *War and the British*, 2; Hylton, *Darkest Hour*, vii.
[144] Matthew 5:30, *The Bible* (New King James Version).
[145] Rose, *Which People's War?*, 72.

to be considered a 'scandalous waste of food and fuel, of man-power and shipping'.[146] Further reports from the church and associated temperance groups claimed drunk industrial workers had caused delays in the production of ships and arms, and this was reprehensible in 'a war which demands mobility, high technical skill and sound health, as well as the highest degree of morale and efficiency'.[147] According to such advocates of morality, the civilian who showed self-control and chastity, and abstained from drink, would be prepared for battle and therefore be a more useful part of the body of society.

In mid-1940 MoI asked M-O to investigate 'the Drink Question' in Scotland, owing to the public's 'general uneasiness' over reports of increasing drunkenness. The investigator observed 'a mild disquiet' among the Scottish public, which was particularly directed at the drinking behaviour of munitions workers, soldiers, labourers and youths. The assumption was seemingly that those involved in the war effort, or those who might soon be called up, should be of sound mind and able to carry out their duties effectively. John Mack, the M-O investigator, suggested that alternative methods of recreation might help to solve the problem, as well as propaganda 'based on patriotic grounds'.[148] The Regional Information Officer for Scotland, Niven McNicoll, agreed, suggesting that '[i]ndirect propaganda (carrying the idea that to drink excessively is to let our country down) would be useful and relatively easy'.[149] In the end, the propaganda was not employed, but the message was clear: restraint of self was seen to be an essential part of the fight against the enemy.

Along with self-discipline, ideals of good citizenship were espoused by various community leaders in Scotland during the Second World War. The Board of Guardians of the Glasgow Synagogue echoed this sentiment about community solidarity, agreeing that '[c]ommon dangers and sacrifices of war time should form the basis of a continuing comradeship and out of our experiences can be welded a higher spirit of human fellowship'.[150] To attain this comradeship, the MP for Greenock Hector McNeil suggested youthful misbehaviour could be channelled into fighting to protect democracy, and the young could be retaught the concept of duty, thereby turning them into 'contributing citizens' who could 'play a part in winning the war'.[151] Within this theory, behaviour that promoted pleasure over sacrifice, or was not in the best needs of society, should be eliminated and

---

[146] NRS, CH1/17/1, Women's Temperance Association, Annual Report 1941; Church of Scotland, General Assembly 1945, Report of the Committee on Temperance.

[147] 'War and temperance', *Life and Work*, November 1939; Church of Scotland, General Assembly 1943, Report of the Committee on Temperance; NRS, CH1/17/1, Women's Temperance Association, Annual Report 1940, 4.

[148] M-O, TC85: Scottish drinking, 6.

[149] Ibid., note by N. McNicoll, 25 September 1940.

[150] SJAC, Glasgow Jewish Board of Guardians, Annual Report, 1941.

[151] Hector McNeil, 'Let's not blame children', *Daily Express*, 6 March 1943.

Figure 2.1 'Weeding and watering': boys' and girls' garden in a city graveyard. (Source: *Life and Work*, September 1941.)

energies redirected into nobler pursuits. In this vein were Church of Scotland youth programmes, which aimed to take 'slum roses' from 'stunting and perverting conditions' and make them into men and women who would be 'ready to serve and co-operate' (see Figures 2.1 and 2.2).[152]

Others warned of a loss of the concepts of duty and citizenship, and felt that these were missing in wartime Scottish society. 'There is little hope of making good citizens of children who live in slums and whose parents are unemployed', wrote a *Glasgow Herald* journalist in 1944.[153] A journalist in the *Sunday Mail* agreed: '[b]etween the two great world wars there has been such a decline in the standard of family life that, in many cases, homes in the real sense of the word do not exist ... [these are] stupid, selfish parents'.[154] He also quoted a local magistrate who had berated parents with these words: '[y]ou bring children into the world, but some of you seem to take less interest in them than you would if you were rearing a pack of whippets'.[155]

---

[152] 'Slum roses', *Life and Work*, September 1941, 198–200; 'A summer play school', *Life and Work*, October 1940, 290–91.
[153] 'Experiment in education', *Glasgow Herald*, 5 January 1944.
[154] 'We've got to help the youngster gone wrong', *Sunday Mail*, 21 December 1943.
[155] Ibid.

Figure 2.2 'Making a wheelbarrow': boys' and girls' garden in a city graveyard. (Source: *Life and Work*, September 1941.)

More worrying was a suggestion that Scotland's pre-war situation had been responsible for a lack of community cohesion and values. 'What more properly concerns us is that this kind of misbehaviour was on the increase before the war', Hector McNeil wrote, in a Saturday column for the *Daily Express*.[156] He felt Scottish working-class sentiment had changed during the years of the Depression, a result of bad housing, unemployment and a loss of the concept of 'duty'. 'We were angry and annoyed, frequently with good reason, and we felt neglected', he stated. 'So we complained of what had been stolen from us and of what was withheld from us, and perhaps because we were so angry and aggrieved, we forgot that if we had rights we also had duties.'[157] This lack of feelings of citizenship may have been a powerful factor in the delinquency crisis. If some Scots felt little connection to the wider community, and lacked a sense of commitment to the war effort and associated sacrifices, this may have played a part in increased delinquency behaviours. In addition, the lack of unity in Scottish society on the eve of war carried over into the war years, prompting morality and law and order advocates to blame delinquent behaviour on the working classes, on heredity and on inbuilt laziness.

[156] 'Saturday column: Hector McNeil, MP', *Daily Express*, 6 March 1943.
[157] Ibid.

Sociologist José Harris wrote that when faced with a common danger, society develops a 'sense of desperate unity' and ideas of national identity condense.[158] Similarly, Sonya Rose claimed the Second World War acted as 'an especially prime historical moment not only for demarcating the national self from that of the enemy, but also for identifying and excluding those who do not exemplify particular national virtues'.[159] She added it was not surprising 'that moral discourses proliferate at such moments . . . when the bases of unity are feared to be fragmented'. Faced with the external threat of war, this may have led Scots to intensify their focus on the enemy within.

'The decline of family religion': the Kirk and secularisation

The sources used throughout this chapter reveal that most of the outcry over wartime delinquency came from groups or individuals with what we might term ulterior motives or self-interest. These included magistrates, sheriffs, bailies and the constabulary, whose daily lives revolved around ensuring law and order was maintained. In addition, frequent opinions were put forward by interest groups such as temperance societies and the British Council for Social Hygiene. By far the most vocal party to belabour Scotland's supposed moral crisis was the Church of Scotland. As the following section will explore, the Kirk had an underlying motive for emphasising levels of wartime delinquency, and this was linked to growing levels of secularisation in Scottish society. This was a factor in the wartime delinquency discussion that was particular to Scotland.

Since 1780, Scotland has enjoyed a 'distinctive religious complexion', and religion has acted as 'the principal agent of national consciousness'.[160] As a result of heavy Protestant influence, temperance, strict moral codes and Sabbatarianism have played a greater part in Scottish cultural history than in other parts of Britain.[161] One vital element of Scottish religious heritage is the prominent role of the Church of Scotland, or Kirk, which has long enjoyed a key place at the heart of Scottish life, society and identity. In the nineteenth and twentieth centuries the Kirk had a significant influence on public and private life: it provided clubs and societies for all age groups; the presence of members on local government committees ensured Church interests were represented in policy and politics; and its congregation gave much time and money to campaigns dedicated to alleviating poverty and providing comfort to those in need.[162] Ultimately, the

---

[158] José Harris, 'War and social history: Britain and the home front during the Second World War', *Contemporary European History* 1, 1 (1992), 17.
[159] Rose, *Which People's War?*, 71–2.
[160] Callum G. Brown, *The Social History of Religion in Scotland Since 1730* (London: Methuen & Co., 1987), 7.
[161] Ibid., 8–9.
[162] Devine, *Scottish Nation*, 364–6.

Church viewed itself as defender of Scottish nationality and identity, and any threat to the Church or its institutions was viewed by the Kirk as a threat to Scotland itself.[163]

Wartime delinquency signalled to Kirk authorities that Christianity was losing its power in Scottish society. In nineteenth- and early-twentieth-century Scotland, the role of the church had been as the nucleus of society and as moral arbiter. The Church of Scotland saw self-control as being essential for the 'correct' functioning of society, and leaders believed that without the influence of religion society would revert to its immoral ways.[164] Church leadership also had strong notions of acceptable behaviour in which the public should engage.[165] Callum Brown has noted Scottish church attendance halved between 1851 and 1951, and Scottish sabbath decline was 'one of the greatest changes in everyday behaviour and morality of the last three hundred years'.[166] As a result, during the Second World War the Kirk was concerned it might no longer have a place at the heart of Scottish society.

One particular aspect of the 'problem family' discussion was its focus on the absence of religion in family life. This was a specific concern of the Church of Scotland, which frequently lamented both the growing degeneracy in Scotland and what it saw as the related loss of religion from daily life. In 1941 the report from the Synod's General Assembly stated that growing degeneracy was 'chiefly an indication of the absence of any vital contact between the Church and many of our Scottish homes' resulting from a lack of 'definite church connection on the part of parents'.[167] In May 1941, the Education Committee of the National Council of Women, meeting in Edinburgh, heard that 36 per cent of the population of Scotland 'were not connected in any way with any Christian church' and, the following year, a leader in the Episcopal Church of Scotland claimed '[f]our-fifths of the nation have no church connection'.[168] For many church authorities and organisations, the lack of religious influence in the lives of Scottish families inflamed the problem of wartime delinquency and gave further support to the belief the country was entangled in a moral crisis.

These concerns about growing levels of secularisation in Scotland continued throughout the years of the war. At the annual assembly of the

---

[163] A. A. MacLaren, 'Introduction: an open society?', in A. A. MacLaren (ed.), *Social Class in Scotland: Past and Present* (Edinburgh: John Donald, 1976), 3; David Sinclair, 'The identity of a nation' in Devine, *Scotland's Shame?*, 179.

[164] Brown, *People in the Pews*, 32.

[165] Edward Royle, *Modern Britain: A Social History, 1750–1985* (London: Edward Arnold, 1987), 238, 241.

[166] Callum G. Brown, 'Spectacle, restraint and the sabbath wars: the "everyday" Scottish Sunday', in Abrams and Brown (eds), *History of Everyday Life*, 153–80, here 157.

[167] Church of Scotland, General Assembly Report 1941, 270.

[168] 'Birch the clergy', *Edinburgh Evening Dispatch*, 11 February 1942; 'Religious teaching: Edinburgh Conference', *The Scotsman*, 1 May 1941.

Women's Home Mission in 1944, attendees were told Glasgow was 'a very black patch as regards juvenile delinquency' and the district which produced the worst misdemeanours was 'the one without a church'.[169] The assembly also heard from the Reverend James Morrison from Blawarthill parish who urged 'it is only the Church that can restore these family relationships and restore the broken-down relationships in the community'.[170] The Church of Scotland summed up its concern in the June 1944 edition of *Life and Work:* 'it is the decline of family religion which is at the root of the failure in character'.[171] Even MoI agreed there was a 'decay in interest in religion in Scotland' and this was linked to the decline of basic virtues and morals.[172] Increasingly, stories of delinquency, intemperance and immoral behaviour served to remind the Kirk of its decreasing influence, and its impassioned response to the moral crisis reveals the fight undertaken by the Kirk to reassert itself in Scottish life.

Previously, the Church had been able to spread its power and influence through youth clubs, education in schools and via 'the army of committed laity who unceasingly carried the message of the gospel into the community'.[173] With delinquency and immoral behaviour seemingly reaching a fever pitch, one way of regaining control of the public was to get families back in contact with Protestant religious organisations. One form of outreach was via Church-led summer holiday programmes, which focused on 'education through play', and included elements of Bible study, nature observation and handcrafts. One holiday school in Edinburgh featured a model housing scheme to 'introduce into the minds of the children the first ideas of the community in which they live'.[174] Alongside homes, post office, hospital and school, the model also featured a church, situated at the heart of the community (see Figure 2.3).

In 1941, the Church of Scotland's annual report lamented, 'Scotland's worst war product is the child criminal . . . there is, too, an indication of the absence of any vital contact between the Church and many of our Scottish homes.' The solution proposed that 'the Church must find a way of enlarging and intensifying its contacts'.[175] A month earlier, the Scottish Office had surveyed 14- to 18-year-olds in the city in relation to membership of juvenile organisations. It was found that out of 28,000 boys and girls only about 9,000 attended Bible classes. 'These figures serve to give some indication of the extent and urgency of the problem', noted the correspondent

---

[169] 'Edinburgh *causerie*', *Edinburgh Evening Dispatch*, 27 May 1944.
[170] Ibid.
[171] 'The house we dare not build', *Life and Work*, June 1944.
[172] SIR: JD Scotland.
[173] Devine, *Scottish Nation*, 369.
[174] 'A summer play school: a new experiment by the Youth Committee', *Life and Work*, October 1940, 290–91.
[175] 'Church warns: war life ruining children', *Daily Express*, 9 May 1941.

Figure 2.3 'At work': a model housing scheme. (Source: *Life and Work*, October 1940.)

for *The Times Educational Supplement*, which reported on this survey.[176] In response, the Scottish Youth Advisory committee was reformed and run by those from Scotland's main Protestant churches. By 1943, 83,200 Scottish youths had joined either girls' clubs, the Church of Scotland Youth Organisation, the Boys' Brigade, the Co-operative Youth Organisation, youth hostels, the Boy Scouts, the Salvation Army or 'a similar appropriate approved organisation [teaching] service, citizenship, healthy habits'.[177]

As earlier discussed, a further cause of panic for the Church was the growing rates of female drinking, crime and immorality. Previously, it had exerted strong influence over Scottish housewives and young women, who were often seen as virtue-keepers, spent much leisure time engaged in church pursuits and made up two-thirds of churchgoers.[178] Callum Brown has written about the religious ideals of feminine morality that existed in Scotland, and the focus on virtue, meekness and the 'commitment to puritanical morality' that were espoused by the ideal woman.[179] When reports

[176] 'Juvenile crime: increase in Scotland', *Times Educational Supplement*, 12 April 1941.
[177] Hansard, HC Deb, 21 July 1943, vol. 391 cols 932–3.
[178] Brown, 'Everyday Scottish Sunday', 175; Brown, *People in the Pews*, 32.
[179] Callum G. Brown, *Religion and Society in Scotland since 1707* (Edinburgh: Edinburgh University Press, 1997), 197–8, 201.

emerged of rising rates of venereal disease, young women 'consorting' with soldiers and women regularly drinking in public houses, this was seen as a rejection of church teaching. These changes were particularly concerning for the Kirk, as they signalled women were moving away from the influence of the Church, and were no longer content in their role as virginal sacrifice on the altar of moral purity.

This female drinking behaviour, in which women willingly and unashamedly chose to drink alcohol, horrified religious moralisers. The Church of Scotland's Women's Temperance Association referred to this practice as 'insidious and treacherous' and noted

> not only has drinking among young women become so comparatively common that it is not looked upon with the disfavour which it would have merited a few years ago but in certain circles it has become a fashionable habit. If this habit persists there is no doubt about the ill-consequences.[180]

The group felt that alcohol 'enfeebles and often paralyses self-control' and lobbied for young women to be protected 'from unnecessary and dangerous facilities' such as alcohol in the workplace.[181] To deal with this danger, the Church undertook a multi-pronged attack: it lobbied for soft drinks to be served in servicewomen's canteens, for alcohol to be banned in workplace canteens and at student dances, spoke on temperance at Girls' Association meetings and in schools, and formed an interdenominational committee to help curb drinking, especially by young women.[182] The Church would do whatever it took to get women back on the path to righteousness.

For the Kirk, the war years and the associated rise in delinquency were grave concerns. In an article in the June 1944 edition of *Life and Work*, the author railed against:

> [t]he decreasing influence of the Church on the community at large, the scant attendance at Divine Worship, the appalling lack of elementary Christian knowledge amongst otherwise well-instructed people, the lost hold on youth, the alienation from the Church of large sections of the industrial population . . . it is the decline of family religion which is at the root of the failure in character.[183]

As we have read, the Kirk was extremely concerned about crime, immorality and drinking. Religious concern over such behaviour was not exclusive to wartime but from 1940–45 this moralising reached fever pitch as the

---

[180] NRS, CH1/17/1, Women's Temperance Association, Annual Reports 1941 and 1943.
[181] Ibid., 1943.
[182] Church of Scotland, General Assembly 1943: Reports by Committee on Temperance, and Women's Temperance Association.
[183] 'The house we dare not build', *Life and Work*, June 1944.

Second World War seemed to have hastened secularisation in Scotland. Delinquency added to already heightened fears about the decline of religion in Scottish life. 'The only hope of bettering this serious development', heard the 1945 General Assembly of the Church of Scotland, 'lies in the deepening of religious life, a fostering of a stronger sense of personal responsibility and a clear declaration by the Church of the duties as well as the privileges of Church membership.'[184] In this arena, the Kirk resisted war's influence, unwilling to give up the fight for Scottish hearts and minds.

While the panic over crime and morality gripped the whole of wartime Britain, in Scotland, the panic was especially intense. Opinions on the causes of degeneracy and its possible solution were offered by members of the public, those in law and order, education or medicine, and religious and moral groups. Beneath this public outpouring of feeling were deeper-laid factors relating to class, national unity and fears the church was losing its place in Scottish society. As this chapter has explained, twentieth-century Scottish nationhood was strongly linked to the Presbyterian identity, thus an observed disintegration of morals which pointed to the declining influence of the church on daily life was, for many Scots, profoundly concerning.[185] While criticisms were voiced over the criminality and morals of Scots during wartime, this masked serious underlying fears. Fundamentally, in Scotland the moral panic was about more than morality: it was about the loss of religion and the search for a new Scottish identity. War appeared to have hastened this conversion.

Concerns over morality and delinquency were not limited to Scotland. However, the research contained within this chapter reveals elements of difference in the Scottish discussion and response to this heated issue. For Scotland, a deeply Presbyterian nation on the eve of the twentieth century, both wars had brought profound change to Scottish society, and the beginning of the removal of religion from public life. If the Kirk was losing its revered place in Scottish communities, and its relevance to the individual, what did this mean for Scottish identity? The microcosm of wartime life revealed a cultural shift taking place in Scotland, and the transition from old notions of morality, 'correct' behaviour and religious adherence, to a new era of public freedom and the search for an identity outside the Church of Scotland. Crucially, the study of Scottish responses to wartime delinquency reveals a key transition in Scottish life and identity.

---

[184] Church of Scotland, Report on Lord's Day Observance, General Assembly 1945.
[185] Brown, 'Everyday Scottish Sunday', 157; Brown, *People in the Pews*, 39.

CHAPTER THREE

'A War of Their Own': Discontent and Subversion on the Scottish Home Front

In March 1941, the Luftwaffe finally launched its long-dreaded attack on Scotland. The raids, which were concentrated on the wider Glasgow area, were on the scale of the heaviest made in Great Britain and casualties were high.[1] Considerable damage was also caused to residential and industrial premises along the River Clyde, particularly those around the shipyards and factories of Clydebank. Following the raids, the chief constable of Dumbarton announced a 'rather serious' supply situation had arisen: the Co-operative Society could not get vans to their bakeries to load bread, owing to blast damage.[2] At the same time, across the shipyards of the Clyde 11,000 apprentices were on strike, protesting over wages. The apprentices came to the rescue, forming a chain 400 yards long, 'over which laden bread boards were passed by hand from the bakery to vans drawn up in a side road at the other end of the chain'. This arrangement enabled distribution of the whole weekend supply of bread to be made to branches 'without any appreciable loss of time or inconvenience to customers'.[3] In contrast to the chief constable of Dumbarton, the Lord Provost of Glasgow declined a corresponding offer of help from a deputation of apprentices. Patrick Dollan, the Provost, publicly criticised the apprentices, stating the best way they could help their city was to resume their work immediately.[4] Industrial outputs were essential to the war effort, and the aftermath of deadly air raids was not the time to continue workplace grievances.

This story symbolises a paradox present in Scotland during the Second World War. During a time of national crisis, workers regularly took strike action and anti-war groups flourished. These activities contrasted with official wartime narratives about self-sacrifice and 'the greater good'.[5] This rhetoric was promoted by Prime Minister Winston Churchill, who spoke of the public as soldiers on the frontline, and called on them to 'do their bit', sacrifice where necessary and put everything into fighting to win the war.[6]

---

[1] NRS, HH55/27, PWD – IR, fortnight to 28 March 1941: *précis*.
[2] Ibid.: Dumbarton.
[3] Ibid.
[4] 'Clyde apprentices' strike', *Glasgow Herald*, 15 March 1941, 10.
[5] Rose, *Which People's War?*, 2, 8–9.
[6] Hansard, HC Deb, 20 August 1940, vol. 364 cols 1160–61; Winston Churchill, 'Be ye men of valour: 19 May 1940, BBC Broadcast', via International Churchill Society, https://

This powerful image of 'everyday sacrifice by ordinary people' endures, and has become part of cultural memory of the British home front.[7] To this end, one recent study found former wartime workers had little memory of dissent and unrest in their workplaces during the Second World War. In the study, historians Juliette Pattinson, Arthur McIvor and Linsey Robb interviewed former reserved workers – those whose labour was considered essential to the war effort. The men, including many Scots, downplayed any involvement in trade unions or strike action, exhibiting a sort of 'collective amnesia' on wartime strikes.[8] The historians felt this omission arose as strikes 'smacked of unpatriotic division and self-interest', and conflicted with wartime narratives framed around personal graft and sacrifice.[9] Such actions also go against the British collective memory of wartime spirit and pulling together, which will be discussed further in Chapter Four.

While cultural narratives cling to nostalgic ideas of wartime graft and sacrifice, academic studies have rediscovered elements of unrest, tension and dissent that existed on the British home front.[10] Angus Calder's seminal *The People's War* exposed the existence of workplace strikes and stoppages, anti-war sentiment, and sedition.[11] In his follow-up work, *The Myth of the Blitz*, Calder further explored the subversive elements that existed during the war, some of these in Scotland. 'The Irish situation', communism, pacifism and rising nationalist movements in Scotland and Wales lay 'far less deeply submerged under the surface of British life' than historians had credited, claimed Calder, and threatened the established and sentimentalised picture of Britain during war.[12] Daniel Todman's recent history

winstonchurchill.org/resources/speeches/1940-the-finest-hour/be-ye-men-of-valour/ (accessed 26 November 2020).

[7] Rose, *Which People's War?*, 5.
[8] Pattinson, McIvor and Robb, *Men in Reserve*, 168–9.
[9] Ibid., 173.
[10] Field, *Blood, Sweat, and Toil*; Penny Summerfield, *Women Workers in the Second World War: Production and Patriarchy in Conflict* (London: Routledge, 1989); Braybon and Summerfield, *Out of the Cage*; Alison Chand, 'Gendered identities in British regions in wartime: women in reserved occupations in Glasgow and Clydeside in the Second World War', *Journal of Scottish Historical Studies* 40, no. 1 (2020): 40–62; Chand, *Masculinities on Clydeside*; John McIlroy and Alan Campbell, 'Beyond Betteshanger: Order 1305 in the Scottish coalfields during the Second World War, part 1: politics, prosecutions and protest', *Historical Studies in Industrial Relations* 15 (2003): 27–72; Pattinson, McIvor and Robb, *Men in Reserve*; J. Phillips, 'British dock workers and the Second World War: the limits of social change', *Scottish Labour History Society Journal* 30 (1995): 87–103; B. Black, 'A triumph of voluntarism? Industrial relations and strikes in Northern Ireland in World War II', *Labour History Review* 70, no. 1 (2005): 5–25; D. Thoms, *War, Industry, and Society: The Midlands, 1939–45* (London: Routledge, 1989); M. Crowley, 'Communist engineers and the Second World War in Manchester', *North West Labour History* 22 (1998): 82–91; Mari A. Williams, *A Forgotten Army: Female Munitions Workers of South Wales, 1939–1945* (Cardiff: University of Wales Press, 2002).
[11] Calder, *People's War*, 17–18, 34, 306–11, 351–7, esp. 393–400.
[12] Calder, *Myth of the Blitz*.

of Britain at war also discussed dissent and unrest, particularly in the Clydeside region of Scotland.[13] While Todman stated that industrial unrest was 'characteristic of British working life', he acknowledged the situation on the Clyde was particularly antagonistic.[14] Alison Chand's timely studies of Clydeside workers have made valuable inroads into understanding this hostility. She explained that local subjectivities and cultural representations profoundly shaped wartime experiences.[15] Similarly, Geoffrey Field's influential study of working-class Britain linked wartime industrial unrest to 'festering' memories of interwar depression.[16] However, he concluded that, while 'regional' identity was an important factor, shared experiences between Britain's industrial workers superseded other loyalties, leading to a 'national' working-class identity.[17] But was this really the case in Scotland, a region of Britain but also a separate nation with a strong sense of national identity, culture and history?

This chapter examines the specificities of the Scottish industrial landscape during the war, and interrogates Field's ideas of (British) national class solidarity. It also explores the local points of tension that exacerbated unrest in Scotland, and the influence of national identity and Scottish history on wartime behaviour and experiences. The chapter focuses on activities that authorities termed 'subversion' or 'sedition', and probes their impact on the Scottish home front.[18] Fresh archival evidence is used to illuminate this anti-war and anti-government activity, and explore the ways this both contests and supports the existing evidence from elsewhere in Britain. Where Calder focused on showing the existence of subversive elements, this chapter will make a deeper study of these groups, examining those that existed on the Scottish home front, and demonstrating they provided a significant challenge to authorities in both Scotland and England.

A wide range of primary sources have been consulted, including newspaper and magazine articles, records from the House of Commons, and intelligence documents from SHD, M-O and MoI. These sources, some previously untapped, provide vital insight into the manifestation of subversion and industrial discontent in wartime Scotland. They also reveal the extent of concern subversive activity aroused in authorities and government agencies in both Scotland and Whitehall. Intelligence summaries generated by agencies in Whitehall or Scotland are also a valuable source. They should be placed into context, though, by considering the priorities and concerns of their authors. Reports may have been coloured by historic tensions,

---

[13] Todman, *Into Battle*, 609–13.
[14] Ibid., 613.
[15] See Chapter 3 of Chand, *Masculinities on Clydeside*; also Chand, 'Gendered identities'.
[16] See Chapter 3 of Field, *Blood, Sweat, and Toil*.
[17] Ibid., 80.
[18] SHD papers on anti-war, pacifist, nationalist, Irish Republican Army (IRA) and communist groups were filed under the headings 'sedition' and 'subversion': see NRS, HH55/656–9.

such as those relating to Red Clydeside or trade unionism, which may have heightened official anxieties in regions with a history of such activity. Even so, these sources provide valuable insights into local points of tension, public behaviour and responses to wartime measures, and reveal regional similarities and points of difference.

This chapter also relies on reports from special interest groups such as political parties and religious groups. In using such sources, the underlying agendas of their authors must be placed in the foreground. Likewise, the scope of influence of each body must be considered. As the Prologue discussed, the Church of Scotland remained a highly influential force in Scottish society, while the Scottish National Party was a fringe element, still in its infancy on the eve of the Second World War. Despite these limitations, these sources illuminate wartime unrest and points of tension and cultural friction, providing valuable insight into the motivations, attitudes and behaviours of those who expressed dissent and discontent towards other workplace authorities, the government and the war itself.

The chapter asks the question 'what forms did subversion take in Scotland and how did government officials and intelligence officers respond?' It begins by investigating industrial discontent, followed by anti-war groups such as communists, nationalists, Jehovah's Witnesses and the Irish Republican Army (IRA). It focuses on the rising challenge of discontent and subversion throughout 1940 up to mid-1941, peaking at the time of the Clydebank Blitz and Germany's invasion of Russia. Following this, the chapter will finish with a discussion of simmering subversion across the remainder of the Second World War. Ultimately, this chapter concludes subversive activity in Scotland was primarily confined to the period before March 1941, though industrial discontent continued to simmer throughout the remainder of the war years.

Industrial discontent

Scotland has a history of industrial discontent, and relations between workers, management and government were particularly volatile in the first few decades of the twentieth century. During this period of instability, grievances related to wages and policies such as dilution, and frustrations over working and living conditions frequently spilled over into strikes, stoppages and demonstrations.[19] Disputes included Clydeside's Singer strike of 1911, protesting at increased workloads for female staff, as well as anti-war demonstrations and strikes over dilution and house rents in 1915

[19] Turner and McIvor, 'Bottom dog men'; Ronnie Johnston and Arthur McIvor, 'The war and the body at work: occupational health and safety in Scottish industry, 1939–1945', *Journal of Scottish Historical Studies* 24, no. 2 (2004): 113–36; Finlay, 'Interwar crisis'; Jacqueline Jenkinson, 'Black sailors on Red Clydeside: rioting, reactionary trade unionism and conflicting notions of "Britishness" following the First World War', *Twentieth Century British History* 19, no. 1 (2008): 29–60.

and 1916.[20] Strikes and a demonstration in Glasgow's George Square in 1919, related to post-war job insecurity, resulted in riots and violent clashes with police, and spread to areas including Liverpool, South Shields and Cardiff.[21] Further, industrial unrest in coal mines resulted in the General Strike of 1926, in which over 1.5 million workers across Britain went on strike. In Scotland, special police were dispatched to quell public disorder, and associated civil unrest continued for several months after.[22]

While strikes and discontent were not exclusive to Scotland, there the 'spirit of rebellion' was especially strong and it continued throughout the interwar period.[23] At this time, socialist ideas flourished in working-class areas and factions such as the Clyde Workers' Committee, the Independent Labour Party and the Glasgow Trades Council saw growing popularity. In industrial areas around the River Clyde, workers' struggles and social radicalism continued, leading to claims of a 'uniquely radical political culture' in the Glasgow area.[24] It was also a time of unparalleled social, political and industrial unrest.[25] These decades became known as Red Clydeside, a play on the popularity of socialism and notions of class struggle. With this history in mind, how did a part of Scotland known for its radicalism and volatility respond to the Second World War?

As in the First World War, Scottish industry played an important role in the Second. At the outbreak of war, Britain's production of vital industrial

---

[20] William Kenefick, *Red Scotland!: The Rise and Fall of the Radical Left, c.1872 to 1932* (Edinburgh: Edinburgh University Press, 2007); Knox, 'Class, work and trade unionism'. For areas outside Scotland, see Chris Wrigley, *A History of British Industrial Relations: 1914–1939* (Sussex: Harvester Press, 1982); Ron Bean, 'Police unrest, unionization and the 1919 strike in Liverpool', *Journal of Contemporary History* 15, no. 4 (1980): 633–53; Peter Schofield, 'Industry and society: a study of the home front in Barrow-in-Furness during the First World War' (PhD diss., University of Central Lancashire, 2017).

[21] Jenkinson, 'Black sailors'; M. Rowe, 'Sex, "race" and riot in Liverpool, 1919', *Immigrants and Minorities* 19, no. 2 (2000), 53–70.

[22] See James E. Cronin, 'Strikes and power in Britain, 1870–1920', *International Review of Social History* 32 (1987): 144–67; A. Mason, 'The government and the General Strike, 1926', *International Review of Social History* 14, no. 1 (1969): 1–21; Sue Bruley, *The Women and Men of 1926: A Gender and Social History of the General Strike and Miners' Lockout in South Wales* (Cardiff: University of Wales Press, 2010).

[23] Paul Griffin, 'Diverse political identities within a working class presence: revisiting Red Clydeside', *Political Geography* 65 (2018): 123–33, here 123.

[24] Chand, *Masculinities on Clydeside*, 58.

[25] Devine, *Scottish Nation*, 311; Griffin, 'Revisiting Red Clydeside', 123; Harvie, *No Gods*; William Kenefick, and Arthur McIvor (eds), *Roots of Red Clydeside 1910–1914: Labour Unrest and Industrial Relations in West Scotland* (Edinburgh: John Donald, 1996); I. McLean, *The Legend of Red Clydeside* (Edinburgh: John Donald, 1983); Nina Fishman, *The British Communist Party and the Trade Unions, 1933–45* (Farnham: Scolar Press, 1995); A. McKinlay, 'From industrial serf to wage-labourer: the 1937 apprentice revolt in Britain', *International Review of Social History* 31, no. 1 (1986): 2–18; John Foster, 'Strike action and working-class politics on Clydeside 1914–1919', *International Review of Social History* 35, no. 1 (1990): 33–70.

Figure 3.1 Group photograph of workers at the Imperial Chemical Industries factory M. S. Powfoot during the Second World War, with dedication written on the back, 'from one pal to another, Jean'. (Source: DPM.2016.138. © The Devil's Porridge Museum.)

products such as steel and machine tools lagged far behind Germany's.[26] In addition, the Treasury predicted every soldier would need three times as much economic support as his equivalent had required in the First World War.[27] In order to meet this demand, and other requirements of war, industrial outputs would be critical. Scottish industry was involved in producing goods for those on the frontline, such as weaponry, munitions and sandbags, as well as larger items such as ships and aircraft (see Figures 3.1 and 3.2). During the Great War, Clydebank had been 'the key centre' of arms production in the British Empire, and it was hoped this significant contribution would extend into the Second World War.[28]

In July 1940 the Conditions of Employment and National Arbitration Order No. 1305 was passed, making strikes and lockouts illegal and effectively forcing any workplace dispute into arbitration.[29] Despite the illegality of strike action, the number of strikes throughout Britain actually increased during the Second World War, with 1944 the highest since the 1880s.[30] From 1942, strikes were most common in coal mines, including at

[26] Field, *Blood, Sweat and Toil*, 79.
[27] Ibid.
[28] Calder, *Myth of the Blitz*, 70.
[29] See TNA, '1951 Cabinet memorandum on ending restrictions on unions', https://www.nationalarchives.gov.uk/cabinetpapers/alevelstudies/1951-cabinet-memorandum.htm (accessed 24 September 2020); Hansard, HC Deb, 28 April 1944, vol. 399 cols 1103–4.
[30] Pattinson, McIvor and Robb, *Men in Reserve*, 169.

Figure 3.2 Thomas Johnston, Secretary of State for Scotland, with female industrial trainees. (Source: *The Scotsman*, 12 May 1942. National Library Scotland.)

collieries in Kent, South Wales, Durham and Yorkshire.[31] Causes included wages and conditions, though stoppages also took place over 'trivialities' such as leaving a pit without formal permission after a fatal accident, and 'going out in sympathy' with other aggrieved workers.[32] Female workers also took part in a range of prominent strikes, including at the Rolls-Royce plant near Glasgow, at an engineering factory in Bristol and in the shipyards of the Clyde.[33]

While strikes occurred across Britain, Scots were 'more militant and strike-prone' than other workers, claimed Daniel Todman.[34] This assertion

---

[31] Calder, *People's War*, 396; Field, *Blood, Sweat and Toil*, 116–17.
[32] Field, *Blood, Sweat and Toil*, 117.
[33] Summerfield, *Women Workers*, 155, 171–3; Chand, 'Gendered identities', 54.
[34] Todman, *Into Battle*, 613.

is borne out by the figures: throughout the war, seventy-one prosecutions of strikers under Order 1305 took place in Scotland, compared to only thirty-eight across both England and Wales.[35] In addition, these prosecutions may represent the tip of the iceberg, as few strikes reached court and many lasted only a matter of days.[36] Scottish wartime unrest began in October 1939 at two biscuit factories in Glasgow, with more than 200 girls protesting an increase in the age at which a wage increase could be obtained.[37] Archival sources reveal that over the next six years strike action continued across Scotland on a weekly basis and across a variety of industries, with most engaged in war production. From coal strippers to rivet heaters, mill boys to works girls, brick workers to tyre makers, hundreds of hours of work time and many thousands of tons of war material were lost to disputes, stoppages and strikes.[38] Scots demanded wage increases, fought over disciplinary action and disagreed over equipment and supplies, among other things.[39] The most frequent strikes occurred in the coal mines and steel works of Lanarkshire, Fife and Midlothian.[40] Figures provided by Scottish chief constables to the SHD reveal hundreds of workers were on strike in Scotland in any given month.[41] One-third of these strikes were prompted by disputes over wages, and discontent was most prevalent in the heavy industries of the west of Scotland, an area which covered eleven counties: more than a quarter of the country. Further, the district contained a population of 3 million, nearly three-quarters of Scotland's population at that time. As MoI summarised, '[i]t is in the main an industrial population, engaged in shipbuilding, mining and heavy engineering; – engaged, that is, on occupations vital to the national effort'.[42]

One authority that showed concern over these activities was the Scottish constabulary. Throughout the war, Scottish police regularly advised the SHD of industrial strikes, stoppages and disputes, and from mid-1940 these reports were forwarded to MoI and the Ministry of Home Security.[43] As a source, police intelligence provides a valuable glimpse into industrial tensions across Scotland and, beneath that, to worker morale. The Regional Commissioner for Civil Defence in Scotland wrote to the Ministry of Home Security in April 1940, stating his confidence in the police intelligence summaries, and declaring the reports were 'the most valuable source of

---

[35] Calder, *People's War*, 396.
[36] See NRS, HH55/26–41, PWD – IR, 17 January 1941–23 February 1945.
[37] NRS, HH55/7, PWD – IR: Daily Reports – Glasgow, 'Letter from Chief Constable City of Glasgow to SHD', 28 October 1939.
[38] See reports from NRS, HH55/7, PWD – IR: Daily Reports, Glasgow; and NRS, HH55/23–42, PWD – IR, 1940–45.
[39] Ibid.
[40] See NRS, HH55/26–41, PWD – IR, 17 January 1941–23 February 1945.
[41] Ibid.
[42] TNA, INF 1/308, Western District Information Committee (WDIC): Scottish Region, 'General review of work by Western (Scotland) District', 9 December 1941.
[43] Ibid.

information about civilian morale which is available to us'.[44] In response to the Minister's request for information on civilian morale in Scotland, and his suggestions on which agencies could supply that information, Tom Johnston, serving as the Regional Commissioner, stated that such reports were 'frequently only expressions of individual opinion'.[45] Reminding the minister '[w]e have had a fair amount of experience here in the collection of information about civilian morale', Johnston declined the request for other reports, restating that those made by police would suffice, as 'they cover the field comprehensively, and are made by Chief Constables with a full sense of responsibility and in the light of extensive local knowledge'.[46] In Johnston's opinion, police intelligence summaries were the best possible source of information on civilian morale in Scotland.

So what does an investigation of these novel reports reveal about Scottish industrial workers? Primarily, the constabulary observed that Scottish workplace discontent was rampant among workers in heavy industries. Coal miners in West Lothian and Fife were particularly prone to stoppages and strikes, but constables also reported frequent disruptions in heavy industry throughout Stirling, Ayrshire, Lanarkshire and the city of Glasgow, as well as in the shipyards of the Clyde.[47] Work stoppages occurred for a number of reasons: days taken in sympathy for deceased colleagues, stoppages over safety matters including concerns regarding sulphur fumes from charcoal, or disputes over quality issues such as inferior supplies of char and coke.[48] Most common, though, were disputes between worker and management, and conflicts over wages.

The morale of Scottish skilled workers was deeply affected by wartime policies such as dilution. Prior to the Second World War, common practice in the Scottish shipbuilding and engineering industries was to train apprentices for five years, after which they would serve one year as an 'improver' then qualify as a 'journeyman' or skilled worker. Apprentices would be paid a set apprentice wage, and journeymen sat at the top of the pay (and status) grade. As a result of wartime worker shortages, employers began to resort to dilution: the employment of unskilled labourers, who would be given basic training by the apprentices. Male trainees received a wage equivalent to that of a journeyman, while women were paid at a level below a journeyman but above

---

[44] TNA, INF 1/673, HO 199/410: Industrial Campaign to Counter Communism in Scotland (also known as the Industrial Areas Campaign, hereafter known as IAC), 1940–42, 'Response from Regional Commissioner of Civil Defence to Minister of Home Security', 13 April 1940.
[45] IAC, 1940–42, 'Response from Regional Commissioner of Civil Defence to Minister of Home Security', 13 April 1940.
[46] IAC, 1940–42, 'Letter from H. Elles, re. morale on the home front', 5 April 1940.
[47] See reports from NRS, HH55/23–42, PWD – IR, 1940–45.
[48] NRS, HH55/34, PWD – IR: 11 November 1942, City of Glasgow; NRS, HH55/35, PWD – IR: 4 December 1942, Fife, Renfrewshire, Greenock.

an apprentice.[49] To many of the young shipyard and engineering apprentices, it was insulting to be paid less than the unskilled workers they were training. Historically, apprentices had inadequate representation in trade unions, a tendency towards militancy, and many displayed 'strong disillusion and bitterness'.[50] In early 1941, this volatile mix led aggrieved apprentices to turn their thoughts into actions. Employers refused to negotiate with a group calling itself 'the Clyde Apprentices Committee', acting as an ad hoc trade union, and the situation escalated.[51] By 11 March, 11,000 apprentices from nearly 50 firms in the West of Scotland had come out on strike, expressing their discontent with the situation and demanding a wage rise. Unrest also spread to apprentices at firms in Lancashire and Coventry.

This unrest had historic roots. Throughout the interwar period, Scottish apprentices had railed against unfair contracts and wage structures, and in 1937 up to 17,000 Clydeside apprentices struck over a similar dispute around workplace wage increases that excluded apprentices.[52] But to undertake a similar action in 1941 was considerably riskier: as 11,000 apprentices downed-tools for up to fourteen days, Allied forces were struggling against the German war machine in North Africa and the Mediterranean. An observer for M-O was horrified by the 'selfish spirit' he observed in the striking apprentices who, in his opinion, were putting self-interest before national interest.[53] At that time, the SHD noted 'almost all' affected firms were engaged on work of national importance, and war production was 'seriously affected' by the stoppages.[54] M-O's observer also noted the local press was disapproving of the strike action, viewing it as ironical in light of the critical stage of the war.[55] A large-scale strike seemed especially ill-timed, given it coincided with a speech by the First Lord of the Admiralty, who declared in the House of Commons on 5 March, '[n]ever in the long history of the growth of our sea power have we had such need of numbers of ships and men'.[56] He had stressed '[w]e must impress upon both employers and workers that in facing the Battle of the Atlantic now opening upon us, we need every ounce of their energy, and ever-increasing production'.[57] As strike action spread throughout Scottish shipyards in the days following this stark announcement, apprentice commitment to the war effort appeared questionable at best and treasonous at worst.

---

[49] M-O, File Report (FR) 604, 'The Scottish shipbuilding and engineering apprentices' strike', 13 March 1941.
[50] M-O, FR600: 'Preliminary report on morale in Glasgow, Addendum to Section III: Apprentice strikes', 32–3; Field, *Blood, Sweat and Toil*, 87.
[51] M-O, FR600: 'Morale in Glasgow, apprentice strikes', 7 March 1941, 33a.
[52] McKinlay, 'From industrial serf to wage-labourer', 14.
[53] M-O, FR600, 'Morale in Glasgow', 7 March 1941, 33.
[54] NRS, HH55/27, PWD – IR, 14 March 1941: *précis* report.
[55] M-O, FR600, 'Morale in Glasgow', 7 March 1941, 34.
[56] Hansard, HC Deb, 5 March 1941, vol. 369 col. 928.
[57] Ibid., col. 931.

Discontent and Subversion

While the apprentice strike is just one example of wartime worker discontent, the frequency of other industrial strikes and stoppages across Scotland revealed to authorities the scale of worker dissatisfaction, and the level to which employer–employee relations had sunk. As M-O's intelligence officer keenly observed, '[i]t is not that Clydeside workers are against the war ... It is rather that [they] are also having a war of their own.'[58] This conflict which pitted worker against management was not new, having repeatedly flared up in Clydeside during the 1915 rent strike, the 1919 riot in Glasgow's George Square and the 1926 General Strike.[59] Additionally, the rise of Labour after the Great War and the consolidation of the power of trade unions had increasingly widened the gap between worker and management.[60] Relations were further strained by the severe economic depression in Scotland between the wars. Years of economic instability, coupled with insecurity of employment, left many Scottish working-class men feeling bitter and distrustful of employers.

When war brought a sudden change in worker fortunes, bringing more jobs, higher wages and employers desperate to hire even those previously seen as undesirable, workers found themselves in a position of power. Furthermore, trade unionism had experienced a resurgence in membership, acting as what Arthur McIvor has termed 'a powerful tool to maintain dignity at work'.[61] This mix of existing disgruntlement, strained relations and newly gained clout led some workers to press the advantage, making the most of the newfound power-shift while it lasted.[62] 'The war has put the Clydeside worker on top again', M-O declared in April 1941, 'from being the "unwanted man" he is now in demand exceeding supply'.[63]

The war had put the worker in 'an almost impregnable bargaining position', and it further served to deepen the gulf between worker and employer.[64] This was a development that concerned authorities in both Scotland and Whitehall. As the pseudo-war between worker and management raged, it dragged time, attention and energy away from the true war. Most importantly, as the power struggle between Scottish workers and management amplified, the resulting strikes, lockouts and absences severely impacted production output. MoI's Regional Information Officer (RIO) for Scotland noted in January 1941 that work per hour per man was less during 1939–1940 than it had been in the year preceding the war, and that production output was only able to reach targets if regular overtime was

---

[58] M-O, FR600, 'Morale in Glasgow', 7 March 1941, 3.
[59] Devine, *Scottish Nation*, 311, 314, 318.
[60] Field, *Blood, Sweat, and Toil*, 87.
[61] Arthur McIvor, 'Was occupational health and safety a strike issue? Workers, unions and the body in twentieth-century Scotland', *Journal of Irish and Scottish Studies* 8, no. 2 (2017), 5–33, here 8.
[62] Pattinson, McIvor and Robb, *Men in Reserve*, 137–8.
[63] M-O, FR631: Summary of Glasgow report, 3 April 1941.
[64] Max Cohen, *What Nobody Told the Foreman* (London: Butler and Tanner, 1953), 142.

devoted.[65] Losing work hours to petty grievances, or outputs to raw materials remaining in the ground, were unacceptable in a situation of national emergency. Inadequate supplies could mean the difference between success and failure for British troops on the frontline. As M-O summarised, the well-established tradition of worker versus boss was 'the direct antithesis of good morale'.[66] Antagonism should be directed towards the enemy rather than those in your own workplace, believed M-O, and such internal divisions could only be detrimental to the war effort at a time when maximum production output was essential.

Communists

The vision of a united Britain during war is further challenged by the existence of groups that actively worked to undermine Britain's war effort. We turn now to consider the most prominent of these: communists. The Communist Party (CP) was the main agitator in wartime Scotland, retaining a place of influence in Scottish workplaces, especially those along the Clyde. Socialism had long been popular in the wider Glasgow area, experiencing a wave of support after the Great War.[67] During the 1920s, the Party gained ground across Britain, and in Scotland its popularity peaked in areas of heavy industry such as Glasgow and Fife.[68] While Scottish support for the CP waned during the 1930s, it retained a hold in the industrial heartlands.[69] Moreover, in the interwar years communist organisations played a prominent part in Scottish trade unions and actively recruited new members.[70] The CP also had 'considerable influence' in central Scotland, particularly in organisations such as the National Union of Scottish Mineworkers.[71] With this history in mind, as the war economy mobilised and investment in heavy industry increased, wary officials in both Scotland and Whitehall likewise prepared for an upsurge in communist agitation.

In early 1940, Niven McNicoll, MoI's Scottish RIO, stated his belief that communists were having undue influence in Scottish workplaces.[72] Later that year, SHD reports also noted there were 'signs of unrest' in industry, which was 'undoubtedly' attributable to communist penetration.[73] Communists were believed to be exploiting existing worker attitudes and grievances, infiltrating trade unions and encouraging strikes, slacking and

---

[65] IAC, 'Letter from McNicoll to Rhodes', 10 January 1941.
[66] M-O, FR600, 'Morale in Glasgow', 7 March 1941, 2a.
[67] Calder, *Myth of the Blitz*, 70.
[68] Hutchison, *Scottish Politics*, 60–62.
[69] Ibid., 97–8.
[70] Field, *Blood, Sweat, and Toil*, 88.
[71] Calder, *Myth of the Blitz*, 70.
[72] TNA, INF 1/308, WDIC, Meeting minutes, 20 June 1940.
[73] IAC, 'Scotland: Communists and Scottish industrial workers summary', 2 December 1940.

sabotage in Scottish workplaces.[74] Such activities were damaging to the war effort because they directly affected war production but also because they encouraged criticism of the government and authorities, promoted anti-war sentiment and affected morale by fostering worker grievances. McNicoll was concerned the cynicism and disillusionment of workers was being exploited by communist factions, who educated their fellow workers in CP doctrine and encouraged them to question the validity of the war. Concerned by these developments, McNicoll actively encouraged the formation of a special committee to monitor communist activities: the Western (Scotland) District Information Committee (WDIC).[75] Members included ministers, councillors, politicians and MoI staff.

Throughout 1940 and early 1941, increasing CP agitation was noted. Intelligence investigators overheard workers expressing known communist rhetoric such as 'war is an imperialist struggle' and 'why should we workers fight to maintain capitalist privilege?'[76] Communist 'mischief-making' was also believed to be involved in strike actions, such as that by Glasgow Corporation Transport workers in January 1941.[77] Additionally, the CP was accused of stoking local points of friction by provoking discussion about the purchase tax and an associated rise in the cost of living, the legitimacy of working after air raid sirens had started and inflaming disputes over workplace conditions and dismissals. As one investigator noted, messages tended towards 'the general denunciation of privilege', and employers were targeted as beneficiaries of an unequal class system.[78] This stirring of tensions and grievances seemed calculated to add further fuel to the fire.

One of the main ways the CP spread its message of subversion was by telling the working classes their safety had been imperilled by those in authority. In the west of Scotland, it was alleged that authorities had made inadequate air raid arrangements for the public, both at home and in the workplace, and the working classes would bear the brunt of this negligence. In industrial premises, prominent communists advised workers to down-tools and head for shelters as soon as sirens sounded, rather than keep working until workplace spotters confirmed an attack was imminent.[79] In January 1941 a shop steward from the Rolls-Royce factory in Edinburgh spoke at a meeting in Glasgow, telling fellow shop stewards no person should be working when air raid warnings had been given, 'as it had been proved that the system of "spotters" and second alarms had failed to work'.[80] As a report from the SHD noted, by the end of 1940 there had

[74] TNA, INF 1/308, WDIC, Meeting minutes, 20 June 1940.
[75] Ibid.
[76] IAC, 'Letter from McNicoll to Rhodes', 10 January 1941.
[77] Ibid.
[78] IAC, 'Scotland: Communists and Scottish industrial workers', 2 December 1940, 3.
[79] Ibid.
[80] NRS, HH55/7, Daily Reports Glasgow, 1940–41, 'SHD Circular No.3732: Intelligence Report No. 70', 7 January 1941.

been no workplace bombings outside Aberdeen and the constant stopping of work caused significant delays to production.[81]

As the war progressed, authorities grew increasingly concerned at the extent to which the CP was attempting to influence Scottish worker morale and behaviour. Speakers at CP events advised Glaswegians that local authority shelter provision was inadequate, and gave examples of similar shelters in London collapsing spontaneously and flooding.[82] This was a theme trotted out repeatedly during 1940 and 1941, with communists demanding that deep or 'bomb-proof' shelters be provided, and even working to infiltrate ARP Coordinating Committees to push this agenda.[83] '[U]rgent action is necessary if the people are not to be slaughtered like sheep for months and years to come', stated the *Scottish Information Bulletin*, a publication of the CP's Scottish District Committee.[84] Throughout Glasgow workplaces, inflammatory leaflets on the topic were distributed regularly. Building upon the deep shelter argument, leaflets further raised the question of worker safety, implying that negligent authorities had made inadequate provision for Glaswegians in the event of air raids. Distributed leaflets included *Glasgow's Air Raid Protection is Inadequate* and *Glasgow Needs More and Better Air-Raid Protection*.[85] Both seemed intended to promote an 'us and them' mentality, further pitting ordinary folk against those in authority.

Other leaflets distributed in Glasgow factories contained the text of provocative speeches, such as one by William Cowe, a Scottish Party member, which accused the government of aiding fascism and called for the 'hated Chamberlain Government' to be overthrown.[86] Many leaflets were markedly anti-war, and emphasised the disproportionate sacrifices such conflicts required of the working classes. One such leaflet, entitled *Women and the War*, stated '[w]e working women, who bring our sons into the world for life – not death – have a right to demand an answer to the question: "Why is it that twice within twenty-five years our boys have been conscripted to perish on the battlefields?"'[87] The leaflet went on to say that all members of the working classes, whether in Britain, France or Germany, were being exploited by the rich. It finished by stating workers must end the war, bring down the capitalist governments and 'refuse to sacrifice millions of human beings for the riches and power of a few'.[88] Those producing such

---

[81] IAC, 'Scotland: Communists and Scottish industrial workers', 2 December 1940, 3.
[82] NRS, HH55/7, Daily Reports Glasgow, 1940–41, 'SHD Circular No.3732: Intelligence Report No. 62', 19 November 1940.
[83] IAC, 'Scotland: Communists and Scottish industrial workers', 2 December 1940, 2; NRS, HH55/7, Daily Reports Glasgow, 1940–1941, 'SHD Circular No.3732: Intelligence Report No. 57', 2 September 1940.
[84] NRS, HH55/7, Daily Reports Glasgow, 1941–43, '*Scottish Information Bulletin*', 1.
[85] Ibid., Daily Reports Glasgow, 1939–40.
[86] Ibid., 'Scotland and the war'.
[87] Ibid., '*Women and the War*', 1.
[88] Ibid., 14.

incendiary and seditious publications would have to be 'tackled vigorously', authorities concluded in December 1940.[89]

It was not only communists who undermined the war effort by spreading anti-war propaganda across Scotland; other subversive groups were similarly active. In Glasgow the No Conscription League encouraged locals to resist conscription, and held regular mock tribunals at which conscientious objectors could practise their arguments in advance of appearances before the real tribunals. The men would also receive coaching in 'the manner in which they ought to present their cases', in order to better succeed in avoiding military or industrial conscription.[90] Other groups and individuals regularly held anti-war meetings or made public declarations against the government and the war. The United Socialist Movement, the Anarchist-Communist Federation, the No Conscription League and the Scottish Peace Council joined the CP and the International Labour Party in agitating regularly throughout the west of Scotland. At one meeting, a speaker announced he had personally contacted the German Legation in Dublin and they would be willing to agree to peace with Britain; another decried 'the Imperialistic war', calling for coal miners to strike and advocate against the war; and another suggested Neville Chamberlain was 'just as big a liar as Hitler'.[91]

Adding to this chorus of sedition was D. N. Pritt, an MP and King's Counsel, and described by the writer George Orwell as 'perhaps the most effective pro-Soviet publicist in this country'.[92] Pritt appeared at a demonstration in Glasgow on May Day 1940. He claimed Chamberlain had 'assisted in building up Fascism in Germany', called for the workers to continue their struggle against the war and emphasised the best time to fight against war was 'while it was prevailing'.[93] Inciting workers into rebellion was clearly a direct contradiction of the ideals of public spiritedness and national community that the government was actively promoting.[94]

Official documents reveal this anti-war and anti-establishment action in Scotland caused anxiety among a range of authorities. Alongside the activities of the WDIC, the City of Glasgow Police compiled daily intelligence reports throughout the war, predominantly noting communist activity, strikes and union agitation in the city. While reports cover all years of the

---

[89] IAC, 'Letter from McNicoll to Rhodes', 17 December 1940.
[90] NRS, HH55/7, Daily Reports Glasgow, 1939–40, 'SHD Circular No.3732: Intelligence Report No. 36', 28 March 1940.
[91] NRS, HH55/7, Daily Reports Glasgow, 1939–1940, 'SHD Circular No.3732: Intelligence Report No. 37', 30 March 1940; 'SHD Circular No.3732: Intelligence Report No. 38', 2 April 1940; 'SHD Circular No.3732: Intelligence Report No. 39', 8 April 1940.
[92] Kevin Morgan, 'Pritt, Denis Nowell (1887–1972)', *Oxford Dictionary of National Biography* (Oxford: Oxford University Press, 2004, online edition).
[93] NRS, HH55/7, Daily Reports Glasgow, 1939–40, 'SHD Circular No.3732: Intelligence Report No. 41', 6 May 1940.
[94] Rose, *Which People's War?*, 85.

war, the thickest files are for 1939 and 1940.[95] Further, officials including Niven McNicoll, Glasgow District RIO Mr Mackinlay, the Regional Commissioner for Civil Defence and representatives of the Scottish Trades Union Congress all expressed alarm at the strength of communist influence in industrial Scotland.[96] Resources were pooled with MoI and the WDIC, and a secret intelligence taskforce was created: the Industrial Campaign to Counter Communism in Scotland, also known as the Industrial Areas Campaign (IAC).[97] This unique response, aimed at stamping out communist influence in Scotland, demonstrates the strength of official concern at this issue.

Under the auspices of the WDIC, the IAC organised factory meetings, showings of films about the importance of war production and War Commentary meetings featuring educated speakers such as local university professors. In late 1940, an MoI adviser stated his belief that the War Commentaries were 'the most important work undertaken' in the district.[98] The IAC also included a 'sustained propaganda-drive'. Under this approach, intelligence officials liaised with the BBC to produce items of 'industrial interest' and leaned on local newspapers in an attempt to have them devote 'a good deal of space' to industrial articles.[99] Officers also hoped to create a Scottish film production unit that could develop content tailored to Scottish concerns.[100] Finally, 'anti-Hitler' leaflets were produced, written to counteract 'the entire long-term problem of the Scottish workers' part in the national effort'.[101] *Co-operative Societies Under the Nazis* was written to 'counteract Communist penetration of the Scottish Co-operative movement', while the leaflet *Mr Smith – Mr Schmidt* was rated 'extremely good', and 'a powerful weapon [which] will also have permanent effects'.[102] The leaflet contrasted Mr Smith, a British worker who can 'ventilate his industrial grievances through his Trades Union', with Mr Schmidt, who lives in fear: '[i]f you are tempted to criticise the national government, you swallow your words. That way lies the concentration camp.'[103]

The IAC increased in intensity as a result of growing strike action and perceived CP agitation in early 1941. In April 1941, an IAC report noted the main effect of disruptive elements in the industrial sector was not strikes, but 'the fostering of cynicism and disillusionment about the war'.[104]

---

[95] See NRS, HH55/7, Police war duties: Daily Reports Glasgow, 1939–40, and May 1940–Jan. 1941.
[96] IAC, 1940–42, 'RIO Scotland to Regional Administration Division', 26 November 1940.
[97] IAC, 1940–42.
[98] IAC, 1940–42, 'Visit to the Scottish Region (No.11) of the Regions' Adviser', 30 November–5 December 1940.
[99] IAC, 1940–42, 'Letter from McNicoll to Rhodes', 10 January 1941.
[100] Ibid.
[101] Ibid.
[102] Ibid.
[103] Herbert Morrison, *Mr Smith and Mr Schmidt* (London: Collins, 1941), 7, 28.
[104] IAC, 1940–42, 'Industrial Areas Campaign (IAC): Report on smaller meetings', 24 April 1941.

Over the next few months, intelligence officials employed a multi-pronged approach to tackle discontent in the west of Scotland. One tactic was to 'help the BBC to obtain items of industrial interest'.[105] Another was to expand the War Commentary meetings, and talks were also given at various groups such as ARP and church debating societies.[106]

One of the most important weapons in the war for morale was Mr William Roberts, a former mechanic from Clydeside, who became the IAC's mole. Roberts was considered 'an advance outpost against Communist infiltration', and ran discussion groups, informal meetings in homes and even visited emergency rest centres, sparking discussions and correcting common misconceptions or untruths about the government and war effort.[107] Small meetings and informal discussion groups were expanded across Bridgeton and Clydebank, and new groups begun in the Glasgow suburbs of Springburn and Govan. Roberts aimed to steer meetings towards war matters, such as the background to the Battle of the Atlantic; discuss current affairs, including the ban of the *Daily Worker*, and help workers who wanted advice for debating communist colleagues.[108] Those behind the IAC noted their plan was to equip industrial workers with better tools to fight subversive 'misrepresentations' in the workplace, but also to tackle apathy about the war. 'The whole summer period . . . should be regarded as a preparation for the problems and stresses of next winter', the April 1941 report concluded.[109]

Over the remainder of the year, intelligence officials continued their efforts to bolster Scottish morale and war support, and to neutralise subversion. The IAC began showing pro-war MoI films at factories such as Scottish Aviation in Prestwick, and at mines across Fife, where the showings were given an 'enthusiastic welcome'.[110] Regular informal discussion meetings continued, as did the public meetings and War Commentaries. MoI film units also toured Scotland and had given 118 shows by the end of May 1941. Film screenings were concentrated in areas with high numbers of labourers, and were tailored to audiences. For example, in Hawick the choice of film was made in conjunction with a Ministry of Labour campaign to enlist more women to work in munitions. In Edinburgh, one film scheme was 'designed to demonstrate the importance of women in war time', presumably to cater to the larger number of female workers in the city.[111] This multi-faceted counter-attack revealed the strong degree of official concern at the fissures developing beneath the Scottish home front.

[105] Ibid., 1.
[106] Ibid.
[107] Ibid., 2–4.
[108] Ibid.
[109] Ibid., 5.
[110] IAC, 1940–42, 'Progress report', 17–31 May 1941, 3.
[111] Ibid., 4.

These efforts also reveal a key difference on the British home front. While industrial unrest and communist agitation were also noted in places such as south Wales, Belfast, Tyneside and Yorkshire, Scotland was treated differently.[112] A search of MoI archives reveals only one Information Committee outside London and the south-east – that in the Western (Scotland) District. Additionally, archival searches locate only one targeted campaign to counter communist influence on the home front – Scotland's Industrial Areas Campaign. While these Ministry records may be incomplete, at this stage archival evidence supports the assertion that officials directed extra attention towards communist subversion in Scotland. While communist agitation was not exclusive to Scotland, this particular response was. This may indicate that Scotland's history of militancy and industrial unrest coloured official responses to wartime subversion there. However, it may also suggest that communist subversion was more prevalent in industrial Scotland than elsewhere in Britain, requiring a more robust response.

Scottish nationalists

Scottish nationalists were another faction attracting the ire of wartime authorities. While war might have brought a halt to nationalism, because of the greater vulnerability of small nation states, in Scotland '[its] resilience was remarkable'.[113] With a small and dwindling membership, and no small element of internal division, the Scottish National Party (SNP) survived the war and the nationalist movement gained several key points of concession for Scotland.[114] The SNP spent the war years arguing *against* conscription – for Scots called both into the military and into war production work in England – and *for* home rule, and key nationalists such as Tom Johnston managed to secure increased powers of administration for Scotland under a *de facto* home rule.[115] Alongside the grievances and concessions, which will be discussed further in Chapters Four and Seven, many

---

[112] On wartime strikes see Todman, *Into Battle*; Daniel Todman, *Britain's War: A New World, 1942–1947* (Oxford: Oxford University Press, 2020); Calder, *Myth of the Blitz*; Calder, *People's War*; James Hinton, *Shop Floor Citizens: Engineering Democracy in 1940s Britain* (Aldershot: Edward Elgar, 1994); James Hinton, 'Coventry Communism: a study of factory politics in the Second World War', *History Workshop* 10 (1980): 90–118; K. Gildart, 'Coal strikes on the home front: miners' militancy and socialist politics in the Second World War', *Twentieth Century British History* 20, no. 2 (2009): 121–51; Field, *Blood, Sweat, and Toil*; Rose, *Which People's War?*; Summerfield, *Women Workers*; Patricia Inman, *Labour in the Munitions Industries* (London: HMSO, 1957).

[113] Harvie, *Scotland and Nationalism*, 34.

[114] For more on Scottish nationalism see chapter 'Celts, reds and conchies' in Calder, *Myth of the Blitz*; Murray G. H. Pittock, *Scottish Nationality* (Basingstoke: Palgrave, 2001); 'Geographies of the nation' in Rose, *Which People's War?*; 'The intellectuals, 1707–1945' in Harvie, *Scotland and Nationalism*; and Gavin Bowd, '"Fortify the Cheviots!": the Nazis and the Scottish nationalists' in Ugolini and Pattinson, *Fighting for Britain?*, 161–84.

[115] Harvie, *Scotland and Nationalism*, 33–4.

nationalist actions were viewed by authorities as subversive and key actors were subjected to enhanced surveillance and security measures.

The Scottish nationalist movement and the associated desire for home rule was, inherently, a threat to the Union. During the war, some adherents argued that the conscription of Scots contravened the 1707 Acts of Union, and others claimed Scotland was not a willing participant in the conflict.[116] Like the CP, Scottish nationalists had their own publications which were often anti-war or anti-establishment in tone. In a 1942 edition of the *Scots Socialist*, the publication claimed the transfer of Scottish workers and machinery to England to undertake war work was a conspiracy by the Bank of England and the English government. In an article entitled 'The Scottish revolution approaches', the women of the Glasgow district of Govan were praised for forming a committee 'to protect the Govan lassies from deportation', proclaiming that, in the conscription of Scottish women, 'our English overlords have gone too far'.[117]

During April and May 1941, under the instruction of MI5, Scottish police executed a number of search warrants upon the homes of known Scottish nationalists. The officers seized personal documents and correspondence, and took some nationalists into custody.[118] In response, a number of incensed letters were sent to the authorities by the affected and their advocates, many addressed to Secretary of State Tom Johnston who was known for his pro-nationalist sympathies.[119] In one reply to a letter of entreaty from a Mr Muirhead, Johnston replied, 'I am indeed personally very sorry that you should have suffered the disturbance and inconvenience you narrate in your letter'. He added 'Scottish self-government advocacy is in no sense a crime'.[120] Johnston also pointed out that all arrests resulting from the search and seize operation were, of course, entirely legal and all came under appropriate laws, such as the Contravention of the National Service Act or unauthorised possession of firearms and ammunition. Nonetheless, many nationalists remained suspicious of the motives behind the raids, and postal censorship revealed that one even suggested petitioning the King to stop the 'systematic violation of Scots law' and associated 'trampling' on civil liberties.[121]

Some nationalists proclaimed the crack-down by authorities was part and parcel of 'English imperialism'. During 1941, the SHD collated a file on nationalist sedition which included records of complaints about raids,

---

[116] Calder, *Myth of the Blitz*, 73.
[117] NRS, HH55/557, Sedition: Police action against Scottish nationalist organisations (hereafter SNO), 1941.
[118] See NRS, HH55/557, Sedition: Police action against SNO, 1941; HH55/558, Scottish Nationalist Party, 'Scottish Nationalists', 12 May 1941.
[119] Macdonald, *Whaur Extremes Meet*, 87.
[120] NRS, HH55/557, Sedition: Police action against SNO, 1941, 'Letter from Johnston to Muirhead', 13 May 1941.
[121] Ibid., 'MoI postal censorship, letter from Grieve to Miller', 24 June 1941.

letters to newspaper editors in defence of nationalism or criticising raids, and details of police control of suspected activists. The language used by those who protested the raids and arrests is revealing: targets had suffered 'monstrous injustice'; raids were 'outrageous' and 'a clumsy blunder'; 'Gestapo methods' had been employed; and the 'cowardly' police actions were 'a gross insult to the whole of Scotland'.[122] As one letter writer acknowledged, 'I quite realise that the main thing just now is to win the war . . . but such actions should not be allowed'.[123] While this nationalist acknowledged a need to focus on war, he revealed a blinkered outlook, unable to see how much concern his actions had caused authorities.

One prominent figure who decried the SHD's crack-down on nationalists was Christopher Murray Grieve, better known by his pen-name Hugh MacDiarmid. A founding member of the National Party of Scotland, Grieve wrote to Johnston protesting the raids on Scots Republicans by 'the English Gestapo', stating '[t]he whole thing is a base English Imperialist manoeuvre to throttle and libel . . . the Scottish Socialist Republican Movement'.[124] He added his belief that if any fifth column traitors were to be found they would be within the aristocracy and government, rather than among Scottish nationalists.[125] The author also pleaded with Johnston to halt the 'victimisation' of Scots, stating

> yourself a distinguished Scottish historian, you must be aware that all the legislation under which conscription and other war-time measures are being applied in Scotland, is utterly illegal and represents a deliberate and systematic violation by the English Government of one of the safeguarding clauses of the Act of Union.[126]

As Johnston had pointed out, Scottish nationalism was not a crime, but the views held by nationalists such as Grieve, pertaining to the legitimacy of the war and feelings that Scottish rights were being violated by 'power-hungry English', certainly caused concern among authorities who were keen to ensure a united home front, with all citizens working together in pursuit of victory.

Elsewhere, nationalist sentiment also chafed against the British war effort. In Wales, Whitehall's push for 'national' unification was perceived by

---

[122] Ibid., and 'letter from Muirhead to Wedderburn', 29 May 1941; letter to the editor: 'Scottish search warrants', *The Scotsman*, 29 May 1941; 'letter from Jamieson to SHD', 20 May 1941; 'letter from Grant to Johnston', 23 May 1941.

[123] NRS, HH55/557, Sedition: Police action against SNO, 1941, 'Letter from Muirhead to Wedderburn', 29 May 1941.

[124] Ibid., 'Letter from Grieve to Johnston', 25 May 1941.

[125] NRS, HH55/557, Sedition: Police action against SNO, 1941, 'Letter from Johnston to Muirhead', 13 May 1941.

[126] NRS, HH55/557, Sedition: Police action against SNO, 1941, 'Letter from Grieve to Johnston', 25 May 1941.

Discontent and Subversion

some as a threat to Welsh culture.[127] Further, the president of Plaid Cymru claimed the war was a clash of imperialists from which Wales had 'nothing to gain, but everything to lose'.[128] Opposition to war was also expressed by the traditionally pacifist Nonconformists, and percentages of conscientious objectors were higher in Wales than in England and Scotland.[129] Martin Johnes has pointed out that while MI5 investigated Welsh nationalist activities, it considered the group's actions to be 'trivial' and of little adverse effect on the war effort.[130] In contrast, while Scottish nationalists may have been a fringe element, their activities aroused anxiety among the authorities, including MI5. Their actions and publications were labelled seditious, and grouped with other 'concerning' activities such as strikes and communist agitation. Many nationalist grievances were also echoed by a significant portion of the public, which will be discussed in Chapters Four and Seven.

Other subversive factions

Other groups whose actions threatened home front stability included the IRA and Jehovah's Witnesses. Jehovah's Witnesses across Europe expressed firm opposition to the war, considering it to be 'the Armageddon by which Jehovah is defeating the enemies of the Theocracy'.[131] Those enemies included all organised government and religion, particularly the Roman Catholic church. Church members were not to take part in the war, as it was believed the Earth would be theirs after Jehovah had used the conflict to defeat all governments and religions. In Nazi Germany, and other Nazi-occupied countries, this stance led to the Witnesses' persecution, incarceration and internment in concentration camps.[132]

In Britain, members of the group refused to be conscripted into military or industrial service, and refused to undertake work 'in support of the war effort'.[133] Additionally, adherents were encouraged to devote their time to the saving of souls, rather than carrying out the edicts of an earthly government.[134] In Scotland, as in England, the group's refusal to support conscription led members to plead their cases at conscientious objection tribunals. 'This direction to take up work in the national emergency does not apply to me, for I claim that I am in holy orders', said one young Scot

---

[127] Rose, *Which People's War?*, 222.
[128] Johnes, *Wales Since 1939*, 25.
[129] Ibid., 27.
[130] Ibid., 28.
[131] NRS, HH55/556, Sedition: Jehovah's Witnesses, 'Security Executive: Conference on Jehovah's Witnesses', 25 August 1942.
[132] See Sabrina C. H. Chang and Peter Suedfeld, 'The faithful do not yield: Jehovah's Witnesses in Nazi camps', *Genocide Studies International* 11, no. 2 (2017): 228–39.
[133] 'Women C. O.s: first Edinburgh appeals', *The Scotsman*, 27 August 1942, 3.
[134] Ibid.

appearing before a tribunal in January 1943.[135] Another claimed if he was required to join the Army that would mean he had a double allegiance, split between God and man. For him to take up military service, he told his conscientious objection tribunal, would be 'to violate his covenant [with God]', bringing 'eternal destruction'.[136]

The difficulty of holding moral or religious objections to war was recognised by MP James Maxton, representing the Glasgow district of Bridgeton. In the House of Commons in April 1941 Maxton proclaimed 'when a man says, "I am not taking my orders from Ernest Bevin; I am taking them from Almighty God" . . . he is standing on a principle, and if he is prepared to stand on it, it must be accepted'.[137] Others did not share this benevolence towards anti-war beliefs. Jehovah's Witnesses were frequently ridiculed by magistrates at conscientious objection tribunals, one deeming the group a 'national menace', while another told a young man to get a job 'instead of lounging about selling books on behalf of an American gang'.[138] The Church of Scotland also issued an information pamphlet on the group, referring to them as a 'strange sect' and 'tireless propagandists'.[139]

The enthusiastic sharing of anti-war beliefs and vocal refusal to support the war effort led the authorities to view the group with concern. In 1942, Home Secretary Herbert Morrison admitted the group's impeding of the war effort was drawing the 'close attention' of security services.[140] Agents at MoI also felt the group was engaging in activities 'which were either directly subversive or at any rate were not likely to advance our war effort'.[141] As a result, the sect was subjected to extra postal and telegraph censorship, and member activities were monitored by MoI, the Ministry of Home Security and in Scotland by police and the SHD.[142] Scottish authorities viewed the group's activities with suspicion, and meetings and rallies were regularly monitored and reported on, and occasionally infiltrated, by government observers.[143]

---

[135] 'District News, Glasgow and West: claimed to be in holy orders', *The Scotsman*, 15 January 1943, 3.

[136] 'A "neutral" Christian: C. O. Appellate Tribunal', *The Scotsman*, 31 January 1941, 3.

[137] Hansard, HC Deb, 1 April 1941, vol. 370 col. 885.

[138] Hansard, HC Deb, 12 March 1942, vol. 378 col. 1183 'Jehovah's Witnesses'; 'Witness ordered out', *The Scotsman*, 17 August 1940, 9.

[139] 'Church news: Jehovah's Witnesses, Church of Scotland pamphlet', *The Scotsman*, 3 February 1941, 7.

[140] Hansard, HC Debs, 12 March 1942, vol. 378 col. 1183; 8 January 1942, vol. 377 col. 9.

[141] NRS, HH55/556, Sedition: Jehovah's Witnesses, 'Security Executive note', 8 February 1945.

[142] See NRS, HH55/556, Sedition: Jehovah's Witnesses; Richard Thurlow, 'The evolution of the mythical British fifth column, 1939–46', *Twentieth Century British History* 10, no. 4 (1999): 477–98.

[143] SHD files term the wartime activities of Scottish Jehovah's Witnesses 'Sedition': see NRS, HH55/556: Sedition: Jehovah's Witnesses.

In contrast to the threat of communist subversion, which was dealt with by a Scotland-specific campaign, the response to this sect's activities was directed from Whitehall. There, intelligence officials struggled to find evidence the sect posed an undue threat to the war effort or contravened any wartime legislation.[144] The chief constable of Glasgow agreed that Jehovah's Witnesses posed little threat to public order in Scotland, and there would be no gain from prohibiting their gatherings.[145] Despite the objections of then MoI head Duff Cooper, members of the Security Executive agreed only to ban the importation of the group's religious literature, rather than to make the sect illegal as it was in other countries such as Germany and Australia.[146] The quantity of literature being imported from the USA declined from 35,156 leaflets in June 1943 to 1,105 the following month when the ban was implemented, and the figure was down to 347 leaflets during September that year.[147] In addition, censorship of Jehovah's Witness literature was implemented at US facilities in order to further reduce quantities arriving in Britain. The ban severely dented the group's ability to proselytise, and significantly eased the burden on British postal censorship facilities.[148]

SHD files make little mention of the group between 1943 and 1945, excepting a small number of censorship violations and member complaints about freedom of speech. This included a letter from a Mr Johnstone of Lanarkshire, who wrote directly to both the Minister of Information and the Secretary of State for Scotland to condemn 'such unwarranted Hitlerite action' as banning the importation of the sect's publications.[149] 'No political propaganda has ever appeared on the pages of these publications', argued one Group Leader in a letter to the MP for Dumbarton Burghs. The complainant, E. E. Durwood, added that banning the magazines strengthened believers' hopes that the Creator would soon 'establish a Righteous Government on this earth'.[150] Copies of publications seized by the SHD included images of Churchill and the Pope, and claims of papal interference in world politics.[151] This provocative text and imagery, arguably, was the very definition of political propaganda. Beyond this, Scottish authorities seem to have taken no further action against the group, and the Britain-wide ban on importing its literature was lifted in February 1945.

---

[144] Ibid., 'Letter from Munro to Calder, SHD', 13 October 1942.
[145] Ibid., 'Letter from DC to Stewart', 4 September 1942.
[146] Ibid., 'Letter from Munro to Calder, SHD', 13 October 1942.
[147] Ibid., 'Security Executive, Jehovah's Witnesses: Note by the Director-General of the Postal and Censorship Department', 27 October 1943.
[148] Ibid.; 'Security Executive Meeting', 14 February 1945.
[149] Ibid., 'Letter from Jas. Johnstone to Brendan Bracken', 12 December 1942.
[150] Ibid., 'Letter from E. E. Durwood to Kirkwood', 2 February 1943.
[151] Ibid., tracts included 'Universal war near', 'Conspiracy against democracy', and 'Who shall rule the world?'

'A considerable fifth column'? The IRA in Scotland

In contrast to the Jehovah's Witnesses, subversion by the IRA was considered a considerable threat to the war effort. During 1939 the IRA had carried out a volatile campaign of 'violent outrages' across Britain, demanding the government withdraw all institutions and representatives from Ireland.[152] Home Office records show IRA members were accused of planning to cause damage at 'vital points' across Britain, such as to power plants or cables, and several members were arrested for possessing stores of illegal explosives.[153] That year, the IRA also carried out attacks at Coventry, London, Blackpool and Liverpool, causing destruction, injury and death.[154] The group's methods of choice included bombs, throwing acid, starting fires and explosives. Driven by fears of further Irish militancy and of a possible German invasion via neutral Ireland, Whitehall stationed troop divisions in Ulster, and requested Irish citizens to voluntarily assist with the war effort.[155] After German raids on Belfast, 'Irish neutrality was effectively pro-British', wrote Angus Calder.[156] In contrast, Sonya Rose termed Irish–British relations 'ambivalent at best'.[157]

In Scotland, the situation was more strained, and suspicions of Irish militancy lingered throughout the war. As discussed in the Prologue, immigration ties between Ireland and Scotland were strong and many of the significant population of Glasgow's Irish Catholic immigrants supported Irish Home Rule.[158] Further, the Kirk's campaign against 'the Irish menace' had heightened hostilities towards migrants and increased beliefs in Irish criminality.[159] As a result, Scottish authorities regularly monitored Irish agitation in Scotland, particularly in the Glasgow region, and were wary of any activity that could be construed as potential IRA sabotage.[160]

In the days before the Second World War, intelligence revealed that 'substantial dumps' of explosive material – gelignite – and possibly arms were unaccounted for, some potentially hidden in Scotland by the IRA.[161] By January 1940, the SHD confessed there was still 'good reason' to believe some of the stolen explosives remained in IRA hands,

---

[152] Calder, *Myth of the Blitz*, 65.
[153] NRS, HH55/658, Irish Republican Army (IRA): sabotage and disturbances (hereafter Sabotage), 'Letter from Home Office', 25 January 1939.
[154] Calder, *Myth of the Blitz*, 65.
[155] Ibid., 66
[156] Ibid.
[157] Rose, *Which People's War?*, 219.
[158] Fry, *Patronage and Principle*, 148; Devine, *Scottish Nation*, 312.
[159] Devine, *Scottish Nation*, 499; Gallagher, *Glasgow: The Uneasy Peace*, 5.
[160] See NRS, HH55/62–75, Irish disturbances, 1920–28; HH55/76, Irish Republican movement, 1929; HH55/77, Irish Republican Army, 1939; HH55/465, Threatened Glasgow disturbance by Sinn Feiners and Orangemen, 1920–22; HH55/655–60, IRA: Sabotage, 1939–55; and HH55/7, PWD: Daily Reports, Glasgow, 1939–40.
[161] NRS, HH55/658, IRA: Sabotage, 'Scottish Office Circular 3656', 31 August 1939.

hidden somewhere in Scotland.[162] Chief constables were reminded to be vigilant in searching for clues as to the whereabouts of the hidden cache. Thoughts that illegal explosives or arms could be in the hands of militant Irish was a concerning possibility. While wartime evidence of such action appeared slim, authorities remained anxious that Irish saboteurs could gain access to explosives stores, such as those kept at quarries or collieries.[163] During 1942, these fears appeared to be confirmed, when a small group of Irish coal miners were caught with explosives in rural Perthshire. Fortunately for the authorities, it turned out the cache was for salmon fishing. Some of the men were sentenced to fourteen days' imprisonment for the illegal possession of explosives, one was placed on probation and another escaped conviction, perhaps shown clemency as a result of having both hands blown off during the poaching expedition.[164] A subsequent investigation could not determine where the men had obtained their store of explosives.

In evidence of the heightened concerns in Scotland, customs, immigration and port officials, as well as chief constables, were also urged to be on the lookout for IRA members attempting to enter Scotland illegally.[165] At that time, illegal entry included 'disembarking elsewhere than at an approved port' or attempted entry by any person named under the Prevention of Violence Act 1939.[166] Special attention was paid to Irish coal boats docking in Ayrshire during 1939 and 1940, in case subversive individuals or goods intended for sabotage were slipped into Scotland.[167] During 1942, Irish seasonal agricultural labourers who frequently travelled between Éire and Wigtownshire for work were also closely monitored for connections to subversive groups.[168] Nothing unusual appears to have been observed, as SHD files on the IRA contain no details of matters arising from either operation.[169]

Nonetheless, a lack of evidence did not stop accusations of Irish 'fifth column' activity. According to Calder, the term 'fifth column' originated during the Spanish Civil War, and referred to an invisible column of soldiers, working from within society to destabilise it.[170] In Britain, the term was often applied to communists, aliens and anyone viewed as pro-German,

---

[162] Ibid., 'SHD Circular 3834', 19 January 1941.
[163] Ibid., 'Letter to Mitchell', 31 August 1940.
[164] NRS, HH55/660, Irish Republicans Sabotage, 'Safe-guarding of explosives', 7 May 1942, 29 June 1942.
[165] NRS, HH55/658, IRA: Sabotage, 'Home Office Direction', 31 October 1939.
[166] Ibid.
[167] Ibid., 'Letter from Chief Constable of Ayrshire to SHD', 21 December 1939, 5 January 1940.
[168] Ibid., 'Wigtownshire Constabulary: return of workers from Eire, March–October 1942', 23 October 1942.
[169] See NRS, HH55/656, 658, 659 and 660 relating to IRA sabotage, disturbances and police actions during the Second World War.
[170] Calder, *Myth of the Blitz*, 111.

but was also used to criticise those perceived to be undermining the war effort. In late 1940, Walter McPhail, managing editor of the *Edinburgh Evening News*, expressed his concern that it was not only communists who were agitating in the shipyards on the Clyde, but also the Irish. McPhail noted that he was worried about the 'enormous Irish element' in the area, believing the Irish to be 'on the make' and 'certain to constitute a considerable Fifth Column'.[171] Intelligence operatives at the SHD also observed that while many Scottish industrial disputes were 'inspired or encouraged by' communists, some were provoked by Irish groups sympathetic to the communist cause.[172]

Alongside historical anti-Irish sentiment in Scotland, this issue was exacerbated by Ireland's neutrality during the war years, along with leader Éamon de Valera's decision to allow Germany to set up a legation in Dublin.[173] In further evidence of this sensitivity about Ireland and its links to Germany, two Dundee lads were arrested in mid-1941 for making two attempts to phone Dublin to reach the German legation. It turned out they were trying to settle an argument over telephone censorship, rather than make contact with Nazi leadership, but nonetheless the youths were sent to prison for three months each.[174]

Similar concerns about an Irish threat were expressed by members of the public, such as Mrs Mary Rennie from Kirkcudbrightshire. Mrs Rennie wrote to Joseph Westwood, the Under-Secretary of State for Scotland, bringing to his attention a potential security risk in her county. She noted that in this, 'probably the most vulnerable part of the whole of the coast of Scotland', there were 600 Irish Catholic labourers working at two nearby explosive works and in the event of an invasion, she wrote, 'they might prove rather a handful to keep in order'.[175] The letter made its way into the hands of the chief constable of Kirkcudbright, who referred the matter to the SHD, adding that some of the Irish labourers had been heard to boast of IRA allegiance.[176] This story serves to remind us that subversion in Scotland during the Second World War was not always tangible; often a *perceived* threat of sedition caused as much concern as concrete actions. Perhaps these anxieties were a result of the Kirk's sustained interwar campaign against alleged Irish criminality and deviance.

[171] IAC, 'Letter from Redpath to Peake', 19 November 1940.
[172] IAC, 'Scotland: Communists and Scottish industrial workers', 2 December 1940, 1.
[173] Calder, *Myth of the Blitz*, 66. See also Clair Wills, *That Neutral Island: A Cultural History of Ireland during the Second World War* (Cambridge, MA: Belknap Press, 2007); Brian Girvin, *The Emergency: neutral Ireland 1939–45* (London: Macmillan, 2006); Eunan O'Halpin, *Spying on Ireland: British intelligence and Irish neutrality during the Second World War* (Oxford: Oxford University Press, 2008); Geoffrey Roberts, 'Three narratives of neutrality: historians and Ireland's war', in Brian Girvin and Geoffrey Roberts (eds), *Ireland and the Second World War: Politics, society and remembrance* (Dublin: Four Courts Press, 2000), 165–79.
[174] 'Tried to phone Nazis in Dublin "to settle a bet"', *The Scotsman*, 25 June 1941, 3.
[175] NRS, HH55/656, IRA: Sabotage, 'Letter from Rennie to Westwood', 24 May 1940.
[176] Ibid., 'Letter from Kirkcudbright Constabulary to SHD', 10 June 1940.

Discontent and Subversion 119

Authorities battled to corral the many subversive elements in Scottish society during the Second World War. Threats of sedition, as this chapter has explained, came in many forms, ranging from the active and destabilising presence of communist agitators to the relatively unquantified risk of the IRA. Whether the subversion was perceived or actual, intelligence officials took this very seriously. All such activity was considered a threat to Scotland's war effort, and presented a solid challenge to official narratives encouraging national community and good citizenship. Moreover, any actions which affected production output could directly affect frontline success, and it is easy to see why this prospect concerned authorities. Whether via the constabulary, SHD, MoI, the Ministry of Home Security or M-O, authorities in Scotland and Whitehall closely watched this volatile situation which had grown to fever pitch during winter 1940 and spring 1941, concentrated around the Clyde.

Simmering subversion

Throughout the period from winter 1940 to spring 1941, Scottish morale, stability and commitment to the war effort seemed to teeter on a knife edge. While some aspects of the situation were not particular to Scotland, such as the threat from the IRA and anti-war lobbyists, others were built on a foundation of local, historic tension, such as the war between worker and management, in uncharted territory after a shift in the balance of power. At the peak of subversive activity in Scotland, in March 1941, MoI commissioned an investigation into morale in Glasgow. The resulting report laid bare the extent of the situation there. The 'lack of close identification with "the English war" is clearly a dangerous tension', wrote M-O investigators. Observing that Glaswegians exhibited little interest in the war, they added that this was in line with 'largely unconscious Scottish thinking about unity and loyalty'.[177] 'Locals talk about the South and London as if they are in another war or another country', investigators noted, adding '[t]here is a big physical distance, there is a bigger psychological distance'.[178] This report, starkly detailing a drop in war commitment in Glasgow and wider Clydeside, must have alarmed authorities at MoI who were already operating with heightened concern as a result of strike action and communist agitation.

Surprisingly, though, after this point CP agitation and industrial discontent tailed off. But why did the two biggest threats to the Scottish war effort reduce after spring 1941? One explanation for the reduction in subversive activity can be linked to the changing fortunes of the CP during early to mid-1941. Beginning with the banning of the CP publication the *Daily Worker* in January 1941, officials in Whitehall and MoI increased

[177] M-O, FR600, 'Preliminary report on morale in Clydeside', 7 March 1941, 2.
[178] Ibid.

their efforts to combat the agitations of the Party. As discussed earlier, this included the special 'Industrial Campaign to Counter Communism in Scotland', which intensified throughout 1941 to combat CP agitation in Scottish workplaces. Moreover, the German invasion of the Soviet Union in August 1941 further reduced the ability of communist agitators to play upon the theme of an unjust imperialist war.[179]

An even more significant impact on Scottish discontent and subversion came via the Luftwaffe. Less than one week after M-O's damning report on Clydeside morale, the industrial areas around Glasgow and Clydeside were heavily bombed.[180] Over two nights of destruction, from 13 to 15 March 1941, nearly 1,200 people were killed, almost all houses in the town of Clydebank were damaged and industrial premises were severely affected, such as the Singer Manufacturing Company in Clydebank and the Royal Ordnance Factory in Dalmuir.[181] In addition, night-shift industrial workers were especially vulnerable, and at Yarrow and Company shipyard in Scotstoun an air raid shelter received a direct hit from a parachute mine, killing forty-seven of eighty employees sheltering there.[182]

While authorities worried about post-raid insurrection, they were surprised to observe that the Blitz seemed to have the opposite effect. In the days immediately following the destructive raids, thousands of Clydeside workers 'made a magnificent answer to enemy terrorism' by returning to their jobs.[183] By 19 March, four days after the end of the air attack, many large industrial firms in Clydeside were at 100 per cent production. Even at Yarrow's shipyard, the scene of terrible human devastation, production was assessed at 50 per cent, though it was acknowledged production 'will be interfered with for some time'.[184] By 25 March officials at the Scottish Office recorded that 79 per cent of men were back working at the largest of Clydebank's shipyards, owned by John Brown and Co.[185] 'The Clyde has never been quieter and more determined about anything than it is just now about finishing with Hitler', observed McNicoll in April 1941.[186] In Edinburgh, where subversive activity was much lower than the Clyde, though still present, the chief constable noted '[i]t may be truthfully said

---

[179] Calder, *Myth of the Blitz*, 85.
[180] 'Long fierce attack on Clydeside town', *Glasgow Herald*, 15 March 1941, 6; 'Clydeside carries on: morale unshaken by brutal attack', *The Scotsman*, 18 March 1941, 3; 'Thursday's heavy raid: indiscriminate bombing over wide area', *Glasgow Herald*, 15 March 1941, 5; 'Clydeside goes on: scarred but not scared', *The Scotsman*, 25 March 1941, 4.
[181] MacPhail, *Clydebank Blitz*, 22–3, 66.
[182] Glasgow City Archives (GCA), D-CD 1, Air raid casualties: 1941, 'Letter from Yarrow and Co. re. casualties'.
[183] 'Home front: editorial notes', *SMT Magazine*, April 1941, 11.
[184] GCA, D-CD 1, Air raid casualties: 1941, 'Report to District War Room at 18.00 hours', 15 March 1941, 'Situation report as at 18.00 hours', 19 March 1941.
[185] GCA, D-CD 1, Air raid casualties: 1941, 'Situation report as at 18.00 hours', 19 March 1941.
[186] IAC, 1940–42, 'IAC: Report on smaller meetings', 24 April 1941.

that for the time at least, pacifist and subversive propaganda have ceased to exist. Those who were once most active in it are now whooping most wildly for unrelenting war.'[187] By January 1942, the *précis* of chief constables' reports concluded '[p]acifism seems on the whole to have gone to ground and its voice has been silenced by an almost universal clamour for war'.[188] While the Blitz may have quelled anti-war sentiment and subversive activity, Angus Calder claimed the bombardment had benefits across Scottish society. It created 'a new feeling of partnership with blitzed English cities', he noted, allowing Scots to integrate into the UK 'people's war'.[189] This claim of partnership and integration will be interrogated in Chapter Four.

While subversion and discontent in Scotland diminished after the peak in Spring 1941, such activity was by no means eliminated. Industrial unrest continued to simmer in Scotland throughout the remainder of the war, particularly in the mining industry. Strikes were especially frequent at collieries in Fife and Lanarkshire, though were not restricted to these counties. Absenteeism at coal pits also was another factor affecting industrial production, and another way the war effort was subverted.[190] From late 1943 compulsion was used to fill labour shortages in coal mines (see Figure 3.3), though many compelled workers were also prone to absenteeism and resentment towards colliery owners.[191]

Figures from the mining industry allow us to gauge some of the impact on war production caused by industrial discontent and slacking. An analysis of chief constables' reports from January 1941 to February 1945 reveals regular strike action across Scotland.[192] These reports also showed that in each month examined, thousands of tons of coal remained in the ground at Scottish collieries as a result of workplace idleness, disputes and strike action.[193] In 1943 Lord Traprain, the Regional Fuel Controller for Scotland, noted weekly output from Scottish coalfields was at 482,100 tons in the month of June.[194] This was down by about 14 per cent on 1939

---

[187] NRS, HH55/29, PWD – IR, fortnight to 15 August 1941: City of Edinburgh.
[188] NRS, HH55/32, PWD – IR, fortnight to 2 January 1942: *précis* report.
[189] Calder, *Myth of the Blitz*, 130.
[190] 'Scottish news: absenteeism at pits', *Glasgow Herald*, 12 July 1943, 5.
[191] Calder, *People's War*, 438–9.
[192] See NRS, HH55/7–41, PWD – IR.
[193] Coal tonnage 'lost', calculated from a selection of PWD reports: HH55/26, fortnight to 17 January 1941 and fortnight to 31 January 1941; HH55/27, fortnight to 28 March 1941; HH55/28, fortnight to 6 June 1941 and fortnight to 20 June 1941; HH55/32, fortnight to 16 January 1942 and fortnight to 2 February 1942; HH55/34, four weeks to 9 October 1942; HH55/35, four weeks to 4 December 1942; HH55/36, four weeks to 29 January 1943 and four weeks to 23 April 1943; HH55/37, four weeks to 18 June 1943 and four weeks to 16 July 1943; HH55/38, four weeks to 3 December 1943; HH55/41, four weeks to 26 January 1945 and 4 weeks to 23 February 1945.
[194] 'Scotland's declining coal output: "war boredom" among miners principal cause', *Glasgow Herald*, 10 July 1943, 2.

Figure 3.3 Photograph of D. McLintoch and four other young men (one of them Albert Murchison) just after their Bevin Boy training in 1943, taken at Muircockhall colliery. (Source: National Mining Museum Scotland. 2008.0058.)

figures and 6 per cent on 1942's figures. Lord Traprain warned coal shortages were a certainty, but added that there were collieries in Scotland where there had been no falling off in production 'because men and officials had been imbued with a real sense of war urgency'. He noted '[i]f that sense of urgency could be spread throughout the industry, many other collieries would increase their output'.[195]

In July 1944 the Ministry of Fuel and Power issued a White Paper on mining disputes across Britain. 'The widespread mining disputes in the first quarter of this year resulted in 2,032,900 tons of coal being

[195] Ibid.

lost to the nation, 1,564,100 man-shifts being also lost. This is by far the biggest loss suffered since at least 1938', the report writers noted.[196] While the greatest losses of output occurred in mines in south Wales and Monmouthshire, Scottish production output also suffered. During the first quarter of the year, 458,820 tons of coal had been lost and, of this amount, 'Lanarkshire was responsible for fully half', stated the White Paper.[197] In the following months and into 1945 coal shortages were recorded across Scotland, and much hardship was suffered during one of the coldest winters on record. 'The recent disclosures by the Ministry of Fuel and Power as to reduced output and increasing absenteeism causes much embittered comment', noted Edinburgh's chief constable in February 1945.[198] The disruption to coal output figures in Scotland demonstrates the ways in which Scotland's war effort was undermined by subversive activities and industrial unrest. The true impact of these activities, though, is difficult to gauge.

The case of the shipyard apprentices, described at the beginning of this chapter, encapsulates the complexity of Scottish wartime discontent and subversion. Most of the apprentices were seeking a fairer wage, yet the strike action by 11,000 of them surely affected wartime ship production on the Clyde. Industrial discontent and subversive activity during this time of national crisis proved a destabilising influence on the home front, and caused worry for authorities anxious to promote national unity and community. While Geoffrey Field concluded that industrial experiences superseded nationality, creating a distinct British working-class identity, Alison Chand argued that 'lived facets of existence in a particular locality' were more influential in shaping identity than shared commonalities with workers elsewhere in Britain.[199] As Sonya Rose wrote, nationhood is an imagined concept of identity and shared commonality.[200] Evidence presented in this chapter has demonstrated that strikers and subversive groups in Scotland were focused on their own goals and generally did not conceive of themselves as part of a greater, British national community.

Despite similarities of experience with other workers across Britain, in Clydeside cultural distinctiveness infused wartime experiences and shaped expressions of dissent and discontent. In the case of the Clyde, home to a 'very distinct and uniquely radical political culture', archival sources reveal the role history and local identity played in wartime unrest and subversion.[201] This local culture also led authorities to develop special committees and campaigns precisely to deal with the problem

[196] 'Strikes lose over 2,000,000 tons of coal', Glasgow Herald, 10 July 1944, 2.
[197] Ibid.
[198] NRS, HH55/41, PWD – IR, four weeks to 23 February 1945: City of Edinburgh.
[199] Field, Blood, Sweat, and Toil, 80; Chand, *Masculinities on Clydeside*, 61–2, 65.
[200] Rose, *Which People's War?*, 11.
[201] Chand, *Masculinities on Clydeside*, 58.

of the west of Scotland and to respond to the perceived threat of the IRA. While Scotland's history of industrial unrest, discontent, radicalism, rising nationalism and anti-Irish sentiment shaped local responses to war, it also shaped official responses to dissent and discontent in Scotland.

CHAPTER FOUR

'We Here in Scotland Can Also Take It': Morale in Scotland, 1939–45

At nine o'clock on the evening of 13 March 1941, air raid sirens began to sound across central Scotland. For the next nine hours, over 200 German bomber planes streaked across Scottish skies to attack Glasgow city and the industrial regions surrounding the River Clyde. Around 272 tons of high-explosive bombs and 1,650 incendiaries were dropped on the targets below.[1] At dawn, the skies finally quietened and a shocked public emerged from beds and armchairs, tenement closes, stairwell refuges and public airraid shelters to take stock of the damage. Fires still raged in Clydebank's industrial premises, many windows across Glasgow were broken and tenement properties were extensively damaged. Essential services were disrupted and all arterial roads into the Clydeside region were blocked by unexploded bombs and debris.[2] The following night, the Luftwaffe again visited Scotland and spent nine more hours bombarding the already devastated Clydeside area. Over the next week, secret civil defence reports gave initial estimates of the damage: more than 12,500 residents were homeless, over 1,600 had suffered injuries and an estimated 600 were believed to have been killed.[3] The death toll was later substantially revised to 1,100.[4]

What effect did this devastating attack, one of the heaviest in wartime Britain, have on Scottish morale? Angus Calder noted that assessors at Home Intelligence considered the raids on Scotland had created '[a] new feeling of partnership with the English blitzed cities'.[5] Calder's evidence was predominantly gathered from London-based intelligence agencies, but do Scottish primary sources support this statement? Were there other events or factors that influenced morale in Scotland? This chapter begins by considering the nebulous nature of morale. It will also discuss the groups concerned with monitoring and maintaining home front morale during the Second World War. The bulk of the chapter, though, assesses Scottish wartime morale, considering the influence of home front and frontline

---

[1] MacPhail, *Clydebank Blitz*, 17, 107.
[2] GCA, D-CD 1, Air raid casualties: 1941, 'Interim situation report Glasgow area at 09.30 hours, 14 March 1941'.
[3] GCA, D-CD 1, Air raid casualties: 1941, 'EMDISCOM, Situation report at 18.00 hours, 22 March 1941'.
[4] Hansard, HC Deb, 1 April 1941, vol. 370 cols 856–7.
[5] Calder, *Myth of the Blitz*, 130.

events, and the impact of factors of particular relevance to Scotland. The chapter finishes with a reflection on Scottish morale and identity.

Few previous studies have attempted to assess morale in Britain's constituent nations.[6] This chapter will address that oversight by examining morale in Scotland, using novel archival evidence to explore the ways this material both contests and supports the existing historiographical research. This chapter also interrogates the influence of local factors and national identity on wartime morale, and considers how the notion of Blitz spirit was portrayed in wartime Scotland. While utilising the well-known sources of HI and M-O, the research contained in this chapter also employs a range of Scottish source material. This includes reports on public morale and behaviour, authored by the Scottish constabulary. It also examines diaries and questionnaire responses written by those resident in Scotland during the Second World War, and themes and language contained in Parliamentary debates, public statements and speeches, and articles in newspapers and magazines.

The history of morale

Public morale was an important aspect of the British home front during the Second World War. With civilians preparing for an expected German invasion, fishermen shot in their boats and families bombed in their homes by Luftwaffe planes, the home front was no longer as removed from war as it had been in earlier conflicts.[7] In a range of stirring speeches during 1940, Prime Minister Winston Churchill told the public their blood, toil, tears and sweat would bring victory; that the people of Britain would never surrender to the enemy, and would fight on the beaches and in fields and streets, if required; and he also implored the public to stand up to the enemy and bear themselves in a way that would be remembered as Britain's finest hour.[8] At this time, public mindset was viewed as central to Britain's victory.

Many within the government and intelligence communities considered that civilian morale was key to winning the war. This included the Minister of Information, Duff Cooper, who believed public willpower was even more important than military strength and, therefore, that home front morale

---

[6] Welsh morale is briefly touched upon in Johnes, *Wales since 1939*; Johnes, 'Welshness, Welsh soldiers and the Second World War', in Ugolini and Pattinson, *Fighting for Britain?*, 65–88. For Scottish morale see Calder, *People's War*; Ch. 6 of Rose, *Which People's War?*; Mackay, *Half the Battle*, 29, 57.

[7] While civilians had been targeted in earlier conflicts, advances in aircraft technology saw this escalate during the Second World War.

[8] Sir Winston Churchill, speeches 'Blood, toil, tears and sweat', 13 May 1940, 'Be ye men of valour', 19 May 1940, 'We shall fight on the beaches', 4 June 1940, 'Their finest hour', 18 June 1940, accessed via https://www.winstonchurchill.org/resources/speeches/.

was integral to British victory.⁹ To this end, values such as united national community, positive spirits and good citizenship were publicly promoted.¹⁰ Contemporary rhetoric also centred on public confidence in Britain's ultimate victory, and good humour and stoicism in the face of difficulty – popularly known as 'Blitz spirit' or 'the spirit of Dunkirk'.¹¹ Official messages designed to raise morale proliferated, and the public was portrayed as 'self-sacrificing, relentlessly cheerful, and inherently tolerant people'.¹² Moreover, the majority of wartime publications were 'coloured by the need to present good face and "high morale" in the eyes of the enemy'.¹³

Attempts to convince the world of Britain's high morale and exemplary stoicism were so successful that this popular narrative became the history of the war, argued Tom Harrisson, founder of social history organisation Mass-Observation.¹⁴ In the official war history, social scientist Richard Titmuss echoed the popular narrative, maintaining that communities were cohesive and united, with rich and poor shoulder-to-shoulder, and that bombing raids helped bring a new resolve to those who felt downtrodden after the Depression.¹⁵ In the following years, historical works echoed these themes of unity, stoicism and support for the war.¹⁶ These ideas also became embedded in British cultural memory of the Second World War.¹⁷ Sonya Rose noted that images of nationhood as 'a unitary collective identity' are common in British civic and popular culture, evidence that community and collective identification are powerful concepts.¹⁸ Lucy Noakes and Juliette Pattinson have also observed the proliferation of wartime themes in modern British popular culture. They noted that the spirit of Dunkirk and Blitz spirit are frequently invoked, 'in order to convey a sense of community spirit, tenacity and stoicism in trying circumstances'.¹⁹ The trope of Blitz spirit has been further popularised by politicians seeking to unite the British public as it navigates a turbulent twenty-first century.²⁰

---

⁹ Henry Irving, 'The Ministry of Information on the British Home Front', in Simon Eliot and Marc Wiggam (eds), *Allied Communication to the Public During the Second World War: National and Transnational Networks* (London: Bloomsbury, 2019), 26.
¹⁰ Mackay, *Half the Battle*, 1; Rose, *Which People's War?*, 85.
¹¹ Calder, *People's War*, 18; Titmuss, *Social Policy*, 346–7.
¹² Rose, *Which People's War?*, 2.
¹³ Harrisson, *Living Through the Blitz*, 324.
¹⁴ Ibid., 324.
¹⁵ Titmuss, *Social Policy*, 346–7.
¹⁶ Henry Pelling, *Britain and the Second World War* (Glasgow: Collins, 1970), 100; Constantine FitzGibbon, *The Blitz* (London: Macdonald, 1970), 114, 118, 268; Taylor, *English History*, 503, 600.
¹⁷ Calder, *People's War*, 18; Noakes and Pattinson, 'Keep calm', 2, 10.
¹⁸ Rose, *Which People's War?*, 7, 11.
¹⁹ Noakes and Pattinson, 'Keep calm', 10.
²⁰ See D. Kelsey, *Media, Myth and Terrorism: a discourse-mythological analysis of the 'Blitz spirit' in British newspaper responses to the July 7th Bombings* (London: Palgrave Macmillan, 2015); Duncan Bell, 'Mythscapes: memory, mythology, and national identity', *The British Journal of Sociology* 54, no. 1 (2003): 63–81; Noakes and Pattinson, 'Keep calm'; Henry Irving, 'What

While the public story of the war years is imbued with unity, stoicism and good cheer, within the historiography wartime morale has been a hotly debated topic. Historians have queried the ways morale can be defined and measured, and contested the overall state of public morale on the British home front.[21] Angus Calder came to a mixed conclusion: yes, the people 'surged forward to fight their own war' and shared experiences of fear and danger created a new unity, but there was also evidence of increasing urban poverty, as well as anti-Semitism and juvenile delinquency.[22] He also reported evidence of public panic, post-raid depression and anti-social behaviour, and concluded these were signs of wavering morale.[23] Harrisson stated that the average experience of war was one of apathy and distress, and that the Blitz had no great effect on British morale – positive or negative. Further, he claimed, the established historiographical view of the civilian experience was so different from his own findings that it spoke of a 'massive, largely unconscious cover-up of the more disagreeable facts'.[24] He argued the British had been brainwashed, and this was 'a form of intellectual pollution: but pollution by perfume'.[25]

In the past twenty-five years, a wave of histories have investigated home front morale further. Rose's comprehensive study also uncovered community tensions over equality of sacrifice and notions of the 'national we', while Penny Summerfield's work on female munitions workers revealed evidence of apathy and cynicism towards the war.[26] Moreover, Harold Smith stated that stories of high morale and public unity obscured increases in crime and delinquency, while other studies uncovered fear, class conflict and hostility towards those deemed community 'outsiders'.[27] While further illuminating home front experiences, these studies also challenge historic ideas about high wartime morale and British national unity. Each discovery of home front conflict and distress also impugns the notion that high public morale was integral to British victory.

---

the Second World War tells us about enlisting "the people" in the fight against COVID-19', Leeds Beckett University, School of Cultural Studies and Humanities blog, 29 March 2020.

[21] See Mackay, *Half the Battle*, 249; Malcolm Smith, *Britain and 1940: History, Myth and Popular Memory* (London: Routledge, 2000); Philip Ziegler, *London at War: 1939–1945* (New York: Alfred A. Knopf, 1995); Todman, *Into Battle*; Todman, *A New World*.

[22] Calder, *People's War*, 18, 41–4, 166, 174, 178, 225–6.

[23] Calder, *Myth of the Blitz*, 120.

[24] Harrisson, *Living Through the Blitz*, 11, 13, 335–6.

[25] Ibid.

[26] Rose, *Which Peoples War?*; Summerfield, *Women's Wartime Lives*.

[27] Smith, *Britain in the Second World War*, 2, 3, 9; Clive Ponting, *1940: Myth and Reality* (London: Hamish Hamilton, 1990); E. Smithies, *Crime in Wartime: A Social History of Crime in World War Two* (London: Allen and Unwin, 1982); Lucy Noakes, *Dying for the Nation: Death, Grief, and Bereavement in Second World War Britain* (Manchester: Manchester University Press, 2020); Amy Bell, 'Landscapes of fear: wartime London, 1939–1945', *Journal of British Studies* 48, no. 1 (2009): 153–175; Paul Addison and Jeremy A. Crang, *The Spirit of the Blitz: Home Intelligence and British Morale, September 1940–June 1941* (Oxford: Oxford University Press, 2020); Smith, *Jim Crow*.

'The woolliest and most muddled concept of the war': defining morale

Early records of the concept of morale date to France in the early nineteenth century, when the term was used in a military context to refer to the discipline, conduct and spirit of a soldier. '*Le moral*', as it was known, essentially denoted the moral condition of a soldier, as opposed to his physique.[28] By the time of the First World War the term had transferred to Britain, had been anglicised to 'morale' and was starting to be used as a general descriptor of non-military conduct. At that stage, the term signified mood, will, sentiment or attitude.[29] This transition from military to civilian usage mirrored a key transformation in warfare, as the distinction between soldier and civilian became increasingly blurred. German Zeppelin raids on English cities during the First World War marked the first time the ordinary citizen was targeted during warfare, and developments in aerial bombing technology saw this tactic also used in conflicts in Iraq, Abyssinia and Spain during the 1930s.[30] By 1939, further advances in weaponry led the British authorities to conclude war would bring large-scale devastation of civilian life and property. Based on public behaviour after the Zeppelin raids and during the Spanish Civil War, authorities assumed wartime air raids would result in nervousness, panic and mass flight from affected areas.[31] In addition, authorities feared demoralised populations might revolt, as they had in both Germany and Russia at the end of the Great War.[32] These behaviours, concluded authorities, symbolised a lack of morale and would need careful monitoring in future conflicts.[33]

During the Second World War, public morale in Britain was measured by a variety of official bodies. This included MoI, its Home Intelligence division (HI), the semi-private organisation M-O, and the Scottish Constabulary. The public also volunteered information on their own morale, through keeping diaries or providing survey responses to M-O, and unknowingly through media such as the government's Postal and Telegraph Censorship Department, which monitored private communications. Amid all this monitoring of morale, however, the notion at its centre remained notoriously difficult to define. Historian Paul Addison, author of the renowned political history *The Road to 1945*, famously summarised morale as 'the woolliest and most muddled concept of the war'.[34] While HI did not provide an official definition of morale, its reports reveal a focus on factors that signified an absence of morale, or what we might conceive of as low morale.

---

[28] Daniel Ussishkin, *Morale, Modernity and British Social Imaginaries* (Oxford: Oxford University Press, 2017), 13, 14.
[29] Ibid., 14, 73.
[30] Mackay, *Half the Battle*, 19, 21. See also Grayzel, *At Home*.
[31] NRS, ED 24/1, War preparations 1935–8; Macnicol, 'The effect of the evacuation', 10.
[32] Mackay, *Half the Battle*, 19.
[33] NRS, ED 24/1, War preparations 1935–8.
[34] Addison, *Road to 1945*, 121.

Things such as rumour, and grumbles about official policies or wartime measures like rationing, were all considered cause for concern.[35]

In contrast, those at M-O considered morale to encompass public state of mind, optimism and commitment to the war effort.[36] Or, as the group summarised, '[m]orale is the amount of interest people take in the war, how worthwhile they feel it is'.[37] In a March 1941 report on morale in Glasgow, M-O investigators provided a more detailed definition of the concept:

> By morale, we mean primarily not only determination to carry on, but also determination to carry on with the utmost energy, a determination based on realisation of the facts of life and with it a readiness for many minor and some major sacrifices, including, if necessary, the sacrifice of life itself. Good morale means hard and persistent work, means optimum production, maximum unity, reasonable awareness of the true situation, and absence of complacency and confidence which are not based on fact.[38]

At MoI, definitions varied with the individual. Duff Cooper, appointed by Churchill in May 1940, claimed public willpower was more important than military strength. As Henry Irving stated, Cooper's words 'betrayed a continued belief that the British people needed to be convinced to join the war effort'.[39] When Cooper was replaced by Brendan Bracken in July 1941, this definition changed. Bracken believed public morale would be stimulated not by being lectured, but by being provided with a steady flow of information and through targeted government campaigns, on such as recycling and salvage.[40] The most comprehensive definition of morale was that used by HI head Stephen Taylor. Taylor deemed morale to be 'ultimately measured not by what a person thinks or says, but by what he does and how he does it'.[41] Taylor further expanded his ideas, stating that morale was made up of two factors: material and mental. Material morale included security of food, work, leisure and safety. Mental factors relied on a series of beliefs: that victory was possible; in equality of sacrifice; that leaders acted with integrity and efficiency; and that war was necessary and just.[42] This was similar to M-O's definition, in which morale was a combination of belief and actions.

These contemporary definitions of morale reveal a more complex set of elements than those often contained within the historiography of British wartime morale. By reducing morale to two polarising camps – one

[35] Mackay, *Half the Battle*, 1.
[36] M-O, FR27, February 1940.
[37] Mackay, *Half the Battle*, 1.
[38] M-O, FR600, Morale in Glasgow, 7 March 1941, 2.
[39] Irving, 'Ministry of Information', 26.
[40] Ibid., 29–30.
[41] TNA, INF 1/292, 'Memo from S. Taylor', 1 October 1941.
[42] Ibid.

featuring crime, apathy or fear; and one in which the public display stoicism and spout cheerful comments in the aftermath of air raids – historians have lost some of the nuance of everyday morale during the Second World War. To address this gulf, Robert Mackay proposed British wartime morale could be better assessed by adopting the wartime definition, in which morale is considered to be an amalgamation of attitude and behaviour.[43] He also suggested the use of a matrix that assesses both 'feelings' and 'behaviour', and that in each of these morale can be 'high' or 'low'. For example, low morale might be expressed through feelings such as panic, apathy or pessimism, or through behaviours such as panic flight, blaming the authorities or strikes. In contrast, high morale would show in feelings of cheerfulness, belief in ultimate victory and commitment to the task in hand, or result in behaviours such as high productivity, volunteering and neighbourliness. This definition of morale as a composite of attitudes and behaviours is useful in the assessment of Scottish wartime morale, and will be applied throughout this chapter.

Morale and the home front

Conditions and events on the home front influenced Scottish morale. Fear of aerial attack was one aspect of home front life that resulted in feelings of anxiety. Three months after the fact, Kingussie schoolteacher Donald Morran could still recall the look of alarm on the faces of his class when an aeroplane had flown over their school in early October 1939, leaving them fearful of air attack.[44] Similarly, Edith Goldberg, a medical student in Edinburgh, remembered the cold shiver that ran down her back when she heard her first air-raid siren.[45] Eileen Offley also dreaded having to go into a Glasgow city basement shelter during an attack, and frequently fretted about what to do if at work during an air raid. 'I am awfully afraid of both darkness and being in a dense crowd', she confessed in July 1940.[46] Such feelings were not limited to Scotland, though. M-O respondents across Britain likewise admitted to feeling terror and apprehension, and dreaming about invasion. To this end, M-O concluded the outstanding feature during the months of the Battle of Britain was 'anticipation of almost immediate invasion'.[47]

Adding to this atmosphere of anxiety was the suppression of news. This strict censorship of events, particularly in the early months of the war, also affected the morale of Scots. Foundry clerk Alistair Goddard complained about sanitised news reports, stating 'there is nothing more

---

[43] Mackay, *Half the Battle*, 3.
[44] M-O, Dir. January 1940, R2019 (Kingussie).
[45] Ibid., R2374 (Edinburgh).
[46] M-O, Diarist 5390 (Glasgow), July 1940.
[47] M-O, FR773, Comparative report: May 1940–May 1941, 5 July 1941, 1.

mentally indigestible than cooked news'.[48] William Stewart, an iron merchant in Glasgow, agreed everyone he knew was 'fed up' with censorship. 'Chamberlain is blacking out our minds as well as our streets', he quipped.[49] Authorities worried that, without censorship, sensitive information could be leaked or defeatist talk spread.[50] In MoI's 'Careless Talk Costs Lives' campaign of summer 1940, the British public was encouraged to stamp out rumour and identify potential fifth columnists.[51] One Glasgow man whose son had been involved in the Dunkirk evacuation openly told neighbours of his belief that Britain would soon be defeated. Afterwards, a number of the neighbours reported the man to the police, and he was subsequently arrested.[52] This defeatist talk, along with the grumbles about censorship, were signs of low morale, according to Mackay's definitions.

These were not the only signs of low morale sparked by life on the home front. At times, Scots also felt pessimism about the future, depression and anxiety. Duncan Watson, a physics student from Aberdeen, expressed resentment that war had spoiled his university education and future career path. Registering as a conscientious objector meant he was sentenced to farm labour while fellow students, many of them also holding pacifist sympathies, were allowed to continue and finish their university courses. 'I still think this was very unfair', Duncan commented, adding, 'I felt very resentful . . . I envied the others, I was annoyed, and very depressed'.[53] Mr Watson felt that, when the war ended, he would be left without prospects, and this left him feeling frustrated and helpless.[54] Another Scot who was concerned about the future was Paul Bruce from Glasgow. He felt the war was making him pessimistic and cynical, and he wished he could live in a 'less great time', adding impassionedly 'I would rather die than live the rest of my life in a Nazi world'.[55] Fellow Glaswegian Gloria Tunner confessed her feelings of despair over the changes brought by war and what it meant for civilisation: 'I am getting to feel old, tired, and cynical', she noted in January 1942, adding, 'I do not find life worth living on the terms on which it is at present offered to me'.[56]

For those who faced the prospect of military service, wartime life brought additional uncertainty. Chemistry student James Wilkinson, who was waiting to hear if he would be allowed to continue his study or would

---

[48] M-O, Dir. January 1940, R2290 (Renfrew).

[49] Ibid., R2121 (Glasgow).

[50] David Welch, 'Forward: communications and propaganda and the Second World War', in Eliot and Wiggam, *Allied Communication*, viii; Jo Fox, 'Careless talk: tensions within British domestic propaganda during the Second World War', *Journal of British Studies* 51, no. 4 (2012), 937.

[51] Fox, 'Careless talk', 936–7.

[52] M-O, Diarist 5390 (Glasgow), 25 July 1940.

[53] M-O, Dir. June 1944, R3361 (Aberdeen).

[54] M-O, Dir. January 1943, R3361 (Aberdeen).

[55] M-O, Dir. January 1942, R2707 (Glasgow).

[56] Ibid., R2910 (Glasgow).

be called up to serve in the military, described feeling 'caught in a net', 'ill at ease' and that his future was 'in the melting pot'.[57] After waiting nine agonising months, James was granted an exception to complete his Honours qualification in chemistry. 'I am somewhat mentally stunned', he observed upon hearing the news.[58] In comparison, 18-year-old Graeme King, a government employee, was wracked with fear at the thought of being called up to serve. 'Shall try to obtain exemption, if I can find courage to go before tribunal . . . Shall try to avoid line of least resistance – join up when called – until have exhausted every loophole', he wrote to M-O in January 1940. The young man's dread of service was evident as he added '[p]erhaps might suicide but religious teachings too strong, as is fear of hereafter'.[59]

While war left some Scots feeling anxious, others chose to detach from the war effort. During July 1940, as nightly bombs rained down on London, Eileen Offley observed the lack of war interest in her friends and family. In the Hyndland suburb of north-west Glasgow, she decided to erect additional protection on her tenement windows. 'I would so like to apply net to our windows at home', she noted, 'but Mother is adamant . . . she will not have the war brought into the house'.[60] A fellow member of the Soroptimists, a group dedicated to the education of women, similarly commented to Eileen 'I have no interest in the war whatever. People say to me "If you were in London you would be interested in the war", and probably I should, but then I am not in London.'[61] Eileen reflected on this, admitting that an interesting project at work 'takes up my thoughts so much that I have little thinking power left for the war. If these pages should happen to survive and one day come to be read by someone who would of course know the *dénouement* of the mighty drama in which we are actors to-day, perhaps that someone will wonder at such indifference as to the future.'[62] The distance from the London Blitz, and even more from the battlefields of North Africa, may also have fostered feelings of disengagement from the war.

These attitudes, according to the definitions of morale discussed earlier, should have concerned intelligence officials. It appears, though, that M-O was the only agency to observe the growing complacency in Scotland. After conducting an in-depth investigation into morale in Glasgow and Clydeside during February and March 1941, the organisation noticed a 'lack of close identification with the English war' and felt this was 'a dangerous tension'.[63] The organisation's fifty-nine-page report concluded while 'the

---

[57] M-O, Diarist 5232 (Aberdeen), 25, 28 September 1939, 7, 19 October 1939.
[58] Ibid., 25 June 1940.
[59] M-O, Dir. January 1940, R2386 (Glasgow).
[60] M-O, Diarist 5390 (Glasgow), 9 July 1940.
[61] Ibid., 10 March 1941.
[62] Ibid., 3 March 1941.
[63] M-O, TC600: Morale in Glasgow, 'Preliminary report on morale in Clydeside', 7 March 1941, 2.

very large majority' of the population were confident in ultimate victory, in general the morale of Glasgow was 'not nearly so good as in other similar places, including even places like Liverpool and Birmingham'.[64] The authors felt the most striking distinctions between Glasgow and elsewhere were 'the apparent lack of interest in much of what is going on in the war', grumbling about wartime inconveniences and a lack of identification with 'the English war'. 'Locals talk about the South and London as if they are in another war or another country', the report noted, adding '[t]here is a big physical distance, there is a bigger psychological distance'.[65]

While morale revealed itself though mindset, it also showed in behaviour. Investigators felt Glaswegians were vastly underprepared for potential air raids, with only 30 per cent expecting heavy raids and a mere one in ten having made any plans to weather those raids.[66] It was strange, the report noted, that so many locals felt Glasgow to be somehow impervious to air attack, and there existed a feeling of extreme distance from the war.[67] Glaswegians were 'living in a fool's paradise' when it came to air raids, investigators stated, and the public were complacent towards the risk of violent attack.[68] In the event of a bombing raid, this could prove 'shattering', the authors predicted. Six days later, these findings would be put to the test.

'Scarred but not scared': Scotland's Blitz

From 13 to 15 March 1941, the Luftwaffe poured down hundreds of high-explosive bombs and incendiaries upon the docks, industries and tenements surrounding the River Clyde. After raids described as 'fierce', 'sustained', 'indiscriminate' and 'greatly destructive', there were 'many harrowing sights'.[69] Demolition, rescue and medical squads spent days digging through masonry to extract victims, many of whom were trapped or suffering severe crush injuries.[70] According to records of the Department of Health for Scotland, across Glasgow and Clydebank the raids damaged more than 14,000 homes, including nearly 2,500 that were totally destroyed or damaged beyond repair.[71] While in Glasgow the bulk of the population were 'disposed to stay put', in Clydebank the situation was vastly different, with 25,000 – half of the town's population – having departed by the

---

[64] Ibid., 1.
[65] Ibid., 2.
[66] Ibid. 4.
[67] Ibid., 7.
[68] Ibid., 3, 7.
[69] 'Long fierce attack on Clydeside town', *Glasgow Herald*, 15 March 1941, 6; 'Clydeside carries on: morale unshaken by brutal attack', *The Scotsman*, 18 March 1941, 3; 'Thursday's heavy raid: indiscriminate bombing over wide area', *Glasgow Herald*, 15 March 1941, 5; 'Clydeside goes on: scarred but not scared', *The Scotsman*, 25 March 1941, 4.
[70] 'Clydeside's second raid: intense anti-aircraft barrage', *The Scotsman*, 17 March 1941, 4.
[71] NRS, HH36/5, Clydeside: Reports on raids of 5/6 and 6/7 May 1941, 'Report on Clydebank', April 1941.

evening of 16 March. Many were transported to evacuation centres in surrounding districts but authorities also noted concerns that a large number had evacuated 'voluntarily and aimlessly'.[72] This was an example of panic flight, a marker of low morale that civil defence authorities had been anxious to avoid.

In total, casualties were worse than first predicted. More than 3,400 people received injuries in the raids, 800 of whom were hospitalised, and more than 50 civil defence volunteers and members of the auxiliary fire services had been killed.[73] Adding to the difficulty of the situation, the Nazi choice of high-explosive bombs and parachute mines meant buildings were devastated and resulting injuries severe.

> It is very difficult to estimate the number of fatal casualties as very few bodies are recoverable [noted officials on 15 March]. The bombing . . . has been almost exclusively by parachute mines or other very heavy H.E. bomb which leaves little or nothing of the smaller-type houses . . . In the case of blocks of tenements or larger-type houses, they leave only a large heap of rubble.[74]

Due to the nature of the raids, recovery and identification of victims was difficult, with many left unrecognisable and only capable of being described by body part or identifying markers such as items of clothing or contents of pockets. Mortuary forms were noticeably scant in detail, with little information to go by for identification: 'housewives' hands, probably due to a lot of work', 'small girl in lemon dress', 'one sock one shoe', 'portion of trunk'.[75] The most common causes of death were falling masonry or bomb blast.

While it could reasonably be assumed that this brutal and destructive attack would devastate local morale, official sources from the immediate period suggested this did not occur. In an initial civil defence report on the raids dated 14 March 1941, amidst reports of death and destruction, authorities noted '[s]ituation in Glasgow very well in hand and morale excellent', in Clydebank 'morale good' and in Dumbarton 'everywhere morale is good'.[76] By Sunday 16 March, a home security report stated, 'the morale of the people is described as magnificent in the circumstances. There are no signs of panic or complaint. A tour of the rest centres today

---

[72] NRS, ED31/528, Letter from SED, 17 March 1941; NRS, MD13, Home Security intelligence summaries: Rep. 16 March 1941.
[73] GCA, D-CD 1, Air raid casualties: 1941; TNA, Western District: analysis of the effects of air raids from June 1940 to Sept 1941, 'Report on the functioning of the casualty services, 13–15 March 1941', 17 March 1941, 4; NRS, MD13, Home Security intelligence summaries: Rep. 18 March 1941; GCA, D-TC 8/10/41, Corporation of Glasgow – ARP casualty services, 18 August 1941.
[74] NRS, MD13, Home Security intelligence summaries: Rep. 15 March 1941.
[75] GCA, D-CD 1, Air raid casualties: 1941.
[76] NRS, MD13/5, Home Security War Room reports, 14 March 1941.

revealed only 2 cases of hysteria and one grouser – A labourer who wished to go back to Ireland.'[77] Similarly, the chief constable of Dunbartonshire, the centre of the attacks from 13 to 15 March, reported:

> During the intensive air raids . . . the conduct of the public in my area was everywhere admirable. In spite of the heavy strain both on the moral and physical resources of the population there was no sign of panic in any form and all behaved with splendid courage. I had the opportunity of personal contact with the people in rest centres, etc., who had lost their homes and found their morale excellent.[78]

To these officials, it seems morale was a catch-all term encompassing state of mind, behaviour and acceptance of hardship without complaint.

Reports were positive, headlines were sensational and press articles were full of gushing praise for the stoic Scots who had shown courage under fire. Post-raid headlines announced: '[a]ttack as severe as any on other areas in Britain', 'Clydeside carries on: morale unshaken by brutal attack', 'Clydeside goes on: scarred but not scared', '"Battle of Clydebank" will rival Waterloo'.[79] The rhetoric contained in them was similar. 'Amazing demonstrations of coolness and courage were witnessed', read one report, while another impassionedly hailed the civil defence workers who were 'unflinching in the greatest peril from the falling bombs', undertaking rescues 'with an utter disregard of their danger from fire and in the midst of a shower of incendiaries'.[80] Other articles told of 'ordinary hard-working families [rising] to epic heights of endurance'; Clydeside workers 'making a magnificent answer to enemy terrorism' by returning to work the day after the attack; and tradesmen reopening their shops with customary good humour – '[b]usiness as usual: to hell with Hitler', the reported sentiment (see Figure 4.1).[81] 'Tell the world that we here in Scotland can also take it,' smiled a post-Blitz evacuee, according to the *Glasgow Herald*.[82]

Officials also promoted this theme of courage under fire. Secretary of State Tom Johnston declared '[t]he morale of the people is magnificent, and the manner in which the women and children have accepted the catastrophe which has fallen upon them is beyond praise. I have not

---

[77] Ibid., 16 March 1941.

[78] NRS, HH55/27, PWD – IR, 28 March 1941: Dunbartonshire.

[79] 'Clydeside under fire', *Glasgow Herald*, 15 March 1941, 4; 'Clydeside carries on: morale unshaken by brutal attack', *The Scotsman*, 18 March 1941, 3; 'Clydeside goes on: scarred but not scared', *The Scotsman*, 25 March 1941, 4; 'Mr H. Morrison: "Battle of Clydebank" will rival Waterloo', *The Scotsman*, 12 April 1941, 7.

[80] 'Thursday's heavy raid: indiscriminate bombing over wide area', *Glasgow Herald*, 15 March 1941, 5; 'ARP workers' heroism: chief magistrate's tribute', *Glasgow Herald*, 15 March 1941, 6.

[81] 'Failure of terror tactics', *Glasgow Herald*, 15 March 1941, 6; 'Home front', *SMT Magazine*, April 1941, 11.

[82] 'Thursday's heavy raid: indiscriminate bombing over wide area', *Glasgow Herald*, 15 March 1941, 5.

Figure 4.1 'Clydeside carries on': photographs from the March 1941 Blitz. (Source: *SMT Magazine*, April 1941. National Library Scotland.)

seen tears since I came here, although there is every justification for them. The women and the children are behaving like the soldiers in the frontline which they really are.'[83] Civil Defence Commissioner for the

---

[83] 'Clydeside's second raid: intense anti-aircraft barrage', *The Scotsman*, 17 March 1941, 4.

district of Western Scotland, Sir Stephen Bilsland, echoed these sentiments. 'Clydeside has stood up magnificently to the brutal Nazi attack', he announced on 17 March, praising the 'undaunted courage' of men, women and children.[84] This theme was repeated by Lord Rosebery, the Civil Defence Regional Commissioner for Scotland, who stated '[t]here is no denying the thoroughness of Hitler's attempt to knock out the Clyde, not by destroying the works, but by smashing the morale of the workers . . . he has failed miserably . . . the morale of Clydeside is even higher than it was before the raids started'.[85] Furthermore, Home Secretary Herbert Morrison termed the event 'the Battle of Clydebank', likened it to the Battle of Waterloo and added his admiration for the 'grit and courage' of Clydesiders. Morrison also played on tropes of Scottishness, stating that he believed the displayed courage was in accordance with 'the best traditions and the highest fighting instincts of the Scottish people'.[86]

This glowing language and themes of courage, lack of complaint or panic, and 'getting on' with life were repeatedly presented in public communications and by prominent officials in the weeks following the Blitz. But was this representative of the mood 'on the ground'? Low morale markers were present in the diary of Eileen Offley, writing after the Blitz. Based in Glasgow, she described her colleagues as 'overwrought', 'utterly exhausted', 'distressed' and suffering strained nerves in the week after the attack.[87] One of Eileen's workmates was particularly distraught after witnessing a neighbouring tenement suffer a direct hit from a bomb. The woman, Helen, had seen the bodies and dismembered limbs of neighbours, and arrived at work 'very nervous and low spirited'.[88] Five days later, Eileen commented in her diary 'Helen remains very depressed'.[89] Further, when retrospectively typing her diary entries on 22 March Elaine realised that rehashing the incident had 'strained me frightfully' and in the days that followed she felt she was 'travelling through a dark tunnel of fear', and confessed to suffering nightmares where '2 or 3 times each night I go through the awfullest blitzing and wake in alarm'.[90] Both of these women showed signs of anxiety and struggled to simply 'get on' with life.

For Nora Mitchel, a writer living in rural Carradale on the Firth of Clyde, the days following the Blitz were also fraught with tension. A friend's Glasgow-based son was missing after the raids, and Mrs Mitchel and some colleagues travelled to Glasgow to assist in the search. Six days after the bombing, the search-party returned from hunting through debris. Their hands were cut and faces 'grimed' with plaster, but they had recovered the

[84] Ibid.
[85] 'Clydeside carries on: morale unshaken by brutal attack', *The Scotsman*, 18 March 1941, 3.
[86] 'Mr H. Morrison: "Battle of Clydebank" will rival Waterloo', *The Scotsman*, 12 April 1941, 7.
[87] M-O, Diarist 5390 (Glasgow), 15, 16, 18, 21 March 1941.
[88] Ibid., 14 March 1941.
[89] Ibid., 19 March 1941.
[90] Ibid., 22, 24, 28 March 1941.

body of their friend.⁹¹ One of the search-party was distraught, a seaman whose ship had recently been torpedoed; he had spent hours adrift in the ocean waiting to be rescued. 'He would sooner that than what he had just done', Mrs Mitchel observed, as the toughened sailor wept over the loss of his friend.⁹² Another friend was later haunted by the memories of a ticking watch buried beneath the rubble, and the sight of his friend's hand sticking up through the debris as if he was asking for help. He took to drinking heavily to cope with the disturbing memories.⁹³ Again, these Scottish residents were deeply affected in the days and weeks after their Blitz experiences.

In sources examined for this chapter, there is some discrepancy between private revelations of fear and anxiety and the officially promoted message of stoicism and high morale. Those who kept diaries wrote of private conversations between friends and office colleagues, as we shall soon read, and they may have kept these sentiments quiet outside these trusted networks, perhaps out of fear of being labelled a defeatist or a 'jitterbug'. After all, the secretary to the Minister of Information had declared in 1940 that the armed forces must stand assured that behind them was a brave civilian frontline, 'not a frightened troupe of shiver-sisters and chatterbugs but a solid wall of national will power'.⁹⁴ This discrepancy between official and private sources was not exclusive to Scotland. In England, private sources also revealed shades of grey, though London morale was generally considered higher than other blitzed towns.⁹⁵ That expressions of low morale were more common in personal writings may explain why the historiography of the British home front has shifted as 'private' sources such as life writings become more widely available to researchers. In more recent years historians have moved away from the confident assertions of high morale so common in the early post-war years, and their studies reveal the shades of experience across the British home front.

Grumbles over the censorship of raid details were another sign of low morale in post-Blitz Scotland. In keeping with this censorial policy, newspaper reports initially referred to bombing that had occurred in 'a west of Scotland town', or that Nazi raiders had visited 'the central district of Scotland', and gave comments from the chief magistrate of 'one Clydeside town'.⁹⁶ Nowhere did reports mention Glasgow, and none approximated a death toll. Numerous industrial premises along the Clyde had been

---

⁹¹ M-O, Diarist 5378 (Campbeltown), 19–21 March 1941.
⁹² Ibid.
⁹³ Ibid., 22 March 1941.
⁹⁴ 'Hitler is not irresistible: need for maximum resistance', *Glasgow Herald*, 1 July 1940, 6.
⁹⁵ Calder, *Myth of the Blitz*, 143. See also Harrisson, *Living through the Blitz*, 285–7; Mackay, *Half the Battle*, 248–9; Bell, 'Landscapes of fear',160–61.
⁹⁶ 'Clydeside's second raid: intense anti-aircraft barrage', *The Scotsman*, 17 March 1941, 4; 'Heavy barrage for central Scotland raiders', *Glasgow Herald*, 15 March 1941, 5; 'Restoring normal life', *Glasgow Herald*, 17 March 1941, 5.

damaged in the raids, including shipbuilding yards and tweed and woollen factories. Further, a number of transport routes had been disrupted, and essential services such as telephone cables and gas and water mains had been damaged, and one major oil tank had 'very serious problems'.[97] From an operational perspective, it was considered crucial that this information not reach the enemy.

Behavioural indicators of low morale soon appeared. The public grew agitated and expressed uneasiness and distrust of officials over the censorship of raid particulars. More than forty-eight hours after the attacks finished, even locals were uncertain of the event specifics. Eileen Offley noted 'I feel lamentably ignorant of what has happened ... Three times to-day I have been told that "Clydebank was worse than Coventry", but no one can tell me in whose opinion.'[98] Details of the raid's location, the extent of damage and the likely death toll were all suppressed, and not even locals could be certain of the true scale of destruction. This official policy was in place for several reasons: to stop the Germans gaining the satisfaction of knowing how much damage was caused, to avoid public panic or fear and so Luftwaffe pilots would not know whether they had located the correct targets in the dark of the black-out.

In the days and weeks afterwards, primary sources revealed the extent to which the event had affected Scottish morale. The suppression of raid details caused alarm for those who had friends and relations in the west of Scotland and were desperate for information on their loved ones.[99] The lack of information also led to the spread of rumours. On 17 March Eileen Offley noted a friend had claimed 'someone she knows from ARP Casualty Services' said 250 had been killed, while a news broadcast on 19 March announced there had been 500 deaths in Clydebank. Eileen's manager 'knew for a fact' that 5,000 had been killed in Clydebank alone, and one colleague announced she would write to Churchill 'demanding that Glasgow should be told the truth about the blitz [as] the figures are ridiculous!'[100] This was representative of sentiment across the wider region. The SHD noted 'adverse comment is made on the official figures given as casualties in the Clydeside raid as it is felt that the numbers were under-estimated. Scepticism, to which this has given rise, may tend to shake public confidence in official communiques on other subjects.'[101] Chief constables across Scotland also reported the lack of specific information had 'caused unnecessary anxiety in many homes', rumour was said to be 'rife' and 'alarming accounts of the damage and casualties have been doing the rounds'.[102]

[97] GCA, D-TC 8/10/99, Messages and reports, Raids, 1941, 'Interim situation report, 14 March 1941', 'Notes on the position of services after air raid on 13/14 March 1941'.
[98] M-O, Diarist 5390 (Glasgow), 17 March 1941.
[99] M-O, Diarist 5378 (Campbeltown), 18 March 1941.
[100] M-O, Diarist 5390 (Glasgow), 17, 19, 20 March 1941.
[101] NRS, HH55/27, PWD – IR, 28 March 1941: *précis*.
[102] Ibid., Berwickshire, City of Edinburgh, City of Dundee.

In a further sign of low morale, the public began to openly condemn official handling of the event. 'Quite a number of people allege that the authorities have withheld the truth from the public and condemn them for doing so', reported the chief constable of Aberdeen. The public in Lanarkshire were showing 'resentment' towards censorship, residents of Ayrshire were 'uneasy' and, in Kirkcaldy, '[t]he details published about other towns that have suffered as a result of enemy action are now being accepted with some dubiety'. 'One had a feeling that there was something being concealed', commented the chief constable of Ayr burgh. In addition, the constabulary in Dumbarton observed: '[p]eople who had seen for themselves what had happened strongly resented the attempt to minimise the real facts. Clydesiders, like the people of other heavily bombed areas[,] feel that "they can take it" and that a frank announcement of the true facts would not have broken their morale.' The chief constable of Glasgow agreed, noting '[p]eople are saying, and rightly so, that if by personal experience they know that an official announcement is untrue, what reliance can there be on similar statements of incidents elsewhere. It shakes the very foundations of public confidence.'[103] In this case, strict censorship resulted in the spread of rumours and anxiety.

Additional upset arose over the burial of unidentified raid victims. Little opportunity was given for public mourning, with no memorial service held and unidentified victims buried in a ceremony without public notification. On 18 March the first unidentified victims were buried in a common grave at Dalnottar Cemetery, near Clydebank. Due to the strict censorship around the event, attendees were restricted and included mainly government and civil defence representatives, military, police and 'a few casual observers'.[104] The sixty-seven bodies were wrapped in shrouds and covered with Union Jack flags, transported to the open pit by policemen acting as pallbearers.[105] Two months later, the misery of these burials was thrown into relief when two Luftwaffe pilots were killed in Stirlingshire during air raids over the Port Glasgow and Greenock area. The area's chief constable reported that 'much bitter criticism' was expressed, especially by Clydeside evacuees, about the 'pomp and ceremony' at the funeral of the two Nazi airmen.[106] In contrast to the Clydeside victims, the Germans were buried in coffins, in individual graves, and afforded an RAF ceremony which included draping the coffins with swastikas, to the 'great indignation' of local priests.[107]

---

[103] NRS, HH55/27, PWD – IR, 28 March 1941: Aberdeen city, Kirkcaldy, Lanarkshire, Ayrshire, Ayr burgh, Dumbarton burgh, City of Glasgow.

[104] 'Mass funeral: many children among the unidentified victims', *The Scotsman*, 18 March 1941, 3; MacPhail, *The Clydebank Blitz*, 77.

[105] 'Funeral of victims: buried in common grave', *Glasgow Herald*, 18 March 1941, 5.

[106] NRS, HH55/28, PWD – IR, 23 May 1941: Stirling.

[107] Ibid; 'Plane crashes: German airmen', *Welcome to Lennoxtown*, https://www.welcometolennoxtown.co.uk/plane_crashes.htm (accessed 16 July 2020).

The growing furore over casualty figures and raid details represented a serious problem on the morale front. 'Rumours, complaints, and grumbles about official policies' were considered by MoI to be indicators of low morale.[108] In what appeared to be a capitulation to public agitation, authorities agreed to address the situation of casualties across Glasgow and Clydeside. Herbert Morrison, the Home Secretary, revealed in the House of Commons that 1,100 had been killed and 1,000 seriously injured in the raids on Scotland between 13 and 15 March. 'I have departed from the usual practice not to give figures in relation to particular incidents', Morrison stated, adding 'I have done so because I felt it important to correct any impression that the original announcements were deliberately designed to minimise the seriousness of the damage sustained . . . this is entirely an exceptional case and I hope that it will not be regarded as a precedent.'[109] With the official release of information, newspapers were also permitted to publish specific raid details. For the first time, print publications could confirm that raid damage was severe in Glasgow and Clydebank, and were even able to name the worst-hit suburbs: Maryhill, Partick, Linthouse and Plantation.[110] It was also confirmed that many schools, churches and public buildings had suffered damage, and 'a large number' of dwelling houses had experienced blast damage, had windows blown in or been demolished entirely by the force of the high-explosives.[111] This extraordinary release of sensitive information went against official censorship policies and betrays the grave concerns authorities held over the state of Scottish morale.

Morale and the frontline

While the home front influenced Scottish morale, so too did events on the fighting front. A series of German successes in north Africa and the Balkans during early 1941 constituted a grave threat to Allied success. In the House of Commons on 9 April Prime Minister Churchill frankly spoke of the 'darkening of the scene' in Libya, admitting valuable airfields had passed into the hands of the Germans, who now held a position of greater strength than the Allies.[112] Churchill gravely detailed the 'remorseless', 'formidable' and 'treacherous' German invasion of the Balkans, warning the public that reverses must be expected and they must be ready 'to take the rough with the smooth'.[113] Those in Scotland responded to this news with 'surprise', 'anxiety' and 'considerable disappointment'. Moreover, Scottish intelligence reports noted the German occupation of Salonika 'came as a shock

[108] Mackay, *Half the Battle*, 1.
[109] Hansard, HC Deb, 1 April 1941, vol. 370 cols 856–7.
[110] 'Clydeside "Blitz": Glasgow and Clydebank bore brunt of attack', *The Scotsman*, 11 April 1941, 4.
[111] Ibid.
[112] NRS, HH55/27, PWD – IR, 11 April 1941: *précis*.
[113] Hansard, HC Deb, 9 April 1941, vol. 370 cols 1587–90.

to most people'. While the prime minister's speech was considered to be 'a much more sobering account than might have been expected', Scots reportedly appreciated its frankness and ability to bring much needed perspective.[114] In the burgh of Coatbridge, the speech was said to have made a deep impression on the public, 'many of whom are only now realizing that the way to victory may be paved by many set-backs'. At the same time, though, Churchill's speech served to reinforce public confidence. 'Public morale remains resolute', stated a report from Peeblesshire, and the chief constable of Dundee recorded a 'high standard of morale' in the city.[115]

In comparison to Scotland, English morale reports at this time were focused on home front events. In the first two weeks of April, there were heavy air raids on London, Birmingham, Portsmouth, Southampton and Plymouth. In addition, a very heavy Blitz on Coventry left a 'dreadful scene of desolation', and one on Bristol was described as 'savage and prolonged'.[116] Government officers assessed the public as being 'mentally unprepared' for the raids, and reactions were said to range from 'vague depression' to 'deep anxiety', clear markers of low morale.[117] Corresponding HI reports focused heavily on responses to the raids and made little comment on the public reactions to the frontline news or Churchill's speech.[118]

As the situation in the Balkans and North Africa deteriorated, Scottish morale faltered. On one hand, intelligence reports from mid-1941 repeatedly stated that morale was high. Chief constables noted public confidence in ultimate victory was unshaken, many believed the war would be won 'no matter how bitter the struggle' and the majority 'now recognise that the fight may be long and severe, but their morale remains high'.[119] Concurrently, intelligence reports also noted markers of low morale. Scots reacted to the war news with 'disquiet', 'great concern', 'a good deal of depression', and from Dundee it was reported that nothing had occurred 'to fully restore the optimism of the ordinary man in the street, so severely shaken as a result of the reverses'.[120] In diary entries, one Scot confessed feeling 'very gloomy' about the prospects in Greece, worrying that the situation would become another Dunkirk, while another commented that the situation was 'as barren as ever'.[121] After the evacuation of the bulk of the Allied forces from Crete, official reports revealed a further drop in morale. In East Lothian public morale appeared 'lower than it has been for a considerable time', and in Ayrshire the withdrawal resulted in 'quite

---

[114] NRS, HH55/27, PWD – IR, 11 April 1941: *précis*.
[115] Ibid., City of Dundee, Perthshire and Kinross-shire, Banffshire, City of Glasgow, Coatbridge, Peeblesshire.
[116] TNA, INF 1/292, HI Reps. 27: 9 April 1941, 28: 16 April 1941.
[117] Ibid., HI Rep. 29: 23 April 1941.
[118] Ibid., HI Reps. 27: 9 April 1941, 28: 16 April 1941, 29: 23 April 1941.
[119] NRS, HH55/29, PWD – IR, 9 May 1941: Midlothian, Aberdeen city, Lanarkshire.
[120] Ibid., Midlothian, City of Edinburgh, City of Dundee, Ayr burgh.
[121] M-O, Diarist 5374 (Campbeltown), 25 and 29 April 1941.

an acute depression'.[122] The chief constable of the city of Edinburgh wrote that public confidence, 'already shaken by events in North Africa and our recent heavy defeat in Greece', had received 'a further shattering blow' after the reverses in Crete. He added '[i]t would not be correct to say that people are becoming defeatist in their outlook, but undoubtedly the unreasoning confidence with which many regarded the ultimate issue has been shattered, and all are made to realise the magnitude of the task before us'.[123] These feelings of depression, worry and lack of confidence all indicate wavering morale.

Throughout 1942, public reflections on the war displayed similar signs of low morale. Many appeared to show little interest in frontline events, and displayed signs of war fatigue. A Mrs Urquhart from Edinburgh felt 1942 would be 'a year of nasty shocks ... and that we'll all get very depressed', while Glaswegian Liam Smith confessed he was 'less and less interested in the war as time goes on', and felt in himself a 'lack of interest almost amounting to apathy to the future'.[124] Likewise, housewife Gloria Tunner admitted her acquaintances 'hardly ever' discussed the war, while the general feeling was 'a more or less dogged keeping on hoping for the best, but only half expecting it'.[125] Katherine Booth's poultry club members in Colinton 'were wondering if this dreadful war would be over by the next general meeting', while Kilbirnie steelworker Ron Muir noted morale had 'never been so poor since the war started'.[126] English reports from this time were similarly bleak, noting 'public spirits have not been high for some time past'.[127] Further, intelligence officials observed feelings of disappointment, a decline in confidence, a lack of enthusiasm and a widespread desire to criticise the government.[128] Furthermore, in February 1942 London morale reached its lowest point of the war. Intelligence officers linked this directly to frontline reverses.[129] Under Mackay's schema, such apathy, depression and war fatigue could all be considered signs of low morale.

While frontline reverses were linked to despondency on the home front, at times rapid rises in morale mirrored key advances on the frontline. In late 1942, news of the Battle of El Alamein began to filter through to the home front, and Scottish constabulary reports noted a significant improvement in local morale. While some celebrations may have been tempered by the high casualties suffered by the 51st Highland Division, in many parts of Scotland 'great excitement and enthusiasm' was observed, morale was

[122] NRS, HH55/28, PWD – IR, 6 June 1941: East Lothian, Ayrshire.
[123] Ibid., City of Edinburgh.
[124] M-O, Dir. January 1942, R2911 (Edinburgh), R2824 (Glasgow).
[125] M-O, Dir. September 1942, R2910 (Glasgow).
[126] Ibid., R2973 (Edinburgh), R1393 (Kilbirnie).
[127] TNA, INF 1/292, HI Rep. 72: 18 February 1942.
[128] Ibid.
[129] M-O, FR2332, War Morale Chart, 6 February 1946.

'much uplifted', and in Inverness the chief constable noted the action in North Africa had a 'wonderful effect upon the morale of the public after what seems to have been a long spell of apparent inaction'.[130] Positive spirits during 1943 similarly reflected frontline success. After German defeats at Stalingrad and in North Africa during February and May 1943, English intelligence reports stated public spirits were 'on a high level', while most Scottish constabulary reports supported this assessment.[131] During June, Scots felt the military actions were 'most stimulating', had given 'the greatest pleasure' and had 'an uplifting effect on the morale of the public'. Chief constables' reports noted 'greatly improved', 'high', 'very high' or 'excellent' morale, as well as the presence of optimism, confidence, buoyancy and inspiration.[132] Among the public, Nora Mitchel in Campbeltown believed most locals thought the war would be over within a year. 'They seem to feel we are sure to win now', she remarked.[133] Other Scots observed optimism and confidence among their fellow countrymen, and a general expectation that an Allied landing in Europe would come 'soon'.[134] 'Everything is going our way [and] nothing can stop us', noted Ron Muir.[135] As Moira Devlin recounted from Glasgow, 'local businessmen were on Monday betting 6–1 that it would be an unconditional surrender of Germany by x-mas'.[136] The odds, though, were not in their favour, and another year ticked over with no end of war in sight.

While 1942's despondency was linked to a lack of breakthrough on the frontline, the despair which appeared during 1944 and 1945 was in response to a war that seemed never-ending. Frontline successes in Europe appeared to have little influence on public morale; instead, Scots showed strain, anxiety and frustration at war's continuation. 'I am feeling a good deal of general strain and tiredness and jumpiness', admitted Nora Mitchel in January 1944.[137] Conscientious objector Duncan Watson noted '[f]eeling of frustration at present tolerable, and directed towards the probable length of the war yet to come'.[138] 'I confess I am getting a little tired of talk about the Second Front', complained Elspeth Musgrove. She continued

---

[130] Glyn Harper, *The Battle for North Africa: El Alamein and the Turning Point for World War II* (Bloomington: Indiana University Press, 2017), 245; TNA, INF 1/292, HI Rep. 111: 19 November 1942; NRS, HH55/35, PWD – IR, 4 December 1942: Peeblesshire, Kirkcaldy, Inverness.

[131] TNA, INF 1/292, HI Rep. 142: 24 June 1943.

[132] NRS, HH55/37, PWD – IR, 18 June 1943: Midlothian, East Lothian, Perthshire and Kinross-shire, City of Edinburgh, West Lothian, Peeblesshire, Kirkcaldy, Banffshire, Moray and Nairn, Orkney, Zetland, Inverness-shire, Ross and Cromarty, Ayr burgh, Clackmannanshire, Dumfries, Greenock, Paisley.

[133] Ibid., R1534 (Campbeltown).

[134] Ibid., R1682 (Edinburgh/Berwickshire), R2490 (Tayvallich), R3324 (Edinburgh).

[135] M-O, Dir. June 1943, R1393 (Kilbirnie).

[136] Ibid., R3247 (Glasgow).

[137] M-O, Dir. January 1944, R1534 (Campbeltown).

[138] Ibid., R3361 (Aberdeen).

'[w]e seem to have been chatting about it for so long and nothing has been happening ... at the moment I am tired of the subject'.[139]

Official intelligence reports reveal some nuance, showing that Scots faced 1944 with confidence but this was tempered with tension and the reality that war would not be over by the end of the year. In January 1944, chief constables' reports repeatedly linked high public morale to events on the frontline. For example, the chief constable of Arbroath stated '[w]ith the continuance of good news from all fronts the public are in a pleasing and expectant frame of mind'. Similarly from Edinburgh, '[m]orale is excellent and hope is high. Great events are imminent and the public contemplate only one outcome, speedy victory.'[140] Six months later, after the successful Normandy landings, officials were ready to admit there had been elements of concern. 'The arrival of the long awaited "D" Day has relieved a feeling of tension and strain which had been constant for some time', a report from Zetland stated. Likewise, the chief constable of Edinburgh admitted the public had been strained, in 'anxious suspense', and 'on tenter hooks' waiting for the landings to happen, and there had arisen a fear 'that our invasion of the Continent would be the signal for concentrated air bombardment'.[141] By December, there was 'solid but sober satisfaction' at the frontline position, and people had 'long been reconciled to the slow grinding advance in Italy'. This had brought home to many people 'the sternness of the fight which still is before us', while others were 'tired of the war and weary for the end'.[142] This weariness and strain demonstrates that morale was often linked to action or inaction – on the frontline.

Low morale markers can also be observed in early 1945, when several Scots confessed their fatigue at entering their sixth consecutive January under the restrictions and pressures of war. 'I think we are all pretty gloomy', noted a housewife in Argyll, while a Kilbirnie steelworker stated 'as far as the war is concerned I would say everybody is fed up with it and wishes it were finished'.[143] Others noted the prevalence of fatigue and stress-related illness. 'We are all easily tired, very easily depressed and liable to get minor complaints', noted Mrs Mitchel. She added 'I would say morale was fairly bad'.[144] Scots in Edinburgh, Renfrewshire and Ayrshire had observed a rise in gastric ulcers, 'nervous strain' and stomach disorders, while solicitor Robert Moore noted he had developed duodenal ulcers as a result of worry, and his wife had been ill in bed with 'sheer exhaustion'.[145] In testament to

---

[139] Ibid., R3545 (Glasgow).
[140] NRS, HH55/39, PWD – IR, 28 January 1944: Arbroath, City of Edinburgh.
[141] NRS, HH55/40, PWD – IR, 16 June 1944: Zetland, City of Edinburgh.
[142] NRS, HH55/41, PWD – IR, 1 December 1944: City of Edinburgh, Ayr burgh.
[143] M-O, Dir. January 1945, R1534 (Campbeltown), R1393 (Kilbirnie).
[144] M-O, Dir. January and February 1945, R1534 (Campbeltown).
[145] M-O, Dir. January 1945, R1682 (Edinburgh/Berwickshire), R2741 (Saltcoats), R2568 (Kilmacolm).

the enigmatic nature of morale, there also existed, simultaneously, feelings of high morale such as an underlying current of determination and belief in ultimate victory. 'The circle in which I move has kept a pretty steady morale for the whole five years', reported Edinburgh solicitor Elaine Meier in 1945.[146] Mr Forster, a chemist in Ayrshire, noted that 'without any doubt ... everyone is quite confident that the war will be won'. He added 'naturally, the morale as far as that sort of thing is concerned is excellent'.[147] Renfrewshire man Robert Moore felt morale was so good 'all would carry on apparently indefinitely' until Germany had agreed to a peace settlement.[148] Thankfully for many, this prediction was short-lived and the war in Europe over within three months.

'Rather an anti-climax': VE Day celebrations

To further complicate the assessment of Scottish morale, archival sources reveal a range of responses to Germany's surrender. In some cases, this momentous event aroused little emotion in Scots on the home front. While the German surrender was a historic moment, officially ending nearly six years of war in Europe, William Craig of Dundee noted only feelings of relief, adding '[d]id not expect to feel much more than that'.[149] For some, the moment had been anticipated for so long as to drain all feelings of novelty. Elspeth Musgrove from Glasgow commented 'the actual announcement of victory was rather an anticlimax after all the crushing defeats and the obviousness of the inevitability of victory for the last few months'.[150] One soldier felt similarly. Upon hearing the peace declaration he was 'not particularly excited ... as the news didn't come as a very great surprise'.[151] Adding to the lacklustre mood of some was the knowledge that the war in the Far East 'still has to be finished'.[152] Similar thoughts were prominent in the mind of Elspeth Musgrove, whose husband was away fighting with the services in Burma. 'I don't feel that I want to whoop with joy at the end of *part* of the war', she commented.[153] These selected sources reveal that for some in Scotland there was little sense of jubilation.

Sources also reveal that feelings of celebration were tempered by memories of loss and sacrifice. Mr Renner, frustrated by Churchill's announcement of peace and accompanying prayers, argued it seemed 'rather hypocritical thanking God for deliverance when it was due to the suffering

---

[146] M-O, Dir. February 1945, R1569 (Edinburgh).
[147] Ibid., R2741 (Saltcoats).
[148] Ibid., R2568 (Kilmacolm).
[149] M-O, Dir. May 1945, R3655 (Dundee).
[150] Ibid., R3545 (Glasgow).
[151] Ibid., R1682 (Edinburgh/Middlesex).
[152] M-O, Dir. February 1945, R1569 (Edinburgh).
[153] M-O, Dir. May 1945, R3545 (Glasgow).

and sacrifice of the ordinary people'.¹⁵⁴ On a rainy Victory in Europe (VE) Day, thoughts of sacrifice were also with Elspeth Musgrove's charwoman who, upon seeing rain on the windowpane, remarked '[t]his'll match some folks' tears, don't you think so? There must be some people feeling pretty sad today who have lost their men.' That evening, Elspeth felt similarly pensive, writing in her diary

> I could see nothing from my window but a little twinkle through the trees and a faint red glow in the sky – very different from the bright red glow on that cold March night when all Clydebank was ablaze and the smoky flames of the oil tanks leapt up in the moonlight. Thank God we'll never see that again and all the desolation that followed it.¹⁵⁵

For this Scot, and those around her, VE Day brought mixed feelings.

The nature of celebrations marking the end of war also reveal mixed markers of morale. After peace was declared on the evening of 7 May, and on VE Day itself, primary sources detailed a range of celebrations that took place across Scotland. Many Scots heard tooting, saw fireworks and bonfires, and heard shouting, singing and dancing in the streets.¹⁵⁶ Besides these rowdy celebrations, some in Scotland heralded war's end with much more muted celebrations. '[P]eople were thronging the streets, walking about quite quietly, but just anxious to be out and seeing what was doing.'¹⁵⁷ A similar phenomenon had been observed by M-O investigators in London after D-Day in June 1944. Observing 'little excitement' and 'discernible anxiety' among the crowds, M O investigators concluded the lack of response was '[p]erhaps, partly, because people had lived over the moment often in the past, expected things to be abnormal and in an undefined way different from any ordinary day'.¹⁵⁸

This lack of excitement over key events heralding the end of the Second World War is seldom noted in popular memory of the Second World War. Lucy Noakes has found an explanation for this in popular memory theory: '[r]epresentations in the public sphere limit or encourage the articulation of personal memories, whilst these dominant representations must have some resonance with the majority of those who experienced the war in order to gain dominance'.¹⁵⁹ In this theory, 'private' memories that conflict with dominant representations may be supressed or struggle to be heard. This may have meant the stories of those who did not carouse in Glasgow's George Square on 8 May 1945 may have been squeezed out

---

¹⁵⁴ Ibid., R1682 (Edinburgh/Middlesex).
¹⁵⁵ M-O, Dir. May 1945, R3545 (Glasgow).
¹⁵⁶ Ibid.
¹⁵⁷ Ibid.
¹⁵⁸ M-O, FR2115, 'We're moving', 14 June 1944, 4; Alan Malpass, *British Character and the Treatment of German Prisoners of War, 1939–1948* (Cham: Palgrave Macmillan, 2020), 75.
¹⁵⁹ Lucy Noakes, 'War on the web: the BBC People's War website and memories of fear in wartime in 21st century Britain', in Noakes and Pattinson, *British Cultural Memory*, 52.

by the more jubilant narrative told in widely read publications such as the *Glasgow Herald*.[160] Noakes concluded that '[t]he social taboo on expressing fear and panic in wartime shaped the many post-war representations of the Blitz in which the courage, cheerfulness and communal spirit that many did display under bombardment took centre stage'.[161]

In Scotland, the end of the war brought a moment of reflection, a chance for many to catch their breath and take stock of the previous six years. Mr McGuire in Glasgow observed that peace was 'rather an anti-climax. Having hoped and prayed as long for peace, now that it has finally come, life does not seem very different after all in these islands.'[162] It is unsurprising that emotions such as contemplation or mournfulness did not make newspaper headlines and have since faded out of public memory. After a restless night in bed contemplating the peace settlement, Eileen Offley felt 'a profound sense of relief, of happiness, and of general bewonderment that out of the terrific happenings in Europe, our home, our town, our nation had escaped'.[163] These introspective reflections on victory may be more representative of public feeling than the expressions of wild revelry contained in British cultural memory. However, these differing accounts may also reflect age and class variation amongst those who are represented in the selected archival sources.

Morale and 'Scottish concerns'

Besides the influences of home front conditions and events, or frontline action and stalemate, Scottish wartime morale was also affected by local concerns. One of the most important issues to cause unrest in Scotland was the sending of Scots girls to England for work. In December 1941 conscription of women began with those between 20 and 30 years of age called into the auxiliary services or to work in industry.[164] By the end of the war, this included women up to the age of 50. Under the Registration for Employment Order, the Minister of Labour obtained power to direct women into employment, such as to industrial plants where labour was in short supply.[165] In March 1942 Mr McCorquodale, the Joint Parliamentary Secretary to the Ministry of Labour, announced that labour shortages across Britain would require many more 'mobile women' – those without

---

[160] See, for example, Deborah Anderson, 'VE Day 75: jubilant scenes across Scotland as people rejoiced the Second World War was finally over', *The Herald*, 4 May 2020, https://www.heraldscotland.com/news/18424885.ve-day-75-jubilant-scenes-across-scotland-people-rejoiced-second-world-war-finally/ (accessed 3 February 2023).
[161] Noakes, 'War on the web', 56.
[162] M-O, Dir. August 1945, R3630 (Glasgow/Northwich).
[163] M-O, Diarist 5390 (Glasgow), 7 May 1945.
[164] Rose, *Which People's War?*, 109.
[165] Hansard, HC Deb, 05 March 1942, vol. 378 cols 820–21; Braybon and Summerfield, *Out of the Cage*, 159–63.

caring responsibilities at home – to be directed into employment. After all, McCorquodale stated, 'the country cannot afford to waste the energies of any single one of us, man or woman, if we are to make victory sure'.[166] He explained that Ministry officials had divided Britain into 'areas into which women must be imported, other areas which balance woman-power within themselves and other areas from which mobile women will be moved'.[167] It was under this scheme that many Scottish and Welsh women would be transported to the Midlands to undertake factory work.

While the Minister of Labour, Ernest Bevin, stressed how desperately workers were needed to meet war production targets, this did not necessarily mean the scheme was well received. The transfer of women was 'a considerable intervention into the realm of private life', and caused upset across both Scotland and Wales.[168] Moreover, an investigation by an MoI official in July 1942 revealed many Scottish mobile workers sent to the English Midlands were struggling to adapt to their new jobs or fit in with English colleagues. The investigator overheard Scots girls saying their lack of choice made them feel they 'might as well be under Hitler', and the girls were 'very much agin the order'.[169] Even so, the investigator admitted, it was a 'noisy and influential' minority that were most discontented over the move, including those displaying communist sympathies by wearing a hammer and sickle badge.[170] An investigation by a Scottish trade union delegation in 1943 similarly concluded many Scotswomen relocated to the Midlands felt isolated and unhappy, and those billeted in rural areas were slow to adjust to new diets and a slower pace of life.[171]

In Scotland, the issue was 'one of the most contentious' of the war and it had a noticeable effect on morale.[172] This was particularly so for Scots with strong nationalist views, who resented Scottish citizens being sent 'abroad' to work.[173] During 1942, when the operation was at its peak, up to 500 Scottish women were transferred to England each month. In August that year, a fiery debate rent the House of Commons, with numerous Scottish MPs expressing bitter frustration over the transfers and

---

[166] Hansard, HC Deb, 05 March 1942, vol. 378 col. 818.

[167] Ibid., col. 822.

[168] Summerfield, *Women's Wartime Lives*, 45; see also Johnes, *Wales since 1939*, 13–14; Reginald Coupland, *Welsh and Scottish Nationalism: A Study* (London: Collins, 1954), 339; Selina Todd, *Young Women, Work, and Family in England, 1918–1950* (Oxford: Oxford University Press, 2005), 131–3.

[169] TNA, INF 1/292/1, HI weekly reports, 'Appendix 1: Scotswomen go south to war work', 9 July 1942.

[170] Ibid.

[171] Scottish Trade Union Delegation to the Midlands, *Transfer of Scottish Girls: Report to Scottish Trades Union Congress General Council and the Organisation of Women Committee* (Glasgow: Scottish TUC, 1943), 15.

[172] Rose, *Which People's War?*, 224.

[173] Ibid., 224–5; Hansard, HC Deb, 05 March 1942, vol. 378 cols 896–7.

displaying 'a nationalistic possessiveness about "their" young women'.[174] MP for Dumbarton Burghs David Kirkwood, a supporter of Home Rule, demanded the Minister of Labour 'issue orders without delay to prevent this transfer of Scottish girls against their will, interfering with war production in Scotland, and to relieve the bitter feeling caused both to the girls and their parents'.[175] Likewise, a number of other MPs described receiving bags of letters from upset mothers and girls, and reported Scottish employers were 'simply wild' that their needs should be deemed less important than those of English firms.[176]

Beneath these concerns also lay anxieties about preserving Scottish nationality. During the debate on 6 August, Glasgow Gorbals MP George Buchanan stated that while Welsh women were also affected by the policy, it had more of an effect on Scotland, as 'we still have some kind of nationality'. Buchanan went on to explain why many in Scotland felt so upset over the scheme: '[t]o-day many of our best women are being picked out and taken away. Scotland is going to be driven ... into a position similar to that of the distressed areas before the war ... As one who has regard for his country', he added, 'I want to see it preserved.'[177] South Ayrshire MP Mr Sloan added his voice, stating 'I do not know any question which has caused so much resentment in Scotland during my lifetime as the transfer of these women from Scotland to England ... The thing has developed into a positive scandal.'[178]

The frustration expressed by these Scottish MPs, and the public anxieties they conveyed, also revealed deeper fears about Scotland and the country's future. Several speakers in the debate spoke of Scotland's depressed areas and damaged industries, and the sacrifices families had made during the Great War. The lack of wartime investment in Scotland was 'a deep social issue', Glasgow Gorbals MP George Buchanan claimed, explaining that his country needed to be preserved.[179] Walter Elliot, former Minister of Health, also expressed concerns that such measures might cause lasting damage and further depress rural areas by removing local skilled labourers. The transfer of women out of Scotland is 'a confession of weakness; it is a gospel of despair', Elliot stated, adding '[t]his is not a party question; it affects all Scottish Members'.[180] 'London policies' were resulting in 'the dereliction of the Highlands', MP David Kirkwood stated, while there was a grave danger, said Elliot, that Scotland would emerge from war, 'not only as a depressed area, but as an area with a potentiality of depression

---

[174] Braybon and Summerfield, *Out of the Cage*, 162.
[175] Hansard, HC Deb, 6 August 1942, vol. 382 cols 1159–60.
[176] Ibid., cols 1160, 1299–300.
[177] Ibid., cols 1289–95.
[178] Ibid., cols 1299–300.
[179] Ibid., col. 1294.
[180] Ibid., col. 1305.

much greater than it has ever had before'.[181] Despite Bevin's protests that he had 'never regarded Scotland as being a separate country', and it must be treated as part of Great Britain, the English were accused of 'denuding Scotland of its womenfolk [in a] systemic, dastardly fashion'.[182] This must not be allowed to happen, MPs urged, and Scotland's population must not be wiped out.[183] To this end, Sonya Rose has noted the paternalistic, protective language used by nationalists, who saw themselves inhabit the role of 'virile defender[s] of national integrity'.[184]

The wide range of protesting voices indicated how deeply this issue affected Scottish morale. In a sense, the transports served as a symbol of English oppression of Scotland and laid bare the fractures beneath the Union. Aside from MPs, dissent was expressed by Thomas Johnston, the Scottish Council of the Socialist Party and the Stirling and Glasgow Town Councils, among other groups.[185] In addition, the Scottish National Party passed a motion opposing the policy, and reminded members of 'the legal and moral right of any Scot to refuse to be directed to work in England'.[186] Further, members claimed the policy was an attack on Scotland and evidence of 'the moral bankruptcy of the British Government'.[187] The organisation also published leaflets, subsequently seized by censors, which proclaimed:

> Since 1707, when the London ruling clique swindled the Scots into a Union, the terms of which have never been honoured by England, BRITISH IMPERIALISM HAS DONE ITS WORST . . . to drive abroad the flower of the Scots race in every generation, now even pressganging Scots women into English factories . . . [and] to root out and stifle everything characteristically Scottish.[188]

These feelings and behaviours represented severely dented morale. As in the case of the clamour over Blitz information, Scottish agitation over transporting mobile women led Whitehall to change its course of action. Beginning in 1942, a Scottish Advisory Council on Industry was established and this took 'active steps' to ensure that, where possible, war production would be established in Scotland, so local labour could be kept in local

---

[181] Ibid., cols 1296, 1303–4.
[182] Ibid., cols 1296–7; 'Mr Bevin's case: transfer of Scottish girls to England', *The Scotsman*, 9 October 1942, 5.
[183] Rose, *Which People's War?*, 226.
[184] Ibid., 225.
[185] 'Scotland's industries: Mr T. Johnston and transfer of girls to England', *The Scotsman*, 23 October 1942, 5; 'Transfer of women workers', *The Scotsman*, 17 September 1942, 8 'Transfer of labour: replies to Stirling's protest', *The Scotsman*, 17 June 1942, 3; 'Scottish girls: transfer to work in England', *The Scotsman*, 4 September 1942, 3.
[186] 'National Party meets: Scots girls in England', *The Scotsman*, 31 May 1943, 2.
[187] Ibid.
[188] SNP leaflet from NRS, HH55/557, Sedition: Police action against SNO, 1941.

factories.[189] Within a year, Scottish industry gained over 2 million square feet of factory space for war production, and there was 'a steady reduction' in the number of transfers.[190] By mid-1943 it was estimated the new war production units would create up to 25,000 jobs, and some Scottish factories were already importing workers from outside the region to meet labour shortages.[191] The groundswell of discontent at the transfers, as we have heard, had been expressed by constituents, business owners, MPs, political parties, civic officers, the Secretary of State for Scotland and some of the women themselves. This demonstrates the extent of public concern over Whitehall's powers to make decisions that were perceived as not in the best interests of Scotland. Moreover, it reveals the ways in which morale was tied to nationalist sentiment in Scotland. Ultimately, though, while some Scots railed against this policy and the implications it might have for Scotland's future, it should be stressed that most mobile women continued to 'do their bit' and, largely, undertook what was asked of them in a time of war.

This provides a challenge to the assessment of Scottish morale during the Second World War. Using Robert Mackay's framework, the Scottish response to work transfers of mobile women indicates low morale in both the 'attitudes' and 'behaviour' categories. Concurrently, Scottish levels of commitment, cooperation and belief in ultimate victory suggests morale was also high in both categories. This apparent conflict indicates the complexity in trying to make judgements about the morale of populations. We can reasonably conclude, though, that Scottish belief in the justness of the war and the public's commitment to 'see it through' were stronger than local concerns about decisions made at Whitehall. While some Scots were comfortable expressing frustrations about 'English imperialism' and concerns over the future of Scotland, they remained committed to the war effort, revealing an underlying strength of character and of morale. Most MPs involved in the fiery debate in August 1942 did not argue that Scotswomen should not be involved in the war effort; rather, that war industries should be established in the home country, to support local industry and keep workers in their own communities.

'The bitter memory of industrial insecurity': legacy of the Depression

Scottish morale was also influenced by concerns about the post-war future. In many respects, this anxiety was tied to memories of the past. Working-class Scots, in particular, worried that the country would suffer maladies similar to those seen after the Great War, such as housing shortages,

---

[189] 'Scotland's industries: Mr T. Johnston and transfer of girls to England', *The Scotsman*, 23 October 1942, 5.
[190] Ibid.
[191] Church of Scotland, General Assembly 1943, Committee on Church and Nation: Scottish industry, 244.

emigration, unemployment and poverty, which had fallen particularly heavily on the working classes. Prior to 1914, much of the housing stock in the wider Glasgow area was considered 'the worst in urban Britain', leading to overcrowding, disease and slum-like conditions in many inner-city suburbs and areas such as Clydebank.[192] With an influx in war workers for the heavy industries, overcrowding worsened. The 1917 Royal Commission on the Housing of the Industrial Population of Scotland estimated 236,000 new houses would be needed to address the problem.[193] New housing schemes were started in the years after the Great War, but stalled when the economy contracted.[194] By 1939, Scottish overcrowding was more than five times worse than in England. Additionally, 40 per cent of the populations in the industrial hubs of Coatbridge and Clydebank and 29 per cent in Glasgow were considered to be living in overcrowded circumstances, compared to 17 per cent in Edinburgh and 7 per cent in Liverpool.[195]

The fates of working-class Scots had been further affected by the interwar depression. The severe economic downturn led to the collapse of many key industries that had propped up the Scottish economy, such as heavy engineering and shipbuilding. This resulted in severe unemployment, especially in the central belt of Scotland which had been the heart of primary industry. Areas such as Airdrie, a coal mining and milling town in Lanarkshire, were hit particularly hard, and in 1936 unemployment in the town was at 30 per cent of the labour force.[196] More generally, between 1931 and 1938 Scottish unemployment averaged 22 per cent, compared to the UK average of 16 per cent.[197] Poverty and deprivation marked the interwar years for the working classes and, as T. M. Devine summarised, memories of the period 'are those of material disaster and social tragedy'.[198] At that time, more than half a million Scots emigrated, partly pulled by opportunities abroad but also pushed by economic depression and severe hardship.[199]

As discussed in Chapter Three, the Second World War brought a revival to Britain's heavy industries, and once again the worker was in demand. Speaking to the House of Commons in August 1940 Churchill declared '[t]he fronts are everywhere. The trenches are dug in the towns and streets . . . The front line runs through the factories. The workmen are

[192] Devine, *Scottish Nation*, 311.
[193] C. H. Lee, 'Unbalanced growth: prosperity and deprivation', in T. M. Devine, C. H. Lee and G. C. Peden (eds), *The Transformation of Scotland: The Economy Since 1700* (Edinburgh: Edinburgh University Press, 2005), 225.
[194] See Ch. 2 in Seán Damer, *Scheming: A Social History of Glasgow Council Housing, 1919–1956* (Edinburgh: Edinburgh University Press, 2018).
[195] Devine, *Scottish Nation*, 319; John Stewart, 'Sickness and health', in Abrams and Brown, *History of Everyday Life*, 230.
[196] Harvie, *No Gods*, 47.
[197] Ibid.
[198] Devine, *Scottish Nation*, 316; Stewart, 'Sickness and health', 232.
[199] McCarthy, *Personal Narratives*, 15, 17–18.

soldiers with different weapons but the same courage.'[200] Lucy Noakes has noted that this appeal served to draw the previously marginalised working-class into the British national community.[201] Churchill's powerful speeches and the associated shared feelings of unity lodged in public memory and went on to form the powerful narratives of the 'people's war' and Blitz spirit.

Primary sources, however, reveal the uptake of this rhetoric was not universal, and the idea of British national unity did not apply to certain communities of Scotland. Rather, identity was localised and Scottish morale shaped by what Alison Chand calls 'lived facets of existence'.[202] In industrial heartlands such as Clydebank, Glasgow and Fife, the legacy of pre-war hardship profoundly influenced wartime morale. As Chapter Three examined, the experiences of many Scottish industrial workers in the interwar period went on to shape both workplace conflict and industrial grievances during the Second World War. While MoI homed in on communism as the chief agitating factor in Scottish industry, this came at the expense of understanding other grievances and anxieties that underpinned discontent and worker morale. This tunnel vision missed much of the picture and, by failing to appreciate the history of industrial Scotland, countering communist influence could only go so far in boosting workplace morale.

While Chapter Three explored the official response to working-class unrest, here I suggest this behaviour was symptomatic of low morale. Prior to the Second World War, work had been 'one of the main "anchorages" of male identity', and the breadwinner ideal was strong in traditional communities oriented around the heavy industries.[203] Historians Juliette Pattinson, Arthur McIvor and Linsey Robb found unemployment 'gnawed' at men's dignity, and in personal memories of the interwar period working-class men displayed 'a sense of shame, impotence and humiliation' over the loss of employment and associated self-worth.[204] These memories, still fresh during the years of the Second World War, had a profound influence on Scottish working-class morale. Throughout the war, workers in the west of Scotland continued to agitate for better conditions and wages, and act on workplace grievances. From mid-1941 communist subversion waned, yet worker discontent continued. This indicates Scottish working-class morale was less tied to communism than the intelligence community had assumed. Rather, worker agitation was linked to fears about the future, as workers worried that a post-war depression might again envelop Scotland.

The anxieties that influenced Scottish worker morale did not go unnoticed by M-O investigators. Their March 1941 report stated that Clydeside workers appeared to be fighting a war of their own and this was 'the direct

---

[200] Hansard, HC Deb, 20 August 1940, vol. 364 col. 1160.
[201] Noakes, *War and the British*, 26–7.
[202] Chand, *Masculinities on Clydeside*, 61, 65.
[203] Pattinson, McIvor and Robb, *Men in Reserve*, 135–6.
[204] Ibid., 137.

antithesis of good morale'. Workers 'cannot forget the numerous battles of the past thirty years', concluded the report, nor could they overcome 'the bitter memory of industrial insecurity'.[205] This conditioning of scepticism and bitterness, observed M-O staff, led workers to feel that, when war was over, things would be worse and 'the scrap heap will be higher than ever'.[206] M-O's conclusions gave an unparalleled glimpse into working-class morale in Scotland during the war. But if this report was a 'smoking gun', why did MoI not act upon it and address Scottish slacking, absenteeism, strikes and apathy towards the war? After all, these were considered key signs of poor morale. One answer comes in the personal communications of Home Intelligence head, Mary Adams. Just one week after M-O submitted its concerning report on wavering morale in Glasgow and Clydeside, Adams wrote to a contact at MoI:

> At the present moment, I've got excellent detailed material about the Glasgow and Clydeside situation but no one is really interested in considering it. There's such departmental jealousy and staggering sensitivity to criticism that this Ministry would never dream of forwarding these reports [to other ministries] . . . There is, of course, terrific pressure everywhere to say (especially in cold print) that everything is alright, that morale is splendid, that people are taking it, etc.[207]

Infighting and fears of criticism, alleged Adams, paralysed MoI from acting on key intelligence. This intelligence baldly stated that morale in industrial Scotland hinged upon the legacy of the pre-war years, and that worker anxieties about the future permeated wartime behaviour. These concerns, however, were overlooked in an environment focused on portraying an image of stoicism and high morale.

'People are looking for change': post-war planning

Uncertainty about post-war regeneration also cast a shadow on Scottish morale in the later years of the war. In response to M-O's Directive for February 1945, which asked about the local state of morale, one Scot commented 'I would say morale was fairly bad . . . There is considerable gloom about prospects.'[208] Another observed, similarly, 'a great discontent is here, and people are looking for change'.[209] A soldier based near Edinburgh commented that morale in his unit was low 'due to uncertainty about post-war life and demobilisation'.[210] Such concerns about post-war life were further aroused by Whitehall's plans for post-war recovery. While Chapter

---

[205] M-O, FR600, 'Preliminary report on morale in Clydeside', 7 March 1941, 3.
[206] Ibid., 16–17.
[207] M-O, 1/C, Adams to 'Harold', 15 March 1941.
[208] M-O, Dir. February 1945, R1534 (Campbeltown).
[209] Ibid., R1393 (Kilbirnie).
[210] Ibid., R1682 (Edinburgh).

Seven on rural Scotland will explore positive reactions to the prospect of rural regeneration, in other Scots these proposals raised anxiety. 'People here are more concerned with post-war problems and are distressed particularly about the housing situation and about the lack of support from the Government for the schemes for Prestwick aerodrome and the Forth Road Bridge', Mrs Musgrove observed in February 1945.[211] Fellow countryman Mr Forster agreed:

> I should say a word on the particular position in Scotland. Almost all Scotsmen regard their future with a black outlook. Recently Scotland has suffered some rebuffs which make her future seem insecure. For example it is perhaps not realised in England that the decision not to make Prestwick the No. 1 airport, in spite of its obvious advantages over all alternative sites, had a very pronounced effect on Scottish morale. The rejection of the Forth bridge scheme was similarly unfortunate, only partly relieved by the promise of a light aluminium industry. I am forced to agree that there are signs that Scottish interests are made to some extent subservient to those of England, and am not surprised at the lower morale in Scotland.[212]

These themes revealed Scottish frustration with Whitehall and, once again, exposed the fissures beneath the Union.

As a result of the history of failed government intervention in the Highlands, certain Scots could only feel cynicism towards this new declaration of support. This cynicism was based on previous experience. In late 1938 Dr Lachlan Grant, chairman of the Highland Development League, had criticised the government for its 'indifference and inaction' that had allowed the Highlands to 'drift to the edge of extinction'.[213] During the previous fifty years, Grant claimed, the 'Highland problem' had been the 'plaything of party politics, conveniently trotted out to serve some ulterior purpose, and just as conveniently forgotten when that purpose was achieved'.[214] Some felt the same would happen after the Second World War. The poem below – a play on the popular song 'There'll Always be an England' – summed up their cynical attitude:

> There will always be an England, As long as Scotland stands
> For it is due to dear old Scotland, That England's wealth expands
> Our friendly neighbour, England, We always will defend
> We'll help her fight her battles, Her broken ships we'll mend
> And when the war is over, And victory has been won
> We'll sing of England's glory, And the victories she has won???[215]

---

[211] Ibid., R3545 (Glasgow).
[212] Ibid., R2741 (Saltcoats).
[213] 'Highland affairs: lack of unity deplored', *The Scotsman*, 9 May 1938, 12.
[214] Ibid.
[215] Poem by John MacDonald, October 1940, in Macdonald, 'Wersh the wine', 110.

Many Scottish nationalists viewed Whitehall's proposals with similar suspicion. Mr A. Moffat in Bridge of Weir was intercepted by Postal and Telegraph Censorship sharing SNP leaflets that lambasted the proposed government scheme for the Highlands. Entitled *1314 Bannockburn, 1943 . . .* the leaflet proclaimed the English were using the war to 'root out and stifle everything characteristically Scottish', and Whitehall's post-war plans would serve to 'strengthen their stranglehold on Scottish land, Scottish industry, Scottish trade and everything Scottish'.[216] In another leaflet, *The Highlands*, frustration was expressed over the government's lack of teeth in dealing with problems laid bare by the Scottish Development Council. The authors of the leaflet also complained that English MPs 'showed open resentment' in the House of Commons during discussions about Highland decline. The leaflet repeated comments from a range of prominent Scots who felt government post-war proposals for Scottish regeneration were 'contemptible', 'completely inadequate' and could 'scarcely be called a policy at all'.[217] The chairman of the Highland Development League made his position clear, stating '[n]o longer must the welfare of our land depend on the whims of civil servants at Whitehall or the decisions of the English Treasury'.[218]

All three examples of specifically Scottish concerns demonstrate how Scotland's history and position within the Union affected wartime morale. These responses also demonstrate the importance of Scottish identity during the war, and the ongoing feelings that Scotland was playing 'second fiddle' to England. The frustrations and 'fraught conversations' reveal the difficulties of Britain being, as Rose deemed, a 'cultural, if not political, "multi-nation"'.[219] Nationalists in both Scotland and Wales fought to retain cultural distinctiveness and identity, and contested the idea of Britain by referring to 'the English government' and 'English imperialism', and repeating themes of local boys fighting 'England's war'.[220] In many respects, these issues reveal that local history and culture was more important to Scots than the idea of 'national' community being promoted by Whitehall. Scots routinely expressed frustrations with government decisions and showed anxiety about the ways their lives would be impacted by these. This is not to say, however, that the majority of Scots were fixated on past legacies. Many demonstrated belief in the underlying justness of the war and showed commitment by complying with wartime conditions or orders, even when resentful of those measures. Ultimately, while Scots often displayed symptoms of low morale, according to Mackay's definitions, Scottish morale did not reach crisis point.

---

[216] NRS, HH55/557, Sedition: Police action against SNO, letter to Lillian Reid, 17 August 1943.
[217] Leaflets from NRS, HH55/557, Sedition: Police action against SNO.
[218] Ibid.
[219] Rose, *Which People's War?*, 197, 231.
[220] Johnes, *Wales since 1939*, 26–8; Macdonald, 'Wersh the wine', 110.

This chapter has attempted to assess Scottish morale during the Second World War. Even acting on the assumption that morale is a composite of attitudes and behaviours, reaching conclusions about public morale is a complex task. At any time, Scots could demonstrate both depression and belief in ultimate victory; grumbling and neighbourliness; defeatism and commitment to the task in hand.[221] The presence of conflicting morale markers demonstrates that public state of mind is multi-faceted. As Robert Mackay concluded, when the historian moves into the terrain of the public mind '[w]hat emerges is a predictably complex picture in which, for every individual, morale was created out of an interplay between the public and the private, the sense of being part of a community and the private need to meet the war on one's own terms'.[222]

So what, then, can we conclude about Scottish morale? As could be expected, frontline success, defeat or inaction both buoyed and frustrated Scots. In similar fashion, uncertain or unfamiliar home front conditions created anxiety and fear. Morale also ebbed and flowed across time, and as fatigue or anxiety crowded out feelings of excitement and anticipation of victory. In contrast to the popular Blitz spirit narrative, which emphasised high morale and confidence in Britain's ultimate victory, archival sources reveal Scottish morale was often low. The government's unprecedented actions, in the release of sensitive particulars about the Clydebank air raids, also emphasises the level of official concern about Scottish morale at that time. In addition, the selected source material has revealed that, in Scotland, the sense of being part of a (British) national community was often conspicuous by its absence. Rather than creating a new feeling of partnership, as Calder proposed, war exposed and sometimes intensified underlying fractures. In fact, as Rose astutely observed, wartime measures and attempts at unifying the public actually fostered 'expressions of cultural distinctiveness' in Britain's constituent nations.[223] Scottish frustrations with Whitehall's decisions, and anger at what was perceived as English domination revealed many Scots would never, truly, buy into the 'national we' that was heavily promoted by wartime politicians and leaders. Alongside the events of war, the legacy of Scotland's complex relationship with England profoundly shaped local morale. As the following chapters will discuss, this tension also infused Scottish responses to the war effort.

---

[221] Mackay, *Half the Battle*, 3.
[222] Ibid., 251.
[223] Rose, *Which People's War?*, 197–8, 231.

CHAPTER FIVE

The Great Escape: Scottish Wartime Holidays

In April 1943, Mass-Observation questioned followers about their plans for holidays after the war. In response, a number of Scots shared their holiday dreams. One soldier wanted to go somewhere quiet and rural, preferably with hills or mountains, 'to get away from crowds of people ... into the open country and relax'.[1] Another wanted to charter a yacht and cruise around Britain and northern Europe.[2] One rural housewife expressed a desire to join a scientific expedition, while another hankered after a holiday in London.[3] A young man wished to holiday in Skye or the Highlands, while a worker on a farm in Aberdeen wanted to hitch-hike around England with only a tennis racket, a bathing suit and 'few complications'.[4] In contrast, a nurse from Glasgow hoped for a holiday in Mexico, writing 'its colour and life appeals to me, its lack of materialism, its freedom'. She added 'I should like the mental shock of dropping out of the sky from Scotland right into Mexico'.[5]

The researcher is left wondering: were holidays merely something to dream about during the long years of the Second World War? Were Scots restricted to dreams and plans of something that might happen 'when the war finished'? Or were holidays a pleasure those in Scotland did not have to forgo during the years of the war? Certainly, popular memory of Britain's home front holds that wartime holidays, if any, were spent at home.[6] In memoirs and oral histories there has also been a reluctance to discuss wartime leisure, amid the dominance of a 'wartime narrative of ... graft and sacrifice for the war effort'.[7] Within this cultural narrative, holidays have slipped from public memory. Author Chris Sladen argued wartime slogans such as the Railway Executive Committee's 'Is your journey really necessary?' have imprinted themselves so strongly upon folk memory that

---

[1] M-O, Dir. April 1943, R1682 (Edinburgh).
[2] Ibid., R2554 (Glasgow).
[3] Ibid., R2490 (Tayvallich), R2973 (Colinton).
[4] Ibid., R2741 (Ayrshire), R3361 (Aberdeen).
[5] Ibid., R3247 (Glasgow).
[6] Chris Sladen, 'Wartime holidays and the "myth of the Blitz"', *Cultural and Social History* 2 (2005), 215–16.
[7] Pattinson, McIvor and Robb, *Men in Reserve*, 245.

the general belief is wartime holidays were uncommon and frowned upon.[8] There also exists in Britain a willingness to promote the war years as a time when the nation pulled together during a time of crisis, and put aside personal interests or pleasure for the greater good of the community.[9] With this in mind, this chapter will challenge these ideas of graft, sacrifice and 'greater good' by exploring holiday experiences in Scotland during the Second World War.

It will build on the work of Chris Sladen, whose two articles on wartime holidays serve as the bedrock in a slim historiography.[10] His article 'Wartime holidays and the "myth of the Blitz"' explored government curbs on leisure travel and wartime holiday patterns, concluding that large numbers of British citizens took holidays during the war, that resorts such as Blackpool prospered and that wartime travel reflected class differences.[11] Sladen gathered his observations primarily from M-O documents, private letters and memoirs, and did not pay particular attention to Scottish aspects of wartime travel. In 2008 Blake Morrison published his undergraduate research into Scottish wartime tourism. Morrison's findings included that holiday patterns were disrupted, Highland travel all but ceased and many Scots chose to holiday 'at home'.[12] This chapter will supplement the work of Sladen and Morrison by adding to our knowledge of wartime holidays, and further exploring Scottish holiday dimensions. It does so by utilising a vast range of sources: these include official records of the Scottish constabulary, MoI and M-O; personal diaries, letters and questionnaire responses; and published articles in Scottish newspapers and magazines. This range of sources provides a valuable view of Scottish wartime holidays, helping us to move beyond the existing narrow frame of reference regarding the subject.

In addition, this chapter provides an alternative slant to the Protestant Work Ethic. According to this ethos, proposed by Max Weber in 1904, Protestant life is dominated by work and the pursuit of money, combined with self-discipline and frugality.[13] In nineteenth- and early twentieth-century Scotland, the Kirk played a prominent role in public culture and Scottish life was dominated by ideas about 'rational recreation' and the

---

[8] Chris Sladen, 'Holidays at home in the Second World War', *Journal of Contemporary History* 37, no. 1 (2002), 68.

[9] James Chapman, 'British cinema and "the people's war"' in Nick Hayes and Jeff Hill (eds), *'Millions Like Us'? British Culture in the Second World War* (Liverpool: Liverpool University Press, 1999), 33.

[10] Sladen, 'Holidays at home'; Sladen, 'Wartime holidays'.

[11] Sladen, 'Wartime holidays', 241.

[12] Alastair J. Durie and Gayle McPherson, 'Tourism and the First World War: a Scottish perspective', *The Local Historian* 29, no. 4 (1999): 240–55; Blake Morrison, 'Down but not out: tourism in Scotland during the Second World War', *Studies by Undergraduate Researchers at Guelph*, 2 no. 1 (2008): 52–8.

[13] Max Weber, *Protestantische Ethik und der Geist des Kapitalismus* [1930] (London: Routledge Classics, 2001),18, 88.

pursuit of morally acceptable forms of leisure.[14] Perhaps for this reason few texts on everyday life in the early twentieth century have explored the topic of holidays.[15] Evidence contained within this chapter challenges the notion that Scottish life was dominated by discipline and a strict work ethic. Simply put, this chapter seeks to answer the question 'how did the war influence Scottish holidays'? It will begin with a brief exploration of the history of holidays, then examine Scottish holidays at home, followed by wartime holidays and the sacrifice of holidays. Following this, the chapter will consider motivations for wartime holiday-making, and explore aspects of similarity and difference to home front holidays in England.

History of holidays

Only from the late 1860s onwards did guaranteed yearly holidays become a common feature in workplaces across Britain.[16] In Scotland, consequently, the late nineteenth and early twentieth centuries were a time of growth for the leisure industry. Rising real wages and the arrival of unpaid summer leave for employees were key developments during this period, allowing greater numbers of Scottish workers to embark on vacations. Moreover, developments in railway networks, and steamship companies offering more pleasure trips, meant holiday-makers had even greater mobility. Popular destinations were Highland villages and coastal resorts, and those from cities commonly holidayed at the seaside.[17] In addition, day trips and excursions were popular.[18] As Irene Maver has pointed out, the change in attitudes towards leisure, and the belief that 'the health-giving qualities of fresh air' were 'vital' for urban dwellers, meant holidays took on an evermore important place in the lives of urban and working-class Scots.[19]

In addition, the Fair holidays in July were a long-established Scottish tradition; a revered part of popular culture where local 'Fairs' (holidays) 'emptied Scotland's industrial towns of all but their poorest and oldest citizens ... as whole populations headed to coastal resorts or back to Highland townships that had once been home'.[20] In Glasgow, these days of respite from work generally resulted in a 'holiday exodus' as locals took off on railways or steamboat pleasure trips to resorts on the Firth of Clyde

---

[14] Brown, 'Rational recreation', 210, 216.
[15] See Macdonald, *Whaur Extremes Meet*, 323–42; Callum G. Brown, 'Charting everyday experience' in Abrams and Brown, *History of Everyday Life*, 19–47; Irene Maver, 'Leisure time in Scotland during the nineteenth and twentieth centuries', in John Beech, Owen Hand, Mark A. Mulhern and Jeremy Weston (eds), *Scottish Life and Society: The Individual and Community Life* (Edinburgh: John Donald, 2005): 174–203.
[16] Sladen, 'Wartime holidays', 217.
[17] Devine, *Scottish Nation*, 357; Maver, 'Leisure time', 178; Macdonald, *Whaur Extremes Meet*, 334.
[18] Maver, 'Leisure time', 178.
[19] Ibid.
[20] Macdonald, *Whaur Extremes Meet*, 332–3.

and beyond.[21] As one historian has summarised, for many citizens the appeal was in exchanging smoke, dirt and noise for clean air and water.[22] Middle-class vacationers could travel by private motor car, allowing greater freedom in planning and choice of destination. In addition, the rising trade in maps and guidebooks during the 1930s gave pleasure motorists further tools to explore remote parts of the country. At that time, 'active leisure' also increased in prominence, and holidays involving cycling, hiking or walking became ever more popular. Pleasure cruises and coach tours were also common.[23] In the twentieth century, the availability of holidays for all classes of society meant, according to historian Peter Borsay, tourism 'became embedded in British leisure culture'.[24]

'Holidays at home'

During the Second World War, the British public was encouraged to forgo holidays away from home and instead spend leisure time in their local surroundings. In July 1941 the Minister of Information observed a 'definite need for a national campaign' to keep holiday-makers from travelling, and that summer a scheme was enacted entitled 'Holidays at Home'.[25] Events were organised by local governments and voluntary groups throughout Britain, and scheduled for the peak summer holiday season. Authorities hoped these alternatives to holidays away from home would help raise the morale of industrial workers and provide urban-dwellers some means of healthy relaxation without resorting to rail travel. The scheme would also keep transport networks free for troop and supply movements, and curb fuel and rubber usage in a time of shortage.[26]

By 1942, the programme was under way in Scotland, and many locals chose to participate in the events 'at home' that summer. Popular events included exhibition sheepdog trials, which were held in both Inverness and Edinburgh. *The Scotsman* reported the Edinburgh trials were 'specially welcomed by the townspeople, and proved of absorbing interest', with spectators 'marvelling' at the control over the sheep by master and dog.[27] Bookstore worker Mrs Booth attended, noting '[g]ood fun. Lovely Day. Home tired and hot. Tea.'[28] Patriotic military displays were also common, such as a performance in the Ness Islands by the band of the Queen's Own Cameron Highlanders, and in Aberdeen a pipe band parade was led by a

---

[21] Maver, 'Leisure time', 178.
[22] Borsay, *History of Leisure*, 174.
[23] Ibid., 171, 186–7; Sladen, 'Wartime holidays', 217.
[24] Borsay, *History of Leisure*, 170.
[25] TNA, INF 1/292B quoted in Sladen, 'Holidays at home', 70.
[26] Sladen, 'Holidays at home', 68–9.
[27] 'Sheep dog trials: a notable display in Edinburgh', *The Scotsman*, 3 August 1942, 3.
[28] M-O, Diarist 5253 (Edinburgh), 1 August 1942.

Figure 5.1 Open-air dancing at the Ross Bandstand, Edinburgh. (Source: *SMT Magazine*, September 1942.)

pipe-major from the Gordon Highlanders.[29] The public was also able to take part in the 'Scotland's Gardens Scheme', which provided a chance to view many of the country's 'famous and romantic' gardens.[30] *SMT Magazine* advertised open days at gardens in Midlothian and Hawick, which offered 'a pleasant escape from bricks and mortar', as well as those of Rowallan Castle in Kilmarnock and Westerdunes in North Berwick, which combined 'the charm of roses, herbaceous borders and water garden, with the topical usefulness of vegetables'.[31]

In Edinburgh an extensive programme was planned, including football, tugs of war, community singing, Punch and Judy shows, treasure hunts, sun-bathing, concerts and open-air dancing in Princes Street Gardens, Leith Links and Portobello Promenade (see Figure 5.1).[32] A Red Cross picnic in Roseburn Park was attended by 6,000 people and included a performance by the City Police Pipe Band, Punch and Judy shows and donkey

---

[29] NRS, HH55/34, PWD – IR, 11 September 1942: Inverness burgh; 'Edinburgh holidays: many workers leave city', *The Scotsman*, 6 July 1942, 2; 'On holiday in Edinburgh: record Sunday crowd at zoo', *The Scotsman*, 21 July 1942, 3.
[30] 'Home front', *SMT Magazine*, May 1942, 11.
[31] Ibid., July 1942, 11.
[32] 'Holidays at home: Edinburgh amusements', *The Scotsman*, 4 July 1942, 6.

rides, which were reportedly 'very popular'.[33] Children's programmes at the Scottish Zoological Park in Corstorphine, Edinburgh, were also well attended by locals. One such programme in late August was attended by 10,000 people and included activities such as sending telegrams to the King and Queen, and to Churchill. Speaking afterwards the city provost, Sir William Darling, lauded the 'value and success' of the day out, which had included theatre, magic, marionettes, a band of Royal Dragoons and the Edinburgh City Police Band.[34]

That year, a glowing editorial in *SMT Magazine* proclaimed the stay-at-home holidays a great success. The editor expressed his pride in Edinburgh locals who had 'taken so enthusiastically to open-air dancing, alfresco concerts, and sports gatherings', and those who had participated in 'the other diversions which compensated for the loss of visits to the country or seaside'.[35] The article finished by linking these wartime sacrifices to the Scottish national character: '[s]o a patriotic necessity helps to foster that love of the out-of-doors which was becoming such a strong national characteristic in the immediate pre-war years'.[36] For the Scots who participated in local 'at home' programmes, a change might not have been as good as a holiday, but at least war did not spoil all attempts to have fun.

During the summer of 1943, the Holiday at Home programme continued. In Edinburgh, locals could enjoy tours to local historic sites, open-air dancing, zoo days, and sports events including football, athletics, swimming galas and cricket.[37] In July the city's chief constable, Sir William Morren, reported the schemes were 'proving very popular and are being largely patronised, particularly the dancing in Princes St Gardens'. He also commended the sightseeing tours of the city, noting '[t]hey not only provide entertainment but are educative as well, and help to stimulate a healthy interest in the city and its history'.[38] Local Mrs Webster went on one of the sightseeing tours, based on the life of Robert Louis Stevenson, during which

> we visited all the spots both in Town and out; associated with the poet. Often on these tours we are accompanied by servicemen of all nationalities and from the Dominions, and all display a keen interest ... We have some very good arrangements here for the holidays at home scheme, and all seems to be well patronised. The open-air dancing attracts tremendous crowds each night, and we have also a fun fair which seems to be popular.[39]

[33] 'Holidays at home picnic', *The Scotsman*, 30 July 1942, 3.
[34] 'Holidays at home: 10,000 at Edinburgh Zoo', *The Scotsman*, 31 August 1942, 3.
[35] 'Home front', *SMT Magazine*, August 1942, 10.
[36] Ibid.
[37] 'Stay-put holidays: Edinburgh scheme outlined', *The Scotsman*, 26 May 1943, 3.
[38] NRS, HH55/37, PWD – IR, 16 July 1943: City of Edinburgh.
[39] M-O, Dir. June 1943, R3324 (Edinburgh).

In Glasgow, a Miss MacLean noted the attractions organised for city folk, which included

> bands in the parks; open air (as well as indoor) dancing; excursions to local places of interest; exhibitions; variety shows; plays; and for the Fair Holidaymakers the '*Express*' Newspapers are sponsoring and meeting the expenses of a series of nightly concerts during the Fair week. [She also observed] picnics, cycling and similar outings are being indulged in. The Shows in town are good, gay, and colourful.[40]

So how successful were these government attempts to alter Scottish holiday habits? Chief constables' reports and newspapers portrayed Holiday at Home programmes as highly successful and well patronised. At the end of summer 1943 *The Scotsman* provided attendance figures for the most popular events held in Edinburgh. The paper noted that over 200,000 people had attended open-air dancing in Princes Street Gardens, and another 40,000 at dancing in Leith Links and Portobello. Park concerts had been attended by over 63,000, which 'showed the reservoir of talent that existed in the localities', while five zoo days had recorded attendances of over 30,000 people.[41] In 1944, Dumbarton's chief constable reported '[h]oliday makers taking "full advantage" of the facilities being provided for them by the local holidays at home committee'.[42] In Greenock, the report from Superintendent McKechnie noted the official events 'were much better patronised than last year'.[43]

In stark contrast, secret intelligence reports compiled by MoI reveal that for the duration of war, support for the Holidays at Home programme was low. MoI gathered details of public sentiment and behaviour from a range of sources, including reports from RIOs, postal censorship, BBC listener research papers and regional press summaries.[44] During summer 1942 the Ministry's sources revealed that while Edinburgh's open-air dancing in Princes Street was 'a huge success', in general the Holiday at Home programme 'appears to be having little practical effect' and Scottish workers were said to be 'arranging to holiday away from home as far as possible'.[45] The feeling across Britain was that the 'Don't travel' campaign 'flounders on', Holidays at Home were 'a broad farce' and there was 'widespread anger and disgust' at the government's lack of response to railway companies advertising holiday excursions and extra train services over the holiday period.[46] Home Intelligence officers also wondered if the running of extra

---

[40] Ibid., R3473 (Glasgow).
[41] 'District news: Edinburgh and south-east', *The Scotsman*, 2 October 1943, 3.
[42] NRS, HH55/40, PWD – IR, 14 July 1944: Dumbarton.
[43] Ibid.: Greenock.
[44] See TNA, INF 1/292/1/2. All HI reports list the sources from which the intelligence was gathered.
[45] TNA, INF 1/292, MoI, HI Rep. 90: 25 June 1942.
[46] Ibid., Rep. 93: 16 July 1942.

trains might have enticed some to travel who might previously have been planning to stay at home.[47]

Life writing sources also challenge the view that Scots were supportive of Holidays at Home. Few Scottish diarists or letter writers consulted for this chapter mentioned participating in the Holiday at Home programmes. Only one writer had enjoyed an open-top bus tour and another had watched others dancing in the Princes Street Gardens.[48] More common were complaints: '[a]nother of the assumptions of the official mind is that a holiday at home meets the case . . . I put it to anyone with a sense of reality whether such a holiday is good enough for these worn out people and their children', wrote 'Rest and Change' to *The Scotsman* in August 1943.[49] Mr Sedgeworth, a 32-year-old clerk from Glasgow, also complained: '[t]he Stay at Home attractions in Glasgow are neither attractive nor adequate. Who wants to look at dolls in national costumes in a museum during the Summer holidays!'[50] Likewise, nurse Moira Devlin was unimpressed with the local programme. 'The stay at home holiday is stodgy', she wrote in her diary, 'who wants to dance in the Park on holiday, you don't get the rich doing that for their holidays'.[51]

The discrepancy between these sources may be attributed to the nature of their focuses. Newspaper reports centred on attendance figures and reported the mass popularity of such events. The impressive attendance figures they promoted do not allow for nuance or repeat attendances. Similarly, chief constables' reports provided a general assessment of local turnout and opinions towards such events. In contrast, MoI reports compared Scottish attendance at these events with numbers departing on traditional vacations. MoI also gathered information on rail patronage, allowing the Ministry to form a better-rounded picture of public sentiment towards the stay-at-home holiday scheme. Moreover, personal sources such as diaries and submissions to M-O allowed authors to express private thoughts about the government's programme. In the letter complaining about the home holiday scheme to the editor of *The Scotsman*, the author was unwilling to provide their name. This implies that the public felt criticism of local events should best be expressed privately or anonymously. Each of these sources provides individual value, and it is only when layered together that the observer can see subtleties emerge.

---

[47] Ibid., and Rep. 92: 9 July 1942.
[48] M-O, Dir. April 1943, R3324 (Edinburgh) and R2973 (Edinburgh).
[49] 'Letter to the editor from "rest and change"', *The Scotsman*, 2 August 1943.
[50] M-O, Diarist 5196 (Glasgow), 13–19 July 1942.
[51] M-O, Dir. June 1943, R3247 (Glasgow).

The wartime holiday

During the Second World War, access to around 40 per cent of Scotland's land mass was prohibited.[52] On 12 March 1940, Highland land northwest of the Great Glen was declared a protected area and unauthorised access was prohibited.[53] In addition, a regulated zone was established along the coast stretching from East Lothian to Caithness, and including the Firth of Forth.[54] Visitors required official approval to visit either zone. Despite war's encroachment on rural Scotland, Scots still managed to take walking, camping and cycling holidays in remote areas of the country (see Figure 5.2). Friends of Frank Balfour spent a long weekend cycling at Callander, in the Trossachs National Park, during 1942.[55] A couple he knew honeymooned at Crianlarich in the Trossachs, while a young friend of Balfour's spent two weeks during summer 1943 camping at Craigellachie, a remote village in Moray.[56] Similarly, the Kerr family spent weeks cycling between Highland hostels in September 1943, and around Inverness and the Caledonian Canal in 1944, averaging nearly 60 miles a day.[57] One reader wrote to the editor of *SMT Magazine* about a cycling trip she planned to take in the Scottish countryside. 'This great urge to see and know something of my own country has been growing on me for some time, fostered by the lure of your fine photographs', wrote Ina Bell in April 1940. She added a motivation for the trip, stating 'I feel it would satisfy some deep longing within myself at the present time: that the eternal majesty and beauty of the hills might in some way lay fingers of peace upon troubled souls at this time'.[58]

Other Scots expressed similar motivations of respite and relaxation for their holiday travel. In September 1942 Katherine Booth and her husband took a seaside holiday near St Andrews. Highlights of the holiday included: '14/9: Lie about in our favourite bathing bay . . . Read thrillers. Very pleasant', '16/9: walk to Rock and Spindle. Very pleasant. Wade about, and then lie on the sands and read another thriller', and 'walk out past Maiden Rock. Rain, but shelter under a ledge and read thriller. BP golfs after tea with Betty.'[59] Despite being in the middle of a war this couple, and others like them, were able to take moments of reprieve from war's effects on their lives.

In *SMT Magazine*, a publication promoting pleasure motoring and Scottish natural and cultural history, regular features and advertisements

---

[52] Alison Campsie, 'When the Highlands went into "lockdown" 80 years ago', *The Scotsman*, 18 September 2020, accessed via *The Scotsman* online.
[53] '"Protection" in force: permits demanded in north', *The Scotsman*, 12 March 1940, 5.
[54] Morrison, 'Down but not out', 58.
[55] Diary of Frank Balfour, 23 August 1942.
[56] Ibid., 6 July 1943, 17 July 1943.
[57] Ibid., 27 September 1943, 6 August 1944.
[58] 'Letter to editor from Ina Bell', *SMT Magazine*, April 1940, 2.
[59] M-O, Diarist 5253 (Edinburgh), 14, 16, 18 September 1942.

Figure 5.2 Members of the Cowgate Boys' Club go camping. (Source: *Life and Work*, June 1941.)

encouraged readers to take rural holidays. The magazine's editor reminded readers in April 1940 that the Highlands was not forbidden to holidaymakers, just restricted, and he encouraged potential vacationers to apply for permits to travel in the region.[60] When one reader wrote in about a potential cycling holiday around the southern Highlands, the editor was happy to suggest an itinerary and said he would be 'delighted' to forward further suggestions from readers.[61] Companies also used advertisements to encourage Scots to travel during the war. In April 1941, one such feature advised readers '[t]here are so many restrictions on holiday resorts that it is wise and prudent to discriminate early in the season. Do not hesitate – now is the time to choose the ideal place where you can get right out of the war atmosphere for a brief respite to rest and play' (see Figure 5.3).[62] Similarly, a full-page advertisement in the magazine during May 1945 advised 'five of Scotland's Premier Hotels offer you just the type of holiday you prefer amidst the most glorious scenery in the West of Scotland'.[63] Most of the suggested holiday locations were in the southern Highlands or on the Firth of Clyde. Such a holiday, the text promised, would 'restore the zest of life in these strenuous days'.[64] Both advertisements were sponsored by the Automobile Club, the Royal Automobile Club and

---

[60] 'Letters to editor – editor's response to Ronald Heald', *SMT Magazine*, April 1940, 2.
[61] Ibid.
[62] 'Where shall we go this summer?', *SMT Magazine*, April 1941, 62.
[63] 'Headquarters for rest and recuperation', *SMT Magazine*, May 1945, 5.
[64] Ibid.

Figure 5.3 'Where shall we go this summer?': Advertisement from *SMT Magazine*. (Source: *SMT Magazine*, April 1941.)

the Royal Scottish Automobile Club. Presumably these organisations were seeking to encourage travel to these locations by private motor car, thus serving as membership advertisements, of sorts, at a time when pleasure motoring was significantly reduced.

Scots had a variety of feelings towards war's intrusion on their holidays. Margaret, an office typist, holidayed on the Firth of Clyde in summer 1942 where she saw 'air convoys, submarines, an aircraft carrier, and sailors galore'.[65] This intrusion of war did not affect the woman's enjoyment of her holiday. In contrast, Eileen Offley, a secretary in Glasgow, liked to escape the war's influence on her life by holidaying in quiet parts of Scotland. In July 1940, she travelled to Helensburgh, a coastal town on the Firth of Clyde, hoping it would be further removed from war's influence. She proclaimed the holiday blissful, especially the 'rest and quiet and removal from war talk'.[66] Summing up her holiday, Miss Offley mused '[t]he stay at Helensburgh is doing us good; fresh air and rest from work count, but as much as anything, I think, the decrease in "war talk". It seems as if the progress of the war were slowed down.'[67] Others found it more difficult to escape the war; for example, Miss Boorman. In July 1940, she planned a holiday in the town of Ayr. 'Forget the war!', a colleague called as she departed on her vacation leave. Miss Boorman replied sadly '[f]orget the war! How can I?'[68]

Despite complaining about war's impact on leisure travel, Miss Offley and her colleagues in Glasgow took holidays every year for the duration of the war. In 1940 the colleagues spoke with 'deep resentment' and 'bitter talk' of the limitation of holidays, as all were restricted to one summer leave period from work.[69] During these summer breaks, all vacationed away from Glasgow. In summer 1940 holidays were taken at Dunoon, Gourock, Port Patrick and Innellan, a collection of coastal locations extending from the Firth of Clyde to the south-west coast of Scotland.[70] Most of these villages had been popular Victorian holiday destinations, reachable by steamboat from Glasgow. In 1941 destinations included Hunter's Quay on the Cowal Peninsula and the seaside town of Ayr.[71] The following summer most of the office again holidayed in rural Scotland: Miss Offley in rural Berwickshire, Miss Boorman in remote Perthshire, another colleague in Hunter's Quay and the office manager on the Isle of Bute.[72] In 1943 Miss Offley holidayed to Berwick with her mother, meeting many servicemen on the train, home

---

[65] M-O, Diarist 5390 (Glasgow), 3 August 1942.
[66] Ibid., 18 July 1940.
[67] Ibid., 16 July 1940.
[68] Ibid., 5 July 1940.
[69] Ibid., 31 July 1940.
[70] Ibid., 23, 30 July 1940.
[71] Ibid., 6 August 1940.
[72] Ibid., 1–4 August 1942.

from Palestine on leave.[73] In July 1944 eastern coastal defence regulations were relaxed, and the travel ban for the wider Firth of Forth and coastal areas south of Edinburgh was lifted.[74] That summer Scottish travellers rushed to visit former coastal haunts, and they included the Offley family who spent a fortnight at the seaside town of Eyemouth, on the coast south of Edinburgh.[75]

Some Scots in rural areas were restricted from leisure travel by wartime responsibilities such as having to meet farm production targets or play host to evacuees, workers or billeted troops. Nonetheless, these Scots helped urban friends and relations to enjoy brief holidays in the countryside as respite from wartime life in the city. In Carradale, near the Isle of Arran, writer Nora Mitchel lamented she could not take a holiday because she had to host several evacuees and billeted workers. Instead, Mrs Mitchel planned to invite friends to stay for the holiday period. 'We plan to ask as many friends as possible, as this would be good for town people; the children also asking friends', she stated in January 1940.[76] It was similar for Mrs Peason, a diarist based at rural Tayvallich on the shores of Loch Sween, with whom visitors often came to escape wartime life in the city. In August 1943, she wrote of a visit from a friend, 'P', and her four children, who were holidaying in a nearby rural croft. Mrs Peason collected her visitors by boat, made scones and sandwiches for lunch, while the children 'occupied their afternoon very happily tinkering with G's sailing boat, with Daphne to sew the sails . . . while P and I turned hay'.[77] That evening Mrs Peason tidied the house ready for the next lot of summer holiday guests, who were also escaping the city for a welcome break from war.

Many Scots did not allow their holidays to be disrupted by the risk of air raids. In August 1942 the Sedgeworth family from Glasgow travelled south for a fortnight's vacation in Manchester, a major centre of industry and attractive target for the Luftwaffe. During the holiday break, the family suffered five air raid alerts and heard and saw both gunfire and flares.[78] Despite the dangers of these air raids, Mr Sedgeworth 'did his best to forget the war and listened to the news but rarely'.[79] Other Scots willing to risk danger on holiday were observed by the chief constable for the city of Glasgow. In summer 1944 the Luftwaffe began a third wave of attacks on London and hundreds of Londoners evacuated to Scotland each week.[80] During the Glasgow Fair week in July that summer, Chief Constable

[73] Ibid., 7 September 1943.
[74] 'Travel warning: raising of Forth area ban', *The Scotsman*, 31 July 1944, 3.
[75] M-O, Diarist 5390 (Glasgow), 15 August 1944.
[76] M-O, Dir. January 1940, R1534 (Carradale).
[77] M-O, Diarist 5314 (Tayvallich), 6 August 1943.
[78] M-O, Diarist 5196 (Glasgow), 1–9 August 1942.
[79] Ibid.
[80] 'Billeting offers wanted: more evacuees in Edinburgh', *The Scotsman*, 17 July 1944; NRS, HH55/40, PWD – IR, 17 June to 14 July 1944: *précis*.

McCulloch noted 'trains leaving the city railway termini have been packed to capacity, and strangely enough bookings to London and the south have been heavy'.[81] At this time, the *Glasgow Herald* also reported that, at the city's St Enoch Station, many hopeful travellers waited in vain to secure a place on the train to London, with flying bombs 'having no deterrent effects generally on those who had decided to spend the Fair in London'.[82] While Londoners were fleeing a wave of deadly air raids on their city, Scots were heading there for a pleasant summer holiday, in defiance of the war's ability to impact their lives.

In addition to leisure travel that ignored the risks of war, Scots also travelled in defiance of official warnings about hampering the war effort. In late May 1942 smallpox broke out in Glasgow and in one month more than thirty cases were recorded.[83] A medical officer advised the public the outbreak was considered 'highly infectious and dangerous', while another said 'this is the most virulent and most infectious type of smallpox that I have encountered in my medical experience ... and the public must be brought to realise the gravity of the position'.[84] The public was warned the coming Glasgow Fair holidays might advance the spread of disease and consequently they should cancel travel plans. Dr Davidson, the Medical Officer of the Department of Health for Scotland, urged Glaswegians to '[b]e vaccinated. Stay at home. Avoid crowded places', and added 'we must have the co-operation of the public'.[85] Over the course of the following week, an estimated 400,000 locals proceeded to get vaccinations. These included some who did so in order to continue with holiday plans, such as Mr Sedgeworth, who wrote in his diary '[o]ur chief fear was not of smallpox itself but of the possibility that if it gets worse we may not be allowed to travel and, of course, holidays are near'.[86] During the following weeks *The Scotsman* reported a stream of leisure travellers leaving Glasgow, in defiance of the official pleas to stay put. On 6 July, the beginning of the trade workers' holiday, 'hundreds of Glasgow holiday-makers' were recorded, train compartments were 'packed to capacity' and officials commented the queue for the 10:30 am train to London was 'the greatest in their experience'.[87] It is unknown how many of these travellers had received vaccinations before departure, but it can be assumed at least some were at risk of spreading a highly infectious disease that might hamper the war effort by infecting workers or troops, or using up valuable medical supplies.

---

[81] NRS, HH55/40, PWD – IR, 14 July 1944: City of Glasgow.
[82] 'Fair holiday rush: Glasgow a city of queues', *Glasgow Herald*, 15 July 1944, 3.
[83] Ian N. Sutherland, 'Some aspects of the epidemiology of smallpox in Scotland in 1942', *Proceedings of the Royal Society of Medicine* 36 (1943), 227.
[84] 'Warning by M.O.H.: most infectious type of smallpox', *The Scotsman*, 6 July 1942, 3.
[85] 'Smallpox outbreak: dangers of the holiday season', *The Scotsman*, 4 July 1942, 3.
[86] 'Smallpox suspected: Glasgow children in hospital', *The Scotsman*, 8 July 1942, 3; M-O, Diarist 5196 (Glasgow), 29 June–5 July 1942.
[87] 'Edinburgh holidays: many workers leave city', *The Scotsman*, 6 July 1942, 2.

Alongside the risk of spreading disease, leisure travellers potentially jeopardised the war effort by affecting production rates in war industries or clogging transport routes that were needed for troops or equipment. To this end, in May 1942 Phyllis West, Welfare Officer for Scotland at the Ministry of Labour, held a press conference reminding Scottish workers not to clog railways or shirk work duties over the summer. Workers were reminded that 'unnecessary travel handicaps war effort', and were encouraged to take only short holidays, so as not to affect the production of munitions or equipment for the frontline.[88] Adding to this was the voice of the Ministry of Transport, which actively encouraged Britons not to travel during the summer season and launched a new campaign, featuring the slogans 'Must you travel?' and 'Don't travel'.[89] A Ministry representative also revealed that more than fifty passenger trains had been lost through enemy air attacks, fast passenger lines were being used to transport munitions, fuel and members of the armed forces, and many extra trains were being run for war workers to get to workplaces in government factories.[90]

Despite these official pleas, in summer 1942 thousands of Scots took holidays. During the Edinburgh Trades Holiday Week in July, '[l]arge crowds which thronged the Waverley and Princes Street Stations on Saturday . . . gave the impression that the Government's advice to stay at home had not been taken at all seriously', reported *The Scotsman*.[91] On Fair weekend in August 1942 Glasgow holiday traffic was 'on a fairly heavy scale', with long queues for southbound trains and for the steamer to the Kyles of Bute.[92] In Edinburgh extra trains were run to Perth and Fife, popular holiday destinations, though many passengers had to stand for their journeys to Glasgow and London.[93] *The Scotsman* also reported the National Union of Scottish Mineworkers had censured thousands of miners who did not resume work after the holiday break. It was claimed that in one colliery in Fife only 400 out of 1,300 men had returned to work after the Fair holiday, in breach of their agreements with pit owners.[94] In response, the union representative stated '[t]his position is the more regrettable when it is known that the Cabinet regard the coal position as serious . . . Every ton of coal is required if we are to win this war speedily. Failure to achieve the desired production can have only one effect – the prolonging of the war.'[95] In such cases, the war seemed to exert little influence over Scottish holiday-making.

[88] 'Holidays at home: people must be kept off railways', *The Scotsman*, 30 May 1942, 7.
[89] 'Raids on our railways: 50 passenger trains lost', *The Scotsman*, 1 August 1942, 4.
[90] Ibid.
[91] 'Edinburgh holidays: many workers leave city', *The Scotsman*, 6 July 1942, 2.
[92] 'Glasgow holiday traffic: people left behind on pier at Wemyss Bay', *The Scotsman*, 3 August 1942, 6.
[93] 'Holiday crowds: congestion at many stations', *The Scotsman*, 3 August 1942, 6.
[94] 'Pit absentees: Scots miners who extended their holiday', *The Scotsman*, 28 July 1942, 3.
[95] Ibid.

Such scenes continued in the following summer of 1943. The public were again exhorted not to travel by train 'during the next few weeks and especially to keep off the railways during the August bank holiday weekend', as crucial troop and equipment movements were under way across Britain.[96] Once again, Scottish leisure travellers defied this plea in order to continue a popular summer pastime. *The Scotsman* noted 'while the "stay put" holiday was obviously the plan of thousands freed from work . . . there were many others who, having presumably convinced themselves that their journey was necessary, were just as obviously prepared to face queues, bustle, congestion and discomfort to make it'.[97] Reportedly, ticket offices were thronged with 'criss-crossing, swarming holiday-makers . . . that made an animated contradiction of the "stay-put" advice'.[98] At Glasgow's St Enoch Station, some travellers queued for over thirteen hours to secure a place on the train to Arran, bringing 'food and flasks of tea . . . in preparation for their vigil'.[99] In Edinburgh, a reporter for *The Scotsman* observed '[i]f a film producer had wanted a flash-back of pre-war holiday traffic scenes at the end of July, Waverley Station, Edinburgh, on Saturday would have given him his subject, unrehearsed and ready made'.[100] Again, it would appear as if the war made little difference to Scottish holiday plans.

In early 1944, Allied preparations for an invasion of France were under way. At that time, Archibald Henderson, the Regional Transport Commissioner for Scotland, announced it was vital to keep the railways free for troops and equipment as, he stated baldly, 'we are hoping to invade the Continent soon'.[101] Henderson beseeched the Scottish public to 'forgo journeys they have hitherto made' and to stagger their holidays more than ever before.[102] The Ministry of Labour also cautioned Britons: 'this is going to be a difficult year, and many sacrifices will be demanded'.[103] In mid-March Henderson again implored Scots to make travel sacrifices during the upcoming holiday season: '[t]he military movements we are all looking forward to must, of necessity, be given absolute, exclusive priority', he stated, adding '[t]he public are tired of our slogans. What we want to appeal to them to do is not to travel.'[104]

Scots again expressed resistance to the pleas of officials, once again choosing to holiday in the face of official advice. Two weeks before the July 1944 Fair holiday, the Glasgow Savings Bank revealed workers were

[96] 'Do not travel', *The Scotsman*, 24 July 1943, 4.
[97] 'Holiday crowds: busy station scenes in Edinburgh', *The Scotsman*, 5 July 1943, 3.
[98] 'Holiday traffic: busy scenes in Edinburgh', *The Scotsman*, 2 August 1943, 3.
[99] 'All-night queue for Arran tickets', *Glasgow Herald*, 12 July 1943, 5.
[100] 'Holiday traffic: busy scenes in Edinburgh', *The Scotsman*, 2 August 1943, 3.
[101] 'Holidays hint: no additional trains this year', *The Scotsman*, 12 February 1944, 3.
[102] Ibid.
[103] 'Workers' holidays: government request that they start and end in mid-week', *The Scotsman*, 18 February 1944, 2.
[104] 'Holidays away: many who have booked may not travel', *The Scotsman*, 11 March 1944, 6.

making 'heavy withdrawals' from their savings in order to travel during the upcoming holiday period.[105] Speaking to *The Scotsman*, the Bank's actuary divulged that nearly £1,000,000 had been withdrawn, 'about double the corresponding figure of last year'. He added 'many people who had done without holidays since 1939 felt they were in need of a change'.[106] Furthermore, over the next few weeks the *Glasgow Herald* reported locals had ignored the railway companies' warnings and appeals, and holiday crowds had been equal to those seen in 1943.[107] In their eagerness to travel over the Fair holiday, some locals had endured 16-hour queues and 1,000 others had camped overnight in Glasgow Central station, in order to get places on trains heading south to Liverpool and Blackpool, or north to Inverness.[108]

The sacrifice of a favoured pastime

In contrast to those whose holidays continued, largely untouched by war, others in Scotland were not so unaffected. The needs of war generally meant those serving in His Majesty's Forces were unable to take a 'proper' holiday, though for many the desire to do so was still strong. For 23-year-old Mr Renner, training in Scotland, the dream of a holiday away from the war was ever-present. 'I have often imagined at some annoying periods of army life how grand it would be to have a month off to do exactly as I pleased without any restrictions', he wrote to M-O in April 1943. 'I should favour somewhere quiet and rural, preferably with hills or mountains, in company with one or two close friends with similar interests.'[109]

War also forced other Scots to sacrifice their holidays. Mr Forster, a chemist in a reserved occupation, wished he could 'take a really quiet holiday in the country, preferably among mountains . . . I have long had a notion of going to Skye and the Scottish Highlands', he confessed in April 1943.[110] Duncan Watson, a conscientious objector who was sentenced to work on a farm in rural Aberdeenshire, longed for the day his sentence would be over and he could 'laze about doing nothing, be my own master, watch people being happy, and see the countryside'. He added, 'I always did like to travel, and it's depressed me no end these last three years that I have hardly been able to move a mile this way or that'.[111] Others were affected by war's impact on their finances or by the availability of fuel. In January 1940, M-O asked its followers what their travel plans were for the year. In Aberdeen, respondent Ian MacLeod noted '[m]y usual holiday up

[105] 'Scottish district news: £1,000,000 for holidays', *The Scotsman*, 10 July 1944, 3.
[106] Ibid.
[107] '"Fair" optimism rewarded', *Glasgow Herald*, 17 July 1944, 4.
[108] 'Fair holiday rush: Glasgow a city of queues', *Glasgow Herald*, 15 July 1944, 3.
[109] M-O, Dir. April 1943, R1682 (Berwickshire).
[110] Ibid., R2741 (Saltcoats, Ayrshire).
[111] Ibid., R3361 (Aberdeen).

to the Highlands is impossible this year due to economy, but I hope to go to a very cheap camp with some friends'.[112] Edith Goldberg in Edinburgh had decided to cancel her holidays for the year, 'both for financial reasons and the difficulty of transport. In addition we should feel distinctly uneasy in strange surroundings if an air-raid came.'[113] Henry Boyd in Glasgow commented that his family 'usually go down to the South of England to see my people, and while we had not fixed to go this year, I have a feeling that this will not be practicable this summer. Furthermore, rising costs will preclude the expensive fares.'[114]

A further group of Scots chose to sacrifice holidays, believing that this would be for the greater good of the war effort. Writing to *SMT Magazine* in August 1942, Mary Hesmondhalgh stated '[t]his year, like many other people, we shall not be able to have a holiday. But each month the *SMT Magazine* brings descriptions and photographs to recall happier days, and with a promise of future happy holidays, I hope, when peace returns.'[115] The editor acknowledged the views of many such readers, writing:

> We are glad to know that the magazine has found such a definite wartime niche in helping lovers of the countryside to visit, in memory at least, the places which for them spell the magic of Scotland ... Through two war-time summer seasons we have tried our utmost, in prose and picture, to offer a mental tonic and escape to the cheerfully uncomplaining army of people who would normally, at this time, be motoring, walking, climbing, fishing, or otherwise enjoying the invigorating beauty of the Scottish scene.[116]

The decision to forgo holidays was not always made enthusiastically. When beautiful weather arrived in Glasgow this produced resentment in Eileen Offley's office, and colleagues complained that owing to wartime restrictions only one week's holiday in the summer was allowed. 'It used to be that when the Fair was over we counted the weeks, and then the days to the September holiday: then we began to look forward to Christmas and New Year, and so on the round of the calendar. The thought of no relaxation whatever for 12 month has psychological effects that are downright harmful to work', Eileen commented in her diary.[117] Resentment was also noted by fellow Glaswegian Miss MacLean, who observed '[i]n the immediate neighbourhood, quite a number of people are spending their holidays at home this year', adding cynically, 'the ones who have up to the present not missed an Autumn, Spring and Summer break are going away, while

---

[112] M-O, Dir. January 1940, R2293 (Aberdeen).
[113] Ibid., R2374 (Edinburgh).
[114] Ibid., R2410 (Glasgow).
[115] 'Letter to the editor from Mary Hesmondhalgh', *SMT Magazine*, August 1942, 1.
[116] 'Home front', *SMT Magazine*, August 1941, 9.
[117] M-O, Diarist 5390 (Glasgow), 31 July 1940.

the faithful members of the community continue to sacrifice'.[118] As we can see, the ability to holiday was not universal; some Scots were forced by the war to sacrifice a favoured pastime.

The continuity of holidays during war

Throughout the Second World War, British newspapers regularly reported on crowds of holiday-makers travelling during holiday periods. A special report into English rail holidays in 1941 over the May Whitsun period and during August bank holidays revealed that despite propaganda campaigns urging curtailment of holiday travel, there had been 'a big increase' in passenger travel compared to levels seen during 1940.[119] Intelligence officials acknowledged that these figures included travel by members of the armed forces, and that half of all passenger transport from London's Euston and St Pancras stations was by servicemen. During Christmas 1941 the Ministry of War Transport attempted to curb London holiday travel by banning all special holiday leave for the Services and ensuring no extra holiday trains were run. Consequently, there was a 'noticeable and remarkable lessening' in pre-Christmas travel from London stations, and travel during the wider festive season was down 50 per cent on pre-war figures.[120] At the August bank holiday in 1942, rail travel was 'lighter than on an ordinary Monday', and seaside resorts 'indicated a quiet week-end'.[121] An article in *The Scotsman* noted, though, that trains from London to York, Newcastle and north Wales were crowded 'but not uncomfortably packed'.[122]

Across both England and Scotland, no extra passenger trains and buses were scheduled over holiday weekends from 1942 to 1945.[123] As was discussed earlier, this appeared to do little to deter Scottish travellers. In England, this led some to take holidays closer to home such as camping and farm holidays, though others braved crowded trains to travel further afield.[124] Destinations in the north of England were popular, and northern resort towns such as Blackpool flourished.[125] Chris Sladen acknowledged that, while specific analysis of railway passenger statistics is complicated, the figures suggest that between a quarter and a third of the civilian population holidayed during wartime.[126] He also noted that changing behaviour in England led people to take holidays closer to home, on farms, and led

[118] M-O, Dir. June 1943, R3473 (Glasgow).
[119] TNA, INF 1/292, MoI, HI Special Rep. 5, 'Holiday travel': 5 February 1942.
[120] Ibid.
[121] 'August Bank Holiday: rail traffic light in England', *The Scotsman*, 4 August 1942, 6.
[122] Ibid.
[123] 'Bank holiday travel', *The Scotsman*, 17 July 1943, 6; Hansard, HC Deb, 9 June 1943, vol. 390 cols 701–5.
[124] Sladen, 'Wartime holidays', 235–6.
[125] Ibid., 238.
[126] Ibid., 227.

to a rise in low-cost holidays such as cycling tours.[127] One important change for London holiday-makers was that traditional seaside destinations on the eastern and southern coasts, such as Margate and Brighton, were out of bounds for civilians. This was because of the high risk of air attack or invasion in these coastal areas. As a result, holiday-makers were forced to adapt, and vacation further north than usual.[128]

One factor behind the steady number of British wartime holidays may have been the state of public morale. In the first half of 1943 a wave of Allied successes in North Africa and Russia and a series of damaging air raids on Hamburg significantly lifted public morale. HI reports noted that across Britain public spirits rose steadily, and reached 'a very high level' with the fall of Tunis and Bizerta in North Africa in May 1943.[129] Across the summer, intelligence reports stated that the public was 'elated' or 'cock-a-hoop', and there was a noticeable increase in optimism about an early finish to the war. Many people were thought to believe 'we're on the last lap now' and the war would be over by the end of the year.[130]

Scottish sources also revealed that local spirits were high. In East Lothian during July 1943, the chief constable stated that the public were satisfied with the war situation, and there was 'a feeling of absolute confidence in the ultimate victory of the Allies'.[131] At that time, locals in West Lothian were said to 'enthusiastically welcome' the invasion of Sicily, and regarded this as 'the beginning of the end'.[132] Similarly, in Dunbartonshire the news about Sicily had 'given lively satisfaction', and in Edinburgh the public were said to regard the military situation in Europe 'with assured confidence'.[133] Edinburgh's chief constable added to his report '[m]orale is excellent'.[134] As discussed earlier, from May to September 1943 Scottish holiday travel was widespread. Intelligence sources concluded the high morale and optimism of the summer were responsible for sustained levels of summer holiday travel across Britain, and that motivation may also have applied in Scotland. The high spirits and belief that victory was just around the corner may have led the public into a state of complacency, and prompted the decision to take holidays during summer 1943, in the face of official pleas to avoid travel.

Conversely, while holidays may have been taken by a public buoyed by optimism, holidays may also have served as an apparatus to raise low morale. Findings by HI in January 1942 concluded that a decrease in workplace production was attributable to fatigue, long work hours and

[127] Ibid., 236.
[128] Ibid., 221, 237.
[129] TNA, INF 1/292, MoI, HI Rep. 136: 13 May 1943.
[130] Ibid., Rep. 136: 13 May 1943; Rep. 139: 3 June 1943; Reps 148–50: 5, 12, 19 August 1943.
[131] NRS, HH55/37, PWD – IR, 16 July 1943: East Lothian.
[132] Ibid., West Lothian.
[133] Ibid., Dunbartonshire, City of Edinburgh.
[134] Ibid., City of Edinburgh.

seven-day weeks. When workers were given greater leisure time and holidays from work, production rose to a level 'substantially above the "pre-emergency level"', the report concluded.[135] In 1943, postal censorship revealed that the public felt they were 'more in need of a holiday than ever, what with war strain and blackout winters'.[136] Intelligence agents also noted the prevalence of tiredness and strain, particularly among women workers and older adults.[137] During September 1943 MoI ordered a special study into complacency in factories, finding that 'fatigue, strain and reduced vitality, both mental and physical' were key factors in reduced production output.[138] Intelligence officials concluded that public determination to have a holiday away from home 'at all costs' was not as a result of good morale, but because of 'the physical and mental need for it'.[139]

Like HI's intelligence agents, a number of Scots also believed that taking holidays was a necessary reprieve from the demands of war. Earlier in this chapter evidence was presented of Scots who holidayed for the purpose of respite, and to 'lay fingers of peace upon troubled souls'.[140] In this sense, holidays served as a form of escapism, and as a means of getting away from the war and its demands on everyday life.

'The absolute necessity of a yearly holiday': entitlement as justification

Scots also expressed the belief that holidays were necessary, particularly for those who held demanding jobs. One anonymous Scot wrote to *The Scotsman* in June 1943 noting their support for 'the absolute necessity of a yearly holiday in the case of the toiling millions'.[141] Glaswegian nurse Moira Devlin espoused similar ideas: 'surely people working hard and living in slums are entitled to a holiday in the Country'.[142] Mr Goddard, a foundry worker from Renfrew, agreed with his fellow countrymen, stating that holidays were needed 'more than ever'.[143] In response to public criticism of the working class taking holidays, Glaswegian Miss Maclean responded '[o]ne cannot blame those who are less fortunate and have to spend most of their life between a stuffy factory and an equally airless house in a none too pleasing environment'.[144] Mr MacLeod, a student in Aberdeen, agreed.

---

[135] TNA, INF 1/292, MoI, HI Rep. 'Appendix – home morale and public opinion': 11 February 1942.
[136] Ibid., Rep. 137: 20 May 1943.
[137] Ibid.
[138] Ibid., Special Rep. 51: 'Complacency in factories', 24 September 1943.
[139] Ibid.
[140] 'Letter to editor from Ina Bell', *SMT Magazine*, April 1940, 2.
[141] 'Letter to the editor from "rest and change"', *The Scotsman*, 4 August 1943, 4.
[142] M-O, Dir. June 1943, R3247 (Glasgow).
[143] M-O, Dir. January 1940, R2290 (Renfrew).
[144] M-O, Dir. June 1943, R3473 (Glasgow).

He wrote '[e]verybody that can afford holidays should by all means take them because they are necessary at all times and more so in a war'.[145]

Primary sources also reveal the public not only felt holidays were needed, but were deserved. A 1941 report by HI on public feeling about war workers taking seaside holidays concluded that the public believed it was 'asking too much to expect people to spend their few moments of leisure in work-a-day surroundings, particularly in blitzed areas'.[146] This sense of public entitlement was also noted in an MoI report from Summer 1942. According to MoI's sources, the public believed they had 'denied themselves real holidays for two years and are now entitled to a complete change'.[147] The following summer, intelligence officials observed a similar sense of public determination and entitlement to take holidays. 'People feel they have a need for, and a right to holidays after four years of war', officials wrote in August 1943, adding '[n]othing short of an invasion will stop them'.[148]

This attitude continued into summer 1944. Intelligence officials assessed the public's reasoning behind holiday travel: they travelled if they were 'badly in need of a change', if they were 'anxious for a glimpse of the sea', or because rest and relaxation were 'necessary after five years of war'.[149] Workers also felt they needed 'a change of air and environment', and that they had earned 'a holiday in better air'.[150] These examples show that throughout the years of the war, public sentiment held that holidays were a necessary form of respite to which they were entitled.

This idea of a change of scenery and 'better air' was a concept encountered earlier, in the discussion of Scottish holiday history. Within Scotland there existed an established tradition that urban dwellers, particularly those from densely populated cities such as Glasgow, needed fresh air and time away from the pollution of the city.[151] This idea of escape was, therefore, a well-established part of Scottish urban culture. Peter Borsay, who specialises in the history of leisure, has suggested holidays are often about 'the pursuit of "other" recreational spaces ... the search for environments different from that which a person occupies in normal life'.[152] During the Second World War, holidaying in one's home locale did not offer a reprieve from the familiar, or a change in environment, and was a pale substitution for traditional seaside or Highland holidays. This may also explain why the Holidays at Home programme enjoyed some popularity but ultimately did not stop Scots from taking holidays. At the end of the day, this was not a satisfying substitute for holidays away from home.

---

[145] M-O, Dir. January 1940, R2293 (Aberdeen).
[146] TNA, INF 1/292, MoI, HI Rep. 44: 6 August 1941.
[147] Ibid., Rep. 91: 2 July 1942.
[148] Ibid., Rep. 148: 5 August 1943.
[149] Ibid., Rep. 204: 30 August 1944; Rep. 202: 17 August 1944.
[150] Ibid., Rep. 196: 6 July 1944; Rep. 195: 29 June 1944.
[151] Maver, 'Leisure time', 178.
[152] Borsay, *History of Leisure*, 177.

'Incapable of realising how grave the situation was': denial as justification

As the philosopher John Locke wrote in 1689, '[e]arthly minds, like mud walls, resist the strongest batteries ... and keep out the enemy, truth, that would captivate or disturb them'.[153] This notion of denial, or the 'emotionally motivated rejection (or embrace) of a factual claim, in the face of strong evidence to the contrary', may have been another factor that prompted Scots to take holidays during the time of crisis that was the Second World War.[154] In essence, self-deception may have prompted Scots to ignore or avoid thinking about the true risks of holiday travel in order to justify decisions to do so.

In June 1943, the Parliamentary Secretary to the Ministry of War Transport stated that no extra passenger transport provisions would be put in place for the summer holiday season. 'I am confident', Mr Noel-Baker asserted, 'that those who are now considering where they will spend their holidays, will decide not to travel by rail, but to leave the limited space which is available to those who, in the interest of the war effort, require it most.'[155] While Noel-Baker had confidence in the public's ability to compromise leisure travel 'for the greater good', this hope was misplaced, and many citizens chose to reject the evidence that summer travel might hamper the war effort. Public willingness to reject the facts was also at play during summer 1944. That year, Scots were told it was 'vital' to keep railways free for troops and equipment, needed for the upcoming invasion of Europe.[156] Even in the face of knowledge that public travel could impede an operation that might finally bring a close to the war, 'earthly minds' chose to reject this truth and head away on summer holidays.[157]

The story of Elspeth Musgrove is an example of the way facts were rejected in order to justify travelling. A resident of Glasgow, Elspeth travelled to Southampton in May 1944 to visit her husband in the armed forces. On the return journey she noticed other girls in the train had also been holidaying to visit their husbands. Elspeth noted one of the other wives had been to visit her husband on five weekends since Christmas, five months earlier, which 'almost equalled my own extensive travel record'.[158] She added 'this made me feel less alone in my guilt at disobeying the Government's instructions about travel'.[159] Even though Mrs Musgrove identified feelings of shame, her desire to see her husband was stronger

---

[153] John Locke, *An Essay Concerning Human Understanding* (Bk IV, Ch. 20, S. 12, published 1689), 715, quoted in Adrian Bardon, *The Truth about Denial: Bias and Self Deception in Science, Politics, and Religion* (Oxford: Oxford University Press, 2019), 1.
[154] Bardon, *Truth about Denial*, 2.
[155] Hansard, HC Deb, 9 June 1943, vol. 390 cols 701–5.
[156] 'Holidays hint: no additional trains this year', *The Scotsman*, 12 February 1944, 3.
[157] 'Holidays away: many who have booked may not travel', *The Scotsman*, 11 March 1944, 6.
[158] M-O, Diarist 5380 (Glasgow), 22 May 1944.
[159] Ibid.

than her guilt over travelling. This is an example of denial: Mr Musgrove, serving in the Forces, would have understood the need to keep transport facilities available for the movement of troops and equipment, especially in light of the upcoming invasion of Nazi-occupied France. Even so, the couple had convinced themselves regular holidays were necessary, even those which required Elspeth to travel from Glasgow to Southampton at a time when the public had been asked to curb leisure travel. This is a simple example of the emotionally motivated rejection of facts that may have prompted wartime travel.

In some cases, the decision to holiday was not a deliberate rejection of truth, but a willingness to ignore that which is discomforting. In the words of the Latin proverb, *quod volumus, facile credimus* – we readily believe what we want to believe.[160] Or, as psychologist Peter Ditto terms it, this is the 'pervasive influence of our hopes and fears on our judgement'.[161] The chief constable of the City of Edinburgh commented in July 1943 'the recent good news of the U-boat campaign has heartened the public greatly, though it must be confessed that many seemed incapable of realising how grave the situation often was'.[162] A similar example of public underestimation of the seriousness of war was noted by MoI. Intelligence-gathering found that Glaswegians who travelled to London during the trades holidays in early August 1944 'returned after a day or two with terrible stories of their sleepless and anxious time'.[163] During the previous weeks, Scottish newspapers had noted the arrival of hundreds of London evacuees, and homeowners had been asked to voluntarily accommodate the arrivals from London.[164] Surely, then, the decision to holiday in London must have been a case of wishful thinking, and of hoping things were not really as bad as had been portrayed.

Defeating the enemy or pre-war tradition? Elements of contrast

Chris Sladen concluded, in his landmark study of wartime British holidays, that it was never intended that holiday travel during war be entirely curbed. Instead, the practice was swept under the carpet, with authorities looking the other way in order to promote the myth of public equality of sacrifice.[165] Sladen also suggested that determination to holiday was

[160] 'Latin proverbs, mottoes, phrases, and words: group Q', *English-Word Information*, https://wordinfo.info/unit/3479/page:4/s:quod%20vide (accessed 15 December 2019).
[161] Peter Ditto, 'Passion, reason, and necessity: a quantity of processing view of motivated reasoning', in Tim Bayne and Jordi Fernandez (eds), *Delusion and Self-Deception: Affective and Motivational Influences on Belief Formation* (New York: Psychology Press, 2009), 23.
[162] NRS, HH55/37, PWD – IR, 16 July 1943: City of Edinburgh.
[163] TNA, INF 1/292, MoI, HI Rep. 200: 3–5 August 1944.
[164] 'Billeting offers wanted: more evacuees in Edinburgh', *The Scotsman*, 17 July 1944; NRS, HH50/40, PWD – IR, 17 June to 14 July 1944: *précis*.
[165] Sladen, 'Wartime holidays', 243.

evidence of public spirit, with Britons convincing themselves they were helping defeat the enemy and displaying a sense of Britishness by 'beating the system and heading off to Blackpool'.[166] In Scotland, primary sources reveal little evidence that taking holidays was about a sense of Britishness, or seen as a way of defeating the enemy. Rather, the Scottish determination to holiday appears linked to continuity of a pre-war cultural tradition, particularly regarding Fair holidays. These were guaranteed leave days for Scottish workers, and were one of few chances for the working classes to gain some respite from the monotony of the workplace. For Glaswegians, it was a yearly working-class ritual to abandon the city *en masse*, and travel to coastal resorts along the Clyde. Holidays away from home are an example of what one historian has termed 'emulation and social competition', a sort of working-class aping of the upper-class Grand Tour.[167] In Scotland, this working-man's Grand Tour, a pleasure cruise along the Clyde or a train ride to the Trossachs, was a privilege Scots were unprepared to sacrifice.

Another factor underpinning wartime holidays in Scotland was the aspect of distance. Scots benefited from having a Scottish Home Department located in Edinburgh, and a certain amount of decision making therefore took place on 'home soil'. In some senses, it was easy for Scots to forget about the effects of war on London, and easier to forget about the war taking place overseas. In the absence of nightly bombings, Scots could, to some extent, put war out of their minds and grow forgetful of its worst effects. The distance from Whitehall and from the Crown also led Scots to show a 'lack of close identification with "the English war"', and intelligence officers noted 'locals talk about the South and London as if they are in another war or another country'.[168] When added to the history of tension within the Union, this physical and psychological distance from London is likely to have played a part in Scots' decisions to continue holidaying during a time of war.

The insularity from war, afforded to Scots by their distance from the frontline, is conveyed in the following example. Agnes Connor, a housewife from rural Helensburgh near Glasgow, travelled south in September 1941. She went to London, 'chiefly to use my clothes coupon. I had thought out carefully what I needed and was going to spend quite a bit of money in getting the best I could.' But she found herself 'disappointed and thwarted', with narrow choices and 'rather dull' clothes. The Scotswoman was also surprised to find the hotel where she usually stayed looked 'desolate' and had been turned into an evacuation centre for Maltese refugees, while her old favourite restaurant 'was just a mass of ruins, mostly mortar and lather ... I was unprepared for the sight of gutted walls and skeleton buildings which I caught sight of in the dusk about 9 pm. And the vision

---

[166] Ibid., 244.
[167] Borsay, *History of Leisure*, 99.
[168] M-O, FR600, 'Preliminary report on morale in Clydeside', 7 March 1941, 2.

gave me a shock. It looked so ghastly and ghostly', she wrote in her diary.[169] After nine months of bombing by the Luftwaffe and the deaths of nearly 30,000 Londoners, how could Mrs Connor have reasonably assumed that she would be able to have a few days' pleasant shopping in the capital and visit her favourite haunts in the ways she had done before the war? This element of distance allowed Scots to 'tune out', in effect, and shield themselves from daily reminders of war in other parts of Britain.

Which explanation of wartime holidays is most convincing, then? In most primary sources examined for this chapter, Scots revealed feelings of entitlement about holidays away from home. This view was strongest amongst the working classes, who may only have had Fair holidays and one week's summer leave during each year of the war. These Scots showed little inclination to forgo this infrequent pleasure. Middle-class Scots, in contrast, were able to holiday more frequently, and in this habit they exhibited an element of denial about the seriousness of the war. This ability to holiday during war was, largely, a result of Scotland's distance from London and the frontline. In this respect, Scots were able to cultivate a certain amount of insularity, allowing themselves to believe their actions posed no threat to the war effort.

While this episode of wartime life has hitherto been overlooked, the evidence presented here suggests that, throughout the war years, those in Scotland resisted wartime disruption of their holidays, choosing to continue established habits and ignore official advice warning against leisure travel. This challenges the prevalent cultural narrative of sacrifice and putting aside personal pleasure for the greater good of the community and the wider war effort. This chapter has also illuminated the complex relationship between 'ordinary' Scots and the state – both in Scotland and in Whitehall. Furthermore, the discovery of the Scottish determination to holiday during a time of crisis undermines the notion that Scottish everyday life was characterised by the Protestant Work Ethic. Ultimately, the Scottish commitment to wartime holidays away from home reveals Scots were not characterised by slavish devotion to work nor driven by strict discipline. Rather, holidays were a cultural tradition and a revered part of Scottish life. Chapter Six will further explore the pleasurable aspects of wartime life.

---

[169] M-O, Diarist 5281 (Helensburgh), 29 September 1941.

CHAPTER SIX

Leisure and Pleasure: Scottish Responses to War's Disruption of Everyday Life

In July 1940, Mr Robert Boothby, Parliamentary Secretary to the Minister of Food, came face to face with the Scottish fondness for sweets. Visiting Scotland to discuss wartime food restrictions, Mr Boothby was outraged at the multitude of cakes displayed in store windows along Edinburgh's renowned Princes Street. In response, he severely criticised both the quantity of cakes and the thickness of the icing, and implied that 'decisive action' would be taken at once to stop such frivolous use of sugar.[1] The general secretary of the Scottish Association of Master Bakers was deeply offended, stating that the trade was 'working loyally on the allocation of sugar given to it by the Ministry of Food and surely they were not doing anything criminal or reprehensible when they made the best use they could of that sugar'. He added, Scotland had 'the finest craftsmen in the baking trade in the world' and Mr Boothby should be giving Scottish bakers a pat on the back for their adaptability and expert craftsmanship 'in applying their allocation of sugar so successfully'.[2] The editor of *The Scotsman* also took up the case, stating that Scots were too focused on duty to even notice the offending cakes. The editorial finished, wryly, '[i]t must have been a moving spectacle to see Mr Boothby moving westward, becoming more and more sunk in gloom before the wanton array of delicatessen, with nothing so much as even a scone to relieve his depression'.[3]

Sugar, cakes and scones are often afforded only a small place in histories of wartime life, as discussions of food culture are dominated by talk of restrictions, rationing and going without.[4] There are similar trends when

---

[1] 'Sugar for jam more important than cakes', *Glasgow Herald*, 1 July 1940, 5.
[2] 'Display of iced cakes in shop windows', *Glasgow Herald*, 3 July 1940, 11.
[3] 'Men and affairs: cakes', *The Scotsman*, 2 July 1940, 4.
[4] Mark Roodhouse, *Black Market Britain: 1939–1955* (Oxford: Oxford University Press, 2013); E. M. Collingham, *The Taste of War: World War II and the Battle for Food* (London: Allen Lane, 2011); Ina Zweiniger-Bargielowska, *Austerity in Britain: Rationing, Controls, and Consumption, 1939–1955* (Oxford: Oxford University Press, 2000); R. J. Hammond, *Food*, Vol. I: *The Growth of Policy* (London: HMSO, 1951); Paul Brassley and Angela Potter, 'A view from the top: social elites and food consumption in Britain, 1930s–1940s' in Frank Trentmann and Flemming Just (eds), *Food and Conflict in Europe in the Age of the Two World Wars* (London: Palgrave Macmillan, 2006): 223–42; Mark Roodhouse, 'Popular morality and the black market in Britain, 1939–1955', in Trentmann and Just, *Food and Conflict*, 243–65.

it comes to wartime leisure more generally, though there is a budding body of work in this area that covers wartime cinema, dancing, sport and holiday camps.[5] In regards to Scotland, the topic of leisure and non-work culture during the twentieth century has received a similarly limited coverage. This may be a result of the legacy of Victorian suppression of working-class leisure (so-called 'rough culture') and the resulting discourse around 'rational' recreation.[6] This may also be a result of the dominance of the Presbyterian work ethic in Scottish life and society.[7] With regards to the Second World War, the discursive silence is not limited to Scotland, though, with historians Juliette Pattinson, Arthur McIvor and Linsey Robb finding that former war workers throughout Britain 'exhibited a reluctance to admit they had any leisure time during the war'.[8] In interviews with those who had worked in reserved occupations during the war, the historians found their subjects 'attempted to skirt the issue altogether', 'batting away' questions on free time, and insisting they had been too busy to indulge in the pursuit of pleasure.[9] Echoes of this sentiment were observed by sports historian Eilidh Macrae when researching women's leisure between 1930 and 1970. In interviews, many of Macrae's subjects failed to mention what they had done for fun during the war years. 'The lack of discussion', Macrae noted of her mostly Scottish interviewees, 'was often quite striking'.[10]

One reason for this collective amnesia regarding wartime leisure and pleasure in Britain may be the prominence of narratives of the 'greater good', argues historian James Chapman. Within this popular picture, he states, the stories of individuals 'were sublimated into the greater story of the whole nation pulling together at a time of national crisis'.[11] This popular 'people's war' mythology promotes an image of 'patriotic sacrifice,

---

[5] Matthew Taylor, *Sport and the Home Front: Wartime Britain at Play, 1939–45* (London: Routledge, 2020); Norman Baker, 'A more even playing field? Sport during and after the war', in Hayes and Hill (eds), *'Millions Like Us?'*, 125–55; R. Nicholson and M. Taylor, 'Women, sport and the people's war in Britain, 1939–45', *Sport in History* 40, no. 4 (2020): 552–75; James Nott, 'The dancing front: dancing, morale, and the war effort in Britain during World War II', *Journal of Social History* 51, no. 2 (2017): 387–406; Christina Baade, '"The dancing front": dance music, dancing, and the BBC in World War II', *Popular Music* 25, no. 3 (2006): 347–68; Richard Farmer, *Cinemas and Cinemagoing in Wartime Britain, 1939–45: The utility dream palace* (Manchester: Manchester University Press, 2016); Chapman, 'British cinema'; Sandra Trudgen Dawson, *Holiday Camps in Twentieth-Century Britain: Packaging pleasure* (Manchester: Manchester University Press, 2011); Claire Langhamer, *Women's Leisure in England, 1920–1960* (Manchester: Manchester University Press, 2000); Field, *Blood, Sweat, and Toil.*

[6] Maver, 'Leisure time', 174–5; Brown, 'Rational recreation', 210–11, 216.

[7] Ibid.

[8] Pattinson, McIvor, and Robb, *Men in Reserve,* 244.

[9] Ibid., 243–4.

[10] Eilidh Macrae, *Exercise in the Female Life-Cycle in Britain, 1930–1970* (Hamilton: Palgrave Macmillan, 2016), 11.

[11] Chapman, 'British cinema', 33.

marathon working hours, destroyed neighbourhoods, separated families, and women tired out from endless queuing and making-do', observed historian Geoffrey Field.[12] Within this popular mythology, some latitude is allowed for the dance hall, which has been cemented as part of the British wartime experience and shall not be considered further here.[13] This chapter sets out to discover whether Scots had other means of leisure and pleasure on the home front, beyond the dance hall. Moreover, the chapter seeks to understand the disruption war brought to popular culture, and to explore the responses of Scots to these challenges.

According to historians Lynn Abrams and Callum G. Brown, 'in the smallest aspect of daily life, in the smallest ritual or rite, is to be found an imprint of the whole of culture'.[14] With regards to the opening story of Robert Boothby visiting Edinburgh to discuss wartime food restrictions, was the defiance shown to this authority figure and to the incoming wartime restraints representative, then, of Scottish culture? Abrams and Brown have suggested the prevailing culture in Scotland during the twentieth century was one of 'everyday resistance', in which the rejection of conformity and rebellion against authority took place 'precisely within the routines of everyday life'.[15] But did this resistance continue during the Second World War? In order to uncover the Scottish response to war's influence, this chapter will focus on four main aspects of everyday life: leisure, fundraising, drink and food. This examination of Scottish wartime life seeks to answer the question: did Scots demonstrate resistance to elements of disruption in their everyday lives, or did they instead accept such transformation and cooperate?

This chapter uses a range of sources, to gain a cross-section of wartime life and leisure. These include letters and diaries, survey responses, newspaper and magazine articles, and intelligence reports from the Scottish constabulary and Whitehall agencies. It will begin by considering wartime leisure, followed by the rise of fundraising as a venture. After that, the chapter will explore drink culture in wartime Scotland, and finish with an investigation of food and diet during the war.

Leisure

At the turn of the twentieth century, working-class leisure in Scotland was associated with the workplace. Employees at the J. P. Coats textile firm in Paisley could enjoy a bowling green, football pitch and tennis court, while those at neighbouring factory Clark's had access to a 'thoroughly equipped sports ground and handsome commodious pavilion' with cricket and

---

[12] Field, *Blood, Sweat, and Toil*, 2.
[13] Nott, 'The dancing front', 391.
[14] Abrams and Brown, 'Conceiving the everyday', 2.
[15] Ibid., 14–15.

hockey pitches, putting greens and lawn tennis courts.[16] For women, leisure needed to be flexible around family and financial constraints. Swimming fitted these requirements and was consequently one of the most popular sporting activities for Scottish working-class women.[17] Developments in the Scottish leisure scene accelerated in the early twentieth-century as a result of changes to the length of work days, the arrival of Saturday half-holidays and Fair holidays, and agitations by trade unions in support of better work conditions.[18] This helped to bring the average worker more free time outside the workplace and led to 'unprecedented levels of consumer interest' in leisure, especially sport and popular entertainment.[19]

During the interwar period, Scottish leisure pursuits were 'largely correlated with class' and, to a lesser extent, influenced by gender.[20] Fiona Skillen referred to this period as one of 'crystallisation, when class boundaries were reinforced within certain activities'.[21] Before the Second World War, football was the most popular leisure pursuit of working-class Scotsmen, in essence 'the new opiate of the people'.[22] It was exceptionally popular in the west of Scotland owing to the concentration of workers in the coal, iron, steel, shipbuilding and engineering industries in this region. During the war almost a quarter of Scotland's insured labour force were employed in such industries, further swelling the population of football-loving working-class men within the wider Glasgow area.[23] Dancing, the music hall, greyhound and horse racing, and boxing were also pastimes popular with the working class.[24] In addition, cinema provided extraordinary value for money and was especially popular with the working classes and with young people.[25] In 1937, a survey of 8,000 children in the West Lothian area found 36 per cent attended the cinema at least once a week.[26]

Popular middle-class activities during the interwar period were often focused on the health-giving properties of physical exercise and the outdoors, and on moral and intellectual improvement.[27] Outdoor pursuits

---

[16] Fiona Skillen, 'Preventing "robotised women workers": women, sport and the workplace in Scotland 1919–1939', *Labour History* 55, no. 5 (2014): 594–606, here 599; 'Opening of Anchor Ground', *Paisley and Renfrewshire Gazette*, 10 June 1922, 4.
[17] Skillen, 'Women, sport and the workplace', 602.
[18] Devine, *Scottish Nation*, 357.
[19] Maver, 'Leisure time', 178, 183.
[20] T. C. Smout, 'Patterns of culture' in Dixon and Treble, *People and Society*, 270.
[21] Fiona Skillen, '"Women and the sport fetish": modernity, consumerism and sports participation in inter-war Britain', *The International Journal of the History of Sport* 29, no. 5 (2012): 750–65, here 752.
[22] Devine, *Scottish Nation*, 361; T. C. Smout, *A Century of the Scottish People, 1830–1950* (London: Collins, 1986), 202.
[23] Devine, *Scottish Nation*, 548. Workers entitled to health and unemployment benefits under the National Insurance Act 1911 were described as 'insured'.
[24] Macdonald, *Whaur Extremes Meet*, 327–9; Maver, 'Leisure time', 176, 187.
[25] Maver, 'Leisure time', 188.
[26] Devine, *Scottish Nation*, 360.
[27] Maver, 'Leisure time', 181.

such as swimming, cycling and golf were in vogue, and exploration of the countryside, including hill-walking and bird-watching, was encouraged as a way of revitalising body and mind.[28] Groups such as the Scottish Mountaineering Club were popular with professional men, and youth clubs often went hiking, a way to 'drink in the hallowed beauty' of the countryside.[29] Membership of choral societies was common, as was listening to classical music on the radio or attending orchestral performances. By the end of 1930, 40 per cent of Scottish homes owned a wireless set.[30] Visiting libraries, galleries and museums, joining philosophical societies or attending lectures, and volunteering one's time were also considered ways the individual could better themselves.[31]

In rural areas of Scotland, traditional field sports such as deer-stalking, grouse-shooting and fishing were common.[32] Water sports were also fashionable, as were curling, shinty and cycling.[33] For practical reasons, rural leisure tended to be individual endeavours, rather than team activities. Rural Scots who worked the land had limited leisure time, and it was common for farmers and labourers to work twelve-hour days. The Saturday half-day was a recent development, having been implemented only during the Great War.[34] War prompted further demands on agricultural workers, as Chapter Seven will explore, and their limited leisure time would be further curtailed. For non-farming Scots, both rural and urban, working and middle class, war would bring differing levels of disruption to daily life and leisure.

'Had a good gallop on the sands': sport and the outdoors

For working-class Scots, war brought longer workdays and more frequent shifts, as well as additional civil defence responsibilities that curtailed free time.[35] However, many citizens still found time for leisure. Between 1941 and 1944, seventy greyhound race meetings took place in Glasgow, and average attendance was around 6,000 per race meet.[36] Boxing competitions were also held regularly, such as one such event at Hampden Park in August 1941 that was attended by 13,000 fans.[37] Even though local men

[28] Ibid., 183.
[29] Ibid., 184; John Burnett, 'Sports in the countryside', in Beech et al., *Scottish Life and Society*, 214.
[30] Devine, *Scottish Nation*, 317.
[31] Maver, 'Leisure time', 174; Royle, *Modern Britain*, 254.
[32] Burnett, 'Sports in the countryside', 204–9.
[33] Ibid., 209–11, 215–16; Maver, 'Leisure time', 185; John Burnett, 'Sport in Scotland', in Beech et al., *Scottish Life and Society*, 229.
[34] Gavin Sprott, 'Lowland country life', in Devine and Finlay, *Scotland in the Twentieth Century*, 178–9.
[35] Pattinson, McIvor, and Robb, *Men in Reserve*, 139, 141, 244.
[36] Information gathered from NRS, HH55/7–42, PWD – IR, 1939–45.
[37] NRS, HH55/29, PWD – IR, 15 August 1941: City of Glasgow.

might be busy with work or serving in the armed forces, competitions still went ahead, with registrations supplemented by servicemen stationed in the locality. In early 1940 and 1941, amateur boxing championships were held in Leith and Glasgow, with servicemen making up 'the bulk' of those taking part in each year's competition.[38]

War did, however, affect the size and number of sporting events. From 1939 to 1942, regulations on crowd sizes at mass sporting events meant small venues were restricted to 8,000 people and larger venues to 15,000. As the frontline war situation grew more grave, mass sporting events, including football and professional boxing, were restricted to days least likely to affect essential war work. This legislation also required horse and greyhound racing to take place only once per track per week, which generally meant matches and race meets were restricted to Saturdays and public holidays. These measures, enacted in March 1942, were designed to increase workplace productivity and free up public transport, but also to convey to the public the seriousness of the war situation.[39]

While war may have reduced the number of football games and the size of crowds that could attend, this did not force the cessation of a favourite pastime. For sports-loving Scots in Glasgow, between January 1941 and December 1944 over sixty senior grade (or higher) football games took place in the city, with an average attendance of 10,000 fans.[40] On special occasions attendance regulations were relaxed, allowing 27,166 to attend a Rangers match at home in Govan during August 1941, while 37,254 watched Rangers take on Celtic in September 1942.[41] Attendance regulations were also waived for international matches such as in April 1943 when 105,000 fans watched England beat Scotland at Glasgow's Hampden Park.[42] Even though war had changed some aspects of the game, Scots welcomed the chance to enjoy a much-loved pastime, whatever its form.

Popular entertainments acted as 'a lubricant rather than a brake on the war machine', according to Home Secretary Herbert Morrison, though this did not stop him from overseeing the restrictions announced in early 1942.[43] Pattinson, McIvor and Robb likewise concluded that British men on the home front viewed sport as 'an important release valve, a mode of escapism, fulfilling the desire to lead a normal life and ... keeping war worries in the background for a few hours a week'.[44] Moreover, Christopher Harvie claimed that playing and watching football was a valuable part of the

---

[38] 'Boxing contests: Glasgow application granted', *The Scotsman*, 23 January 1940, 12; 'Boxing: Scottish amateur titles', *The Scotsman*, 13 January 1941, 8.
[39] M-O, FR6: Sport in wartime, 29 October 1939, 1.
[40] See NRS, HH55/7–42, PWD – IR, 1939–45.
[41] NRS, HH55/29, PWD – IR, 15 August 1941: City of Glasgow; NRS, HH55/34, PWD – IR, 11 September 1942: City of Glasgow.
[42] NRS, HH55/36, PWD – IR, 23 April 1943: City of Glasgow.
[43] 'Restrictions on petrol and entertainment', *The Scotsman*, 13 March 1942, 5.
[44] Pattinson, McIvor and Robb, *Men in Reserve*, 247.

Scottish war effort, as this gave working-class men a chance to escape from wearying work and join in solidarity against a judgemental middle class.[45]

In contrast to curbs on mass sporting events, war brought little disruption to middle-class leisure pursuits, meaning many Scots could continue activities they had enjoyed in peacetime. Cycling and rambling in nearby green spaces were two popular pursuits in which the urban middle class regularly indulged.[46] Edinburgh resident Katherine Booth often walked around the villages of Balerno and Juniper Green, situated to the south-west of Edinburgh.[47] Similarly, Edinburgh lawyer Frank Balfour frequently spent his leisure time exploring the green spaces around Edinburgh, walking, cycling and watching birds.[48] While many of Mr Balfour's evenings were taken up with Home Guard exercises and many nights were spent at a local war command room, he rejected war's influence on his life by spending as much time as possible in the great outdoors, enjoying the balm of nature. Evening and night walks also served as a distraction from the absence of his family, evacuated to Canada for their safety. Where possible, Mr Balfour walked and cycled in Edinburgh's Holyrood Park or in the Pentland Hills, south-west of the city, even at night-time.[49] 'Took byke on train to Balerno tonight & came thro' Highland Glen to Flotterston. A most lovely night, and very enjoyable run; birds plentiful', he commented in May 1943.[50] Despite the intrusion of war on his daily routines, Mr Balfour managed to find time for simple pleasures.

Scots in rural areas were also able to continue pre-war leisure. Diary entries noted that popular outdoor leisure activities such as walking, gardening, sailing, shooting and fishing continued much as usual during the war years.[51] In some cases, wartime leisure came with additional benefits. Living on the remote Kintyre peninsula, Mrs Mitchel commented that shooting was her main recreation, 'largely because the results are so good to eat'.[52] Similarly, war benefited rural schoolteacher Miss Mellon who found that the shortened workday, a result of sharing classrooms with evacuated children, allowed for extra leisure time. After only three hours of teaching on 22 April 1941, the teacher was able to spend her afternoon planting potatoes, fishing for flounder in the bay and pony-riding. 'Had a good gallop on the sands and then climbed up to the cairn with the

[45] Harvie, *No Gods*, 119–20.
[46] See M-O, Diarists 5281 (Helensburgh), 5253 (Colinton, Edinburgh), 5380 (Glasgow), 5390 (Glasgow); Diary of Frank Balfour.
[47] M-O, Diarist 5253 (Colinton), 1 May 1940, 30 August 1942.
[48] Diary of Frank Balfour, 23 August 1942, 6 July 1943, 17 July 1943.
[49] Ibid., 1 February 1941, 14–15 March 1941, 27 May 1943, 31 July 1943.
[50] Ibid., 6 May 1943.
[51] M-O, Diarist 5314 (Tayvallich, Argyllshire), 5 and 6 August 1943; Diarist 5281 (Helensburgh), 22 and 24 July 1941; Diarist 5374 (Campbeltown), 22 April 1941; letters of the Mackintosh family, 4 January 1942.
[52] M-O, Dir. March 1942, R1534 (Campbeltown).

ponies', she noted in her diary.[53] In this case, leisure not only continued, but was extended by war.

While most forms of leisure continued, largely, as they had in peacetime, war did have an influence on this aspect of daily life. War's influence was reflected in sports tournaments, gala days and matches that were held in support of charities or war-savings campaigns and often featured members of the armed forces as competitors. Scots responded with welcome to these war-themed sports events. During summer 1941 an army commando day was held in Glasgow to raise money for the City of Glasgow Central War Relief Fund. The day featured obstacle races by teams of commando troops and displays by the Home Guard and Air Training Corps, and was attended by a crowd of 25,000.[54] In similar fashion, an American Services Sports Meet held at Glasgow's Hampden Park during November 1942 gathered a crowd of 29,645 and was attended by Anthony Eden, the Secretary of State for War.[55] Other events included Scottish universities' athletics days, which featured teams of students and service personnel in seven-a-side rugby tournaments, golf, cricket and hockey matches.[56] One Scot who was fond of attending charity sports days was Agnes Connor, based in Helensburgh. In summer 1941, Mrs Connor attended a swimming gala featuring her husband as captain of the Navy's polo team; a sports day, which saw the town 'crowded with visitors'; and a swimming gala in aid of the Red Cross.[57] She noted that the Red Cross event was 'crowded with spectators; members of the three Services coming to cheer their comrades who were competing. No-one could have imagined this bright, happy gathering was enjoying itself in wartime, but for the uniforms. Small boys shouted themselves hoarse.'[58] 'In this instance, war-themed leisure not only provided pleasure but also encouraged camaraderie between the public and the fighting forces.'

'Wide-eyed and absorbed': cinema

Scottish love for the cinema was a pleasure that was little affected by war, continuing as one of the most popular forms of entertainment across all social classes.[59] In response to a 1943 M-O questionnaire on cinema habits, Scottish respondents mentioned the pleasure of being able to lose oneself in a film featuring a favourite actor, going to the cinema 'for a good laugh' and using film as a way of escaping 'from the usual fit of depression of

---

[53] M-O, Diarist 5374 (Campbeltown), 22 April 1941.
[54] 'Athletics: commando event at Glasgow sports', *The Scotsman*, 13 July 1941, 2.
[55] NRS, HH55/35, PWD – IR, 31 October 1942: City of Glasgow; 'Mr Anthony Eden at U.S. sports gala in Glasgow', *The Scotsman*, 2 November 1942, 3.
[56] 'Another Heriot's success', *The Scotsman*, 12 April 1943, 2; 'Cricket: Red Cross match', *The Scotsman*, 2 August 1943, 2.
[57] M-O, Diarist 5281 (Helensburgh), 12 and 22 August 1941.
[58] Ibid., 2 August 1941.
[59] See NRS, HH55/7–42, PWD – IR, 1939–45.

a Saturday afternoon'.[60] Edinburgh restaurateur Isabelle Ritchie used cinema as a form of escapism, rating a Fred Astaire film in 1943 as 'silly, but cheerful and didn't mention the war which is the one thing I really require on Saturday'.[61] Likewise, Glaswegian nurse Moira Devlin enjoyed the break a Charlie Chaplin film afforded from the seriousness of war. 'I laughed again and was delighted that I could do so', she commented.[62]

Some Scots used cinema to avoid war even as it raged around them, as was reported by the deputy chief constable of Ayrshire. After the heavy two-night Blitz of Clydeside in March 1941 he noted '[o]n the second night of the attack when the people were able to interpret the noise they were hearing, there was no panic, and very little use was made of public shelters. The only people to leave the cinemas were the Civil Defence personnel.'[63] These hardy Scots were not about to miss the end of their film just for a few bombs.

Examples of the dominance of cinema in Scottish wartime lives can be found in many primary sources. In 1944 Glaswegian novelist George Woden compiled a survey of an unnamed neighbourhood of the 'better artisan class' to gauge local leisure habits. He surveyed thirty-seven families and found that, in one month, sixty-four Sunday papers were taken, thirty-nine individuals borrowed books from free libraries and none went regularly to the theatre. In sharp contrast, each week there were over 200 visits to the cinema.[64] For those living in this Glasgow suburb, cinema was clearly the most favoured wartime leisure pursuit. This was not unique to Glasgow, however, and the broad appeal of cinema was recorded in reports from across Scotland. In the Highlands and Islands, Orkney's chief constable commented that local cinemas were 'crowded out', in Moray and Nairn on the north-east coast they were 'well patronised' and in Greenock, near the mouth of the River Clyde, Superintendent William McKechnie reported that 'house full' notices had to be shown at 'practically every performance'.[65] Likewise, in Edinburgh the city's chief constable observed '[c]ertain cinemas have now been opened on Sunday evenings. Houses are filled to capacity and numbers are turned away.'[66] These reports tell us that cinema was enjoyed the length and breadth of wartime Scotland.

While war may not have affected the ability of Scots to attend the cinema, film itself did not remain unchanged. During the Second World War, a war flavour permeated all aspects of the cinema experience. In general, Scots did not resist this change and continued to enjoy a favoured leisure pursuit in whatever form it was offered. In 1943, M-O asked subscribers to list their

---

[60] M-O, Dir. November 1943, R1682 (Berwickshire), R3361 (Aberdeen).
[61] M-O, Diarist 5415 (Edinburgh), 8 May 1943.
[62] M-O, Dir. November 1943, R3247 (Glasgow).
[63] NRS, HH55/27, PWD – IR, 28 March 1941: Ayrshire.
[64] 'Drama in Glasgow: Citizen's Theatre symposium', *The Scotsman*, 31 January 1944, 2.
[65] NRS, HH55/38, PWD – IR, 5 November 1943: Orkney; NRS, HH55/26, PWD – IR, 31 January 1941: Moray and Nairn; NRS, HH55/26, PWD – IR, 31 January 1941: Greenock.
[66] NRS, HH55/34, PWD – IR, 11 September 1942: City of Edinburgh.

ten favourite films of the past year. Three out of the top ten films rated by Scottish respondents had been subject to state influence, with their content approved by the armed forces and government ministries. *We Dive at Dawn* featured submarine crews from the Royal Navy and its content required the approval of the Admiralty, while *The First of the Few* told the story of RAF pilots and planes.[67] The film most frequently viewed, highly rated by M-O's Scottish respondents, was *In Which We Serve*, a patriotic story of the crew of HMS *Torrin*, torpedoed during the Battle of Crete in mid-1941.[68] The film was well received and won an Oscar for lead actor and director Noël Coward, but was, essentially, thinly veiled propaganda backed by MoI.[69] In 1943, Edinburgh woman Isabelle Ritchie attended this film at an Inverness cinema with her family. She 'thought it excellent and so did sister-in-law who had admitted to me her horror of all "war" films'.[70]

Scottish moviegoers were also influenced by government news shorts and short propaganda films, which were generally played before a feature film. Three such films shown in Scotland were *Malta G.C.*, *Convoy* and *Squadron 992*. *Malta G.C.* was a short propaganda documentary produced by the Crown Film Unit, a division of MoI, which focused on the heroic efforts of the Maltese people in withstanding heavy Axis air attacks. It was viewed by Mrs Ritchie, who noted it was 'immensely interesting to look at the first-rate pictures ... as a production this one served not only the propaganda and educational purposes it was intended to serve but also succeeded in being a really artistic piece of work'.[71] In a similar vein was *Squadron 992*, a film about balloon barrage defences during a Luftwaffe raid on Edinburgh's Firth of Forth in October 1939. Again produced by the Crown Film Unit, it was rated by *The Scotsman*'s reviewer as follows: 'They have given their film a human interest which is ultimately more compelling than obvious dramatics, and they have given reality and meaning to one aspect of life under war conditions. In its quiet purposefulness the film is more stimulating than a dozen perfervid appeals.'[72] The reviewer also called the film 'exciting', 'arresting' and an 'excellent' example of propaganda, which 'urges us to be up and doing'.[73] This reviewer had correctly noted the purpose of such films – to raise public support for the war and to encourage people to get behind the war effort. The positive reaction of Scots to this official propaganda demonstrates a willingness to accept war's disruption of life. The success of these films, sanctioned, produced and sometimes written by state propagandists,

---

[67] Figures gathered from M-O, Dir. November 1943, and NLS, ACC11356, Diaries of Muriel Kerr.
[68] See M-O, Dir. November 1943.
[69] Lee Pfeiffer, '*In Which We Serve*', *Encyclopaedia Britannica*, https://www.britannica.com/topic/In-Which-We-Serve (accessed 9 December 2019).
[70] M-O, Diarist 5415 (Edinburgh), 15 April 1943.
[71] Ibid.
[72] 'The cinema: balloon barrage film', *The Scotsman*, 9 July 1940, 7.
[73] Ibid.

also reveals a Scottish acceptance of government involvement in popular leisure, challenging the notion of everyday resistance to authority.

Short films about the home front were also a useful way to appeal to local sensibilities, and let audiences feel their efforts were not going unrecognised. In Scotland, cinemagoers were shown films such as *Warwork News No. 19: The Other Man's Job*, about workers in Glasgow producing locomotives for the war in Europe, and *Fighting Fields: Feeding the Nation During Wartime*, on the importance to the war effort of Scottish agricultural workers and the Women's Land Army.[74] One such film, *Scotland At War*, was summarised in glowing terms by a writer for *SMT Magazine:*

> The people of Scotland, with that deep love of freedom which made them resist aggression in bygone days, have entered with all their energies into the nation-wide drive for victory over the Nazi regime. In field and factory, on land and sea, they are 'going to it', a great army of civilian workers standing shoulder to shoulder with their kinsfolk in the Services.[75]

Film historian James Chapman believes that such films played an important role in influencing the public by presenting a general message of national unity and reminding the public why Britain was at war.[76] Shorts, as they were known, could express direct and urgent messages to a wide audience, suitable for disseminating propaganda that needed to be spread as widely as possible.[77] In the mid-twentieth century, cinema admission charges were very low, ranging from 1d to 6d, or between 16p and £1 in 2020 terms.[78] With the Scottish love of cinema ensuring a steady stream of audiences, this was indeed a valuable medium for disseminating information.

Even Scots in rural areas were not immune to war – and state – influence on leisure. MoI made sure that government messages reached rural communities by employing a mobile film technician to tour isolated parts of Britain.[79] A 1941 film tour of the Isles of Lewis and Harris was rated by

[74] Ministry of Supply and Paramount, *Warwork News No. 19: The Other Man's Job*, 1943, viewed at *Scotland on Screen*, https://scotlandonscreen.org.uk/browse-films/007-000-000-225-c (accessed 12 October 2019); MoI, Scottish Department of Agriculture, and Scottish Film Productions, *Fighting Fields: Feeding the Nation During Wartime*, 1941, viewed at *Scotland on Screen*, https://scotlandonscreen.org.uk/browse-films/007-000-000-089-c (accessed 12 October 2019).

[75] '*Scotland at War*: the new Ministry of Information film', *SMT Magazine*, December 1940, 24–5.

[76] James Chapman, *The British at War: Cinema, State and Propaganda, 1939–1945* (London: I. B. Tauris, 1998), 113.

[77] Ibid., 112.

[78] Devine, *Scottish Nation*, 360. Conversion calculated using the National Archives Currency Converter, https://www.nationalarchives.gov.uk/currency-converter/#currency-result (accessed 16 December 2020).

[79] 'Home front', *SMT Magazine*, April 1944, 11.

government intelligence officials as 'one of the most successful yet carried out by the film units'.[80] The welcome shown by locals to film crews was assessed as 'phenomenal', and after viewing the MoI films, locals were said to have 'a great enthusiasm for the Ministry's work'.[81] Similar shows were given in Fort William, Nairn and Ross and Cromarty, while one film screening in Dingwall was attended by over 700 people.[82] An MoI film projectionist also braved the snowy Scottish Highlands to take the film show to Tomintoul, a small village in the Cairngorms. There was no cinema in the village and the area was 15 miles from the nearest railway station, so many locals had never before seen a film.[83] An article in *SMT Magazine* lauded the success of the event, claiming that the town hall was packed out with children and adults who were 'wide-eyed and absorbed', and the film had brought 'tangible proof . . . that the world has not forgotten those who work in unpublicised obscurity far away from the centres of war administration'.[84] Such programmes provided a valuable opportunity for MoI to influence Scottish lives, but Scots also benefited from this arrangement. What was previously a habit limited to those in towns and cities was now accessible to those in remote areas. In this respect, war had brought a new leisure habit to rural Scots.

'An evening of real satisfaction': cultural entertainment

In similar fashion to other popular forms of entertainment in Scotland, cultural pursuits were largely unaffected by war, and able to continue much as they had during peacetime. Attendance of galleries and museums, listening to classical music, and membership of libraries and educational, charitable or philosophical societies had been popular pastimes of the middle classes in pre-war times.[85] Ten diaries and one series of letters examined for this chapter, written predominantly by middle-class Scots, mention engaging in such forms of leisure during the war.[86] Other popular pastimes were

---

[80] TNA, INF 1/673, IAC, 'Progress report', 17–31 May 1941.
[81] Ibid.
[82] Ibid.
[83] IWM, D22617, 'Film show at highest village in the Highlands: Ministry of Information film screening, Tomintoul'. See associated photographs D22615–22631.
[84] 'Home front', *SMT Magazine*, April 1944, 11.
[85] Royle, *Modern Britain*, 254.
[86] M-O, Diarist 5196 (Glasgow), 15–21 June 1942, 1–9 and 24–30 August 1942; Diarist 5177 (Berwickshire), 3 September 1942, 4 August 1943; Diarist 5232 (Aberdeen), 16 September 1940; Diarist 5253 (Colinton), 28 April 1940, 3 April 1942, 3 July 1942, 8 August 1942, 14 September 1942; Diarist 5281 (Helensburgh), 31 July 1941, 13 August 1941; Diarist 5380 (Glasgow), 21, 24, 28 May 1944; Diarist 5390 (Glasgow), 1 and 10 August 1941; Diarist 5415 (Edinburgh), 13 August 1942, 10 September 1942, 24 April 1943, 14 and 27 May 1943; BBC People's War, A3220057, letter from Anne Westlands, 1 December 1940; Diary of Frank Balfour, January 1940, May 1943, December 1943, January 1944; NLS, ACC11356, Diaries of Muriel Kerr, 'List of books read during 1943'.

painting, folk-dancing, ballet and attending meetings of clubs such as the Soroptimists and the Tree Lovers Society.[87]

Despite the mantle of war, cultural entertainers continued to tour wartime Britain. The Scottish Orchestra performed regularly, though there were also many visits from such groups as the Hallé Orchestra, the London Philharmonic Orchestra and the National Symphony Orchestra.[88] After praising a 'magnificent' concert in Edinburgh's Usher Hall during September 1943, a correspondent for *The Scotsman* noted that music was 'enjoying a large measure of public favour at present'.[89] Scottish ballet fans also enjoyed regular visits from popular troupes, with the Sadler's Wells Ballet and the International Ballet Company touring during 1941, the Ballets Jooss in 1943 and 1944, and the Anglo-Polish Ballet between 1941 and 1944.[90] In Edinburgh Isabelle Ritchie attended the ballet with a member of the Women's Royal Naval Service during August 1942. 'I gave her dinner and took her to the Sadler's Wells Ballet which was pure joy', Mrs Ritchie noted in her diary. She added 'I haven't had such an evening of real satisfaction for a long time'.[91]

Satisfaction was also found in theatre performances, such as a stage adaptation of Jane Austen's *Emma* that was performed in Glasgow during May 1944. That month, Elspeth Musgrove reported that she had been to the play with her mother-in-law. 'How beautifully it was acted and how popular Jane Austen is! It all seems so utterly remote from the present war', she observed, adding '[i]s Jane's present popularity escapism I wonder?'[92] The quality of theatre was high, and included the Old Vic performing *King John* in Edinburgh during June 1941, the H. M. Tennent Players performing early releases of popular West End plays and the Glasgow Citizens' Theatre, formed in 1943 to perform 'the best type of play with the best possible company, and the encouragement of Scottish drama'.[93] Theatre lovers in rural areas did not miss out either, and often benefited from the programmes of the Entertainments National Service Association (ENSA)

---

[87] M-O, Diarists 5380 (Glasgow), 1 December 1943, 24–25 May 1944; Diarist 5415 (Edinburgh), 13 August 1942; Diarist 5390 (Glasgow), 29 July 1940, 4 August 1941, 25 June 1944.

[88] 'National Symphony Orchestra: Pouishnoff', *The Scotsman*, 20 September 1943, 4.

[89] Ibid.

[90] *The Scotsman*, entertainment listings for 4 November 1941, 16 March 1943 and 8 February 1944; 'Ballets Jooss', *The Scotsman*, 31 March 1944, 3; 'Edinburgh theatres, Kings: the Anglo-Polish Ballet', *The Scotsman*, 4 February 1941, 6; 'Edinburgh theatres, Lyceum: the Anglo-Polish Ballet', *The Scotsman*, 5 August 1941, 3.

[91] M-O, Diarist 5415 (Edinburgh), 13 August 1944.

[92] M-O, Diarist 5380 (Glasgow), 10 May 1944.

[93] 'Entertainments', *The Scotsman*, 24 June 1941; 'Repertory drama: for Edinburgh and Glasgow, West End company', *The Scotsman*, 19 February 1940, 3; 'Citizens' Theatre: Glasgow plans for coming season', *The Scotsman*, 18 August 1944, 3; 'James Bridie's *Holy Isle*: opening performance at Citizens' Theatre in Glasgow', *The Scotsman*, 12 October 1943, 4.

Leisure and Pleasure 199

and the Council for the Encouragement of Music and the Arts (CEMA) which toured Scotland with theatre performances, variety shows and mobile cinemas (see Figure 6.1). During late 1941, ENSA toured to 'lonely outposts of the Highlands', 'solitary lowland hamlets' and into the Western Isles, Orkney and Shetland.[94] Similarly, CEMA was responsible for a 1943 tour by the Perth Repertory Company to remote Highland and Island localities, considered by *SMT Magazine* to be 'possibly one of the most exciting theatrical journeys ever attempted'.[95]

Scots interested in art or museums were also able to continue this interest during war. Groups such as the Royal Scottish Society of Painters in Water Colours, the Edinburgh College of Art, the Royal Scottish Academy and the Royal Glasgow Institute of the Fine Arts held frequent exhibitions during the war years.[96] CEMA also took art exhibitions to locations such as Montrose, Arbroath and Fife, ensuring that Scots outside the big cities were not starved of other forms of cultural entertainment during the war.[97] Scottish galleries and museums were not left completely unaffected by war, though. In Glasgow and Edinburgh large facilities chose to send their most valuable items to country houses for safe-keeping. In the case of the Kelvingrove Art Galleries and Museum in Glasgow, this was a fortuitous move as the facility was badly hit in the Clydeside Blitz and suffered extensive damage.[98] Director Tom Honeyman was pleased to report his gratitude that the safety measures had ensured 'nothing of any real value' was lost from the collection.[99] At the National Gallery of Scotland and the Scottish National Portrait Gallery most possessions were distributed between a variety of country lodges and castles, though large pieces such as a Van Dyck and wax models by Michelangelo were kept in a reinforced room at the National Gallery.[100]

Edinburgh's National Museum of Scotland, at that time known as the Royal Scottish Museum, was more affected by war than many other galleries and museums, as the majority of its collections were sent for safe-keeping to country houses and castles, and most of the museum was closed to the public until 1944.[101] Director Thomas Rowatt admirably adapted to these wartime disruptions, though. He arranged for a series of lectures

[94] 'With ENSA in Scotland', *SMT Magazine*, December 1941, 26–7.
[95] 'With CEMA in Scotland', *SMT Magazine*, August 1943, 29.
[96] *The Scotsman* reports exhibitions of these groups on 25 January 1941, 25 April 1941, 10 May 1941, 27 June 1941, 21 August 1941, 26 November 1941, 27 April 1942, 27 April 1943, 1 May 1943, 10 June 1943, 7 August 1943, 2 October 1943, 13 November 1943, 22 April 1944, 25 August 1944 and 14 October 1944.
[97] Euan McArthur, *Scotland, CEMA and the Arts Council, 1919–1967* (Abingdon: Routledge, 2016), 152–3.
[98] 'Kelvingrove Art Galleries', *The Scotsman*, 21 March 1941, 4.
[99] NMS, director's correspondence, letter to Thomas Rowatt, 25 March 1941.
[100] 'How Scotland's treasures were safeguarded', *The Scotsman*, 19 July 1945 via NRS, ED3/362, National treasures in an emergency.
[101] NMS, The Royal Scottish Museum, Report for the year 1940, 7.

Figure 6.1 'Music for the Fleet': 28 March 1944, on board HMS *Duke of York* at Scapa Flow. (Source: © Crown Copyright. IWM.)

to be given to members of His Majesty's Forces at two anti-aircraft stations in Scotland, enabling servicemen to escape the war for an evening. Topics included 'Modern business methods', 'Art of cinema photography' and 'Land transport through the ages'.[102] The museum was also able to lend specimens to other galleries, continue school holiday classes and provide visits to schoolchildren from Edinburgh, Fife, West Lothian and Peeblesshire.[103] When the museum officially reopened in 1944, public lectures included 'Scotland's contribution to metallurgy', 'The mountains of Scotland' and 'Woollens'.[104] The cultural theme continued in exhibitions, including 'Spinning and weaving', which featured Scottish textiles, tartan weaving demonstrations, films and lectures, and 'Meet Scotland', which was based on the geography, resources and industries of Scotland.[105] A very patriotic programme, indeed.

One change during wartime was the emergence of art and museum exhibitions that fostered support for the war. At the National Gallery of Scotland exhibitions tended to have a 'war flavour', such as the 1940 exhibition of photographs in aid of the Polish Relief Fund and a 1941 exhibition entitled 'Inter-Allied art', featuring works by Czech, Polish, Norwegian and Belgian artists.[106] An article in *SMT Magazine* praised the exhibition as an 'artistic *entente* [that] augurs well for the future not only of art but of human relations in post-war Europe'.[107] By July 1945 the Scottish National Gallery had held over seventy exhibitions, averaging a new exhibit every three weeks, and 'the flags of practically all our Allies had flown from the pole above the gallery door . . . a memory of happy collaboration with many friends and with artists from all over Europe', commented the director in 1945.[108] By speaking of 'allies', '*entente*' and 'collaboration' these exhibitions cultivated a martial flavour and directly appealed to public sentiment. In a way, they fostered the idea that patronising these entertainments was also a way to support the collective war effort.

Another popular exhibition that roused public support for war was the 'RAF exhibition of war' collection. Displayed at Glasgow's Kelvingrove Art Galleries during August 1942, the exhibition featured photographs of damage caused by RAF bombers, souvenirs from German planes that had been shot down and a silk parachute, among other things. On the surface,

---

[102] NMS, director's correspondence: letter to Thomas Rowatt from The Edinburgh and South-East Scotland Regional Committee for Adult Education in HM Forces, 11 December 1940.
[103] NMS, letter from Thomas Rowatt to Mrs Jardine, National Gallery of Scotland, 1 March 1943; Annual Reports 1939 and 1945.
[104] NMS, The Royal Scottish Museum, Report for the year 1945, 2.
[105] Ibid.
[106] 'Exhibition of inter-Allied art', *The Scotsman*, 30 May 1941, 6; 'How Scotland's treasures were safeguarded', *The Scotsman*, 19 July 1945.
[107] 'Home front', *SMT Magazine*, July 1941, 10.
[108] 'How Scotland's treasures were safeguarded', *The Scotsman*, 19 July 1945 via NRS, ED3/362, National treasures in an emergency.

such an exhibition seems a chance for the public to indulge their interest in war. Examined more closely, however, the items exhibited included what could be described as trophies of war. The exhibition also celebrated attacks on the enemy, such as detailing the tally of German planes brought down by the 'very fine' local squadrons such as the 603 City of Edinburgh fighter squadron.[109] The exhibition, curated by the Air Ministry and MoI, toured the length of Britain but enjoyed unparalleled popularity in Scotland. Miss Offley reported that it was 'the most crowded exhibition I've been to yet . . . hundreds of boys in their teens and all wildly enthusiastic . . . Also many adults really anxious to see'.[110] Reporting on its reception in Glasgow, *The Scotsman* noted '[a]ttendance records have been broken . . . in no other city where the exhibition has been staged have so many visitors seen the exhibits'.[111] The wild popularity of such a display shows how successfully public support for war could be fostered.

A further example of a display that played upon public sentiment about war was the 'Exhibition of art from enemy prison camps', held at the Scottish National Gallery in September 1944. The display featured artworks by men of Scotland's 51st Highland Division, two-thirds of whom had been imprisoned in Germany since the Dunkirk evacuation in 1940 and 'needed the utmost help we could give them to keep them occupied and to keep their hope and self-respect and reason as they were before the war', said the exhibition organiser.[112] Surely nothing could play upon public sympathies like the misfortunes of the revered Division. An article in *The Scotsman* speculated that the exhibition would also appeal to relatives of the prisoners, who would have a chance to see what camp life was like for their loved ones.[113] Unfortunately, no accompanying tally of visitor numbers could be found.

The government was behind many of these attempts at fostering pro-war sentiment or raising public morale. At the National Museum of Scotland the most popular wartime exhibitions were those organised by MoI. This ministry specialised in propaganda and the influencing of public morale, and it is a measure of its success that exhibitions curated by those intent on public persuasion were the very exhibitions most popular with the public. While the 'Scottish fisheries exhibition' received 32,000 visitors in nearly five months, the immensely popular 'War against Japan' exhibit received 30,738 attendees within only two weeks.[114] 'Mulberry', on the topic of portable harbours deployed in France, was also popular with Edinburgh audiences, receiving more attendees there than in any other showings

---

[109] 'RAF exhibition in Edinburgh: Scottish squadrons' fine work', *The Scotsman*, 21 August 1941, 3.
[110] M-O, Diarist 5390 (Glasgow), 23 August 1942.
[111] 'Glasgow and west: RAF exhibition in Glasgow', *The Scotsman*, 25 August 1942, 3.
[112] 'Prisoners' pictures: Edinburgh exhibition opened', *The Scotsman*, 27 September 1944, 3.
[113] 'Art in captivity: pictures from prison camps', *The Scotsman*, 26 September 1944, 3.
[114] NMS, The Royal Scottish Museum, Report for the year 1945, 1, 4.

across Britain.[115] Another popular exhibition was 'Marine', which included lectures on naval operations and propaganda films such as *Heroes of the Atlantic* and *Clyde Built*, about shipyards along Scotland's River Clyde. The Museum's director in 1944, Dr Allan, noted that while average Sunday attendance was 1,000 patrons, during 'Mulberry' and 'Marine' attendances ranged between 2,000 and 3,000 visitors per Sunday.[116] These Scots responded with enthusiasm to these entertainment media, embracing war and state influence over this area of their lives.

Fundraising

Scots also responded to war by vigorously committing themselves to fundraising campaigns. Such campaigns were common across Britain, raising money for charities such as the Red Cross, for war weaponry or to encourage the public to participate in savings schemes. In many cases these campaigns also included displays of military weaponry or parades by the armed forces, which was a way for the public to feel more connected with those on the frontline. The first campaigns began in 1940 and were marketed as donations to purchase new Spitfire and bomber planes, or even components for them. By telling people that their donation of 8 shillings had purchased a spark plug, or their community's donation of £2,000 had purchased a Spitfire wing, the public was left with the impression that every donation, however small, directly helped the war effort.[117] Fundraising efforts across Scotland were varied, and included such events as a garden fête at Lochinch Castle in Wigtownshire, a military sports gala and performance by the pipe band of the Argyll and Sutherland Highlanders held in rural Stirling, and in Galashiels a 'Braw Lad' fund offering work in exchange for donations, which reached £324 in two weeks.[118]

War Weapons Weeks were another element of wartime life to which Scots responded positively. These were a series of campaigns encouraging the public to contribute to the National Savings Scheme.[119] During 1940, Edinburgh events included a pageant that, according to *SMT Magazine*, focused on 'the cause of freedom, particularly as illustrated in Scottish history'.[120] Scots gave generously to this scheme, with Edinburgh donations totalling £10,000,000 during 1940's savings week. Run alongside War Savings Weeks were Tank Days, events that allowed the public to indulge

---

[115] Ibid. Attendance for 'Mulberry' is harder to calculate, as this was running at the same time as the popular 'Meet Scotland' exhibition.
[116] NMS, The Royal Scottish Museum, Report for the year 1945, 2.
[117] Greig Watson, 'Spitfire funds: the "whip-round" that won the war?' *BBC News*, 12 March 2016, https://www.bbc.com/news/uk-england-35697546 (accessed 28 February 2020).
[118] 'Spitfire funds in Scotland', *The Scotsman*, 25 September 1940, 8; 'Spitfire and bomber funds', *The Scotsman*, 23 September 1940, 3.
[119] 'Home front', *SMT Magazine*, December 1940, 11.
[120] Ibid.

their curiosity about military weaponry (see Figure 6.2). In summer 1941 Miss Offley attended Glasgow's Tank Day, observing '[t]he tanks stood at Radnor Street for thirty minutes and the police had their hands full getting the traffic through the dense crowds. Little boys swarmed over the tanks until they looked like human anthills.' She added '[t]here was no doubt of the desire of the public to see the tanks'.[121] The editor of the *Glasgow Herald* agreed, noting '[t]he crew of Matilda, along with the tank, disappears in a twinkling under a score of children absorbed in climbing over everything'.[122] These events were not just fundraisers, explained an editorial in *SMT Magazine*, but also demonstrated how money invested in war savings could be 'turned into a deadly, efficient war weapon'.[123]

Scots also cooperated with the war effort through their commitment to 'Wings for Victory' savings campaigns. The accompanying propaganda proclaimed the events as a chance for every citizen 'to express their admiration of, and gratitude to, the men of that superb force to whom the many owe so much': the Royal Air Force.[124] Across Scotland, fifty-five savings weeks were organised, taking place from Shetland in the north to Wigtownshire in the south. One of the main features of the campaign was that it gave the public the chance to view a military procession and war machinery. In Edinburgh, events in 1943 included a Services parade, an RAF exhibition and band performances. In addition, numerous Air Force planes were displayed around the wider Edinburgh area, and an 8,000-lb bomb put on display at the Mound in Edinburgh's heart.[125] During the campaign, Edinburgh local Frank Balfour went to see a Lancaster bomber on display in Bruntsfield Links, south of the city.[126] This plane was considered to be a big attraction for the public, and that attraction extended to a writer for *The Scotsman*, who gushed that upon arrival at an airbase in the south-east of Scotland the plane had 'taxied with ponderous majesty and a thunderous roar of engines'.[127]

Glasgow received its own Lancaster bomber (see Figure 6.3), one that had taken part in forty-seven 'operational sorties', including important raids on Berlin and the submarine bases at St Nazaire, on the west coast of France.[128] Lord Provost J. M. Biggar, welcoming the plane and its crew to Glasgow, said he hoped it would help the city 'hit the target and blast it to pieces'.[129] Events in the city also included a band contest, the releasing of

[121] M-O, Diarist 5390 (Glasgow), 10 August 1941.
[122] 'An editorial diary: speed the tanks', *Glasgow Herald*, 11 August 1941.
[123] Ibid.
[124] British Pathé, *Wings for Victory Week* (film), 1943. Viewed at https://youtu.be/xfuAfIzc_c4 (accessed 11 October 2019).
[125] 'Wings for Victory: varied attractions for Edinburgh week', *The Scotsman*, 1 May 1943, 4.
[126] M-O, Diarist 5415 (Edinburgh), 17 May 1943; Diary of Frank Balfour, 17 May 1943.
[127] 'Lancaster bomber for display in Edinburgh', *The Scotsman*, 29 April 1943, 4.
[128] '"Veteran" bomber: Lancaster for Glasgow', *The Scotsman*, 6 May 1943, 3.
[129] Ibid.

Figure 6.2 Tanks at Edinburgh Castle for War Savings Week, 1941. (Source: *SMT Magazine*, September 1941. National Library Scotland.)

Figure 6.3 Wings for Victory plane, Glasgow, 1943. (Source: © Newsquest (*Herald & Times*) 000-000-124-058-R.)

1,350 pigeons – 'one for each £10,000 of the city's target of £13,500,000' – and medals and souvenirs from the collection of a deceased squadron leader, a Glasgow lad.[130]

Scots gave enthusiastically, surpassing all savings predictions for the Wings for Victory events. While the target for Edinburgh had been set at £10,000,000, the city finished the savings period having raised over £12,000,000.[131] Glasgow had reached a 'splendid' £16,262,317, a higher result than all of Scotland's previous Wings for Victory campaigns.[132] Scots in the regions also showed support for the war by beating their local targets. The best results came from Newton of Falkland, where donations equalled an astonishing £112 per head of population. Following close behind were two rural areas: Strathyre, a village in the Trossachs, with £90 per head; and Cove and Kilcreggan on the north shores of the Firth of Clyde, with £63 per head.[133] Across Scotland the amount saved totalled £62,250,000 – more than £2 million above target, or enough to purchase 12,000 fighter planes.[134] *The Scotsman* noted that this was higher than 'Warships Weeks', which had raised £57,754, 446, and 'War Weapons Weeks', which had seen Scots donate £50,028,675.[135] At this time, figures indicated that since the beginning of the war Scots had contributed more than £500 million to savings campaigns.[136] This level of support indicates some acceptance of the disruptions of war, with Scots going above and beyond to donate in support of the war effort.

It is difficult to assess the popularity of such events across the duration of the war. While MoI museum exhibitions in Edinburgh attracted record visitor numbers during summer 1944, this was not the case for a pro-war fundraising event held at the same time in Glasgow. The Army Exhibition, held at Queen's Park Recreation Grounds in Glasgow during July 1944, was 'the most comprehensive exhibition of Army equipment ever staged', and was run in tandem with a fundraising drive.[137] The equipment display covered 2 million square feet, twice the acreage displayed when the exhibition was staged in Manchester, and featured 'practically every "non-secret" vehicle, weapon, and ancillary service of the modern British Army'.[138] Despite the extra square footage, attendance in Glasgow fell 'notably short' of that it had garnered in English cities, with only 544,200 Scots viewing the display.[139] This worked out to roughly half the population of the city,

[130] 'Wings for Victory: Glasgow campaign opens to-day', *The Scotsman*, 29 May 1943, 3.
[131] 'Edinburgh lends £12,050,000', *The Scotsman*, 24 May 1943, 5.
[132] 'Target exceeded', *The Scotsman*, 2 July 1943, 3.
[133] Ibid.
[134] Ibid.
[135] Ibid.
[136] Ibid.
[137] 'The modern army: public to see equipment', *The Scotsman*, 14 July 1944, 3.
[138] Ibid.
[139] 'Attendance below record: army exhibition ends', *Glasgow Herald*, 1 September 1944, 6.

compared to Birmingham where three-quarters of residents attended, and Manchester where attendance was equal to the city's population.[140] Perhaps the problem was the timing of the event, occurring during August when many Glaswegians were away on trades holidays. Surprisingly, while attendances were lower than hoped, charitable donations were high. Scots donated over 40 per cent more (in ratio to attendance) than visitors to the same exhibition in London, Manchester or Birmingham. This led the chairman of the Scottish Advisory Committee of the MoI to declare the display 'the finest exhibition' since the Empire Exhibition of 1938, and praise its 'atmosphere of victory'.[141]

Regardless of 'low' attendances at the Army Exhibition, the primary sources discussed here reveal that, without doubt, Scots gave generously to fundraising campaigns throughout the war. Such generosity may have been influenced by interwar theories of good citizenship, in which leisure could be used as 'a social good'.[142] Alternatively, behaviour may have been influenced by what historian Sonya Rose termed 'the potency of the national "we"'.[143] Messages about 'public spirit', images of Britain as a unified community and discussions about how to be 'active contributors' to a democratic society played an important part in public discourse during the war years.[144]

The importance of playing one's part was also reflected in the persuasive language of the savings campaigns. Aside from fundraising weeks, poster campaigns from the Scottish Savings Committee were frequently used to exhort the public to take part in national savings campaigns or to buy war bonds.[145] Slogans linked domestic action to frontline action, putting the individual in a role of importance: 'Convoy your country to victory', 'Save for the brave', 'The most you can save is the least they deserve', 'Lend to defend the right to be free' and 'We at home have a battle to win – support your savings group'.[146] These messages portrayed the notion that through the action of saving money an individual had agency, while through inaction the outcome of war might be altered, and it was thus up to the

---

[140] Ibid. Attendance figures calculated on data gathered from Federal Cultural Foundation, Germany, 'Manchester/Liverpool II' (Leipzig: Shrinking Cities, unpublished report, 2004), 41.
[141] Ibid.
[142] Robert Snape, 'The new leisure, voluntarism and social reconstruction in inter-war Britain', *Contemporary British History* 29, no. 1 (2015): 51–83, here 51.
[143] Rose, *Which People's War?*, 9.
[144] Ibid., 84–5.
[145] Posters were used across Britain by the National Savings Committee, the Scottish Savings Committee and the Ulster Savings Committee.
[146] IWM, PST 20952, 'Convoy your country to victory', n. d.; IWM, PST 18454, 'Save for the brave', n. d.; Australian War Memorial (AWM), ARTV03352, 'The most you can save is the least they deserve', n. d.; IWM, PST 15575, 'Lend to defend the right to be free – buy defence bonds', n. d.; IWM, PST 15568, 'We at home have a battle to win – support your savings group', n. d.

individual to act for the greater good of society. Savings Committees harnessed this message, even going so far as to link an individual's act of saving money and the battlefront. In this manner, during 1943 Lord Alness advised the people of Edinburgh that the savings stamps they purchased would be attached to a bomb that would then be 'dropped on a target in Germany' (see Figure 6.4).[147] In effect, this allowed the public to play a direct role in the frontline war effort. Messages telling citizens their actions would have a direct bearing on the outcome of the war, and that this was what responsible citizens should do, must surely have spurred the generous giving seen in Scotland. Or perhaps Scots were driven by the spirit of competition, eager to outbid their English neighbours.

'The drink'

The Scottish population's close relationship with alcohol was historically well established in national culture. According to historians T. C. Smout and Sydney Wood, Scots 'have a reputation for being free to the point of abandon' in their drinking habits.[148] The consumption of alcohol had a central place at Scottish *ceilidh*, as well as at funerals, during Hogmanay or on almost any other occasion.[149] As *The Scotsman* summarised in May 1850, '[t]hat Scotland is, pretty near at least, the most drunken nation on the face of the earth is a fact never quite capable of denial'.[150] In the eighteenth and nineteenth centuries, popular writers presented Scotland as a place of conviviality, portraying 'a robust image of drinking and tavern life'.[151] Historically, the public house was a safe haven for Scottish men, providing the ability 'to wrap themselves in the safe cloak of alcohol'.[152] Pubs also functioned as meeting places and as a sort of community hub for social interaction.[153] In essence, alcohol acted as a social lubricant, and drink culture was a fundamental part of pre-war Scottish society.

In the early years of the war, Scots fought to resist war's influence on drinking culture. One way they rebelled was by circumventing the 'bona fide traveller' law. The Forbes-Mackenzie Act of 1853, as it was formally known, had decreed public houses were prohibited from opening on Sundays but hoteliers were permitted to serve alcohol to bona fide travellers.[154] During 1940 and 1941 law enforcement officials regularly reported evasion

---

[147] 'Savings weeks: Scotland's "Wings for Victory" campaign', *The Scotsman*, 25 March 1943, 5.
[148] Smout and Wood, *Scottish Voices*, 147.
[149] Devine, *Scottish Nation*, 352; Alan Dean, 'Alcohol in Hebridean culture: 16th–20th century', *Addiction* 90, no. 2 (1995): 277–88, here 285–6.
[150] Untitled article, *The Scotsman*, 22 May 1850, quoted in Devine, *Scottish Nation*, 350.
[151] Maver, 'Leisure time', 176.
[152] Edwin Muir, *Scottish Journey* (Edinburgh: Mainstream, 1979 edition), 19.
[153] Devine, *Scottish Nation*, 352.
[154] Maver, 'Leisure time', 180.

Figure 6.4 Lord Alness sticking a savings stamp on a bomb, 1943. (Source: *The Scotsman*, 25 March 1943. National Library Scotland.)

of this law, as large numbers of Scots travelled on the sabbath seemingly for the sole purpose of consuming alcohol.[155] Officials were also concerned at the use of private motorcars to travel to public houses, as this contravened wartime curbs on leisure travel and calls to conserve petrol and rubber for the war effort.[156]

[155] See NRS, HH55/19–31, PWD – IR, 1940–41.
[156] Ibid.: Aberdeen City, Lanarkshire.

'Drink travel' was concentrated in rural areas near large cities. This was the case in the burgh of Kincardine where local constables observed 'obvious signs of abuse' of the bona fide traveller privilege at weekends, when those from the nearby city of Aberdeen travelled to public houses in rural parts of the burgh. Likewise in Stirling, the chief constable complained in August 1941 that the number of persons obviously travelling for the sole purpose of obtaining drink on Sundays appeared to be increasing. In Lanarkshire, the county in which Glasgow is situated, the constabulary noticed locals using public transport to go drinking on Sundays, which caused 'considerable congestion' on transport services. Similarly, in rural Aberdeen complaints were received about Sunday drinking in villages within twenty miles of Aberdeen city, and also over overcrowding on late buses as a result of these 'drinking expeditions'.[157] This behaviour was frowned upon, as the overcrowding of public transport could potentially interfere with the commuting of essential workers.

While these Scots resisted the war's restriction of a favoured pastime, this defiance was not to last. In mid-1941, while Germany rampaged through Russia and the Allies signed the Atlantic Charter, Scottish authorities agreed wartime drinking had to be restrained. As a result, the Licensing (Restriction of Supply on Sunday) (No.1) Order 1941 was drafted, coming into effect on 17 August 1941. Under the terms of the order, drinking in 'the most populous counties in Scotland' would be restricted, hopefully curbing Sunday drink travel.[158] Immediately, the Scottish constabulary noted a 'marked decrease' in Sunday drinking and in travelling to obtain drink.[159] As the law was implemented, authorities recorded public responses: in Edinburgh, the legislation was said to be 'well received by all'; in Glasgow and Clydeside the change was 'quietly accepted'; and among 'the travelling public' in Greenock the ban was 'well received'. In Ayrshire the chief constable commented that the legislation was 'generally welcomed', and there was a public feeling of satisfaction that the government had, at last, moved on the matter. Satisfaction at the change was not limited to 'the fanatical pussyfoots only', the chief constable added.[160] A fortnight later, the chief constable of Lanarkshire reported drink traffic was down by over 75 per cent since the regulation had been implemented.[161] Over the next four years of war, the majority of Scots continued to cooperate with this restriction and most regions of the country reported further decreases in drink travel in each subsequent

[157] NRS, HH55/29, PWD – IR, 15 August 1941: Kincardine, Stirlingshire, Lanarkshire, Aberdeen.
[158] Ibid., 29 August 1941: *précis*.
[159] Ibid.
[160] NRS, HH55/29, PWD – IR, 15 August 1941: City of Edinburgh, City of Glasgow, Greenock, Ayrshire.
[161] Ibid., 29 August 1941: Lanarkshire.

year of war.¹⁶² In this aspect of Scottish everyday culture, resistance was notable by its absence.

In the early years of the Second World War, Scots managed to continue their warm relationship with alcohol, and this was observed by local constabulary, who provided regular reports to the SHD.¹⁶³ These reports noted drinking was most common at weekends and in areas with high proportions of labourers and servicemen, and Sunday drinking was 'increasingly prevalent'.¹⁶⁴ While the constabulary reported no increase in concern over Scottish drinking, temperance groups and moralisers stood convinced war had caused Scottish drinking to rise to alarming levels. During summer 1940, as the Battle of Britain raged over London skies, the SHD asked MoI to investigate what it termed 'the drink question in Scotland'. M-O's intelligence agent observed that in some areas such as Clydeside there was 'a great deal' of drinking at weekends, which was said to be prevalent among Scots who had struggled on low wages or with limited employment in the interwar period.¹⁶⁵ As a result of higher wages and better employment opportunities these Scots, according to the investigator, initially grappled to make sensible choices with their newfound riches. The investigation also found munitions workers in Scotland had increased their alcohol consumption, most likely as a result of larger pay packets and the 'greatly increased strain' of wartime production outputs.¹⁶⁶ Moreover, greater numbers of women had taken up drinking, including in public houses and local establishments, accompanied by servicemen.¹⁶⁷

Despite these initial attempts by Scots to hold fast to the familiar, before long they came to accept war's disruption of drink culture. The biggest disruption to Scottish consumption of alcohol was to come in the form of supply shortages. Beginning in spring 1941, liquor shortages were reported in Kilmarnock, where intelligence reports noted 'an effort is being made by local hotel keepers to discourage Sunday drinking, by closing their premises earlier and by increasing their charges'. In Greenock, supplies were so limited that public houses restricted their opening hours, and local magistrates had recommended only beer should be sold in the evenings in order to conserve supplies of other liquor.¹⁶⁸ Within three months, the shortages had spread to other regions of Scotland. During

---

¹⁶² See NRS HH55/39, PWD – IR, 18–28 January 1944; HH55/41, PWD – IR, Month ending 26 January 1945; HH60/485, Drunkenness: 'Number apprehended in the four large cities in Scotland for offences involving drunkenness', September 1942 to August 1944.

¹⁶³ See 'drunkenness' reports in NRS, HH55/23–9, PWD – IR, 1940–41.

¹⁶⁴ NRS, HH55/23, PWD – IR, 2 August 1940, 16 August 1940: SHD: *précis* report; HH55/28, PWD – IR, 20 June 1941: *précis*.

¹⁶⁵ M-O, TC85: Scottish drinking, 'Public opinion and the drink question in Scotland', 25 September 1940, 2–3.

¹⁶⁶ Ibid.

¹⁶⁷ Ibid., 6.

¹⁶⁸ NRS, HH55/28, PWD – IR, 23 May 1941: Kilmarnock, Greenock.

August 1941, in the city of Aberdeen supplies of beer and spirits were so low that public houses began to close three to four hours early to preserve supplies. In addition, Scots in locations such as Dumbarton and Glasgow were affected by weekly half-day closures of public houses 'to overcome supply difficulties'.[169] In May 1943, Edinburgh restaurateur Isabelle Ritchie announced her intention to start stockpiling wine supplies, due to shortages. 'Still, I suppose it is marvellous to be getting anything at all at this stage of a total war', she commented.[170] Shortages continued throughout the war and in March 1945 the chief constable of Edinburgh stated his belief that the shortage of supply and high cost were chiefly responsible for low levels of drinking across the city.[171]

In war, as in peace, the consumption of alcohol had a central place in the leisure time of men. Male workers and servicemen across Scotland battled against war's effect on their alcohol-fuelled revelry. From 1940, increasing numbers of contract labourers and foreign forestry workers were brought to rural Scotland to address labour shortages and contribute to wartime construction and industry. Many of these labourers chose to spend their down-time drinking in local public houses. During 1940 and 1941 Scottish police officers observed a marked increase in drunkenness in areas where there were high concentrations of labourers on government contracts.[172] In Orkney, unskilled labourers who received generous wages for working on defence projects caused consternation with their 'lavish and ostentatious' spending on alcohol and their drunken behaviour in Kirkwall at weekends.[173] In Ayr burgh, on the south-west coast of Scotland, Irish labourers working on a local aerodrome regularly imbibed and upset locals with their drunken antics.[174] Problems also arose in Berwickshire where male labourers were regularly seen under the influence of drink, becoming 'a nuisance and an eyesore' in local villages.[175] There were also problems with the drink behaviour of men on labour squads in Argyllshire, in the Western Isles and in Banffshire on the edge of the Moray Firth.[176]

In addition to the drunken exploits of labourers, drinking to excess was common with servicemen. Large numbers of British servicemen were stationed in Scotland, as were sailors from Norway, members of the Polish armed forces and, as the war progressed, those from the Antipodes,

---

[169] NRS, HH55/28, PWD – IR, 6 June 1941: Dumbarton; HH55/29, PWD – IR, 15 August 1941: Aberdeen City, Inverness-shire; HH55/29, PWD – IR, 29 August 1941: City of Glasgow.
[170] M-O, Diarist 5145 (Edinburgh), 12 May 1943.
[171] NRS, HH55/41, PWD – IR, 23 March 1945: City of Edinburgh.
[172] NRS, HH55/26, PWD – IR, 3 January 1941: *précis*, see also HH55/23–9, PWD – IR, 1940–41.
[173] M-O, TC85: Scottish drinking; NRS, HH55/26, PWD – IR, 14 February 1941: Orkney.
[174] NRS, HH55/27, PWD – IR, 14 March 1941: Ayr burgh.
[175] NRS, HH55/29, PWD – IR, 15 August 1941: Berwickshire.
[176] NRS, HH55/27, PWD – IR, 28 March 1941: Argyllshire.

Canada and the United States of America, among others. Foreigners and locals alike regularly spent leisure time consuming alcohol and merry-making in Scottish public houses and local towns. In the bigger cities, especially Glasgow, large populations of troops on leave regularly engaged in heavy drinking.[177] A plethora of intelligence reports attested to similar problems in other parts of Scotland. Norwegian naval ratings in West Lothian were reported to 'imbibe rather freely', there was 'drunkenness and general unruliness' among naval personnel at Kyle of Lochalsh and in the Hebridean town of Stornoway a 'considerable increase' of drunken behaviour had been observed, particularly among Naval, fleet auxiliary and Norwegian personnel.[178] In the Highland region of Moray and Nairn the chief constable reported to the Home Office in June 1941 '[t]here is still a considerable amount of liquor being consumed particularly at the week-ends. With the influx of troops from the surrounding districts to the Burghs of Nairn, Forres and Elgin on Fridays and Saturdays of each week, licensed premises are doing considerable business.'[179] Drunkenness among service personnel, particularly the RAF, was also reported in Argyllshire and Ross and Cromarty during 1941.[180] In the coastal burghs of Banff and Aberchirder, the 2nd Seaforth Highlanders also prompted comment with their excessive drinking and consequent disorderly behaviour at weekends.[181] While the working lives of these men were spent in a state of alertness, in their leisure time servicemen revealed a desire to escape war's clutches by relaxing in the mind-numbing haze of alcohol.

This drunken respite would soon be curtailed. In 1941, frustrated Scottish officials, along with the Kirk and temperance campaigners, agreed something must be done to curb wartime drinking rates among servicemen. In England and Wales, during 1940 entertainment venues had been permitted to open on Sundays to provide entertainment for bored servicemen, but the same privilege had not been granted in Scotland.[182] This was not surprising, as Scottish society had been confined within the strictures of Sabbatarianism since the early nineteenth century. In Victorian times, observing the sabbath was 'a fairly strict affair', and the Protestant churches exerted 'a huge influence in public life'.[183] From 1853, legislation required Scottish public houses to close on Sundays, and cultural tradition dictated that travel and

---

[177] M-O, TC85: Scottish drinking.
[178] NRS, HH55/26, PWD – IR, 31 January 1941: West Lothian, Ross and Cromarty; February 1941: Ross and Cromarty; HH55/28, PWD – IR, 6 June 1941: Ross and Cromarty.
[179] NRS, HH55/28, PWD – IR, 6 June 1941: Moray and Nairn.
[180] NRS, HH55/26, PWD – IR, 31 January 1941: Argyllshire; 14 February 1941: Argyllshire; HH55/27, PWD – IR, 28 March 1941: Argyllshire; HH55/29, PWD – IR, 15 August 1941: Ross and Cromarty.
[181] NRS, HH55/29, PWD – IR, 29 August 1941: Banffshire.
[182] NRS, HH55/26, PWD – IR, 28 February 1941: Aberdeen, City of Edinburgh, Ayr burgh.
[183] Brown, 'Sabbath wars', 155; Devine, *Scottish Nation*, 364.

retail on the sabbath should be avoided.[184] In addition, cinemas, shows and exhibitions, and municipal spaces were controlled on Sundays by local authorities. This influence continued into the twentieth century, and the Scottish sabbath maintained its 'unusually strict' character.[185]

Special times called for special measures, and wartime drunkenness resulted in the abandonment of long-established Sabbatarian principles. While the pull of alcohol was strong, male boredom was stronger and the provision of Sunday entertainments soon curbed drunkenness among servicemen. Sunday concerts were first provided in Berwickshire during March 1941, and the initiative was rated by authorities as 'very successful'.[186] It was not until September 1942 that this strategy would be used elsewhere in Scotland, with entertainments 'for the fighting services and their friends' provided on Sunday evenings in the city of Perth.[187] A month later, Edinburgh cinemas were opened on Sundays 'for service personnel who may be accompanied by one civilian friend', though attendance was lower than desired.[188] This was not the case elsewhere, though, and in many areas organised entertainment on Sundays proved 'very popular'.[189]

Throughout 1943, as ever-increasing numbers of servicemen spent time in Scotland, a range of Sunday entertainments were provided for service personnel. In Peeblesshire, 'bi-weekly' concerts for the armed forces were 'successfully inaugurated', and in Moray and Nairn, Kirkcaldy, Aberdeen and East Lothian cinemas were successfully opened for troops on Sundays.[190] In Midlothian, Arbroath and Kilmarnock, Sundays saw cinemas opened, concerts held and even MoI evening meetings, which were reportedly 'very popular'.[191] While these Sunday entertainments helped to control drunkenness among military men and labourers, it did not mean the habit was eradicated, and the chief constable of Edinburgh pointed out that service personnel would continue to drink and wander the streets 'whatever counter-attractions may be provided'.[192]

The Scotsman's 1850 labelling of Scotland as close to 'the most drunken nation on the face of the earth' could certainly not be applied to its citizens during the Second World War.[193] Despite the accusations of moralisers, primary sources reveal claims of widespread drunkenness were generally unfounded, and Scottish alcohol consumption actually

---

[184] Brown, 'Sabbath wars', 156.
[185] Ibid., 157.
[186] NRS, HH55/27, PWD – IR, 14 March 1941: Berwickshire.
[187] NRS, HH55/34, PWD – IR, 11 September 1942: City of Perth.
[188] NRS, HH55/35, PWD – IR, 4 December 1942: City of Edinburgh.
[189] Ibid.: SHD, précis report.
[190] Ibid.: Peeblesshire; HH55/36, PWD – IR, 29 January 1943: Moray and Nairn, Kirkcaldy, East Lothian; 23 April 1943: Aberdeen City.
[191] NRS, HH55/38, PWD – IR, 5 November 1943: Arbroath, Midlothian; 3 December 1943: Kilmarnock.
[192] NRS, HH55/35, PWD – IR, 4 December 1942: City of Edinburgh.
[193] Untitled article, The Scotsman, 22 May 1850, quoted in Devine, Scottish Nation, 350.

decreased over the years of war. Police intelligence reports from 1940 to 1945 provide excellent insight into the ways Scottish drink culture changed over the course of the war. During 1940 and 1941 chief constables regularly noted high levels of weekend drinking, and drunkenness among working-class men. From 1942 to 1945, this trend reversed, and alcohol consumption was rarely considered cause for comment.[194] Where it was mentioned, predominantly reported was drunkenness of Irish workers, labour squads and servicemen, or female drinking in public houses. Officials agreed the situation was nowhere near the scale of that experienced in the Great War, when severe restrictions on alcohol had to be introduced to curb the problem.[195]

Statistics provided by the Scottish police also showed that in the main cities, charges for drunken offences steadily decreased throughout the war.[196] In addition, a report by the Edinburgh Constabulary noted apprehensions for drunkenness in 1944 were the lowest ever recorded in Edinburgh.[197] The next lowest year was 1918, when alcohol had been subject to severe restrictions.[198] Throughout the years of the war, apprehensions for drunkenness were highest in 1940, but rapidly declined in the subsequent years. While drunkenness is not the only measure of alcohol consumption, the constabulary reports provide an unparalleled glimpse into Scottish drink culture throughout the war years. The lack of complaint detailed in intelligence reports in response to liquor shortages, price rises, reduced public house opening hours and Sunday drink travel reveals that – for the most part – Scots did not fight the incursion of war into this longstanding relationship with alcohol.

Food and diet

Before the war, Scottish food culture had not been known for its sophistication or nutritional excellence. The urban diet was generally extremely poor, largely as a result of poverty, poor food supply and lack of fresh fruit and vegetables.[199] Rural Scots were traditionally more reliant on oats, potatoes, vegetables and fish, but cheap refined carbohydrates increased

---

[194] See NRS, HH55/19–31, PWD – IR: 1940–41 and HH55/32–42, PWD – IR: 1942–5.
[195] M-O, TC85: Scottish drinking, 2; see also Callum G. Brown, 'Piety, gender and war', in Macdonald and McFarland, *Scotland and the Great War*, 188–9.
[196] M-O, TC85: Scottish drinking, 1; NRS, HH60/485, Drunkenness, 'Number apprehended in the four large cities in Scotland for offences involving drunkenness, from Sept 1942', 'Drunkenness statistics – four cities', 'Drunkenness convictions Scotland'; HH60/427, Juvenile Delinquency: Statistics.
[197] NRS, HH 60/427, Juvenile Delinquency: Statistics, 'Edinburgh City Police: Annual Report, 1944'.
[198] Ibid.
[199] Maisie C. Steven, 'Diet and health in Scotland', in Beech et al., *Scottish Life and Society*, 133–53, here 140–41.

in prominence in the years after the Great War.[200] The popular historiography of Scottish food culture during the Second World War has focused predominantly on social changes as a result of food and milk schemes for the urban poor. Measures included wider availability of school meals, provision of milk, oranges and blackcurrant syrup for impoverished children, and greater rations of milk for mothers and infants.[201] As a result of this increased government intervention, it has been said, many Scots reached the end of the war far healthier than they had been before it.[202] Besides improved health among the impoverished, little is known about war's impact on the diet and food culture of other Scots. This section explores the ways in which Scottish diet was disrupted by war, and the ways Scots responded to this interference.

War rapidly affected Scottish diets from the outset as foreign food shipments, transported to Britain in shipping convoys, were attacked by German submarines. As the Battle of the Atlantic heated up in late 1940, British food shortages became increasingly pronounced, and home-produced supplies were insufficient to meet demand. Everyday life was affected by the rationing of basic household goods such as sugar, bacon and butter, which were restricted from January 1940. By 1942 many other foodstuffs, including meat and eggs, joined the list of rationed goods.[203] As a result of these restrictions, food supply in Scotland fluctuated. This included shortages of fruit and tomatoes, particularly as the country was reliant on external markets for both fresh and tinned stocks. The public was quick to respond when new shipments arrived, such as in this incident observed at a Glasgow grocer in 1942. When word got out that blackcurrants and gooseberries were finally in stock after a period of shortages, the resulting queue, according to one local, was 'as long as for an execution'.[204]

As a result of erratic supply, food availability in Scotland varied across regions. During summer 1941 some parts of the countryside noted limited supplies. Mrs Peason in rural Argyllshire commented 'I suppose there are oranges in the country as I occasionally see orange peel about, but certainly people who live as far away from shops as we do never get a chance at them'.[205] In rural Inverness-shire the chief constable pointed out that oranges and bananas had 'entirely disappeared', while tomatoes and apples

---

[200] Ibid., 143.
[201] Ibid., 144; see also Royle, *Time of Tyrants*, 207; Macnicol, 'The effect of the evacuation', 19–24; Pete Alcock, Howard Glennerster, Ann Oakley and Adrian Sinfield (eds), *Welfare and Wellbeing: Richard Titmuss's Contribution to Social Policy* (Bristol: Policy Press, 2001), 85.
[202] Devine, *Scottish Nation*, 550–51.
[203] IWM, 'What you need to know about rationing in the Second World War', https://www.iwm.org.uk/history/what-you-need-to-know-about-rationing-in-the-second-world-war (accessed 3 November 2020).
[204] M-O, Diarist 5390 (Glasgow), 15 August 1942.
[205] M-O, Diarist 5314 (Tayvallich), September 1941.

were 'almost unprocurable'.[206] Tomatoes and eggs were also in short supply in Helensburgh on the Firth of Clyde, but the landlady of a Mrs Connor was easily able to obtain these items when on holiday in the central region of Stirling. In contrast, the landlady reported there was 'less food in Stirling than there is here, meat especially being scarce'.[207] Regional variation was also noted by residents of Coatbridge, east of Glasgow, when returning from summer holidays during 1941. They carried reports that in the holiday resorts of western Scotland necessities were 'practically unobtainable', while other holiday-makers claimed that in districts they had visited 'no difficulty was experienced in obtaining ample supplies, even of luxury foods'.[208] Variation was not limited to Scotland, and holiday-makers returning from England in mid-1942 were struck by the contrast between fruit supplies in Kent and what was available locally in Scotland. One vacationer commented that Kent was 'overrun' with tomatoes, while in Scotland they were 'as scarce as scarce can be'.[209]

Wartime shortages of raw materials also led food manufacturers to implement regional restrictions on supplies. In July 1943, owing to shortages, Scottish manufacturer McVitie and Price announced a zoning scheme for Scotland which would see supplies reduced to selected counties, including the Highlands and Islands and Edinburgh. 'Customers outside these areas will, we are sure, appreciate the necessity of this restriction and will accept it loyally in the National Interest', the company stated.[210] Local Eileen Offley was distraught, bemoaning 'Glasgow, where so many biscuits are made, Glasgow that did have biscuits when the people in the South revelled in their onions and fruit. Is our ewe lamb to be taken from us?'[211] In 1944, biscuit manufacturer Macfarlane Lang's followed suit, advising customers in Glasgow their favourite Rich Tea variety would not be available as 'the needs of the Fighting Forces come first'.[212] A humorous opinion piece in *The Scotsman* bemoaned that the biscuit had 'lost its freedom of movement', but the writer accepted it was better to have the total disappearance of a friend than to see 'the sight of one who was once strong and handsome in a state of depression and ill-health'.[213]

'You would never guess there was a war on': food supply and shortage

During 1942, Japan captured Singapore and Burma, Germany occupied Vichy France and the House of Commons was told of the escalating

---

[206] NRS, HH55/29, PWD – IR, 15 August 1941: Inverness-shire.
[207] M-O, Diarist 5281 (Helensburgh), 4 August 1941.
[208] NRS, HH55/29, PWD – IR, 29 August 1941: Coatbridge.
[209] M-O, Diarist 5390 (Glasgow), 15 September 1942.
[210] 'McVitie & Price's biscuits: zoning scheme for Scotland', *Glasgow Herald*, 1 July 1943, 3.
[211] Ibid., 21 May 1943.
[212] 'Macfarlane Lang's biscuits', *Glasgow Herald*, 17 July 1944, 4.
[213] 'Biscuits and cheese', *The Scotsman*, 11 November 1944, 4.

execution of Jews in Germany. Events in foreign theatres of war were grim, and intelligence reports described a growing awareness of this among the public. Towards the end of the year, reports by Scottish chief constables attested to public acceptance of wartime disruption in their everyday lives, a result of their newfound cognisance that the war effort teetered on a knife edge. 'The people realise that they are still a long way from experiencing anything like real hardship', reported the chief constable of Edinburgh in October 1942. His counterpart in Coatbridge agreed, noting that people had come to realise, 'after three years of war . . . we have suffered no hardship'. In East Lothian, the public 'fully understood' further restrictions on the supply of foodstuffs were likely 'and the public willingness to endure them is apparent', the chief constable wrote.[214] While Scots demonstrated a willingness to accept wartime hardships as par for the course, it is possible they did not rail against these restrictions as they were not as restricted by them as we may have assumed. The following sub-section explores the range of ways in which Scots, despite this rhetoric of acceptance, actually resisted war's influence on their diets.

Scots who were responsible for household food shopping often altered their daily routines to obtain desired supplies of food. 'Shops are often very crowded and women state that the procuring of food is a very strenuous and difficult business', the chief constable of Ayr pointed out in June 1941.[215] Those with flexible work arrangements, such as Katherine Booth, could rearrange the day to visit the grocers in the morning, 'as there is nothing left in the shops later'.[216] Despite these difficulties, shoppers regularly stood in long queues to obtain particular foods they wanted, such as meat, onions and oranges.[217] The chief constable of Ayrshire noted there were daily queues at bakers and tea shops for luxury goods such as cakes and tea bread, when 'plain ordinary bread' was in ample supply.[218] Similarly, Miss Offley's desire to lose weight by eating salad led her to spend her lunch breaks scouring greengrocers for lettuce.[219] As these examples demonstrate, oftentimes Scots were willing to rearrange their days to obtain desired food items.

In some respects, rural Scots found it easier to resist wartime dietary restrictions. They could supplement their diets with animal products such as eggs, milk or butter, or via hunting, foraging and fishing. As a result, rural diets contained greater variety and larger quantities of meat. Mrs Peason, in Tayvallich on the shores of Loch Sween, ate a diet rich in meat, fish and game. An average day began with porridge followed by fried bread or potato,

[214] NRS, HH55/34, PWD – IR, four weeks ending 9 October 1942: City of Edinburgh, Coatbridge, East Lothian.
[215] NRS, HH55/28, PWD – IR, 6 June 1941: Ayr burgh.
[216] M-O, Diarist 5253 (Colinton), 21 March 1942.
[217] Ibid.: City of Glasgow; NRS, HH55/34, PWD – IR, 9 October 1942: Greenock; HH55/39, PWD – IR, 28 January 1944: City of Glasgow, Ayr burgh.
[218] NRS, HH55/29, PWD – IR, 15 August 1941: Ayrshire.
[219] M-O, Diarist 5390 (Glasgow), 27 August 1941.

with bacon, egg or fish on the side. Lunch generally contained some form of meat, followed by pudding or fruit and custard. Meat choices included beef, haggis, haddock or trout, grouse and rabbit. Foraged items such as brambleberries and gulls' eggs supplemented these options.[220] Similarly, Miss Mellon and Mrs Mitchel, both living on the Kintyre peninsula, added to their food choices by collecting whelks and hunting rabbits.[221] One family in Helensburgh also had a diet that was varied and rich. On one single day in August 1941 Mr and Mrs Connor ate veal for lunch, and dined for supper on vegetable soup, baked rabbit, bacon scraps and a cornflour pudding. However, Mrs Connor complained, 'last year, I was putting six [rabbits] of that size into one pie'.[222] Visiting Comrie in Perthshire, Anne Westlands commented on this dietary variety during war: '[i]n this part of the world you would never guess there was a war on at all . . . We are all living perfectly normal lives and get plenty of food.'[223]

Scots also avoided the full impacts of wartime dietary restriction by supplementing their diets with occasional luxuries. In May 1942 Edinburgh restaurateur Isabelle Ritchie was pleased to be able to provide a last drink of champagne for an 'aristocratically-minded' friend. The restaurateur commented 'I feel it's only right that she should have the champagne while it's going . . . So let her enjoy the sort of party she likes till the cellar runs dry at last!'[224] Katherine Booth observed fellow Edinburgh women eating in Crawford's café during March 1942, and noted '[o]ne woman at the table has a chocolate biscuit with her coffee, and all the others ask [for] one. The waitress dispenses them reluctantly, as if they were made of gold.'[225] In some cases, the choice to indulge in treats over-rode one's better judgement. In September 1943, Eileen Offley's employer was gifted a block of ice cream and the naval captain promptly shared it among his colleagues. 'Ice cream does not suit me, but I ate this immense helping', Eileen noted, adding 'I enjoyed the slice – like everyone else, and felt no ill effects in the afternoon, but at time of writing, 8:30, feel very sick'.[226] Likewise, Mrs Peason in rural Argyllshire displayed mixed feelings towards food. She noticed herself obsessing over a 'marvellous' sugary cake a guest had brought to her child's birthday party, but felt shame over her response to the food. 'How disgustingly greedy and keen on one's food this war makes one! I never remember taking as much interest in my food and being so anxious to eat as much of any sweet things that are going – even in the last war', she noted in September 1941.[227]

---

[220] M-O, Diarist 5314 (Tayvallich), March, April and August 1943.
[221] M-O, Diarist 5374 (Campbeltown), 22 April 1941; Dir. March 1942, R1534 (Campbeltown).
[222] M-O, Diarist 5281 (Helensburgh), 23 August 1941.
[223] BBC People's War, RA3219842, Anne Westlands, 20 August 1940.
[224] M-O, Diarist 5145 (Edinburgh), 6 May 1942.
[225] M-O, Diarist 5253 (Colinton), 18 March 1942.
[226] M-O, Diarist 5390 (Glasgow), 17 September 1943.
[227] M-O, Diarist 5314 (Tayvallich), September 1941.

These infrequent treats provided Scots momentary pleasure, helping them to weather the inconveniences of war. Diaries and letters written during the Second World War contain many details of favourite meals, and authors expressed a range of emotions towards food.[228] The detailed diary entry of an Edinburgh professor recalled one memorable experience: 'Last night I called on Rev Paterson ... he pressed me to stay and have a most scrumptious supper with him and his sister. We had boiled eggs, toast, a chocolate cake, jam, fruit cake, and lovely chocolate biscuits. Oh, how I enjoyed it.'[229] Similar food-related reactions of pleasure were frequently noted in the diaries of Miss Offley. During May 1942 her mother was in 'a state of ecstasy' about apple rings she had found in a local grocer; in August an acquaintance 'nearly went off her head with emotion' at the mention of rare blackcurrants; and in September Miss Offley's purchase of a doughnut the size of a tea-plate 'caused a sensation both at the office and at home'.[230] The choice of descriptors such as 'scrumptious', 'marvellous', 'ecstasy' and 'off her head with emotion' reveals the visceral response food evoked in Scots. It also demonstrates the pleasure they gained from rebelling against wartime dietary restrictions – and the regret experienced after overindulgence.

Scots who were unhappy with mediocre wartime diets found ways to get around this. One American diplomat based in Glasgow took to using his rank as a naval captain to entitle him to inspect ships at 11:45 am as 'then they have to invite him to lunch; lunch on an American scale of plentitude and variety'.[231] Similarly, Eileen Offley was grateful for her membership of the Soroptimist Club, partly for the *camaraderie* but also for the generous lunches. 'The small band of Soroptimists who attend faithfully during the off season don't have to wait till they get to heaven for their reward, they get it right now, in a most marvellous lunch', Miss Offley commented.[232] The Connor family, holidaying in summer 1941, found a creative way to fight limited food choice. Staying in the Highland village of Crianlarich, Agnes Connor was disappointed with the local food offerings, commenting '[f]ood at hotel was most inadequate ... I was awake with hunger most of the night'.[233] Rather than accept the bland wartime diet, Mr and Mrs Connor phoned home for additional sugar and butter supplies to be sent. Agnes spent the rest of her holiday finding ways to get extra food, including discovering a packet of biscuits on sale at the local post office, 'which my husband devoured in the night'.[234] She also observed that

---

[228] See M-O, Diarists 5390 (Glasgow), 5314 (Tayvallich), 5015 (Glasgow), 5145 (Edinburgh).
[229] University of Edinburgh Special Collections, BAI 2/8, papers of Professor John Baillie and family, 5 February 1941.
[230] M-O, Diarist 5390 (Glasgow), 23 May 1942, 4 August 1942, 15 September 1942.
[231] M-O, Diarist 5390 (Glasgow), 11 September 1943.
[232] Ibid., 4 August 1941.
[233] M-O, Diarist 5281 (Helensburgh), 15 August 1941.
[234] Ibid., 16 August 1941.

another hotel guest hung around after breakfast, waiting for other guests to leave so she could scrounge their unwanted pieces of toast for her teenaged son. These were certainly inventive tactics to supplement a restricted diet.

Scots also circumvented wartime restrictions by selling or swapping foodstuffs with friends and colleagues. Eileen Offley in Glasgow purchased tomatoes from a colleague who lived in Lanarkshire where they were abundant, and sold some of her bacon ration to her American manager, who was struggling on what he felt was a meagre British diet.[235] She and her mother also regularly swapped their sugar rations or sold them to others, sometimes in exchange for other food such as fruit.[236] In September 1943 Eileen noted '[p]eople who have tea four times a day get obliged by neighbours who like coffee. The commodity in which most swopping takes place must be sugar, housewives who like making jam stopping at almost no limit to get [it].'[237] Alastair Bain, a schoolboy in Glasgow, noted in September 1941 that he had received 'an amazing parcel of wartime scarcities. Nine eating apples, ½-lb block of plain chocolate & ½-lb box of liquorice allsorts'.[238] Another time he received a box of tomatoes from a friend in London, writing '[t]hese are very welcome indeed for the last times our greengrocer has had them we have been allowed only two'.[239] Similarly, one Scot received parcels of green vegetables, another was sent a halibut by his father, and one soldier, based near a fishing town in Caithness, was 'able to send 3 lovely fresh haddocks or plaice by the mail bus last night' to friends who experienced difficulties obtaining fish in their local area.[240] In November 1942 the government announced that to give rationed foodstuffs as presents was illegal. Nonetheless, most Scots whose writings were studied for this chapter mentioned sending or receiving food during wartime, suggesting this was commonplace.

This behaviour was not limited to Scotland, and historian Mark Roodhouse has noted the emergence of a 'grey market' in Britain. In this, food took on the role of a legal currency, and dealing took place outside official channels.[241] Such dealing was not conducted 'for profit alone', and involved such actions as gifting and swapping of surplus coupons or rations, as well as dealing in home-grown produce or locally procured items. Roodhouse states the practice was proportionally more common in Britain than in the rest of Western Europe and that 'none of them saw how transferring this personal property caused direct or indirect harm to

---

[235] M-O, Diarist 5390 (Glasgow), 12 August 1941, 11 September 1943.
[236] Ibid., 4 August 1942.
[237] Ibid., 11 September 1943.
[238] M-O, Diarist 5015 (Glasgow), 25 September 1941.
[239] Ibid., 9 September 1941.
[240] M-O, Diarist 5281 (Helensburgh), 7 August 1941; Diarist 5015 (Glasgow), 1 March 1942; University of Edinburgh Special Collections, BAI 2/8, papers of Professor John Baillie and family, 'letter from Ian Baillie', 18 June 1942.
[241] Roodhouse, *Black Market Britain*, 51.

third parties'.²⁴² This sentiment is reflected in primary sources used for this chapter. None of the Scots whose writings were studied gave any indication they believed their actions were wrong or against the law.

Owners of grocery and fruit stores also resisted war's influence on their businesses, operating in similar grey areas by keeping food 'under the counter'. When shopping at a store close to home, and being told there were only damaged tomatoes in stock, Miss Offley went home to her mother who 'went straight around and got a pound from under the counter. She is a known customer there whereas I am seldom in that shop.'²⁴³ This was a practice that took place even in rural parts of Scotland. From Helensburgh Mrs Connor reported 'spied oranges under the counter and was allowed 2 for 7d'.²⁴⁴ Similarly, shopping in Peacock's grocery, Eileen Offley was beckoned by a young assistant, who asked if she would like apricots. 'She impressed on me three times to tell no-one', Eileen added.²⁴⁵ As this demonstrates, while citizens might have claimed ignorance at the legality of swapping foodstuffs, retailers knew it was not allowed and took pains to hide or deny such practises.

Diet was one area in which Scots were able to push back against war's influence on their everyday lives. It is surprising, then, that cultural memory of the war years is often oriented around food shortages and rationing.²⁴⁶ Food historian Lizzie Collingham has claimed government food rationing and equitable supply distribution ensured public morale remained steady throughout the war.²⁴⁷ 'Rationing had the effect of levelling out the diet of everyone in the country to the standard of the prewar skilled worker', she wrote in an article on the wartime British diet.²⁴⁸ But wartime diet was not restricted to what was available 'on the ration'. As this chapter has demonstrated, Scottish rural diets were supplemented with hunted or foraged food, and urban Scots could visit multiple retailers and procure items from 'under the counter'. Scots also chose to swap and sell rations, and access occasional luxuries. Despite demonstrating a willingness to accept dietary hardship, in their actions Scots showed rebellion against war's influence on diet. Perhaps this everyday resistance had more of a positive effect on Scottish morale than government assurances of food equity. In addition, food brought pleasure, and this may have helped Scots to endure hard times. Sharing meals or swapping supplies with others served as a social

---

[242] Ibid., 53.
[243] M-O, Diarist 5390 (Glasgow), 19 August 1942.
[244] M-O, Diarist 5281 (Helensburgh), 6 August 1941.
[245] M-O, Diarist 5390 (Glasgow), 19 May 1942.
[246] See for example Juliet Gardiner, *War on the Home Front: Experience Life in Britain during the Second World War* (London: Carlton and IWM, 2012); Royle, *Time of Tyrants*, 206–7; Pattinson, McIvor and Robb, *Men in Reserve*, 278.
[247] Lizzie Collingham, 'Birthday onions: Second World War rationing and the British diet', *Times Literary Supplement* 6107 (2020), 27.
[248] Ibid.

connection: creating moments of shared happiness and forging common bonds. These factors may have contributed to Scottish rejection of war's influence on food culture.

In contrast to the subjects interviewed by Pattinson, McIvor and Robb, who insisted they had no time for leisure during war, the sources detailed in this chapter reveal some Scots had ample time for leisure and pleasure during the Second World War. The selected sources show that many Scots were able to enjoy popular entertainments from pre-war days, as well as new forms of war-tinged leisure. Moreover, those in remote rural areas were treated to forms of leisure they could not often access during peacetime. While generally existing on a restricted diet, those in Scotland also found ways to access foods they could not purchase locally, and indulged in treat foods where possible. Scots no doubt made sacrifices, and were dedicated workers in demanding environments. It is, therefore, understandable that this is the dominant memory of the war years. However, this is not the complete picture and, as this chapter has uncovered, everyday life also contained many moments of pleasure and of respite.

This chapter has also revealed that war challenged some aspects of Scottish tradition and culture. Firstly, alcohol was scarcer, and responses to the problem of intoxicated men dealt a severe challenge to the Scottish Sabbatarian tradition by opening entertainments on the previously sacred Sunday. Furthermore, while food culture was one area in which Scots demonstrated resistance to both war and the authorities, the research contained within this chapter has revealed that, in life outside the workplace, the Scottish wartime experience was not generally one of resistance and revolt. Finally, war brought an unprecedented level of state involvement in Scottish lives. In response, Scots demonstrated a degree of receptiveness to these messages, enjoying state-produced films and exhibitions and responding positively to the 'good citizen' rhetoric behind fundraising campaigns. This acceptance indicates that in some areas of wartime life Scots did view themselves as part of a wider culture: a 'national' British community, united behind the war effort and the government. If everyday behaviour leaves an imprint of wider culture, then this study of wartime life reveals adaptation, acceptance and cooperation with the war and with the authorities.

CHAPTER SEVEN

'Scotland's Fighting Fields': The Transformation of Rural Scotland

In March 1941, the First Lord of the Admiralty addressed the House of Commons with a stark warning: after the collapse of France, and Italy's subsequent entry into the war, Britain had lost a powerful naval ally and Germany had gained one. 'The collapse of France did more than turn Mussolini into the accomplice of a pirate; it gave the pirate himself new lairs from which to sally forth against us', stated Mr A. V. Alexander, political head of the Royal Navy.[1] The German conquest of French ports on the Channel and Atlantic coast enabled German submarines to more than halve the distance to their 'hunting grounds' in the Atlantic, and allowed German aircraft to reach British shipping convoys further out to sea.[2] This signalled the start of a new phase of war: unrestricted submarine warfare.

This was a concerning development which could potentially starve Britain into submission. On the eve of the Second World War, the nation had been reliant on overseas food supplies to feed its population. Meat was procured mainly from the Dominions, eggs often from Europe and butter from New Zealand and Australia.[3] In addition, 96 per cent of timber supplies – used in important industries such as transport, mining and communications – came from overseas producers.[4] A large amount of material to be used as feedstuff for animals was also imported.[5] This over-reliance on international markets put Britain in a position of extreme vulnerability. In the three months to May 1941, U-boats sank 142 Allied merchant ships and a further 179 were lost to air attack.[6] In April this resulted in losses of nearly 700,000 tons of shipping. By way of comparison, prior to December 1940 the average tonnage lost per month had been under 300,000.[7] According to R. J. Moore-Colyer, this German barrage reduced Britain's imported

---

[1] Hansard, HC Deb, 5 March 1941, vol. 369 col. 928.
[2] Ibid.
[3] Hansard, HC Deb, 1 August 1939, vol. 350 col. 2144; HC Deb, 8 November 1939, vol. 353 col. 278.
[4] Emma Vickers, '"The forgotten army of the woods": the Women's Timber Corps during the Second World War', *The Agricultural History Review* 59, no. 1 (2011), 101–12, here 101, 104.
[5] Hansard, HC Deb, 25 January 1940, vol. 356 cols 824–5.
[6] Calder, *People's War*, 231.
[7] Ibid., 231–2.

food supplies by 85 per cent from pre-war levels.[8] Britain's self-sufficiency and ability to feed its population were under threat. The over-reliance on imported supplies was a dangerous risk when merchant ships were at the mercy of U-boats. With the threat of potential famine looming, the need to secure domestic food supplies and timber resources was critical. Coming on the back of severe economic depression and labour shortages, though, it was unclear whether British primary industries could rise to the occasion.

Certainly, in Scotland the ability to meet this challenge appeared slim. From the late 1700s onwards, rural Scotland had been a place of 'rapid, profound and comprehensive' transformation.[9] Industrialisation, urbanisation and the Clearances resulted in the abandonment of large tracts of rural Scotland, along with mass migration pushed by rent increases, famine and land dispossession.[10] After the land evictions ceased, the depopulation of rural areas continued. Population decline was severe, and more than 230,000 residents left the Highlands between 1861 and 1931, taking the region's population from 16.4 per cent of the total Scottish population at the beginning to 6.1 per cent at the end of this period.[11] With industrial jobs providing a powerful lure, Scotland's cities beckoned to agricultural workers 'driven by desperation and self-preservation'.[12] In 1851, 30 per cent of Scotland's male employed population worked in agriculture. By 1911, this figure had dropped to 11 per cent.[13] Population decline was further exacerbated by the Great War, in which an estimated 100,000 Scotsmen perished, including many from rural areas.[14] On the eve of the Second World War rural Scotland lay in a state of dereliction. Communities had been slowly drained of their lifeblood over nearly 200 years of land clearances, famine, failed government interventions, economic depression, mass migration and war. It would take drastic changes for Scottish agriculture and forestry to reach ambitious government targets for wartime food and timber production.

Scholarship on rural Britain during the Second World War has focused on two broad themes: assessing agricultural outputs and changes; and charting the experiences of workers.[15] On the first of those themes, works by Brian

---

[8] R. J. Moore-Colyer, 'The call to the land: British and European adult voluntary farm labour, 1939–49', *Rural History* 17, no. 1 (2006): 83–101, here 83.

[9] Devine, *Scottish Clearances*, 1.

[10] Ibid., 353–4.

[11] Adam Collier, *The Crofting Problem* (London: Cambridge University Press, 1953), 128–9.

[12] Smout, *Century of the Scottish People*, 61.

[13] Devine, *Scottish Nation*, 253.

[14] Stephen McGinty, 'Great War worst for Scots troops "a myth"', *The Scotsman*, 10 August 2014, https://www.scotsman.com/arts-and-culture/great-war-worst-scots-troops-myth-1529401 (accessed 1 May 2020); Trevor Royle, 'The First World War', in Spiers, Crang and Strickland, *Military History of Scotland*, 530.

[15] On agriculture see R. J. Hammond, *Food and Agriculture in Britain, 1939–45* (Stanford, CA: Stanford University Press, 1954); K. A. H. Murray, *History of the Second World War: Agriculture* (London: HMSO, 1955); J. Martin, *The Development of Modern Agriculture: British Farming*

Short, Angus Calder and Ewen Cameron have brought valuable insight into the wartime mechanisation and modernisation of the agricultural sector, in Scotland as elsewhere, and have assessed the production yields of that sector.[16] Adding to this small but significant history is a burgeoning body of scholarship on worker experiences, including female labour in the Women's Land Army and Timber Corps; male farmers; child and adult volunteers; and prisoners of war.[17] This chapter adds to this rich scholarship by interrogating the ways rural Scotland was reshaped by war and the drive for self-sufficiency. It uses government and parliamentary records, material from newspapers and magazines, life writings and intelligence documents to explore the influences of war on rural life and work. The chapter begins with an analysis of war's effect on agriculture, and covers themes of state intervention, adaptation and resistance. It will then examine the ways war reshaped rural populations, uncovering tension between incoming workers and local communities. The final section investigates the role war played in renewing Scottish hopes for rejuvenation of the rural sector.

'Scotland's fighting fields': the reshaping of Scottish agriculture

On the eve of war, British agriculture was in a state of decline after two decades of economic depression. Life was difficult for Scottish farm workers, with the interwar period characterised by high unemployment and life lived 'precariously close to the breadline'.[18] In Ross and Cromarty,

---

since 1931 (Basingstoke: Palgrave Macmillan, 2000); John A. Burnett, *The Making of the Modern Scottish Highlands, 1939–1965: Withstanding the Colossus of 'Advancing Materialism'* (Dublin: Four Courts, 2011). On worker experience see Vickers, 'The forgotten army'; Bob Powell and Nigel Westacott, *The Women's Land Army* (Stroud: History Press, 2009); Joanna Foat, *Lumberjills: Britain's Forgotten Army* (Stroud: History Press, 2019); Elaine M. Edwards (ed.), *Scotland's Land Girls: Breeches, Bombers and Backaches* (Edinburgh: NMS, 2010); Affleck Gray, *Timber! Memories of Life in the Scottish Women's Timber Corps, 1942–46* (Edinburgh: Tuckwell Press, 1998).

[16] Calder, *People's War*, 231–2; Brian Short, *The Battle of the Fields: Rural Community and Authority in Britain during the Second World War* (Woodbridge: Boydell Press, 2014); B. Short, C. Watkins, W. Foot and P. Kinsman, *The National Farm Survey, 1941–1943: State Surveillance and the Countryside in England and Wales in the Second World War* (Wallingford: CABI, 2000); Ewen A. Cameron, 'The modernisation of Scottish agriculture', 184–207, in T. M. Devine, C. H. Lee and G. C. Peden (eds), *The Transformation of Scotland: The Economy Since 1700* (Edinburgh: Edinburgh University Press, 2005); Ewen A. Cameron, 'The Scottish Highlands as a special policy area, 1886–1965', *Rural History* 8, no. 2 (1997): 195–215.

[17] Robb, *Men at Work*; R. J. Moore-Colyer, 'Call to the land', and 'Kids in the corn: school harvest camps and farm labour supply in England, 1940–1950', *The Agricultural History Review* 52, no. 2 (2004): 183–206; Michelle Moffat, '"Scotland's fighting fields": the mobilisation of workers in rural Scotland during the Second World War', *Rural History* 33, no. 2 (2022): 231–49; Johann Custodis, 'Employing the enemy: the contribution of German and Italian prisoners of war to British agriculture during and after the Second World War', *Agricultural History Review* 60, no. 2 (2012): 243–65.

[18] Catherine Maclean, 'Getting out and getting on: Scottish Highland migration in the first half of the twentieth century', *Rural History* 11, no. 2 (2000), 231–48, here 236.

'the most seriously depressed of the Scottish counties', nearly half of all insured workers – those normally earning a wage – were unemployed at that time.[19] Scottish farming was also heavily reliant on the horse and slow to mechanise. War would rapidly change the status quo. Agriculture was viewed as central to Britain's victory. Upon the outbreak of war, Whitehall quickly implemented policies to increase home-produced food supplies 'by hook or by crook'.[20] Some changes were simple, such as raising the minimum wage for agricultural workers and making agriculture a reserved occupation, meaning employers in other industries were forbidden from hiring agricultural workers.[21] More complex proposals included incentives and benefits for farmers, which included guaranteed prices for staple products, assured markets and subsidies for those who made use of previously unproductive land.[22] Under one subsidy scheme, farmers would be paid £2 per acre of old pasture put to the plough. By 1945, over £2,000,000 in subsidies had been paid in Scotland alone, and more than 1 million acres of old grassland had been ploughed.[23]

As well as bringing financial benefits, war also reshaped Scottish farming practices. Before the war, Scottish agriculture had been dominated by 'significantly more' oats, potatoes and turnips than in England and Wales, where wheat was the main crop.[24] Within a few weeks of war's outbreak, all farmers across Britain were immediately ordered to plough 10 per cent of their grassland and to sow wheat, in the main, followed by potatoes, barley and oats.[25] In addition to these crop changes, wartime policies also led to the cultivation of land previously considered undesirable for farming. Apart from old pastures, many parts of Scotland were less suitable for cropping or heavy stock grazing, mainly due to difficult topography and harsh climates.[26] In order to increase production in such areas, the Department of Agriculture for Scotland introduced numerous assistance schemes for those who could improve the prospects of such land. One such scheme offered up to 50 per cent of the cost of cultivation for farmers who tilled marginal lands, which would otherwise be uneconomic to plough.[27] These were, indeed, attractive inducements.

While war brought government-funded incentives, it also required farmers to submit to the *Diktat* of Agricultural Executive Committees (AEC). These were the main apparatus for administering the state's

[19] Calder, *People's War*, 416.
[20] Devine, *Scottish Nation*, 546.
[21] 'Farming notes: war-time policy', *The Scotsman*, 7 June 1940, 10; 'Farming on a war-time basis', *Glasgow Herald*, 1 July 1940, 4.
[22] Devine, *Scottish Nation*, 547.
[23] Short, *Battle of the Fields*, 306.
[24] Macdonald, *Whaur Extremes Meet*, 58.
[25] Hansard, HL Deb, 28 September 1939, vol. 114 col. 1200.
[26] Short, *Battle of the Fields*, 298.
[27] Ibid., 312.

wide-ranging campaigns, and the forty Scottish AECs were roughly organised along county lines and staffed by farmers, landowners or estate agents. Scottish AECs were responsible for allocating acreage payments, quotas and issuing compulsory cropping notices, and could even requisition rural land.[28] Before the war, significant portions of Scottish land had been in the hands of a small number of landowners. Much was used primarily for game shooting, including 2 million acres of Highland land kept free of grazing stock so as not to interfere with deer stalking. In the AEC region of Ross and Cromarty, for example, 73 per cent of the land was deer forest, considered by the authorities to be a waste of land suitable for cultivating or grazing.[29] Between November 1939 and May 1941 over 100,000 acres of land in Scotland were compulsorily acquired 'in the interests of national food production'.[30] This included Department of Agriculture for Scotland acquisitions of twenty farms, two deer forests covering in total over 55,000 acres and a range of smaller properties.[31] This illustrates the extent to which the state was involved in land usage and ownership during the Second World War.

The need to meet government targets also reshaped the techniques and technologies used in Scottish farming, and led to the abandonment of traditional farming methods. Before the war, Scottish agriculture had relied on a system of ley farming – with land generally left fallow and planted with a cover crop for up to seven years, to allow the soil to rest before being ploughed and resown.[32] This improved soil fertility for future years' crops. To meet high AEC targets for crop production, farmers could no longer rely on this traditional practice, instead, choosing to embrace the large-scale use of fertiliser to increase soil fertility. As the land was further depleted by heavy crop loads, this became ever more important. By 1941, supplies of traditional fertilisers such as basic slag, bones and potash were in short supply and farmers were advised they would have to rely on chemically manufactured superphosphate. The parsimony of existing supplies was also advocated, with instructions to use it only for those crops that would give the best return.[33] Farmers were also told that they 'need not fear any disastrous effects on soil fertility' as a result of the substantial increase in artificial fertilisers.[34] Those who wanted to meet targets had no real choice in the matter, though, as leaving fields to rest and recover was no longer a viable option.

---

[28] Ibid., 301, 306.
[29] Ibid., 312.
[30] 'Land taken over: 105,717 acres in Scotland', *The Scotsman*, 8 May 1941, 8.
[31] Ibid.
[32] Short, *Battle of the Fields*, 299.
[33] 'Farming notes: the fertilisers position', *The Scotsman*, 28 February 1941, 8.
[34] 'The essence of fertility', *The Scotsman*, 26 September 1941, 8. Excess use of artificial fertilisers can cause soil acidification and degradation, mineral depletion and lead to pollution of waterways. See S. Savci, 'An agricultural pollutant: chemical fertilizer', *International Journal of Environmental Science and Development* 3, no. 1 (2012): 77–80.

War required farmers to embrace new methods, such as the relatively new process of ensiling. This was a practice to help with stock feeding, more common on North American farms, which involved cutting young grass and storing it in a pit or tower to ferment.[35] The resulting product – silage – was described as 'a dilute succulent concentrate', the food value of which was only 10 per cent less than fresh grass.[36] In contrast, hay had 25 per cent less food value. The Ministry of Agriculture distributed leaflets to farmers explaining the new method, and facilities such as the Boghall Experimental Farm at the Edinburgh and East of Scotland College of Agriculture gave demonstrations showing best methods for ensiling.[37] Farmers were also able to apply to the Agricultural Requisites Assistance Scheme for supplies of molasses, to help the silage ferment, or for materials to construct structural silos.[38] They were warned there would be 'no more lavish and uneconomical feeding', and they must embrace new technologies for growing foodstuffs.[39]

In addition to new techniques, wartime targets required Scottish farmers to grapple with novel machinery. On the eve of war, Scottish farming was known for its reliance on the horse, and there were only 6,250 tractors in private ownership.[40] Scottish farmers could no longer rely on old methods to plough, sow and harvest the acreage required to meet the new food production targets: it was time to mechanise. During 1941, the Department of Agriculture for Scotland provided farms with 550 tractor-and-binder outfits, 25 threshing units and 60 for digging potatoes.[41] Further, by the start of July 1943 17,000 tractors were at work in Scotland. This new machinery, commented Tom Johnston, Secretary of State, meant Scotland was 'rapidly becoming one of the most intensively mechanised farming countries in the world'.[42]

While farmers were 'commonly accused of being old-fashioned and suspicious of new-fangled methods', stated Sir Patrick Laird of the Department of Agriculture for Scotland, they had 'proved themselves capable of adapting in an amazing degree' to wartime requirements.[43] This ability to adapt led to impressive results and, by the end of 1943, Scotland's harvest was 'the largest that the country has ever known', with crops of both potato and sugar beet among 'the best ever grown'.[44] Figures released in July 1944

---

[35] John Moran, *Tropical Dairy Farming: Feeding Management for Small Holder Dairy Farmers in the Humid Tropics* (Collingwood: Landlinks Press, 2005), 84.
[36] 'Farming notes: war-time policy', *The Scotsman*, 7 June 1940, 10; 'Agricultural affairs: face of countryside transformed', *The Scotsman*, 26 April 1940, 12.
[37] Ibid. (both).
[38] Ibid.
[39] Ibid.
[40] Short, *Battle of the Fields*, 309.
[41] 'Agriculture: Department's harvesting machines', *The Scotsman*, 7 October 1941, 6.
[42] 'Scotland's record farm crops', *The Scotsman*, 3 July 1943, 3.
[43] 'Strain on man-power, doubling the Land Army', *The Scotsman*, 1 February 1943, 2.
[44] 'Scotland grows more: year's record harvest', *The Scotsman*, 31 December 1943, 6.

confirmed the successes: there had been a 43 per cent increase in Scottish acreage under crops compared to 1938 and, as a result, Scotland was providing 14 per cent of the total UK food production yield.[45] This was truly a remarkable achievement in under six years.

'They are not going to be dictated to': resistance to change

While many Scottish farmers adapted to war's influence on their lives, others actively opposed wartime disruptions and resisted state influence. During January 1943, at a meeting of the Council of the National Farmers' Union (NFU) and the Chamber of Agriculture of Scotland, attending farmers expressed 'strong criticism' of the structure and 'dictatorial' powers of AECs.[46] The representative for Nairn, Mr Pottie, reported those in his area had expressed 'a tremendous number' of complaints about the Committees. In general, most farmers were upset that the Committees had power to determine the actions of others and could dictate what farmers should do on their own land, as if the AEC knew more about the farms than those who worked the land. One farmer from Dornoch, in Sutherland, voiced his frustration about the seemingly arbitrary process of AEC distribution of assistance to farmers. 'They could allocate to Tom and Dick, but not to Harry, for reasons known only to themselves', he said.[47] Mr Douglas from Fearn in Ross-shire agreed. 'Farmers are all out for greater production', he stated, 'but they are not going to be dictated to by Committees . . . whether these are good for the country or not.'[48] Certainly these *Diktats* were unpopular, though such meetings were more an expression of frustration than a sign of active rebellion.

There were, however, a small number of cases where resentment translated into open defiance. In July 1940 George Simpson, farming near Loanhead, south of Edinburgh, was charged with 'failing to cultivate 12 acres of his land'.[49] Simpson, a grocer in the city, was too busy to attend to his smallholding and had refused an AEC order to plough the twelve acres. The Sheriff said Simpson appeared 'defiant' towards the orders, so he fined the farmer £10 – approximately £400 today.[50] The following day, a farmer from Hoddom appeared before the Dumfries Sheriff court, pleading guilty to having failed to plough and crop two fields, as ordered.[51] Thomas Bryden, the farmer, was also fined £10 or given the option of

---

[45] 'Farming: "Scotland's largest industry"', *The Scotsman*, 5 July 1944, 4.
[46] 'NFU and powers of country Executive Committees', *The Scotsman*, 7 January 1943, 8.
[47] Ibid.
[48] Ibid.
[49] 'Failed to plough land', *Glasgow Herald*, 5 July 1940, 6.
[50] Conversion calculated using the National Archives Currency Converter: 1270–2017, The National Archives, https://www.nationalarchives.gov.uk/currency-converter/ (accessed 8 May 2020).
[51] 'Failed to plough fields', *Glasgow Herald*, 6 July 1940, 9.

sixty days' imprisonment. It is easy to see how farmers struggled with the new system, which allowed a distant committee the power to dictate what farmers did on their own land.

At times, the powers of AECs seemed to be enforced without consideration of circumstances. Two such cases appeared before the Cupar Sheriff Court in Fife, during February 1942. Robert Mathieson, farming near the village of Pittenweem, was ordered by the East Fife AEC to plough 190 acres of his land, and then to plant some acres with sugar beet.[52] Mathieson 'set his mind to do it' but was already behind on farm work after the long winter of 1941 and struggled to find additional labour to help with the large task. In a similarly difficult position was farmer Andrew Simpson from Kingsbarns who was ordered to plant six acres with sugar beet. The farmer explained to the Sheriff that he already had to dispose of 100 sheep to comply with a previous order from the AEC, and had lodged an objection with the Committee.[53] The AEC was not inclined to negotiate, so both men appeared before the court. Each was fined only a nominal amount. These cases serve to remind us that some farmers decided to resist state influence in wartime life and work.

'Slaves of that duty': additional challenges and pressures

While some farmers fought against increased state intervention, others battled additional challenges. Some, particularly in the Highlands and Islands, faced their old nemesis – the weather. The trials of a heavy winter were nothing new to Scottish farmers, but those during the Second World War were exceedingly harsh. In January 1940 Britain's 'most severe freeze-up' since 1894 arrived, bringing large snowdrifts and freezing solid some Highland lochs.[54] The following winter was equally severe. In January 1941 there were very heavy snowfalls in the northern Highlands and on the Isle of Skye, severe storms elsewhere and parts of Sutherland and Caithness were cut off for several days. Some rural communities even had to receive parcels of emergency rations via aeroplane drops.[55] Farmers were hit particularly hard (see Figure 7.1). According to the *Glasgow Herald* several shepherds lost their lives in the storms of January 1941 searching for stock in snow drifts as deep as thirty feet.[56] The effect of the storms on hill sheep farms was grave, and when sheep were gathered for clipping in June losses were 'far greater than anticipated'.[57] At one farm in Ross-shire, there were 166 lambs compared to 630 at the same time in 1940, and at

---

[52] 'Agriculture: Fife farmers fined', *The Scotsman*, 25 February 1942, 8.
[53] Ibid.
[54] 'Big freeze up: most severe spell for nearly fifty years', *The Scotsman*, 29 January 1940, 6.
[55] 'A wintry January: persistent and severe frost, heavy snowfalls', *The Scotsman*, 17 February 1941, 7.
[56] 'Agricultural news: hill sheep losses', *Glasgow Herald*, 21 June 1941, 8.
[57] Ibid.

Figure 7.1 'A picturesque scene from last month's great freeze-up': a Midlothian shepherd carries two new-born lambs through the snow. (Source: *SMT Magazine*, February 1941.)

a farm in Sutherland losses were estimated at £3,000 – the equivalent of about £120,000 in 2022.[58] 'These losses', stated the *Glasgow Herald*, 'are representative of those sustained by other hill farmers throughout the Highlands'.[59] Such severe losses must have impacted heavily upon farming incomes, production targets and future plans.

The winter of 1944/5 was another severe trial for Scottish farmers. Described as 'arctic', the winter brought heavy snowstorms to Perthshire and Kinross-shire, Loch Lomond was frozen from Balloch to Luss, and a foot of snow even fell at sea level in Oban.[60] To add to the woes of farmers, in both north Argyll and Sutherland hundreds of sheep, cattle and deer perished in blizzards and acute frosts.[61] Crops were also badly affected, especially potatoes, for which there was a serious loss in yield.[62]

[58] Conversion calculated using The National Archives Currency Converter: 1270–2017, The National Archives, https://www.nationalarchives.gov.uk/currency-converter/#currency-result (accessed 8 May 2020).
[59] 'Agricultural news: hill sheep losses', *Glasgow Herald*, 21 June 1941, 8.
[60] NRS, HH55/41, PWD – IR, 26 January 1945: Perthshire and Kinross-shire.
[61] 'Arctic weather continues: Scotland's coldest spell for 50 years', *The Scotsman*, 29 January 1945, 2.
[62] 'Farming notes: potato prices', *The Scotsman*, 19 January 1945, 8.

This created severe shortages across Scotland during early 1945, leaving some regions with an 'almost total absence' of potatoes for purchase.[63] All of this added to the sense of pressure on the farmers who bore responsibility for feeding a nation at war.

On top of this responsibility, many rural Scots were also required to serve in the Home Guard. In addition to their work duties, farmers had to attend Home Guard meetings or training sessions, even if this meant a tramp of 'four or five miles down the glen or over the hill in the darkness of winter nights' to attend classes.[64] For those on night watch, duties generally involved patrolling the countryside or spending hours in wait at likely landing beaches on watch for enemy agents.[65] In the Moray region, some relief came when bathing huts from the beach at Lossiemouth were loaned to the local battalion, who placed them at sentry posts, 'so that the men could obtain some shelter on cold and wet nights, and a little sleep when not actually on duty'.[66] Perhaps a small measure of comfort for those facing cold, lonely nights on the shores of the North Sea.

War also brought the emergence of a discourse around farmers as heroes and key players in the war on the home front. The 'veneration of the farming profession' appeared in a range of sources, including films, magazines and newspaper articles.[67] The text and themes running through these sources often portrayed farmers as heroic and strong, playing an important role in the war effort. An article in *The Scotsman* in April 1940 spoke of the farmer's 'will to win on the home front', which was reportedly 'so strong that the seemingly impossible' had happened – record amounts of land had been ploughed and sown.[68] The Secretary of State for Scotland also claimed that, by their actions, farmers had maintained 'the enviable reputation of Scottish ploughmen of a bygone generation'.[69] Similar themes of agricultural workers as heroic fighters were evident in a 1941 film entitled *Fighting Fields*.[70] Produced for MoI and the Department of Agriculture for Scotland, the film showcased the ways Scotland was feeding its population during the war, and the methods and adaptations employed in the drive to increase production. Focusing on the contributions of rural workers, footage showed labourers and volunteers cultivating, growing and harvesting food, and rapidly increasing

---

[63] NRS, HH55/41, PWD – IR, Month ending 26 January 1945.

[64] 'Highland Home Guard: how equipment was issued in remote areas', *The Scotsman* 20 February 1941.

[65] NLS, MSS.3817, Records of Scottish Home Guard, 1939–1945: North Highland District: Orkney and Shetland; Hebrides Battalion Home Guard.

[66] Ibid.: 1st Moray Battalion Home Guard.

[67] Robb, *Men at Work*, 20–22.

[68] 'Agricultural affairs: face of countryside transformed', *The Scotsman*, 26 April 1940, 12.

[69] Ibid.

[70] Scottish Film Productions and GB Instructional, *Fighting Fields*, 1941, accessed via NLS, Moving Image Archive, https://movingimage.nls.uk/film/0456 (accessed 2 December 2020).

production yields to meet the needs of war. The film finished with these words:

> In the old fields of Scotland and in the new fields . . . the farmers work side-by-side with the Scottish seamen, and the men that clear the sea in the armed trawlers, side-by-side with the men of the air force and with the men of the army. These men and women, these old people and children who are working on the land, together with the fighting services, are defending Scotland. They are striking their blow for freedom on Scotland's fighting fields.[71]

The underlying message of this short but stirring clip was that rural work was as valuable as that undertaken by the armed forces. In essence, the turnip fields were as essential to the war effort as the deserts of North Africa.

This message of heroism was similarly promoted through an MoI exhibition entitled 'New Life to the Land', which toured Scotland in 1941. Opening the exhibition in Aberdeen, Sir Patrick Laird declared food production had increased owing to the 'gallant and united efforts' of farmers.[72] The display, he said, would 'bring home to the urban population how much the many owed to the few who produce the bread, the porridge, the meat, and the milk'.[73] These phrases 'the many' and 'the few' echoed the words used by Prime Minister Churchill in praise of the Royal Air Force during August 1940.[74] This was a powerful choice of words, to liken farmers to the aircraft pilots who had repelled the Luftwaffe in the Battle of Britain.

Other important figures placed similar emphasis on the role of agricultural workers. After the record harvest of 1943, the Department of Agriculture for Scotland described farmers as 'the agricultural heroes of this war'.[75] Similarly, Tom Johnston, speaking in Parliament in July 1944, echoed these sentiments:

> Agriculture is more than our largest industry. It supplies the lifestream of the nation. Without continuous contact and reinvigoration from agriculture, our urban population would wither and die. In war-time we should have been starved into surrender, had not our farmers, farm-workers, scientists, technicians, and administrators united to increase the yield from our flocks, from our herds, and from our fields.[76]

This message of the vital role of farmers, sustaining a nation that would otherwise 'wither and die', placed these workers in a prominent and important

---

[71] Ibid.
[72] 'Agriculture: "new life to the land"', *The Scotsman*, 25 October 1941, 3.
[73] Ibid.
[74] Winston Churchill, 'The few: 20 August 1940', via International Churchill Society, https://winstonchurchill.org/resources/speeches/1940-the-finest-hour/the-few/, accessed 11 May 2020.
[75] 'Scotland grows more: year's record harvest', *The Scotsman*, 31 December 1943, 6.
[76] Hansard, HC Deb, 04 July 1944, vol. 401 col. 1012.

place in society. This role, while flattering, also brought the pressure of heavy responsibility. One Scottish farmer wrote of this sense of duty and pressure to perform:

> War is the gaunt background to all we do. To grow the best crops possible and to harvest them securely becomes our savage duty. We are the slaves of that duty and slaves have neither heart nor peace to rejoice in their labours until they are free. [He added] We have learned painfully that the best we can do, our utmost effort, is just barely enough and we've got to do more.[77]

This message, of pressure, pain and struggle, provides valuable insight into the lived experiences of Scottish farmers in wartime Scotland. While mechanisation, modernisation and state intervention reshaped agricultural methods and practices, the pressure and rhetoric that accompanied wartime farming also reshaped those who worked the land.

Reverse of population decline: migrant workers

Another significant way that war influenced rural Scotland was by stalling – and in some cases reversing – population decline. The wartime rural workforce was swelled by labourers from Ireland; women of the Timber Corps and Land Army; North American and Honduran lumberjacks; and prisoners of war. These experiences of these workers, and the resentments and frictions that arose between the new arrivals and local communities, provide a compelling glimpse into rural life and society during the war. Further, they reveal the ways war reshaped rural communities.

Irish labourers were one such group that made a significant contribution to the Scottish rural workforce.[78] These labourers often worked in agriculture and on government contracts, such as for aerodromes or defence purposes. As discussed earlier in this work, the Irish were 'always unpopular in Glasgow', and the Second World War saw this sentiment spread to rural communities where high concentrations of Irishmen were working.[79] In a sense, these Irish outsiders acted as a tangible representation of the political uncertainty of war. HI reports during 1940 regularly noted the Scottish public were worried about a Nazi invasion coming via the politically neutral Éire. Scots were said to be 'uncertain', 'concerned', 'worried' and full of a 'deep and growing distrust' of Éire and its leader, Éamon de Valera.[80] Scottish farmers also expressed a reluctance to hire the Irish to dig potatoes, supposedly because of concerns about Irish neutrality.[81] Such logic

---

[77] Ian Macpherson, 'Harvest 1942', *SMT Magazine*, October 1942, 16–17.
[78] See Enda Delaney, 'Irish migration to Britain, 1939–1945', *Irish Economic and Social History* 28 (2001): 47–71; Webster, *Mixing It*.
[79] M-O, Diarist 5390 (Glasgow), 9 July 1940.
[80] TNA, INF 1/264, HI Reps. 15: 3 June 1940; 29: 19 June 1940; 33: 24 June 1940.
[81] Ibid., Rep. 29: 19 June 1940.

often served as a thin veil for prejudice, as it seems unlikely that potato diggers would act as a conduit for a German invasion.

Irish agricultural workers were also criticised for a range of other behaviours, including requesting extra wages to work on Sundays, or dodging military service.[82] After two years' uninterrupted labour in Britain, a worker was liable to be called up for British National Service. By returning to Ireland at the end of a job contract, Irish workers could avoid this obligation. Some locals viewed this with suspicion, believing the workers were returning home between contracts to shirk their obligations.[83] By far the most avid criticism of Irish workers, however, related to heavy alcohol consumption. In areas with high numbers of contract labourers there was a 'marked increase' in drunkenness and, likewise, a rise in disorderly behaviour.[84] In the burgh of Ayr, on the south-west coast of Scotland, Irish labourers working on a local aerodrome caused 'a fair amount of trouble' with their drunkenness.[85] Chief Constable J. Lowdon told the SHD that he would be glad when construction finished and the Irish workmen left, as the problem should abate. Similarly, Irish aerodrome workers in Berwickshire were noted for heavy drinking. 'Numbers of these men are seen under the influence of drink', the chief constable noted, 'and become a nuisance and an eyesore in the small villages near the Aerodromes'.[86]

Historian Enda Delaney has cautioned that oral testimony reveals little evidence of 'overt hostility' towards Irish migrants, and many Irish were positive about their experiences in wartime Britain.[87] It is also notable that, despite Scotland's pre-war history of sectarianism, most wartime criticisms of Irish labourers in Scotland did not extend to religion; rather, they focused on the men's alcohol consumption or potential role as spies. This indicates that during the war not only were rural communities focused on the preservation of traditional conservative values, but also gripped by fears of invasion. Perhaps in some cases these worries over-rode long-standing religious hostility.

'No woman can learn much about farming': the Women's Land Army and Timber Corps

Female labour was also a crucial part of wartime efforts, and women from across Britain migrated to rural Scotland to assist with farming

---

[82] NRS, HH55/38: PWD – IR, 5 November 1943: Berwickshire; HH55/36, PWD – IR, 23 April 1943: City of Edinburgh.
[83] NRS, HH55/36, PWD – IR, 23 April 1943: City of Edinburgh. See also Webster, *Mixing It*, 79–80.
[84] NRS, HH55/26, PWD – IR, 3 January 1941: *précis*.
[85] NRS, HH55/27, PWD – IR: Ayr burgh, 14 March 1941.
[86] NRS, HH55/29, PWD – IR: Berwickshire, 15 August 1941.
[87] Enda Delaney, *Demography, State and Society: Irish Migration to Britain, 1921–1971* (Montreal: McGill-Queen's University Press, 2000), 139.

and forestry. One such group was the Women's Timber Corps (WTC). Established by the Ministry of Supply during April 1942 in England, and in Scotland the following month, the WTC came under the auspices of the Home Grown Timber Department. These women quickly had to adapt to rural life and the demands of forestry work. In Scotland, women were recruited from age 17 and worked in the physically demanding jobs of felling, snedding (stripping the side branches off a felled tree), loading lorries and trains, and in sawmills.[88] The volunteers were often billeted in huts or hostels, which were generally of an austere standard. Former lumberjills, as they were known, spoke of basic camp conditions such as having only one bathroom between ten girls, and only enough water for three girls to take a bath per day.[89] Tibby Scotland said the work left her 'hungry, sore and tired', but 'I felt I was doing a good job . . . something worthwhile'.[90] Another woman who worked in Aberdeenshire, Margaret Lynch, summed up her service with fondness: 'I loved working in the woods. I'm glad I joined the Timber Corps. I loved every minute of it. It was great. I often return to Banchory on holiday. I go back to the woods we felled.'[91]

Estimates vary regarding the number of women who served in the WTC during the Second World War. Emma Vickers has suggested a figure of 6,000 across Britain, while Kate Schaefer puts the total closer to 8,500.[92] Joanna Foat's research found that 1,400 women served in Scottish forests, though other sources suggest membership may have been closer to 4,000.[93] All Public Record Office files relating to the WTC have been destroyed, so it remains difficult to know the finer details of the Corps and its members.[94] One archive that survives, though, is a film about the WTC in Scotland, entitled *Jolly Good Fellers*. Produced by film company British Pathé in December 1942, the film shows lumberjills going about their work 'somewhere in Scotland'.[95] 'Felling trees may harden the muscles, but see what it does to the dimples', the cheerful voiceover intones over film of smiling women sharpening axes. The short film is heavy on gender

---

[88] 'Women's Timber Corps', *Forestry and Land Scotland*, https://forestryandland.gov.scot/learn/heritage/world-war-two/womens-timber-corps (accessed 8 September 2020).

[89] BBC, '*The One Show*: The Lumberjills', via https://forestryandland.gov.scot/learn/heritage/world-war-two/womens-timber-corps (accessed 8 September 2020).

[90] Ibid.

[91] Christian Auer, '108. Margaret Lynch, Women's Land Army Timber Corps, 1943', in *Scotland and the Scots, 1707–2007: A Reader* (Strasbourg: Presses Universitaires de Strasbourg, 2013), 322–4.

[92] Vickers, 'The forgotten army', 101; Kate Murphy Schaefer, 'Land Girls and lumber jills', *Historic UK*, https://www.historic-uk.com/HistoryUK/HistoryofBritain/Land-Girls-and-Lumber-Jills/ (accessed 9 September 2020).

[93] Foat, *Lumberjills*, 53–4; Gray, *Timber!*, 170.

[94] Foat, *Lumberjills*, 15.

[95] *Jolly Good Fellers*, British Pathé, 1942, via https://www.youtube.com/watch?v=lq6LhFzFMMI (accessed 2 December 2020).

stereotype, also telling the viewer 'there's a knack and a great deal of effort in swinging an axe. Especially for a girl who's never swung anything heavier than a handbag.' Often such films were produced for MoI, to encourage women to enlist, or to keep up public support for the war effort by revealing the contributions of fellow citizens. In this case, there is no surviving bibliographical information to reveal clues to why or for whom this specific film was produced. The film does, however, show the methods used by the women to chop and prepare trees for milling, giving a valuable insight into the demanding conditions of forestry work for women of the WTC in Scotland.

Aside from lumberjills, the chief source of women workers was through the Women's Land Army (WLA). Initially formed late in the First World War to assist with redressing food shortages, the organisation was resurrected in 1939 and reached peak membership in 1943.[96] The WLA was essentially a semi-private organisation, administered by Lady Denman, the president of the National Federation of Women's Institutes. In Scotland, the group came under the purview of the Department of Agriculture for Scotland and much of the administration was carried out via AECs.[97] The women were often accommodated in hostels, while others boarded with families or in properties on farm steadings. Wages were low and, for those accommodated on farms, a portion of the pay-packet was given directly to the farmer for food and board. According to the research of Elaine Edwards, at that time male agricultural workers in Scotland earned less than half of what other unskilled labourers did, bringing in an average of £1 18 shillings a week, while members of the Scottish WLA were entitled to only £1 8 shillings.[98] In February 1943, Laird from the Department of Agriculture for Scotland issued a statement calling for more women to help on Scottish farms. He complimented the 'Land Girls' on their efforts, but explained that the strain on labour was growing more severe and the war at sea meant thousands of extra tons of grain were required.[99]

Members of the SWLA soon adapted to their new conditions, though there were many challenges. Workers were often given physically demanding tasks such as hoeing, spreading manure, pulling turnips and digging potatoes. Church of Scotland support workers noted city girls who had previously undertaken little manual labour found these tasks backbreaking, and many struggled to 'accustom themselves to country life'.[100] This was especially so for those accommodated in hostels, where living conditions could be basic. Correspondence between officers at the Department

---

[96] Vickers, 'The forgotten army', 103.
[97] Field, *Blood, Sweat, and Toil*, 168; Edwards, *Scotland's Land Girls*, 16, 24.
[98] Edwards, *Scotland's Land Girls*, 21.
[99] 'Strain on man-power, doubling the Land Army', *The Scotsman*, 1 February 1943, 2.
[100] Scottish Film Productions, *Fighting Fields*, 1941.

of Agriculture for Scotland and the Ministry of Works regularly recorded problems with hostel accommodation, and requests for alterations and improvements. One hostel in Dalrymple had a leaking roof; another in Fife had had its washtub removed and 'the girls now have nowhere to wash their personal belongings', while all four radiators at another hostel were recorded as 'defective'.[101] Furthermore, a hostel officer for the Young Women's Christian Association remarked that while new hostels in Inverness-shire and Aberdeen were 'very bright and attractive', she was 'very sorry to say [they] appear to have been planned by someone who has no practical knowledge of running a hostel or of what is really required'.[102]

Alongside the challenges of hard work and poor accommodation, sources also reveal evidence of friction between Land Girls and farmers. 'On the first day the farmer regarded "the government wench" with covert suspicion', wrote columnist Sheila Watson in the *Glasgow Herald* in July 1940. She continued 'he still insists that no woman can learn much about farming. At the same time, he overcomes this prejudice enough to produce a line of jobs ... which keep me trotting around from dawn till dusk.'[103] An article in *The Scotsman* similarly noted that while 'Scottish farmers were slow at first to believe that the land girl could be of value', by the end of February 1943 5,500 women were working the land on 3,500 Scottish farms.[104] Of these women, 3,000 had earned long-service badges, proof, according to *The Scotsman*, 'that their powers of endurance are sufficient to enable them to "stick it" through all the vagaries of the climate and varying conditions of employment'.[105]

Female farm workers were also vulnerable to the temperament of farmers and their wives. After employing the same Land Girl for more than three years, one farmer unexpectedly telephoned the SWLA to end the employment arrangement. In May 1943, Mr Munro from a poultry farm at Muirhouse, north of Edinburgh, told an SWLA representative that the female worker they had supplied was 'dumb stupid' and it was 'quite impossible for her to take any responsibility unless she [was] very carefully watched'.[106] This came after three years of employing the same girl. In response, the Land Girl expressed surprise at being asked to leave, noting that she 'worked hard and did everything she could' to please the farmer's wife, who was considered 'very difficult and always nagging, constantly changing her mind about how the work should be done'.[107]

---

[101] NRS, AF59/12/2, Women's Land Army: hostels, 'letter from Macintyre to McGlashan', 24 March 1944, 'letter to Sorrell at Ministry of Works', 19 November 1943.
[102] Ibid., 'letter from YWCA Scottish Division', 15 September 1943.
[103] Sheila Watson, 'To be a farmer's girl', *Glasgow Herald*, 8 July 1940, 3.
[104] 'Women's Land Army: big drive for Scottish recruits', *The Scotsman*, 24 February 1943, 6.
[105] Ibid.
[106] NRS, AF59/245, 'WLA: Elizabeth Robson', memo of 4 May 1943.
[107] Ibid., letter of 10 May 1943.

Despite these challenges and the evidence of friction between workers and farmers, memoirs and oral histories of Land Army members have tended to emphasise the fun and *camaraderie* experienced by the women. Geoffrey Field has noted such narratives tend to foreground 'individual adaptability to new ways of life', through themes such as rapid maturation, gaining in confidence and meeting new people.[108] Scotswoman Mona McLeod said '[t]he Land Army opened up a whole new world for me. The long-term effect of this was a wonderful escape from the very narrow life in which I had been brought up.'[109] In the view of one historian, these oral histories tend to be, primarily, the record of those who 'stuck with it ... the survivors, and the pictures painted must be seen in that light'.[110] This was also observed by researcher Elaine Edwards when interviewing former Scottish Land Girls. Edwards noted 'those who responded to my appeal for information tended to be the ones that enjoyed their time in the Women's Land Army'.[111] One such Land Girl was Jean Forbes Paterson, who reflected, 'even when doing the most mundane jobs, we managed to sing, laugh and enjoy life with all its ups and downs'.[112]

In 2012, a memorial to the SWLA was unveiled by (then) HRH Prince Charles. Situated in Moray, the steel sculpture features seven young women standing on a gate, smiling and waving.[113] Mrs McLeod was one of the former Land Girls consulted over the memorial's design, but she was unimpressed, feeling that the chosen design was 'a false picture ... an insult'.[114] Shovelling manure was neither romantic nor fun, 'but that was the reality of the Land Girls', Mrs McLeod added. Time, perhaps, has helped to gloss over the more difficult experiences of female labourers on the Scottish home front. As Field observed, the realities of harsh or monotonous work and frequent prejudice have been overshadowed by memoirs and oral histories, written decades after the fact, in which companionship and maturation are emphasised.[115] Memory, Lucy Noakes has pointed out, is 'notoriously slippery', and involves forgetting, 'almost as much as it does remembering'.[116]

---

[108] Field, *Blood, Sweat and Toil*, 171–2.
[109] Edwards, *Scotland's Land Girls*, 129.
[110] Keith Kirby, 'Review of Mairi Stewart, *Voices of the Forest, A Social History of Scottish Forestry in the Twentieth Century*', *Northern Scotland* 8, no. 1 (2017), 117.
[111] Edwards, *Scotland's Land Girls*, 9.
[112] Ibid., 39.
[113] 'First permanent memorial to Women's Land Army gets Royal seal of approval', *NFU Scotland*, 9 October 2012, https://www.nfus.org.uk/news/news/first-permanent-memorial-women-s-land-army-gets-royal-seal-approval (accessed 8 February 2023).
[114] Murray Scougall, '"I can't honestly remember spending a massive amount of time swinging on gates and waving my hat in the air": Mona, 95, says sculpture is no fitting tribute to WWII's land girls', *The Sunday Post*, 19 February 2018, https://tinyurl.com/ycksb7zc (accessed 11 May 2022).
[115] Field, *Blood, Sweat, and Toil*, 171–2.
[116] Noakes and Pattinson, 'Keep calm', 4.

'A great bunch of boys': lumberjacks from Newfoundland, Canada and British Honduras

Scotland's rural population was further buoyed by migrant foresters from North America and the Caribbean. This was a tradition established during the Great War, when Canadians and Newfoundlanders had worked as lumberjacks in British forests.[117] Timber was crucial both to the military and to industry, being used for a range of purposes such as pit-props for coal and other mines, telegraph poles and for houses or air-raid shelters.[118] During the Great War, half of Britain's best trees had been used to address wartime production needs. While replacements had been planted, by the eve of the Second World War few were of sufficient size to be much use.[119] By 1939, Britain produced on home soil only 4 per cent of its timber needs, importing the remainder from overseas producers.[120] This was unsustainable and risky during war, especially as Atlantic shipping routes came under increasing levels of attack from German naval forces. To add to the problem, home-grown timber was reliant on the availability of labour, which was in short supply as forestry workers enlisted or moved into essential industries. It soon became clear that additional labourers would be needed to meet ambitious wartime timber targets.

The biggest group of migrant lumberjacks were the Canadian Forestry Corps, which came under the authority of the Canadian military (see Figure 7.2).[121] Thirty companies and nearly 7,000 men were deployed to Scotland over the course of the war. 'A large percentage' were of Scottish descent and, in reflection of this, the Corps had its own pipers.[122] These men were lumberjacks by trade and brought with them modern equipment and new methods of lumbering.[123] The Canadians also impressed locals with their work ethic and skills. One commander, Major F. J. Dawson, told *The Canadian Press* '[t]he Scots around these parts are amazed at us. They say we no sooner get into a piece of timber than it's gone.'[124]

---

[117] 'Newfoundland Forestry Corps', *Newfoundland and Labrador in the First World War*, https://www.heritage.nf.ca/first-world-war/articles/forestry-corps-en.php (accessed 8 September 2020).

[118] David Sneddon, 'Newfoundlanders in a Highland forest during WWII', *Journal of Conflict Archaeology* 3, no. 1 (2007): 233–66, here 239.

[119] Foat, *Lumberjills*, 28.

[120] Vickers, 'The forgotten army', 101, 104.

[121] See William C. Wonders, *The 'Sawdust Fusiliers': The Canadian Forestry Corps in the Scottish Highlands in World War Two* (Montreal: Canadian Pulp and Paper Association, 1991).

[122] Angela Forbes, 'The British Empire and the war effort: a comparative study of the experiences of the British Honduran Forestry Unit and the Newfoundland Overseas Forestry Unit', unpublished MA dissertation: University of the Highlands and Islands, 2015, 5; IWM, H23592, 'Canadian Forestry Corps', 5 September 1942.

[123] Ross Munro, 'N.B. Soldiers with Canadian Forestry Corps in Scotland', *Telegraph-Journal*, 4 June 1941.

[124] Ibid.

Figure 7.2 Personnel of an unidentified company of the Canadian Forestry Corps moving a log, Scotland, 19 May 1943. (Source: Library and Archives Canada/ Department of National Defence fonds/a180712.)

The war correspondent for *The Canadian Press* was also impressed with the men's work, after visiting a number of Canadian mills across Scotland. He observed that the workers were 'hard-working', worked with 'team-like precision' and were able to keep a mill going 'even during a terrific snowstorm'.[125]

Another group of migrant workers came from Newfoundland, a former British dominion.[126] In total, over 3,400 Newfoundland lumberjacks volunteered, with 69 out of 71 of the resulting forestry camps based in Scotland.[127] 'It is not easy to train a man, however strong and fit he may be, to become a good lumberjack', stated the manager of the Newfoundland Overseas Forestry Unit (NOFU) in 1941.[128] By 1943, six new forestry camps

---

[125] Ibid.
[126] T. Curran, *They Also Served: The Newfoundland Overseas Forestry Unit, 1939–1946* (Newfoundland: Jepherson Press, 1987), 105.
[127] Forbes, 'The British Empire', 5; Drew Scott, 'Timber Corps', *East Lothian at War*, http://www.eastlothianatwar.co.uk/ELAW/Timber_Corps.html (accessed 7 May 2020).
[128] 'Newfoundlander Overseas Forestry Unit (NOFU)', *Forestry and Land Scotland*, https://forestryandland.gov.scot/learn/heritage/world-war-two/newfoundlander-overseas-forestry-unit-nofu (accessed 8 September 2020).

had been opened to accommodate the Newfoundland lumberjacks. 'Work in this area has never been so plentiful', reported the chief constable of Moray and Nairn.[129] The accommodation was basic, though, with no heating and lighting only by paraffin lamp.[130] In their spare time, many of the men volunteered with local Home Guard battalions. In Inverness-shire there were enough Newfoundlanders to form their own grouping, the 3rd Inverness (Newfoundland Forestry) Battalion Home Guard. Formed in September 1942, the response was 'quick and excellent', with 750 men enrolling by the end of the year. Training was undertaken at weekends, as work duties permitted.[131]

Unlike some other groups of wartime labourers in rural Scotland, North American lumberjacks were generally welcomed into local communities. The men frequently drank at nearby public houses and attended local dances. Canadians were especially popular with local women, and several marriages took place during their service in Scotland. A remarkable example of this came from the No. 4 Company of the Canadian Forestry Corps, based near the Moray town of Forres. When reaching the end of its stay in Scotland, the Corps' war diarist noted on 4 April that eight men had recently married, 'seven with permission and one without'. He also noted that, over the previous 12 months, 33 out of 180 men had married local women. The diarist added 'perhaps it is well for the sake of those who still remain unmarried that the unit is leaving Scotland tomorrow'.[132]

While relations were often positive, there were also elements of tension between migrant foresters and local Scottish communities. Throughout their time in Scotland, both Canadians and Newfoundlanders became known as heavy drinkers, and authorities regularly noted their 'considerable' and 'excessive' drunkenness.[133] During 1941, police in Inverness-shire commented on the 'increased drunkenness' of Newfoundland lumbermen, especially on Sundays, while those from the Canadian Forestry Corps aroused the ire of police in both Inverness-shire and Ross and Cromarty.[134] Friction between foreign forestry workers and local authorities was a regular occurrence between 1941 and 1944. During these years, constabulary across the Highland regions of Inverness-shire, Ross and Cromarty, Perth and Moray and Nairn noted 'numerous complaints' from the public,

[129] NRS, HH55/36, PWD – IR, 29 January 1943: Moray and Nairn.
[130] 'Newfoundland Overseas Forestry Unit', *East Lothian at War*, http://www.eastlothianatwar.co.uk/ELAW/Timber_Corps.html (accessed 8 September 2020).
[131] NLS, MSS. 3817: Home Guard Records, historical record of 3rd Inverness (Newfoundland Forestry) Battalion Home Guard.
[132] Libraries and Archives Canada, RG24 vol. 16423, War Diary: No. 4 Company, Canadian Forestry Corps, 4 April 1945.
[133] NRS, HH55/29, PWD – IR, 15 August 1941: Ross and Cromarty; HH55/34, PWD – IR, 11 September 1942: Inverness-shire, Ross and Cromarty.
[134] NRS, HH55/29, PWD – IR, 15 August 1941: Inverness-shire, Ross and Cromarty.

and repeatedly raised concerns over the lumberjacks' excessive drunkenness and 'drunken antics'.[135] The village of Strathpeffer, north-west of Inverness, was also a particular hot-spot for the 'drunk and disorderly behaviour' of Newfoundland lumberjacks. In June 1943, the region's chief constable complained there was 'a certain amount' of ill-feeling between the Newfoundlanders, who travelled to the town to drink at weekends, and members of the Canadian Forestry Corps, stationed nearby. '[I]n drink they quarrel and sometimes fight', he commented.[136] This behaviour and the higher level of police activity required to deal with it somewhat soured the relationship between these workers and their local Scottish communities.

Alongside Newfoundlanders and Canadians, workers from central America also supplemented the Scottish rural labour force during the Second World War. In total, around 800 foresters from British Honduras came to Scotland to work, with the first contingent arriving in August 1941.[137] The group was privately recruited by a Scottish timber importer, W. Robertson, who told the *Glasgow Herald* he had been to British Honduras to personally recruit this 'great bunch of boys'.[138] British Honduras, now known as Belize, was well known for its mahogany industry and the workers who arrived in Scotland were expert axemen, bringing their own axes, handles and hatchets which were used for cutting down large mahogany trees, and superior to the tools available in Scotland.[139] The recruits were initially destined for the south of Scotland where, it was thought, the climate would better suit the men. Later contingents were sent to camps in the Highland regions of Sutherland and Ross-shire, which must surely have come as a shock to these men from the sub-tropics.

Perhaps not unexpectedly, these new arrivals struggled to adapt to Scottish rural life and conditions. In 1942, a group of the men wrote to the Ministry of Supply in Edinburgh expressing a grievance about conditions in the forestry camps. The men's concerns were not taken seriously, however, and the resulting investigation concluded their allegations were 'largely unjustified'.[140] An intelligence officer for MoI took up the case and his solution was to introduce a programme of films and speakers to 'help to break the monotony of life' for the Hondurasians.[141] When he visited with a film projectionist months later, the official reported that conditions in the

---

[135] NRS, HH55/36, PWD – IR, 23 April 1943: Ross and Cromarty; HH55/37, PWD – IR, 18 June 1943: Ross and Cromarty, Perth, Inverness burgh; HH55/39, PWD – IR, 18–28 January 1944: Moray and Nairn.
[136] NRS, HH55/37, PWD – IR, 18 June 1943: Ross and Cromarty.
[137] Forbes, 'The British Empire', 6; 'Empire axmen for Scotland: British Honduras lumberjacks', *Glasgow Herald*, 23 August 1941, 6.
[138] Ibid.
[139] Ibid.
[140] TNA, INF 1/293, HI Special Rep. 34: 3 December 1942, 1.
[141] Ibid.

forestry camps were 'according to our standards . . . bad'.¹⁴² The road into one of the camps was 'a quagmire' and the MoI film van had to be towed in by a tractor, there was no electric light, the huts were described as full of 'chaos, dirt and confusion' and – in the middle of a Scottish winter – on-site canteens did not supply hot drinks, only aerated water. Moreover, in response to 'many' complaints the MoI intelligence officer sampled the camp food, finding it to be 'ill-cooked, unappetising, and difficult to analyse'.¹⁴³ One can only imagine how these lumberjacks felt working far from home, living in cold and primitive conditions in the wilds of Scotland.

Like the Canadians and Newfoundlanders, the lumberjacks from central America were also known for drinking. When under the influence of alcohol, the men became 'very excitable', and in the town of Duns in Berwickshire so many disturbances had taken place that some local pubs and hotels refused to serve the lumbermen.¹⁴⁴ An MoI intelligence officer heard talk of 'wild scenes' and instances where the men had become involved in altercations that resulted in police laying charges. 'We were well liked until we started drinking', commented one lumberjack from the camp at Duns.¹⁴⁵ The Hondurasians were also dogged by rumours of local women abandoning their husbands to move in with the men, and of prostitutes from as far away as Newcastle arriving 'regularly, and especially on pay nights'.¹⁴⁶ In response, MoI investigators suggested that the problem lay with the women, not the Hondurasians, and that officials were 'considering getting powers to keep women out of the camps, especially at night'.¹⁴⁷

Early historiography of the British Honduran Forestry Unit (BHFU) concluded that the 'appalling' conditions and treatment of the men was largely due to government and individual racism.¹⁴⁸ In contrast, a 2015 study by Angela Forbes discovered men in the NOFU and BHFU had relatively similar experiences, with both camps poorly fitted out and conditions 'leaving much to be desired'.¹⁴⁹ Forbes also concluded the Hondurasians had 'largely positive' relations with the local population, while experiences of the Newfoundlanders were 'comparatively negative', the men being subjected to taunting and regularly getting into fights with locals.¹⁵⁰

---

¹⁴² Ibid.
¹⁴³ Ibid.
¹⁴⁴ TNA, INF 1/293, HI Special Rep. 34: 3 December 1942, 2.
¹⁴⁵ Ibid.
¹⁴⁶ Ibid.
¹⁴⁷ Ibid., 3.
¹⁴⁸ See A. A. Ford, *Telling the Truth: The Life and Times of the British Honduran Forestry Unit in Scotland, 1941–44* (London: Karia Press, 1985); Marika Sherwood, '"It is not a case of numbers": a case study of institutional racism in Britain, 1941–43', *Immigrants and Minorities* 4, no. 2 (1985): 116–41; Marika Sherwood, *The British Honduran Forestry Unit in Scotland, 1941–43* (London: One Caribbean, 1982).
¹⁴⁹ Forbes, 'The British Empire', 24–5.
¹⁵⁰ Ibid.

Figure 7.3 A band formed from the Honduran Timber Corps playing in Tranent. (Source: East Lothian at War.)

The research in this chapter buttresses Forbes' findings, and the selected archival sources generally portrayed Hondurasian lumberjacks as being welcomed into local villages. The men were well liked by locals, and expressed 'delight' that white women wanted to associate with them.[151] Government investigators noted the 'dance mad' men regularly attended dances, enjoyed mixing with locals at public houses, and some were welcomed into evening classes in nearby villages.[152] Many had musical talent and some had brought hand-made instruments with them from British Honduras, which they used to play in local bands, including at Tranent and Kirkpatrick Fleming (see Figure 7.3).[153]

After the War, some Hondurasian migrants stayed on in Scottish communities. Sam Martinez was one wartime migrant who remained, living in Edinburgh until his death in 2016. In an interview with *The Herald* in 2006, Martinez said

> we were very willing and happy to come here during the war and do our bit for the mother country. We heard about the war and the destruction that was going on, and didn't hesitate. We volunteered to

[151] TNA, INF 1/293, HI Special Rep. 34: 3 December 1942, 2.
[152] Ibid., 1.
[153] 'British Honduran Forestry Unit', *East Lothian at War*, http://www.eastlothianatwar.co.uk/ELAW/Timber_Corps.html (accessed 11 September 2020); 'Empire axmen for Scotland: British Honduras lumberjacks', *Glasgow Herald*, 23 August 1941, 6; TNA, INF 1/293, HI Special Rep. 34: 3 December 1942.

come in good spirit, prepared for anything. We knew the soldiers had suffered and we were prepared to suffer the same.[154]

While the sharp edges of memory may have been smoothed by the passage of time, these words provide valuable insight into the lived experience of this wartime migrant.

'Excellent workmen': prisoners of war

Scotland's rural workforce was also swelled by the arrival of 'enemy agents'. In the drive to find labourers to undertake vital farming, forestry and construction work, officials turned to compulsion as a means of filling vacancies. Prisoners of war (POWs) were such a source of labour. Predominantly German and Italian men, POWs in Scotland were initially the crew of downed aircraft or seamen from captured or sunk vessels.[155] As war progressed, prisoners captured in the Mediterranean, North Africa and Italy were transported to internment camps in places such as Canada and Australia. This practice was halted after the *Arandora Star* was torpedoed in July 1940. The ship, carrying POWs and enemy aliens to Canada, sank and 865 lives were lost.[156] From then onwards, POW internment in Britain increased, with the numbers of Italians peaking in early 1945, and Germans in August 1946.[157] In Scotland, by 1945 there were up to 12,000 Italians and 8,000 Germans, accommodated in 45 camps.[158] POW camps were situated across Scotland, from Orkney in the north to Wigtownshire in the south, often in locations where POW labour could be used in nearby agriculture and construction projects.[159]

Primary sources reveal evidence of tension in rural communities between locals and Italian POW workers. One reason for this was that the Italians quickly earned a reputation for being troublesome and provocative. One such incident occurred in October 1942, and involved Italian prisoners working on a farm 'somewhere in Central Scotland'. Reports claimed that when travelling to work through the local town, prisoners flew a swastika from the POW lorry. Townsfolk were further incensed by the men calling

---

[154] Vicky Allan, 'The last lumberjack', *The Herald*, 15 January 2006, https://tinyurl.com/bddk2s46 (accessed 11 May 2022).
[155] Malpass, *British Treatment of German POW*, 5.
[156] Alison Campsie, 'Scotland and Italy remember "atrocious" sinking of *Arandora Star* 80 years on', *The Scotsman*, 2 July 2020, https://www.scotsman.com/heritage-and-retro/heritage/scotland-and-italy-remember-atrocious-sinking-arandora-star-80-years-2902334 (accessed 8 February 2023).
[157] Malpass, *British Treatment of German POW*, 5–6.
[158] Royle, *Time of Tyrants*, 246; 'Farmers must not feed prisoners of war', *The Scotsman*, 13 July 1945, 6.
[159] 'POW camp summary WWII', *Secret Scotland*, https://www.secretscotland.org.uk/index.php/Secrets/PoWCampSummaryWWII (accessed 14 September 2020).

out '*Duce, Duce*', and making jest of the popular 'V' sign.[160] One morning an irate local coalman 'held up' the lorry, threatening the occupants with a chair leg. After details of the incident appeared in *The Scotsman*, the story quickly spread across the country, causing 'considerable' public comment.[161] That same week, newspapers reported Germany was manacling a group of POWs, Allied servicemen captured in Dieppe. Public 'anger and consternation' was expressed across Britain.[162] In Scotland, the sight of Italian POWs brazenly flying a swastika as they travelled in relative comfort to local farms must have rubbed salt into the wounds.[163]

Throughout the war, Italian agricultural workers continued to cause friction in rural Scottish communities. Rumblings came from Berwickshire and Ayrshire, where Italian POWs were criticised for their 'considerable latitude' in freedom of movement, and accused of bringing 'a little trouble' through their relationships with local women.[164] In Dundee, when two Italians refused to do certain farm tasks they were fired by the unimpressed farmer. Three of their comrades quit in consternation. Outraged at this conduct, the Dundee branch of the NFU requested support from the county AEC, and asked the organisation to enforce discipline better among POW workers.[165] Problems were also noted over Italian workers who demanded wages from Scottish farmers. Authorities condemned the practice, advising farmers that payment would result in POW labour being withdrawn, and reminding POWs this was a punishable offence.[166]

The Italians also raised resentment among servicemen home on leave from the Italian theatre of war. This was noted by the chief constable of Berwickshire, who mentioned the case of one Scottish soldier, home on leave in 1944. The man had lost a comrade back in Italy – 'treacherously shot by a Fascist' – and when out walking in his Scottish hometown had come across a group of Italians. The soldier was enraged to see enemy POWs freely roaming the streets of Scotland.[167] In some cases, these tense undercurrents spilled over into brawls. During 1945, three Italians were admonished at Tayport Police Court for an altercation with local men.[168] Later that year, an Italian POW faced a serious assault charge in Fife. Following an argument, and some provocation, the POW had stabbed

---

[160] 'Italians cause fracas: prisoners' swastika emblem rouses Scot to action', *The Scotsman*, 2 October 1942, 3.
[161] See NRS, HH55/34, PWD – IR, 9 October 1942: especially Kirkcaldy.
[162] Douglas Williams, 'Highland Division: story of gallant action along French coast', *The Scotsman*, 13 July 1940, 7.
[163] TNA, INF 1/264, HI Rep. 106: 15 October 1942; NRS, HH55/34, PWD – IR, 9 October 1942.
[164] NRS, HH55/37, PWD – IR, 16 July 1943: Berwickshire; HH55/38, PWD – IR, 5 November 1943: Ayrshire.
[165] 'Agriculture: Italian prisoners on farm work', *The Scotsman*, 19 May 1943, 8.
[166] 'Agriculture: Italian P.o.W. demanding money', *The Scotsman*, 1 August 1945, 3.
[167] NRS, HH55/40, PWD – IR, 14 July 1944: Berwickshire.
[168] NRS, HH55/42, PWD – IR, July to September 1945: Fife.

a Cowdenbeath man in both arms with a table knife.[169] These incidents reveal the simmering tension between Italian POWs and rural Scots.

In contrast, German POWs experienced less friction with local communities. During 1945, the Scottish constabulary was asked to report on POW workers in rural areas of Scotland. The most common comment about Italians was that they were 'satisfactory'.[170] In contrast, German workers were lauded, frequently praised for their work and temperament. Farmers spoke well of the men, their work was considered 'highly satisfactory' and they were 'excellent workmen', 'docile and obedient'.[171] Unfortunately for Italians working in rural Scotland, their conduct and work effort paled in comparison to those of the Germans. In both Berwickshire and Kirkcaldy farmers said German workers were 'preferred to Italians', in Perthshire and Kinross-shire they were 'far better workers than Italians' and in Kincardineshire the Germans were working well, 'far ahead of the Italians'.[172] The German labourers had clearly impressed locals with their work ethic, in stark contrast to the more troublesome Italians.

While archival sources reveal strong antipathy towards Italian POWs, it is important to remember the complex nature of public feeling towards Italy at the time of the described interactions. Intelligence reports noted the British public often viewed Italy with bitterness and distrust, considering the country to be a friend that had stabbed them in the back.[173] In addition, Italy was perceived as traitorous for choosing to ally itself with Germany, and then capitulating and offering to fight alongside Britain when things were going the Allies' way.[174] These negative perceptions may have coloured interactions with Italian POWs. It may also be possible that resentment towards Italian workers, who were often Catholic, was linked to existing sectarianism. As discussed in Chapters One and Two, religious tension had been a common feature of pre-war life in Scotland, and hostility between the Kirk and Catholicism had increased in intensity during the interwar period.[175] This may have been a factor in the treatment of Scottish Italians, who were often ridiculed for their Catholicism and subjected to xenophobic prejudice. Wendy Ugolini's research into the experiences of members of the Italian diaspora in Scotland found that many were labelled fascists and 'desperate characters', and ridiculed for their Catholicism.[176]

---

[169] Ibid.
[170] See NRS, HH55/42, PWD – IR, July to September 1945.
[171] NRS, HH55/42, PWD – IR, July to September 1945: Kirkcaldy, Berwickshire, Ayrshire, Greenock.
[172] NRS, HH55/42, PWD – IR, July to September 1945: Berwickshire, Kirkcaldy, Perthshire and Kinross-shire, Kincardineshire.
[173] TNA, INF 1/292, HI Rep. 154: 16 September 1943.
[174] Ibid.
[175] Devine, *Scottish Nation*, 491.
[176] Wendy Ugolini, 'Memory, war and the Italians in Edinburgh: the role of communal myth', *National Identities* 8, no. 4 (2006): 421–36, here 422, 429–30.

When faced with an influx of Italian POW labourers, such existing sentiment may have inflamed tensions in rural communities of Scotland.

Wendy Webster has observed that British responses to wartime migrants were 'complex and varied', and that popular attitudes shifted across time.[177] The sources selected for this chapter illustrate this complex response, demonstrating that while migrant workers made a significant contribution to Scottish primary industry, their presence also brought tension, raised concerns and required communities to adapt. Wartime migration also reshaped communities on a more permanent basis as some migrants chose to remain after war's end. The following section will further explore the longer-reaching effects of the war.

Renewed hope for the future: prospect of rural rejuvenation

War transformed rural Scotland, bringing hope for the future. Wartime migration hinted at a reversal of population decline, and the regeneration of primary industries brought the tentative signs of economic upturn. Amid the focus on self-sufficiency in food and timber production came discussions about how Scotland could begin the post-war years on a secure footing, and the ways in which rural areas could continue to thrive after war's conclusion. In late 1940, politicians and planners renewed discussions on Scotland's future, anxious to avoid a return to the years of depression that had followed the Great War.[178] With this in mind, the inquiry into the economic development of the Highlands and Islands was reopened. This subject had been examined by the Scottish Development Council in 1938, but the uncertainty in the international situation had seen its practical suggestions shelved. The Council's Highlands and Islands Committee, announced *The Scotsman* in January 1941, would now reopen the inquiry and investigate the ways in which Scottish resources 'can and should be developed'.[179] This announcement heralded a new era for Scotland's remote communities, and promised the chance of avoiding the mistakes made after the Great War.

For many, the discussion on post-war planning was invigorating. Primary sources reveal much talk about the opportunities war could provide for the Highlands, including self-sufficiency and economic revival. It was hoped this local regeneration would bring greater national security. Reinvigoration of the agricultural and fishing industries was seen as a 'first line of defence', bringing greater food security to Scotland and potentially reversing Highland depopulation.[180] The president of the NFU and Chamber of

---

[177] Webster, *Mixing It*, 16.
[178] 'The Highlands', *The Scotsman*, 3 January 1941, 4.
[179] Ibid.
[180] Ibid.; 'Planning for post-war agriculture: Highland Society to consider proposal', *The Scotsman*, 9 January 1941, 8.

Agriculture of Scotland, Mr W. Graham, said regeneration was dependent upon upgrades to roading and transport infrastructure, as well as improvements to housing stock. 'We stand to-day on the threshold of an era which is going to bring unbounded advancement to agriculture', stated Graham, adding that good planning for that era was essential.[181] The Highland and Agricultural Society agreed, issuing a memorandum expressing its wish to see wartime Agricultural Committees retained and the Secretary of State for Scotland acting as regulating authority for agriculture. The body also argued for retaining some wartime measures: controls of the meat industry, national wage regulation and state loans for equipment. The continuation of such measures would ensure agriculture was maintained in 'a state of reasonable prosperity'.[182] The measures of state control introduced during the War were, in some ways, desirable to Scots, seen as a necessary means of injecting new life into rural industry and community.

The future of Scotland's forestry was also under consideration. In July 1943, the government Forestry Commission tabled a report into the future of the industry, and in the House of Commons the Commissioner announced his desire for a cash injection to the Forestry Fund, so that the industry might prepare 'for a great expansion'.[183] Scottish MPs argued over the report and its suggestions for post-war forestry in Britain. Henry Wedderburn, representing West Renfrew, felt there was much more land available for forestry in Scotland than the report had assumed, and it was important to balance the tension between forestry and hill sheep farming. Ultimately, Wedderburn concluded, timber was of a 'higher value to the country' than sheep, and more land should be given over to forestry.[184] Malcolm MacMillan, MP for the Western Isles, disagreed, feeling that the report was excellent, and would give Scotland 'a first-class forestry policy'.[185] Even so, MacMillan added, it was better to have plenty of food than plenty of wood.[186]

Together with this reflective consideration of past mistakes, and the desire to plan better for Scotland's future 'this time around', came new strategies for post-war prosperity. From 1941 onwards Johnston 'was intent on preparing Scotland for the post-war era on his own terms'.[187] A Labour MP and a fervent patriot, Johnston was involved in setting up the Scottish Industrial Council, the Scottish Building Committee and the Clyde Valley Regional Planning Committee, among other groups.[188] The jewel in the

---

[181] 'Agriculture: on threshold of new era for farming', *The Scotsman*, 10 December 1942, 8.
[182] 'Stability in agriculture: Highland Society's five essentials', *The Scotsman*, 6 November 1943, 4.
[183] 'Forestry expansion: bold and vigorous policy', *The Scotsman*, 7 July 1943, 4.
[184] Ibid.
[185] Hansard, HC Deb, 6 July 1943, vol. 390 col. 2000.
[186] Ibid., col. 2003.
[187] Graham Walker, *Thomas Johnston* (Manchester: Manchester University Press, 1988), 153.
[188] Macdonald, *Whaur Extremes Meet*, 87.

crown of post-war Scotland, Johnston proposed, would be hydro-electric power. Under this plan, several major hydro-electricity schemes would be developed across the Highlands. It was hoped this would lead to jobs, regional revitalisation and flow-on effects such as better transport networks.[189] Johnston promised hydro-electricity would be a 'partial remedy' for repopulating the Highlands, and vowed that remote areas would receive transmission lines where possible and domestic consumers in the north of Scotland would receive subsidised electricity.[190] As Christopher Harvie summarised, Johnston successfully sold hydro-electric power as 'an agency for regenerating the Highlands, a national investment, and a triumph for Scots autonomy'.[191]

Public curiosity was piqued. Numerous articles and letters to the editor were published on the topic in *The Scotsman* during 1942 and 1943. Some were sceptical, wondering if the influx of 'alien' workers on hydro-electric schemes would result in 'further reduction of the Celtic language, culture, and ways of life'.[192] Others were concerned that the dams and power stations would impinge on the picturesque Highland scenery, or on its 'unspoiled character'.[193] The loudest voices were from supporters, who argued power schemes could only be to Scotland's benefit, by providing domestic power to isolated communities but also by bringing employment, workers and prosperity back to neglected parts of the country.[194]

Finally, in July 1943 the Hydro-Electric Development (Scotland) Act 1943 was passed, and the North of Scotland Hydro-Electric Board was established.[195] Johnston went on to chair the board from 1945 to 1959, realising his dream. To help achieve Highland regeneration, the Board was given the role of promoting 'economic development and social improvement' in the region.[196] The Act for Scottish hydro-electric development was 'a great measure, a great instrument for the rehabilitation, and what I hope is the future prosperity, of a neglected area', stated the deputy chairman of the Board in November 1944.[197] Without power, he added, the traditional

---

[189] Ibid., 182.
[190] Hansard, HC Deb, 24 February 1943, vol. 387 cols 182–3.
[191] Harvie, *No Gods*, 58.
[192] John McIntyre, 'Letters to the editor: a plan for the Highlands', *The Scotsman*, 17 December 1942, 7.
[193] James Hunter, *Last of the Free: A Millennial History of the Highlands and Islands of Scotland* (Edinburgh: Mainstream, 1999), 345.
[194] John Bowman, 'Letters to the editor: architects and engineers', *The Scotsman*, 22 January 1943, 4; Hunter, *Last of the Free*, 345–6.
[195] Colin T. Reid, Aylwin Pillai and Andrew R. Black, 'The emergency of environmental concerns: hydroelectric schemes in Scotland', *Journal of Environmental Law* 17, no. 3 (2005): 361–82, here 365.
[196] Hydro-Electric Development (Scotland) Act 1943, s. 2(3). See Hansard, HL Deb, 7 July 1943, vol. 128 col. 323.
[197] 'Hydro-electric power: rehabilitation of the Highlands', *The Scotsman*, 24 November 1944, 3.

Highland industries – agriculture and fishing – could not intensify. Once again, war had brought Scotland's future to the forefront, and prompted plans for Highland regeneration and its future economic prosperity. This investment in rural Scotland would culminate in 1965 in the formation of the Highlands and Islands Development Board.

While time would only tell whether these post-war interventions would bring the long-hoped-for revival, at the close of war Whitehall's schemes had brought to Scottish agriculture rapid mechanisation, increased prosperity and greater outputs. Much progress had also been made towards the goal of home-grown timber sufficiency.[198] As production rose, so did earnings. Between 1938 and 1942, across the United Kingdom agricultural incomes rose faster than wages, salaries, professional earnings and profits.[199] In Scotland, average net incomes for farmers increased 107 per cent and, according to historian Angus Calder, hill sheep farmers 'thrived on lavish Government subsidies'.[200] This was a dramatic contrast to the bitter years of the Depression.

By the end of 1942, Scottish production of wheat and barley had doubled, potatoes increased by 70 per cent and oats by 40 per cent.[201] During 1943 Scotland exported 300 per cent more potatoes to England than it had done in 1939; to assist production on marginal lands, grants during 1943 had been given totalling an average of £20 per farm assisted; and dairy cattle numbers had increased by 9 per cent on 1939 figures.[202] Moreover, nearly 450,000 acres of land had installed drainage schemes, and over 2 million acres were under crops, an increase of 43 per cent on the last pre-war year. The increased push for mechanisation also meant tractor equipment had risen from 6,250 units before the war, to more than 20,000 by mid-1944.[203] This rapid mechanisation and modernisation was a profound change for a sector reliant on antiquated methods and technology prior to war.[204] As Brian Short observed, 1943 was a peak year for Scottish farming and figures did not increase as dramatically over the following two years of war.[205] Operations were scaled back from 1943 as reserves dwindled.[206] Nonetheless, Scottish wartime agricultural output was equal to that of England, and for some foodstuffs greater.

Population records further explain the significance of these wartime efforts. In 1931, Scotland had a population of 4,842,554, nearly half

---

[198] Short, *Battle of the Fields*, 320.
[199] Devine, *Scottish Nation*, 547.
[200] Ibid.; Calder, *People's War*, 417.
[201] Short, *Battle of the Fields*, 307.
[202] Hansard, HC Deb, 4 July 1944, vol. 401 cols 1013–14.
[203] Ibid., col. 1014.
[204] Maclean, 'Getting out', 236; Short, *Battle of the Fields*, 299.
[205] Short, *Battle of the Fields*, 306–7.
[206] Vickers, 'The forgotten army', 112.

of whom lived in the counties of Lanarkshire and Midlothian.[207] Over 1.5 million people resided in Glasgow, Edinburgh and the industrial hub of Clydebank, while fewer than 190,000 lived in the four sizeable counties north of the Great Divide.[208] These census figures demonstrate Scotland was a heavily urbanised nation in the years before war's outbreak. Further, government estimates also suggest Scotland made up less than 10 per cent of the 1941 UK population of 48 million.[209] However, estimates from 1944 show Scotland was producing 14 per cent of total UK food output.[210] When we consider that more than half of Scotland's population lived in urban areas, this contribution is even more significant. These figures reveal that a small proportion of the British population had a large impact on its wartime food supply. In essence, rural Scotland had a significant impact on British self-sufficiency during the Second World War. Without the work of farmers and migrant labourers, stated Johnston in 1944, '[w]e should have been starved into surrender'.[211]

In summary, war had an indelible effect on rural Scotland. In a short number of years, the nation rapidly modernised and mechanised agriculture, and altered established farming practices. This also laid bare the tension between resistance and cooperation that farmers faced as a result of greater state involvement in everyday life and work. War also reshaped rural communities, by slowing long-term population decline and bringing new faces to rural parts of Scotland. However, while wartime labour went some way towards redressing pre-war depopulation and depression, it also provoked animosities relating to gender, ethnicity and behavioural norms.

Those who worked the land played a valuable part in Scotland's war effort, responding with a mix of cooperation, adaptation and sheer hard work. Undeniably, their labour was critical, helping to rescue Britain from what may have been the brink of starvation. Moreover, the importance of Scottish primary industries during wartime helped to raise questions about the country's future self-sufficiency, and provided impetus for rural rejuvenation projects. But at the end of the Second World War it was too soon to know whether this wartime success would leave post-war Scotland on a more secure foundation than it had been for many years prior to war.

---

[207] Census of Scotland, 'Preliminary Report on the Fourteenth Census of Scotland. Part III – Population Tables' (Edinburgh: HMSO, 1931), 1.
[208] Ibid., vii–xiv.
[209] Joe Hicks and Grahame Allen, *A Century of Change: Trends in UK Statistics Since 1900* (House of Commons Library, 1999), 6.
[210] Hansard, HC Deb, 4 July 1944, vol. 401 col. 1015.
[211] Ibid., col. 1013.

EPILOGUE

A Story Worth Telling?

In 2004, Scottish historian Catriona Macdonald stated '[a]n integrative account of Scotland's war-time experience ... is absent in our historiography: there is no adequate Scottish history of the war beyond the fragments readers must piece together for themselves from a great variety of sources'.[1] Macdonald pondered, is the story not worth telling? Can it not be found? Are the sources hidden? Has the history of 'Britain's War' been written?[2] For over twenty years these questions have gone unanswered.

Two decades later, *Scottish Society in the Second World War* has attempted to address this oversight and, in doing so, asserts that the story of Scotland's war years *is* worth telling. This study has provided an original overview of Scottish society during the Second World War and has aimed to significantly illuminate Scotland's lived experience of the War. Throughout this work, chapters have highlighted areas of similarity with the British experience of war, but have also drawn out aspects of cultural difference. The selected archival sources revealed that, in some aspects of wartime life, Scottish experiences of war were similar to those of other parts of Britain. Common experiences included friction over the evacuation scheme, worries about juvenile crime and delinquency, and unrest in industrial heartlands. In addition, signs of apathy, war fatigue and depression were noted across Britain. While similarities exist, there are a number of aspects that distinguish experiences of war in Scotland.

It is striking that conflict infused many facets of Scottish wartime life. The research contained here suggests that in Scotland, responses to war were influenced by existing class-based tension, sectarianism, the urban/rural divide and ethnic discord. Sources reveal this friction permeated the evacuation scheme and responses to delinquency and drunkenness, and shaped industrial workplaces and rural communities. While these factors were also present in wider Britain, tension was a notable feature of the Scottish war experience. Moreover, while Scotland's history of industrial unrest, radicalism, rising nationalism and anti-Irish sentiment shaped local responses to war, these tensions also shaped official responses, resulting in special measures and campaigns to manage Scottish dissent and discontent – tactics that were possibly unique to Scotland. While further archival research is needed, that contained within this book indicates that,

---

[1] Macdonald, 'Wersh the wine', 111.
[2] Ibid., 106.

in this area, there may be aspects of difference between Scotland and what is known of the wider British home front.

In many aspects of wartime society, Scottish actions appeared to be moulded by a tension between resistance and conformity. Before the war, Scottish daily life was characterised by resistance to power and authority, and the challenging of hegemonic ways of being.[3] The research presented here implies that in almost every aspect of home front life, Scots battled wartime disruption and the increasing influence of the state. The tension between conformity and non-conformity was particularly evident in Scottish responses to the evacuation scheme, agricultural targets and wartime leisure. In many cases, Scots adapted to wartime disruption and, ultimately, chose to cooperate with official measures and systems. In contrast, this study also uncovered instances of resistance and revolt, in which Scots displayed opposition to official *Diktats* or were reluctant to let war command their everyday lives. When it came to diet, holidays and industrial workplaces, Scots were especially unwilling to accept war's hegemony.

This study has also proposed that Scottish war experiences were coloured by identity. On an official level, the wartime Scottish Office had powers to administer the nation separately from England and Wales, being given responsibility for health, education, agriculture and home affairs. In addition, the evacuation scheme and both the Women's Land Army and the Women's Timber Corps were separately administered by Scottish authorities. Further, the Scottish constabulary compiled its own reports on daily life and morale, outside the structure of Whitehall's Ministry of Information. On the ground, tropes of Scottishness infused wartime culture, with pipe bands, tartanry, the 51st Highland Division and Scotland's martial heritage playing a visible part in daily life and leisure. In addition, war laid bare the cultural influence of the Kirk, especially over Sabbatarianism, temperance and morality. Additionally, in the panic over perceived wartime immorality and delinquency, primary sources revealed an underlying uncertainty about Scotland's cultural identity and concerns over growing secularisation in a country previously defined by its religiosity.

The war years were also suffused with discussions of nationhood and national identity. Here, chapters on subversion, morale and the rural sector expose an uncertainty about Scotland's identity and place within Britain. Nationalism, anti-English sentiment and Scottish questioning of Whitehall's dedication to post-war promises alluded to underlying concerns about Scotland's role in the Union. An investigation of morale, especially in the wider Glasgow region, also revealed some wavering support for the war effort, and traces of the sentiment that this was England's war, not Scotland's. Scottish feelings of distance from London, Westminster and the war effort may also have reflected feelings of political and cultural distance between Scotland and England. This was also a period of national

---

[3] Abrams and Brown, 'Conceiving the everyday', 14–15.

and cultural transition, as Scotland grappled to re-establish its identity after years of political, economic and social upheaval.

While wartime rhetoric revolved around community, unity and civic virtue, Scottish war experiences appeared to be characterised by fracture and tension, and there was little evidence of a united British community, let alone a united Scottish community. In 1939, Scotland was a deeply divided country, and this legacy of fragmentation did not abate upon the outbreak of war. These old divisions continued to widen, and in many cases wartime disruptions seemed to cause new fissures to appear. Socio-cultural differences, such as pre-war sectarianism, class division and the influence of the Kirk in Scottish life, meant concerns about morality, secularisation and urban/rural tensions appeared more prominent in Scottish responses to war than they appear to have been elsewhere in Britain. In addition, the severity of Scotland's interwar depression and associated rates of emigration, unemployment, poverty and decline drove wartime industrial discontent, influenced Scottish morale and suffused discussions about the post-war future. Moreover, internal fragmentation seemed to divert attention from the war effort, particularly in heavy industry, in response to evacuation, and in rural communities buoyed by migrant labourers and servicemen.

Past studies on experiences of war in Britain have been broad in focus, and most have failed to take into account the subjectivities and experiences of those within Britain's constituent nations. This is a substantial oversight. In undertaking a national study of the lived experience of war, *Scottish Society in the Second World War* has taken a step towards addressing this shortcoming. This study has proposed that examining wartime life through a national lens significantly adds to our understanding of wartime Britain. In applying a 'four nations' approach, this work has also elicited elements of cultural distinctiveness and illuminated local subjectivities and points of difference. This approach has also revealed similarities and interactions across Britain's internal borders. Future comparative studies of the nations of Britain will extend or refine the suggestions made within this monograph, and further enrich public knowledge of the lived experiences of war throughout the regions and nations of Britain.

In conclusion, this research has considerably advanced our understanding of Scottish lived experiences of war, and of Scottish life and culture in the twentieth century. This study has also uncovered a variety of responses to war, ranging from resistance to adaptation to willing engagement. Moreover, this research has suggested that Scottish society remained deeply divided throughout the war, and that experiences differed widely across regions, classes, genders and ethnicities. Ultimately, this text has demonstrated that Scotland's war years were a period of transformation, bringing conversations about national and cultural identity, reshaping communities and offering the prospect of recovery to a country deeply wounded by the Great War and the interwar depression.

Bibliography

PRIMARY SOURCES

Diaries and letters
Balfour, Francis. Diaries, 1939–1945. Private collection.
Canadian Forestry Corps, Number 4 Company. War Diary: No. 4 Company, 02/1942–04/1945. RG24 volume 16423. Libraries and Archives Canada.
Mackintosh family. Letters, 1939–1944. Private collection.
Westlands, Anne. Letters from Anne Westlands, 1940–1944. A3219572, A3219626, A3219842, A3219941 A3220002, A3220057, A3225485, A3225511, A3225584, A3225656, A3225773, A3219699. BBC, *WW2 People's War*. References accessed 6 May 2020, https://www.bbc.co.uk/history/ww2peopleswar/stories/26/a3219626.shtml.

Church of Scotland Records
General Assembly Reports, 1939–1946.
Life and Work magazine, 1939–1946.

Edinburgh University Special Collections
BAI 2/8, Papers of Professor John Baillie and family, 5 February 1941.

Glasgow City Archives
D-CD 1. Glasgow Corporation Civil Defence Department, 1939–1965.
D-CD-3. Mortuaries.
D-TC 8/10/39. Casualties – Recording and Notification – July to August 1940.
D-TC 8/10/41. Casualties – Burial Arrangements.
D-TC 8/10/61. Evacuation Scheme.
D-TC 8/10/62. Evacuation, 1939–1941.
D-TC 8/10/99. Messages and Reports, Raids, 1941.
D-TC 8/10/343. Women's Emergency Services 1939–1940.

Glasgow University Archives
GUA 24394–24461. Enlistment of students for National Service, 1941–1946.
GUA 32829. Correspondence concerning women students re. war service 1942–44.

GUA 32832. Further Education and Training Scheme.
GUA 53764, GUA 53766, GUA 53770. Scottish Universities Entrance Board 1939–1946.

Mass Observation Archive (M-O)
M-O, 1/C, Adams to 'Harold', 15 March 1941.

File reports
6: Sport in Wartime. 29 October 1939.
27: US. 2 February 1940.
600: Morale in Glasgow and Apprentice Strikes. 7 March 1941.
604: The Scottish Shipbuilding and Engineering Apprentices' Strike. 13 March 1941.
631: Summary of Glasgow Report. 3 April 1941.
773: Comparative Report. May 1940-May 1941, 5 July 1941.
932: The Clyde Situation. October 1941.
2115: We're Moving. 14 June 1944.
2332: War Morale Chart. 6 February 1946.

Topic collections
3_2860, Illegitimate births in Scotland.
85: Scottish drinking.

Directives
Directives for November and December 1939; January 1940; January, March, September 1942; January, April, June, November 1943; January and June 1944; January, February, May, August 1945.

Directive respondents
Respondents 1302; 1363; 1393; 1534; 1569; 1574; 1682; 2019; 2121; 2290; 2293; 2374; 2386; 2410; 2490; 2554; 2568; 2707; 2741; 2824; 2910; 2911; 2973; 3247; 3324; 3361; 3473; 3545; 3630; 3655.

Diarists
Diarists 5015, Glasgow; 5048, Kilmacolm; 5069, Prestwick; 5145, Edinburgh; 5146, Glasgow; 5177, Berwickshire/Edinburgh; 5196, Glasgow; 5232, Aberdeen; 5253, Colinton; 5281, Helensburgh; 5302, Glasgow; 5314, Tayvallich; 5364, Kingussie; 5374, Campbeltown; 5378, Campbeltown; 5380, Glasgow; 5390, Glasgow; 5415, Edinburgh.

National Library of Scotland
ACC11356. Diaries of Muriel Kerr, 1941, 1943.
MSS.3817. Records of Scottish Home Guards, 1939–1945.

National Museum of Scotland
Director's correspondence, 1939–1946.
The Royal Scottish Museum, Reports for the years 1939–1946.

National Records of Scotland
AF59/12/1. Women's Land Army, 1940–43.
AF59/12/2. Women's Land Army, 1943–1948.
AF59/23/7. Children and agricultural work.
AF59/245. WLA personnel files: Elizabeth Robson, 1940–1949.
CH1/17/1. Files of the Women's Temperance Association.
ED3/362. National treasures in an emergency.
ED24. Second World War files, 1935–1953.
ED31/528. Air raids on Glasgow and Clydebank, March 13/14 and 14/15, 1941.
ED39/23. Social and community services: behaviour of girls and women in wartime.
ED48/745. Sedition, teaching in schools: Hamilton Academy.
GD193/32/1. Women's Voluntary Service.
GD194/46/5. Records from Sauchieburn House.
HH36/5. Clydeside: reports on raids of 5/6 and 6/7 May 1941.
HH55/7. Police war duties, daily reports Glasgow, 1939–1940.
HH55/7–42. Police war duties – intelligence reports, 1939–1945.
HH55/556. Sedition: Jehovah's Witnesses.
HH55/557. Sedition: Police action against Scottish nationalist organisations.
HH55/558. Scottish Nationalist Party.
HH55/656. IRA: sabotage and disturbances, 1940–1955.
HH55/658. IRA: sabotage and disturbances, 1939–1946.
HH55/659. IRA: sabotage and disturbances, 1940.
HH55/660. Irish republicans sabotage, 1939–1943.
HH60/421. Juvenile Delinquency Enquiry, 1939–1942.
HH60/422. Children and young persons juvenile delinquency, press cuttings.
HH60/425. Juvenile delinquency during wartime, 1941–1942.
HH60/426. Juvenile delinquency, 1942–1943.
HH60/427. Juvenile delinquency, statistics, 1942–1948.
HH60/428. Juvenile delinquency, 1942.
HH60/485. Drunkenness statistics, 1942–1945.
MD13. Home Security intelligence summaries.
MD13/5. Home Security War Room reports.
SC19/27/1944/4. Fatal accident inquiry, Margaret Toner, Land Girl.

Scottish Jewish Archives Centre
Records of the Glasgow Jewish Representative Council, 1930–1940.
Garnethill Synagogue, minutebook.

Glasgow Jewish Board of Guardians, annual reports 1940–1945.
Records of the Edinburgh Hebrew Congregation, 1939–1941.

The National Archives
HO 199/198. Western District: analysis of the effects of air raids from June 1940 to September 1941.
HO 199/410. Ministry of Home Security: Intelligence Branch. Monthly reports from regional commissioners, 1940–1944.
HO 199/428. Morale reports: region 11 (Scotland), May 1942–January 1943.
INF 1/264. Ministry of Information: home intelligence, daily reports, 1940.
INF 1/292. Ministry of Information: home intelligence, weekly reports, 1940–1944.
INF 1/293. Ministry of Information: home intelligence, special reports, 1941–1944.
INF 1/308. Ministry of Information: Western District Information Committee: Scottish Region (Glasgow), 1940–1943.
INF 1/673. Ministry of Information: Industrial Campaign to Counter Communism in Scotland, 1940–1942.

Miscellaneous films
British Pathé, *Wings for Victory Week*, 1943, British Pathé, accessed 2 December 2020. https://www.britishpathe.com/video/wings-for-victory-week.
—— *Jolly Good Fellers*, 1942, YouTube, accessed 2 December 2020. https://www.youtube.com/watch?v=lq6I_hFzFMMI.
Ministry of Supply, and Paramount, *Warwork News No. 19: The Other Man's Job*, 1943, Scotland on Screen, accessed 2 December 2020. https://scotlandonscreen.org.uk/browse-films/007-000-000-225-c.
Scottish Film Productions and GB Instructional, *Fighting Fields: Feeding the Nation During Wartime*, 1941, National Library of Scotland: Moving Image Archive, accessed 2 December 2020. https://movingimage.nls.uk/film/0456.
Scottish Educational Film Association, *Youth Takes a Bough!* 1940, National Library of Scotland: Moving Image Archive, accessed 2 December 2020. https://movingimage.nls.uk/film/3247.

Hansard
House of Commons Debates
- 1 August 1939, volume 350.
- 14 September 1939, volume 351.
- 1 November 1939, volume 114.
- 8 November 1939, volume 353.
- 21 November 1939, volumes 351, 353.
- 25 January 1940, volume 356.
- 13 May 1940, volume 360.
- 4 June 1940, volume 361.

- 18 June 1940, volume 362.
- 20 August 1940, volume 364.
- 5 March 1941, volume 369.
- 1 April 1941, volume 370.
- 9 April 1941, volume 370.
- 29 May 1941, volume 371.
- 30 July 1941, volume 373.
- 8 January 1942, volume 377.
- 05 March 1942, volume 378.
- 12 March 1942, volume 378.
- 8 July 1942, volume 381.
- 6 August 1942, volume 382.
- 24 February 1943, volume 387.
- 9 June 1943, volume 390.
- 6 July 1943, volume 390.
- 21 July 1943, volume 391.
- 28 April 1944, volume 399.
- 4 July 1944, volume 401.
- 2 November 1945, volume 415.
- 19 November 1945, volume 416.

House of Lords Debates
- 28 September 1939, volume 114.
- 7 July 1943, volume 128.

Newspapers and magazines
SMT Magazine and Scottish Country Life, 1938–1946.
The Scotsman, 1939–1945.
The Glasgow Herald, 1939–1945.
Also selected articles from *The Jewish Chronicle, Dundee Courier and Advertiser, Daily Express, Edinburgh Evening News, Daily Record, Edinburgh Evening Dispatch, Glasgow Evening Citizen, Sunday Mail.*

Miscellaneous
Churchill, Winston, 'Winston Churchill speeches', The International Churchill Society, accessed 25 November 2020. https://www.winstonchurchill.org/resources/speeches/.
NRS, 'Scotland's Census, 1931', accessed 6 March 2019. https://www.scotlandscensus.gov.uk/1931.
Census of Scotland, *Fourteenth Census of Scotland* (Edinburgh: HMSO, 1931).
Morrison, Herbert, *Mr Smith and Mr Schmidt* (London: Collins, 1941).
Scottish Trade Union Delegation to the Midlands, *Transfer of Scottish Girls: Report to Scottish Trades Union Congress General Council and the Organisation of Women Committee* (Glasgow: Scottish TUC, 1943).

SECONDARY SOURCES

Books and edited collections

Abrams, Lynn and Callum G. Brown, eds. *A History of Everyday Life in Twentieth-Century Scotland.* Edinburgh: Edinburgh University Press, 2010.

Addison, Paul. *The Road to 1945: British Politics and the Second World War.* London: Jonathan Cape, 1975.

Addison, Paul and Jeremy A. Crang. *Listening to Britain: Home Intelligence Reports on Britain's Finest Hour – May to September 1940.* London: Vintage Books, 2011.

Ash, Marinell. *The Strange Death of Scottish History.* Edinburgh: Ramsey Head Press, 1980.

Bardon, Adrian. *The Truth about Denial: Bias and Self Deception in Science, Politics, and Religion.* Oxford: Oxford University Press, September 2019.

Beech, John, Owen Hand, Mark A. Mulhern and Jeremy Weston, eds. *Scottish Life and Society: The Individual and Community Life.* Edinburgh: John Donald, 2005.

Borsay, Peter. *A History of Leisure: The British Experience since 1500.* Basingstoke: Palgrave Macmillan, 2006.

Boyd, William. *Evacuation in Scotland. A Record of Events and Experiments.* Bickley: University of London Press, 1944.

Braybon, G. and P. Summerfield. *Out of the Cage: Women's Experiences in Two World Wars.* London: Routledge, 2012.

Brown, Callum G. *Religion and Society in Scotland since 1707.* Edinburgh: Edinburgh University Press, 1997.

—— *Religion and Society in Twentieth Century Britain.* London: Routledge, 2014.

—— *The People in the Pews: Religion and Society in Scotland since 1780.* Glasgow: Economic and Social History Society of Scotland, 1993.

Calder, Angus. *The Myth of the Blitz.* [1991]. London: Pimlico, 2008.

—— *The People's War: Britain 1939–45.* London: Jonathan Cape, 1969.

Cameron, Ewen. *Impaled Upon a Thistle: Scotland Since 1880.* Edinburgh: Edinburgh University Press, 2010.

Chand, Alison. *Masculinities on Clydeside: Men in Reserved Occupations, 1939–1945.* Edinburgh: Edinburgh University Press, 2016.

Chapman, James. 'British cinema and 'the people's war', in *'Millions Like Us?': British Culture in the Second World War,* edited by Nick Hayes and Jeff Hill, 33–61. Liverpool: Liverpool University Press, 1999.

—— *The British at War: Cinema, State and Propaganda, 1939–1945.* London: I. B. Tauris, 1998.

Curtice, John, David McCrone, Alison Park and Lindsay Paterson, eds. *New Scotland, New Society? Are Social and Political Ties Fragmenting?* Edinburgh: Polygon, 2002.

Devine, T. M. *The Scottish Clearances: A History of the Dispossessed.* Milton Keynes: Penguin, 2019.

—— *The Scottish Nation: 1700–2000.* [1999]. London: Penguin, 2006.
—— ed. *Scotland's Shame? Bigotry and Sectarianism in Modern Scotland.* Edinburgh: Mainstream, 2000.
Devine, T. M. and R. J. Finlay, eds. *Scotland in the Twentieth Century.* Edinburgh: Edinburgh University Press, 1996.
Devine, T. M. and Jenny Wormald, eds. *The Oxford Handbook of Modern Scottish History.* Oxford: Oxford University Press, 2012.
Devine, T. M., C. H. Lee and G. C. Peden, eds. *The Transformation of Scotland: The Economy Since 1700.* Edinburgh: Edinburgh University Press, 2005.
Dickson, A. and J. H. Treble, eds. *People and Society in Scotland,* Volume III, *1914–1990.* Edinburgh: John Donald, 1992.
Edwards, Elaine M., ed. *Scotland's Land Girls: Breeches, Bombers and Backaches.* Edinburgh: NMS, 2010.
Eliot, Simon and Marc Wiggam, eds. *Allied Communication to the Public During the Second World War: National and Transnational Networks.* London: Bloomsbury, 2019.
Emmons, Robert A. and Michael E. McCullough, eds. *The Psychology of Gratitude.* New York: Oxford University Press, 2004.
Field, Geoffrey G. *Blood, Sweat, and Toil: Remaking the British Working Class, 1939–1945.* Oxford: Oxford University Press, 2011.
Finlay, Richard J. 'The interwar crisis: the failure of extremism', in *The Oxford Handbook of Modern Scottish History,* edited by T. M. Devine and Jenny Wormald, 569–85. Oxford: Oxford University Press, 2012.
—— *Modern Scotland: 1914–2000.* London: Profile Books, 2004.
Foat, Joanna. *Lumberjills: Britain's Forgotten Army.* Stroud: History Press, 2019.
Fraser, W. Hamish and Irene Maver, eds. *Glasgow,* Volume II: *1830 to 1912.* Manchester: Manchester University Press, 1996.
Fry, Michael. *Patronage and Principle: A Political History of Modern Scotland.* Aberdeen: Aberdeen University Press, 1987.
Gallagher, Tom. *Glasgow: The Uneasy Peace: Religious Tension in Modern Scotland.* Manchester: Manchester University Press, 1987.
Harris, José. *Private Lives, Public Spirit: A Social History of Britain, 1870–1914.* New York: Oxford University Press, 1993.
Harrisson, Tom. *Living Through the Blitz.* London: Collins for the Trustees of the Mass Observation Archive, 1976.
Harvie, Christopher. *No Gods and Precious Few Heroes: Twentieth-Century Scotland.* Edinburgh: Edinburgh University Press, 1998.
—— *Scotland and Nationalism: Scottish Society and Politics 1701 to the Present,* 4th edn. Abingdon: Routledge, 2004.
Hinton, James. *Nine Wartime Lives: Mass-Observation and the Making of the Modern Self.* Oxford: Oxford University Press, 2010.
Hutchison, I. G. C. *Scottish Politics in the Twentieth Century.* Basingstoke: Palgrave, 2001.
Hylton, Stuart. *Their Darkest Hour: The Hidden History of the Home Front 1939–1945.* Stroud: Sutton, 2003.

Johnes, Martin. *Wales Since 1939*. Manchester: Manchester University Press, 2012.

Jones, Greta. *Social Hygiene in Twentieth-Century Britain*. London: Croom Helm, 1986.

Kellas, James G. *Modern Scotland*. London: George Allen & Unwin, 1980.

McCarthy, Angela. *Personal Narratives of Irish and Scottish Migration, 1921–65: 'For Spirit and Adventure'*. Manchester: Manchester University Press, 2007.

McCrone, David. 'Tomorrow's ancestors: nationalism, identity and history', in *Scottish History: The Power of the Past*, edited by Edward J. Cowan and Richard J. Finlay, 253–71. Edinburgh: Edinburgh University Press, 2002.

—— *Understanding Scotland: The Sociology of a Stateless Nation*, 2nd edn. New York: Routledge, 2001.

Macdonald, Catriona M. M. *Whaur Extremes Meet: Scotland's Twentieth Century*. Edinburgh: John Donald, 2009.

Macdonald, Catriona M. M. and E. W. McFarland, eds. *Scotland and the Great War*. East Linton: Tuckwell Press, 1999.

Mackay, Robert. *Half the Battle: Civilian Morale in Britain During the Second World War*. Manchester: Manchester University Press, 2002.

MacLaren, A. A., ed. *Social Class in Scotland: Past and Present*. Edinburgh: John Donald, 1976.

MacPhail, I. M. M. *The Clydebank Blitz*. Dumbarton: West Dunbartonshire Libraries, 1974.

Macrae, Eilidh. *Exercise in the Female Life Cycle in Britain, 1930–1970*. Hamilton: Palgrave Macmillan, 2016.

Malpass, Alan. *British Character and the Treatment of German Prisoners of War, 1939–1948*. Cham: Palgrave Macmillan, 2020.

Marwick, Arthur. 'People's war and top people's peace? British society and the Second World War', in *Crisis and Controversy: Essays in Honour of A.J.P. Taylor*, edited by Alan Sked and Chris Cook, 148–64. London: Macmillan, 1976.

Marwick, Arthur and Harold Chapman. *The Home Front: The British and the Second World War*. London: Thames and Hudson, 1976.

Muir, Edwin. *Scottish Journey*. Edinburgh: Mainstream, 1979 edition.

Noakes, Lucy. *War and the British: Gender and National Identity, 1939–91*. London: I. B. Tauris, 1998.

Noakes, Lucy and Juliette Pattinson, eds. *British Cultural Memory and the Second World War*. London: Bloomsbury, 2014.

Pattinson, Juliette, Arthur McIvor and Linsey Robb. *Men in Reserve: British Civilian Masculinities in the Second World War*. Manchester University Press, 2017.

Pelling, Henry. *Britain and the Second World War*. Glasgow: William Collins Sons & Co., 1970.

Pugh, Martin. *'We Danced All Night': A Social History of Britain Between the Wars*. London: The Bodley Head, 2008.

Robb, Linsey. *Men at Work: The Working Man in British Culture, 1939–1945*. Cham: Palgrave Macmillan, 2015.

Roodhouse, Mark. *Black Market Britain: 1939–1955*. Oxford: Oxford University Press, 2013.

Rose, Sonya O. *Which People's War? National Identity and Citizenship in Wartime Britain 1939–1945*. Oxford: Oxford University Press, 2003.

Royle, Edward. *Modern Britain: A Social History, 1750–1985*. London: Edward Arnold, 1987.

Royle, Trevor. *A Time of Tyrants: Scotland and the Second World War*. Edinburgh: Birlinn, 2011.

Scottish Women's Group on Public Welfare, and Minna Galbraith Cowan. *Our Scottish Towns, Evacuation and the Social Future, a Report by the Scottish Women's Group on Public Welfare*. Edinburgh: W. Hodge, 1944.

Short, Brian. *The Battle of the Fields: Rural Community and Authority in Britain during the Second World War*. Woodbridge: Boydell Press, 2014.

Smith, Harold L. *Britain in the Second World War: A Social History*. Manchester: Manchester University Press, 1996.

—— ed. *War and Social Change: British Society in the Second World War*. Manchester: Manchester University Press, 1986.

Smout, T. C. *A Century of the Scottish People: 1850–1950*. London: Collins, 1986.

Smout, T. C. and Sydney Wood. *Scottish Voices: 1745–1960*. London: Collins, 1990.

Spiers, Edward M., Jeremy A. Crang and Matthew J. Strickland, eds. *A Military History of Scotland*. Edinburgh: Edinburgh University Press, 2012.

Summerfield, Penny. *Reconstructing Women's Wartime Lives: Discourse and Subjectivity in Oral Histories of the Second World War*. Manchester: Manchester University Press, 1998.

Taylor, A. J. P. *English History 1914–1945*. Oxford: Clarendon Press, 1965.

Titmuss, Richard M. *Problems of Social Policy*. London: HMSO, 1950.

Todman, Daniel. *Britain's War: Into Battle, 1937–1941*. Oxford: Oxford University Press, 2016.

Turnbull, Mattie. *Days of Apprehension and Adventure: Experiences of Scottish Evacuees During World War Two*. Pittsburgh, PA: Dorrance, 2016.

Ugolini, Wendy. *Experiencing War as the 'Enemy Other': Italian Scottish Experience in World War II*. Manchester: Manchester University Press, 2011.

Ugolini, Wendy and Juliette Pattinson, eds. *Fighting for Britain? Negotiating Identities in Britain During the Second World War*. Bern: Peter Lang, 2015.

Webster, Wendy. *Mixing It: Diversity in World War II Britain*. Oxford: Oxford University Press, 2018.

Weight, Richard and Abigail Beach, eds. *The Right to Belong: Citizenship and National Identity in Britain, 1930–1960*. London: I. B. Tauris, 1998.

Welshman, J. *Underclass: A History of the Excluded, 1880–2000*. London: Continuum, 2006.

Woodward, Guy. *Culture, Northern Ireland, and the Second World War*. Oxford: Oxford University Press, 2015.

Articles

Calvin, Catherine, Jeremy Crang, Lindsay Paterson and Ian Deary. 'Childhood evacuation during World War II and subsequent cognitive ability: the Scottish Mental Survey 1947', *Longitudinal and Life Course Studies* 5, no. 2 (2014), 227–44.

Chand, Alison. 'Gendered identities in British regions in wartime: women in reserved occupations in Glasgow and Clydeside in the Second World War', *Journal of Scottish Historical Studies* 40, no. 1 (2020), 40–62.

Collingham, Lizzie. 'Birthday onions: Second World War rationing and the British diet', *Times Literary Supplement* 6107 (2020), 27.

Cullen, Stephen M. 'The fasces and the saltire: the failure of the British Union of Fascists in Scotland, 1932–1940', *The Scottish Historical Review* 87, no. 2 (2008), 306–31.

Eley, Geoff. 'Finding the people's war: film, British collective memories and World War II', *The American Historical Review* 106, no. 3 (2001), 818–38.

Field, Geoffrey. 'Perspectives on the working-class family in wartime Britain, 1939–1945', *International Labor and Working-Class History* 38 (1990), 3–28.

Finlay, Richard J. 'National identity in crisis: politicians, intellectuals and the "end of Scotland", 1920–1939', *History* 79, no. 256 (1994), 242–59.

Griffin, Paul. 'Diverse political identities within a working class presence: revisiting red Clydeside', *Political Geography* 65 (2018), 123–33.

Harris, José. 'War and social history: Britain and the home front during the Second World War', *Contemporary European History* 1, no. 1 (1992).

Macdonald, Catriona M. M. '"Wersh the wine o'victorie": writing Scotland's Second World War', *Journal of Scottish Historical Studies* 24, no. 2 (2004), 105–12.

Maclean, Catherine. 'Getting out and getting on: Scottish Highland migration in the first half of the twentieth century', *Rural History* 11, no. 2 (2000), 231–48.

Macnicol, John. 'Reconstructing the underclass', *Social Policy and Society* 16, no. 1 (2017), 99–108.

McIvor, Arthur. 'Was occupational health and safety a strike issue? Workers, unions and the body in twentieth-century Scotland', *Journal of Irish and Scottish Studies* 8, no. 2 (2017), 5–33.

McKinlay, Alan. 'From industrial serf to wage-labourer: the 1937 apprentice revolt in Britain', *International Review of Social History* 31, no. 1 (1986), 2–18.

Moffat, Michelle. '"Scotland's fighting fields": the mobilisation of workers in rural Scotland during the Second World War', *Rural History* 33, no. 2 (2022), 231–49.

Moore-Colyer, R. J. 'The call to the land: British and European adult voluntary farm labour, 1939–49', *Rural History* 17, no. 1 (2006), 83–101.

Morrison, Blake. 'Down but not out: tourism in Scotland during the Second World War', *Studies by Undergraduate Researchers at Guelph* 2, no. 1 (2008), 52–8.

Peniston-Bird, Corinna M. '"All in it together" and "backs to the wall": relating patriotism and the people's war in the 21st century', *Oral History* 40, no. 2 (2012), 69–80.

Preston, A. M. 'The evacuation of schoolchildren from Newcastle upon Tyne, 1939–1942: an assessment of the factors which influenced the nature of educational provision in Newcastle and its reception areas', *History of Education* 18, no. 3 (1989), 231–41.

Sindall, R. S. 'Criminal statistics of nineteenth-century cities: a new approach', *Urban History Yearbook* (1968), 28–36.

Skillen, Fiona. 'Preventing "robotised women workers": women, sport and the workplace in Scotland 1919–1939', *Labour History* 55, no. 5 (2014), 594–606.

—— '"Women and the sport fetish": modernity, consumerism and sports participation in inter-war Britain', *The International Journal of the History of Sport* 29, no. 5 (2012), 750–65.

Sladen, Chris. 'Wartime holidays and the "myth of the Blitz"', *Cultural and Social History* 2 (2005), 215–46.

—— 'Holidays at home in the Second World War', *Journal of Contemporary History* 37, no. 1 (2002), 67–89.

Smith, David. 'Official responses to juvenile delinquency in Scotland during the Second World War', *Twentieth Century British History* 18, no. 1 (2007), 78–105.

Stewart, John and John Welshman. 'The evacuation of children in wartime Scotland: culture, behaviour and poverty', *Journal of Scottish Historical Studies* 26, no. 1–2 (2006), 100–120.

Summerfield, Penny. 'Dunkirk and the popular memory of Britain at war, 1940–58', *Journal of Contemporary History* 45, no. 4 (2010), 788–811.

Summerfield, Penny and Nicole Crockett. '"You weren't taught that with the welding": lessons in sexuality in the Second World War', *Women's History Review* 1, No. 3 (1992), 435–54.

Sutherland, Ian N. 'Some aspects of the epidemiology of smallpox in Scotland in 1942', *Proceedings of the Royal Society of Medicine* 36 (1943).

Todd, Selina. 'Young women, work, and leisure in interwar England', *The Historical Journal* 48, no. 3 (2005), 789–809.

Ugolini, Wendy. '"Spaghetti lengths in a bowl?" Recovering narratives of not "belonging" amongst the Italian Scots', *Immigrants & Minorities* 31, no. 2 (2013), 214–34.

Vickers, Emma. '"The forgotten army of the woods": the Women's Timber Corps during the Second World War', *The Agricultural History Review* 59, no. 1 (2011), 101–12.

Welshman, John. 'Evacuation and social policy during the Second World War: myth and reality', *Twentieth Century British History* 9, no. 1 (1998), 28–53.

Unpublished

Forbes, Angela. 'The British Empire and the war effort: a comparative study of the experiences of the British Honduran Forestry Unit and the Newfoundland Overseas Forestry Unit', unpublished MA dissertation: University of the Highlands and Islands, 2015.

Hess, S. J. 'Civilian evacuation to Devon in the Second World War', PhD dissertation, University of Exeter, 2006.

Jack, Jo. 'The impact of Second World War evacuation on social welfare in Scotland (incorporating an analysis of oral testimony from Scottish evacuees)', MPhil thesis, University of Stirling, 2017.

Index

Note: *italic* page number indicates an illustration

Aberdeen
  alcohol, 211, 213
  armed forces' entertainments, 215
  fascism, 22
  military displays, 164
  'New Life to the Land' exhibition, 235
  social conditions, 24
  Women's Land Army hostels, 240
Abrams, Lynn, 3, 188
Acts of Union (1707), 9, 111, 152
Adams, Mary, 156
Addison, Paul, 8, 12, 129
agricultural workers
  earnings, 239, 254
  hiring of, 228
  leisure, 190
  portrayal of, 234–5
  see also Women's Land Army
agriculture, 227–36
  Agricultural Executive Committees (AEC), 228–9, 231–2
  crop production, 229, 230–1
  importance of, 235–6
  machinery, 229, 254
  reinvigoration of, 251, 254
  and resistance, 231–2
  silage, 229
  subsidies, 228
  volunteers, 234–5
  and weather, 232–6
  see also Department of Agriculture for Scotland

air raids, 48–9, 93, 120, 125, 131
  air raid precautions (ARP), 78, 106, 109
  Clydeside, 136–8
  First World War, 129
  Glasgow, 93, 106, 120, 125, 134, 135, 138, 142
  victims of, 135, 141–2
  see also Blitz
Airdrie, 25, 154
alcohol, 209–16
  and behaviour, 72–3, 81
  culture of, 209, 215–16
  'drink travel', 210–12, 216
  licensing, 211
  lumberjacks and, 244–5, 246
  and morale, 83–4
  shortages, 212–13
  women and, 72, 91
  see also drunkenness; temperance
Alness, Lord, 209, *210*
anti-Semitism, 56
anti-war groups, 93, 107; *see also* conscientious objectors
apprentices, 101–3, 123
armed forces
  alcohol consumption, 213–14
  cultural pursuits, 199, 201
  entertainment, 214, 215; *see also* Entertainments National Service Association (ENSA)
  fundraising, 203–9
  and morale, 142–9
  recruiting campaigns, 26–7
  and sports, 192–3

armed forces (*cont.*)
   and travel, 176, 178, 183
   volunteers, 27
   see also conscription; military displays; military service; Royal Air Force
army: exhibitions, 207–8
art exhibitions, 199, 201–2
art galleries
   Edinburgh, 199, 202–3
   Glasgow, 199, 201–2
arts *see* Council for the Encouragement of Music and the Arts (CEMA), 199; music
Ayr
   alcohol consumption, 213
   evacuees, 48
   as a holiday destination, 171
   morale, 141
Ayrshire
   alcohol licensing, 211
   delinquency, 75
   evacuees, 41, 48, 52, 61
   food shortages, 219
   industrial unrest, 101, 117
   morale, 141, 143–4, 146–7

BBC, 108, 109
   'WW2 People's War' website, 14
Balfour, Frank (diarist), 168, 192, 204
ballet, 198
Banff: evacuees, 46–7
behaviour, 6–7, 15, 64
   alcohol consumption and, 72–3, 81; *see also* drunkenness
   evacuees, 44, 52
   see also delinquency; immorality; Mass-Observation (M-O)
Bevin, Ernest, 150, 152
Bevin Boys, *122*
Blackpool, 161, 178
Blitz, 134–42
   Clydebank, 50
   Clydeside, *137*
   and evacuation, 48
   and memory, 148–9
   and morale, 127, 128
   and subversion, 120, 121
   see also air raids
Booth, Katherine, 144, 192, 219, 220
Boothby, Robert, 186, 188
Borsay, Peter, 163, 181
boxing, 190–1
Boyd, William, 31, 33–4, 40, 43, 53–4, 71, 75
Bracken, Brendan, 130
Braybon, Gail, 6, 64
Bridge of Allan: evacuees, 47
British Council for Social Hygiene, 73, 87
British Medical Association, 77
British Union of Fascists (BUF), 22
Britishness, 8, 10, 184
Bromley, Catherine, 15–16
Brown, Callum G., 3, 65, 88, 188
Buchanan, George, MP, 151

Calder, Angus, 5, 94, 116, 117, 121, 125, 128
car clubs, 169, 171
Catholics
   and Church of Scotland, 25–6, 250
   and evacuation, 53–4, 56
   Irish, 25–6, 53, 56, 118
   and Jehovah's Witnesses, 113
   and Mass-Observation, 14
   and politics, 21
   and religious tensions, 22, 25, 26, 56
   and social class, 59
   see also Italians
CEMA *see* Council for the Encouragement of Music and the Arts
censorship, 114, 115, 129, 131–2, 140–1, 142, 158, 180
Chamberlain, Neville, 107

Chand, Alison, 2, 10, 95, 123, 155
Chapman, James, 187, 196
children
   and air raids, 136–8
   child guidance clinics, 75–6
   cinema attendance, 58, 189
   clubs for, 89, 90, *169*
   and crime *see* delinquency
   cultural pursuits, 201, 202
   and food, 222
   pre-World War II, 24
   programmes for, 85, 89
   and Tank Day, Glasgow, 204
   see also evacuation; evacuees; youth
Church of Scotland
   and alcohol, 72; *see also* Women's Temperance Association
   and Catholicism, 25–6, 250
   Committee on Temperance, 83–4
   and evacuees, 54–5, 57
   and identity, 87–8
   influence of, 87–92, 96, 257, 258
   and Jehovah's Witnesses, 114
   and leisure, 161–2
   and morality, 65, 73–4, 82
   and sectarianism, 25–6
   Synod records, 14
   youth programmes, 85
Churchill, Winston, 4, 6–7, 35, 38, 47, 83, 93, 126, 142–3, 154–5
cinemas
   armed forces' access to, 215
   attendance, 193–7, 203
   children and, 58, 189
   damage to, 69
   rural areas, 197–8
Clyde Workers' Committee, 21, 97
Clydebank
   air raids, 93, 125, 134–5, 136, 142
   arms production, 98
   communism, 32
   evacuation, 32, 39, 48, 49
   morale, 155
   overcrowding, 154

   population, 255
   youth delinquency, 68
Clydeside
   air raids, 120, 136–8, *137*
   alcohol licensing, 211
   identity, 10, 123
   industrial unrest, 13, 96, 97
   morale, 133, 141
   politics, 20–1, 95
   war commitment, 119
   see also Clydebank; Glasgow; Port Glasgow
coal mining, 20
   absenteeism, 121
   Bevin Boys, *122*
   holidays, 174
   production, 121–3
   strikes, 98–9, 101, 121
Coatbridge
   Catholics, 25
   morale, 143
   overcrowding, 154
communists, 104–9, 150, 155
   Communist Party of Great Britain (CPGB), 21, 104, 119
   and industrial disputes, 118
Connor, Agnes (diarist), 184–5, 193, 220, 221–2, 223
conscientious objectors, 107, 114, 132, 176
conscription
   Jehovah's Witnesses and, 113–14
   No Conscription League, 107
   Scottish National Party and, 110
   women and, 11, 149–52, 153
Cooper, Duff, 115, 126–7, 130
Council for the Encouragement of Music and the Arts (CEMA), 199
Crang, Jeremy A., 2, 12
crime, 66, 128, 131
   women and, 90
   youth *see* delinquency
cultural pursuits, 197–203; *see also* arts; cinema; music

cycling, 163, 166, 168, 179, 190, 192

Daily Express, 71, 74, 76, 86
Dalwhinnie: war memorial, 1
Darling, Sir William, 165
Davies, Russell, 2
de Valera, Éamon, 118
delinquency, 63–92, 128
   beliefs about, 66–80
   causes, 67, 71–80, 92
   Church of Scotland and, 89–92
   official responses to, 64
   punishment of, 69–71
   statistics, 66
   treatment of, 75–7
Department of Agriculture for Scotland, 228, 230, 235, 239–40
Department of Health for Scotland, 32, 39, 46, 47, 134, 173
Depression: legacy, 153–6
Devine, T. M., 2, 23, 26, 154
Devlin, Moira (diarist), 145, 167, 180, 194
devolution, 22
disability: and evacuation, 34, 35–6
dissent, 94–5, 96, 123–4, 256
diversity, 9; *see also* identity
divisions
   cultural, 26
   social, 23, 59, 61, 62, 78, 258
   workplace, 94, 104
drunkenness, 60, 64, 73, 80, 81
   culture of, 209
   and industrial production, 84
   labourers and, 213, 237
   lumberjacks and, 244–5
   measures to prevent, 214–15
   servicemen and, 213–14
Dumbarton
   air raids, 135, 136
   alcohol shortages, 213
   evacuation, 32, 39
   'holidays at home', 166

Dundee
   evacuation, 32, 35
   morale, 143
   social conditions, 24
   youth delinquency, 68
Dunkirk, 8, 127

economy
   and industry, 154
   pre-World War II, 18–20, 23, 27
Edinburgh
   abstinence, 75
   alcohol, 211, 213; drunkenness, 81, 216
   art galleries, 199, 202–3
   bakeries, 186
   Castle: War Savings Week (1941), *205*
   children's holiday scheme, 89, 90
   cinema-going, 194, 215
   cultural pursuits, 198
   dancing, open-air, *164*
   evacuation, 32, 35
   fascism, 22
   food restrictions, 220
   holidays, 164–5, 166, 167, 174
   morale, 144, 179, 183
   National Museum of Scotland, 199, 201, 202
   population, 255
   prostitution, 81
   savings campaigns, 204, 207
   sheepdog trials, 163
   social conditions, 24, 154
   War Weapons Weeks, 203–4
   Women's Auxiliary Police Corps, 74
   youth delinquency, 68, 69–70, 71, 80
Edwards, Elaine, 239, 241
emigration, 20, 23, 154; *see also* migrants; migration
employment: pre-World War II, 18; *see also* unemployment

England
  Blitz, 143
  evacuation, 29, 32, 33, 34, 38–9, 49, 50, 52, 56, 61
  food supplies, 218
  morale, 144
  religious differences, 53
  Scottish attitudes to, 157–8
  social conditions, 24, 31
  strikes, 97, 98–9, 102
  see also Blackpool; Liverpool; London
entertainment
  cultural, 197–203
  Sunday, 214, 215
  see also cinemas; leisure; sports
Entertainments National Service Association (ENSA), 198–9
Episcopal Church of Scotland, 79, 88
evacuation
  Air Raid Precautions Department, 32
  background, 31–9
  Committee on Evacuation, 32
  and disability, 34, 35–6
  Government Evacuation Scheme (GES), 28, 29–30, 35, 49, 62
  hospital patients, 36, 38
  Operation Pied Piper, 28–9, 35–9, 50
  zones, *33*
evacuees, 28–62, *37*
  behaviour, 44, 52
  billeting allowance, 34
  Catholic, 53–4, 56
  Children's Overseas Reception Scheme, 48
  clubs for, 40
  deaths, 48
  economic and social concerns, 51–62; class conflict, 59–62; poverty, 62; religious tensions, 53–6; urban–rural divide, 56–8
  education of, 35
  and gratitude, 52–3
  hosts, 32–3, 39–62; hostility of, 46–62; perceptions of, 41–9
  Irish Catholic, 53–5
  Jewish, 53, 55–6
  from London, 183
  and morale, 131
  mothers of, 34, 41, 43, 45–6, 47, 50, 55, 59
  physical condition of, 42–3
  and poverty, 29–31, 42, 61–2
  return of, 49–50
  and sanitation, 43
  and social change, 30
  sources, 31
  volunteers and, 39, 40

farmers
  incomes, 254
  portrayal of, 234
  and prisoners of war, 249
  and Women's Land Army, 240–1
farming *see* agriculture
fascism, 22, 107
Field, Geoffrey, 9–10, 29, 56, 64, 95, 123, 188, 241
Fife
  agriculture, 232
  delinquency, 71, 76
  evacuees, 47, 50–1
  exhibitions, 199
  holidays, 174
  MoI films, 109
  morale, 155
  prisoners of war, 249–50
  strikes, 100, 101
fifth column
  definition, 117–18
  Irish as, 117
films
  propaganda, 109, 195–6, 203
  Women's Timber Corps (WTC), 238–9
  see also cinemas
Finlay, Richard J., 19, 22

Firth of Forth
  air raids, 32, 195
  evacuation, 32
  travel, 168, 172
fishing industry, 251, 254
food
  as currency, 222–3
  and diet, 216–24
  evacuees and, 28, 44, 45; Jewish, 55–6
  imported, 225–6
  lumberjacks and, 246
  production, 230–1, 234
  rationing, 217, 222, 223
  restrictions, 186–7
  shortages, 51, 217, 218, 219
  see also nutrition
football, 189, 191
Forbes-Mackenzie Act (1853), 209
forestry, 251–2; *see also* timber; Women's Timber Corps
Forth Road Bridge, 157
Franchise Act (1918), 21
fundraising, 203–9
  savings campaigns, 204–9
  War Weapons Weeks, 203–4

gardens
  children and, 44, 68, *85*
  'Scotland's Gardens Scheme', 164
girls
  and delinquency, 68, 76
  and sexual immorality, 73, 81
  and strikes, 100
  see also women
Glasgow
  air raids, 93, 106, 120, 125, 134, 135, 138, 142
  alcohol, 211, 213, 214
  art galleries, 199, 201–2
  boxing, 190–1
  charity sports days, 193
  cinemas, 58, 69, 194
  dance halls, 58
  delinquency, 89
  economy, 18, 19
  and Empire, 26
  evacuation, 32, 34, 35–6, 39, 40, 48, 52
  evacuees, Jewish, 56
  food shortages, 217, 218
  football, 191
  greyhound racing, 190
  holidays, 162–3, 166, 167, 173, 174, 175–7, 184
  Irish immigrants, 18, 25, 116
  morale, 119, 130, 133–4, 141, 144, 155
  Notre Dame Clinic, 76, 78
  politics, 21, 22
  population, 255
  savings campaigns, 204, 207
  sexual immorality, 74, 81
  smallpox, 173
  social conditions, 24, 56–7, 154
  socialism, 104
  strikes, 97, 100, 101
  theatre, 198
  Wings for Victory plane, *206*
Glasgow Herald, The, 38, 85, 136, 149, 173, 176, 204, 232, 233, 240, 245
Glasgow Trades Council, 21, 97
Grant, Dr Lachlan, 157
Greenock
  alcohol shortages, 212
  bombing, 48
  evacuation, 32, 39
  'holidays at home', 166
  youth delinquency, 70
greyhound racing, 190, 191
Grieve, Christopher Murray, 112

Hardie, Agnes, MP, 68
Harris, José, 30, 87
Harrisson, Tom, 15, 127, 128
Harvie, Christopher, 25, 191–2, 253
health
  cities, 56–7

and diet, 217
holidays and, 162
pre-World War II, 24
see also British Medical Association; Department of Health for Scotland; smallpox; syphilis; vaccinations; venereal disease
Helensburgh, 171, 193, 218
Herald, The, 247–8
heredity, 65, 86
Highlandism, 26–7
Highlands
access to, 168, 169
development, 251; Highland Development League, 158
schemes, 157, 158
travel, 161
weather, 232
Highlands and Islands Development Board, 254
holidays, 160–85
armed forces, 176
Fair, 162–3, 184
history of, 162–3
'at home', 163–7, 181
plans for, 160
reason for, 181
sacrifice of, 176–8
sources, 161
wartime, 168–76, 178–85
home front, 4, 5, 12–13, 83
morale, 128, 131–42
Home Guard, 234, 244
home rule
Irish, 21, 116
Scottish, 22, 110, 111
horse racing, 191
housing
pre-World War II, 24
schemes, 89, *90*, 154
hydro-electric power, 253

IRA, 116–19
identity, 7–10, 22, 87, 257–8
Church of Scotland and, 87–8
and community, 4–5
and cultural distinctiveness, 8, 26–7
and morale, 158
and morality, 92
working class, 95, 155
see also Britishness; Scottishness
illegitimacy, 81
immigrants *see* Irish; migrants; migration
immorality, 64, 65, 66
sexual, 73–5, 81–2, 91
see also delinquency; prostitution
Imperial Chemical Industries workers, *98*
Independent Labour Party, 97
Industrial Areas Campaign (IAC), 108, 109
industrial unrest, 95, 96–104, 118, 121; *see also* strikes
industry, 97–8, 152–3, 174, 179–80; *see also* coal mining; shipbuilding
International Labour Party, 107
Inverness
prostitution, 81–2
sheepdog trials, 163
Women's Land Army hostels, 240
Ireland: home rule, 21, 94, 116; *see also* IRA
Irish, 18
as agricultural workers, 236–7
Catholic, 25–6, 53, 56, 118
and drunkenness, 213, 216, 237
and evacuation, 53–5, 56
and 'fifth column' activity, 117
hostility to, 25–6
and Irish Home Rule, 116
and Liberal Party, 21
and Mass Observation, 14
Italians
diaspora, 9, 250
prisoners of war, 248–50, 251

Jehovah's Witnesses, 113–15
Jewish Chronicle, 55
Jews
   Board of Guardians of the Glasgow Synagogue, 84
   as evacuees, 53, 55–6
Johnes, Martin, 2, 113
Johnston, Thomas, MP, 67, 75, *99*, 101, 110, 111, 136–7, 152, 230, 235, 252–4, 255
Jones, Greta, 65, 79–80

Kilmarnock
   abstinence, 75
   alcohol shortages, 212
   armed forces' entertainments, 215
   evacuees, 41
Kincardine
   'drink travel', 211
   evacuees, 51
Kircaldy
   armed forces' entertainments, 215
   prisoners of war, 250
Kirk *see* Church of Scotland
Kirkwood, David, MP, 151–2
Kushner, Tony, 56

Labour Party, 21, 59; *see also* Independent Labour Party; International Labour Party
Laird, Sir Patrick, 230, 235
Lanarkshire
   alcohol, 211
   censorship, 141
   coal mining, 123
   strikes, 100, 101, 121
   see also Airdrie; Coatbridge
leisure, 186–90
   active, 163
   and memory, 7, 187–8, 224
   'rational recreation', 25, 162
   and social class, 189
   working class, 59
   see also cinemas; cultural pursuits; entertainment; holidays; sports
Leith
   boxing, 191
   fascism, 22
   'holidays at home', 164, 166
Liberal Party, 20, 21
Life and Work (magazine), 54, 89, 91
Liverpool
   IRA attacks, 116
   industrial unrest, 97
   overcrowding, 154
Locke, John, 182
London
   Army Exhibition, 208
   morale, 139, 144, 148
   travel from, 178
   travel to, 172–3, 183, 184–5
lumberjacks, 242–8
   Canadian Forestry Corps, 242–3, *243*, 244
   Honduran Timber Corps, 245–8, *247*
   Newfoundland Overseas Forestry Unit (NOFU), 243–4, 246
lumberjills *see* Women's Timber Corps
Lynd, Robert, 58

MI5, 111, 113
McCorquodale, Mr (Parliamentary Secretary), 149–50
McCrone, David, 10, 15–16
MacDiarmid, Hugh *see* Grieve, Christopher Murray
Macdonald, Catriona, 3, 256
McEwen, Captain, MP, 62
Macfarlane Lang's (manufacturer), 218
McIlvanney, William, 9
McIvor, Arthur, 7, 94, 103, 155, 187, 191
Mack, John, 72, 84
Mckay, Robert, 131, 153, 159
MacMillan, Malcolm, MP, 252

McNeil, Hector, MP, 84, 86
Macnicol, John, 30, 62, 64–5
McNicoll, Niven, 84, 104–5, 108, 120
MacPhail, Walter, 118
Macpherson, Ian, 1–2
MacVitie and Price (manufacturers), 218
Marwick, Arthur, 30
Mass-Observation (M-O), 13, 14–15, 84, 102, 103–4, 131, 133, 148, 155–6, 160, 194–5
Maver, Irene, 162
Maxton, James, 114
Mellon, Miss (diarist), 53, 192–3, 220
memories
  and Blitz, 148–9
  and leisure, 7, 187–8, 224
  popular memory theory, 148–9
  strikes and, 94
  and unity, 127, 128, 155
middle class
  cultural pursuits, 197
  and evacuees, 30, 59–62
  and holidays, 163, 185
  and leisure, 189–90, 192
  and Mass-Observation, 14, 61
  attitude to poverty, 31, 60
  and radicalism, 22
  and 'rational recreation', 25
  and social mobility, 25
  and unemployment, 22, 25, 59
migrants, 6
  attitudes to, 251
  lumberjacks, 247–8
  workers, 236–48
  see also Italians: diaspora; prisoners of war
migration, 23–4, 226
military displays, 163–4
military service, 132–3
  avoidance of, 237; see also consciencious objectors
Ministry of Fuel and Power, 122–3

Ministry of Health, 82
Ministry of Information (MoI), 11, 12, 68–9, 76, 81, 89, 100, 108, 114, 119, 132, 139, 155, 156, 166, 167, 197, 202, 245–6
  films, 109
  Home Intelligence division (HI), 129, 130, 143, 179, 181, 237
  'New Life to the Land' exhibition, 235
  Scottish Advisory Committee, 208
Ministry of Transport, 174
Mitchel, Nora (diarist), 138–9, 145, 172, 220
Moore-Colyer, R. J., 225–6
morale, 125–59, 258
  defining, 129–31
  exhibitions and, 202–3
  and food, 223
  frontline, 142–9
  Glasgow, 119, 130, 133–4, 141, 144, 155
  history of, 126–31
  and holidays, 163, 179
  and home front, 128, 131–42
  and nationality, 151–2
  and women's conscription, 149–51
morality see immorality
Morren, Sir William, 165
Morrison, Blake, 161
Morrison, Herbert, 114, 138, 142, 191
Morrison, Reverend James, 89
mountaineering, 190
museums, 199, 201, 202
Musgrove, Elspeth (diarist), 145–6, 148, 157, 182–3, 198
music
  choral societies, 190
  listening to, 190, 198
  lumberjacks and, 247
  see also Council for the Encouragement of Music and the Arts

nation-building, 5–6
national character, 8
National Council of Women, 88
National Federation of Business and Professional Women, 76
National Party of Scotland, 22
nationalism, 8–9, 22; *see also* Scottish National Party; Scottish nationalists
nationality, 151–2
nationhood, 22, 123; *see also* Britishness; identity; Scottishness
Noakes, Lucy, 5, 10, 127, 148–9, 155, 241
Nonconformists, 113
nutrition, 24–5; *see also* food

Offley, Eileen (diarist), 39, 42, 47, 53, 58, 131, 133, 138, 140, 149, 171–2, 177, 202, 204, 218, 219, 220, 221, 222, 223
orchestras, 198
Orkney
  alcohol consumption, 213
  cinema-going, 194
  Entertainments National Service Association (ENSA), 199
  prisoners of war, 248
Orr, John Boyd, 24–5
Our Scottish Towns report, 44

pacifism, 94, 113, 121; *see also* conscientious objectors
Paisley
  workplace leisure, 188
  youth delinquency, 68
Pattinson, Juliette, 7, 10, 94, 127, 155, 187, 191
Peason, Mrs (diarist), 172, 217, 219–20
Perth
  armed forces' entertainments, 215
  evacuees, 47, 48
  juvenile delinquency, 63
planning, 156–9
police
  and IRA, 117, 118
  intelligence reports, 107–8
  and Scottish nationalists, 111
  and sexual immorality, 74
  and strikes, 97, 100–1
  see also Scottish constabulary reports
politics: interwar, 20–3
population, 254–5
Port Glasgow
  bombing, 48
  evacuation of, 32, 39
poverty, 30, 128
  Church of Scotland and, 87
  and diet, 216
  evacuees, 29–31, 42, 61–2
  middle class attitude to, 31, 60
  pre-World War II, 19, 27, 154
Presbyterianism, 92; *see also* Church of Scotland
Prestwick aerodrome, 157
prisoners of war (POWs), 202, 248–51
prostitution, 81–2
Protestant Action, 22
Protestant Work Ethic, 161–2, 185
psychiatry, 77
pubs, 209, 214, 246, 247

racism, 6, 26, 246; *see also* anti-Semitism
radicalism, 22
rambling, 192
reserved occupations, 187, 228
Ritchie, Isabelle (diarist), 194, 195, 198, 213, 220
Robb, Linsey, 7, 94, 155, 187, 191
Roberts, William, 109
Rolls-Royce, 99, 105
Roodhouse, Mark, 222

Rose, Sonya O., 5, 7, 8, 9, 30, 64, 65, 83, 87, 116, 123, 127, 152, 158, 159, 208
Rosebery, Lord, 138
Ross and Cromarty
  armed forces' drinking, 214
  evacuees, 51
  films, 197
  food shortages, 51
  land usage, 229
  lumberjacks, 244
  sheep losses, 232–3
  unemployment, 227–8
Royal Air Force: fundraising for, 204–7
Royal Scottish Society for the Prevention of Cruelty to Children (RSSPCC), 78
Royle, Trevor, 8–9
rural areas
  alcohol consumption, 211, 213
  cinema-going, 196–7
  cultural pursuits, 198–9
  food and diet, 216–17, 219–20
  fundraising, 207
  leisure, 190, 192–3
  rejuvenation of, 251–5
  unemployment, 228
  see also agriculture

SMT Magazine, 11, 168–9, *170*, 177, 196, 197, 199, 201, 203
Sabbatarianism, 214–15
Salvesen, Lord Edward, 70
sanitation, 43, 60
savings campaigns, 204–7
schools, 67
Scots Socialist (magazine), 111
Scotsman, The, 36, 38, 40–1, 47, 70, 76, 163, 166, 167, 173, 174, 175, 176, 178, 180, 186, 195, 198, 202, 204, 207, 209, 215, 218, 234, 240, 249, 251, 253
Scottish Advisory Council on Industry, 152–3
Scottish Co-operative movement, 108
Scottish constabulary reports, 12, 48, 54, 61, 80, 101, 141, 144, 145, 211, 212, 216, 244–5, 250, 257
Scottish Development Council, 158, 251
Scottish Education Department (SED), 32, 57, 67, 111–12
Scottish Home Department (SHD), 11, 67, 70, 73, 102, 104, 116–17, 118, 140, 184
Scottish Motor Traction group (SMT), 11
Scottish National Party (SNP), 96
  and fascism, 22
  membership, 15
  and proposed Highlands scheme, 158
  and women's conscription, 152
Scottish nationalists, 110–12, 113
Scottish Office, 89, 257
Scottish Party, 22
Scottish Savings Committee, 208
Scottish Temperance Alliance, 72, 75
Scottish War Savings Committee, 27
Scottish Women's Group on Public Welfare (SWG), 44, 45, 57
Scottish Youth Advisory committee, 90
Scottishness, 9, 10, 138, 257
sectarianism, 25–6
secularisation, 88–92, 257, 258
sedition, 94, 95, 111–12, 119
servicemen *see* armed forces; army; Royal Air Force
shelters, 106, 120
shipbuilding
  air raids, 120
  output, 18, 19, 20
  strikes, 101, 102
  subversion, 123

ships
  Arandora Star, 248
  City of Benares, 48
  Duke of York, 200
  losses, 225
Short, Brian, 254
Skillen, Fiona, 189
Sladen, Chris, 160–1, 178–9, 183–4
slogans, 160–1, 174, 208
smallpox, 173
Smith, David, 64, 82
Smith, Harold, 128
Smout, T. C., 3, 209
social class
  communists and, 105
  conflict, 128
  differences, 25, 59–62
  and identity, 10
  and leisure, 189
  see also middle class; underclass; working class
social conditions, 23–6, 30, 56–7; *see also* housing; poverty; sanitation
socialism, 21, 104; *see also* Scots Socialist
Soroptimists, 133, 221
sports, 190–3
  country, 190
  crowds, 191
  workplace, 188–9
  see also football; mountaineering; swimming
Stephen, Campbell, 40, 49
Stewart, John, 31, 61
Stirling
  'drink travel', 211
  evacuees, 42, 47, 54–5
  food shortages, 218
strikes, 96–104
  apprentices, 93, 103
  coal mining, 101, 121
  communists and, 105
  General Strike (1926), 97

  and memory, 94
  police and, 100
  shipbuilding, 102
  women and, 99, 100
submarine warfare, 225
subversion, 94, 95, 107, 109, 111, 114–15, 116, 117, 119–24
suffragettes, 21
Summerfield, Penny, 6, 64, 128
Sunday Mail, The, 85
swimming, 189, 190, 193
syphilis, 82

tartanry, 26
Taylor, Stephen, 130
temperance, 72, 74–5, 214
  Church of Scotland Committee on Temperance, 83–4
  Scottish Temperance Alliance, 72, 75
  Women's Temperance Association, 72, 73, 75, 91
timber, 225, 226, 242, 254; *see also* forestry; lumberjacks; Women's Timber Corps
Times Educational Supplement, The, 71, 75–6, 90
Titmuss, Richard, 30, 31, 61, 127
Todman, Daniel, 94–5, 99
tourism, 161; *see also* holidays
trade unions, 9, 96, 103
  apprentices and, 102
  communists and, 104–5, 107–8
  and leisure, 174, 189
  and strikes, 94
trains
  damage to, 69
  and holidays, 166–7, 173, 175, 176, 177, 178, 182
  munitions, 174
transport *see* Ministry of Transport; tourism; trains
Traprain, Lord, 121–2
travel
  'drink travel', 210–12, 216

Sunday, 214–15
see also tourism

Ugolini, Wendy, 2, 6, 250
underclass, 64–5
unemployment, 19, 27, 59, 154, 228
Unionist Party, 23
unity
  Church of Scotland and, 66
  and discontent, 123
  films and, 196
  and identity, 8, 87
  and loyalty, 119
  and memory, 127, 128, 155
  and morale, 4, 128, 130
  and morality, 86
  threat to, 7

VE Day, 147–9
vaccinations, 173
venereal disease, 73–4, 75, 82
Vickers, Emma, 238
volunteers
  and agriculture, 234–5
  armed forces, 27
  civil defence, 135, 190
  and evacuees, 39, 40
  and Mass-Observation, 14–15, 129
  and morale, 131
  see also Home Guard; lumberjacks; Women's Institute; Women's Timber Corps; Women's Voluntary Services

Wales
  evacuation, 32, 33, 34, 49, 50, 61
  national identity, 2, 8
  nationalism, 112–13, 158
  religious differences, 53
  social conditions, 24
  strikes, 97
War Commentaries, 108, 109
war memorials, 1

Watson, Duncan, 132, 145, 176
Webster, Wendy, 6, 251
Weight, Richard, 7–8
Welfare State, 29–30
Welshman, John, 30–1, 61
West, Phyllis, 174
Western (Scotland) District Information Committee (WDIC), 104, 108, 110
Woden, George, 194
women
  and air raids, 136–8
  and alcohol, 72, 91, 212, 216
  conscription of, 111, 149–52, 153
  as evacuees, 34–5, 41, 43, 45–6, 50, 51–2, 55, 59
  as industrial trainees, *99*
  and leisure, 189
  and morale, 180
  and morality, 65, 90–1
  and pay, 101–2
  and strikes, 96, 99
  and war work, 109
  see also evacuees: mothers of; girls; National Council of Women; National Federation of Business and Professional Women; Soroptimists; suffragettes
Women's Auxiliary Police Corps, 74
Women's Home Mission, 89
Women's Institute, 46
Women's Land Army (WLA), 239–41
Women's Temperance Association, 72, 73, 75, 91
Women's Timber Corps (WTC), 238–9
Wood, Sydney, 3, 209
working class
  and alcohol, 212, 213, 216
  and community cohesion, 86
  and evacuation, 60–1
  factions, 97
  and holidays, 162–3, 184, 185

working class (*cont.*)
   and identity, 10, 95
   and leisure, 59, 188–9, 190–2
   and Mass-Observation, 10
   and moral panic, 65
   and morale, 153–6
   and politics, 20–1
   social conditions of, 24, 29–30, 59, 62
   social judgement of, 64
   see also agricultural workers
workplace relations, 20–1; *see also* industrial unrest

youth
   and crime *see* delinquency
   organisations for, 90
   see also children

EU representative:
Easy Access System Europe
Mustamäe tee 50, 10621 Tallinn, Estonia
Gpsr.requests@easproject.com

www.ingramcontent.com/pod-product-compliance
Lightning Source LLC
Chambersburg PA
CBHW050209240426
43671CB00013B/2268